Quality in Teaching and Teacher Education

Key Issues in Teacher Education

POLICY, RESEARCH & PRACTICE

Series Editors

Joanna Madalinska-Michalak (*University of Warsaw, Poland*)
Maria Assunção Flores (*University of Minho, Portugal*)
Marco Snoek (*Hogeschool van Amsterdam, the Netherlands*)

Editorial Board

Björn Åstrand (*Umeå University, Sweden*)
Eve Eisenschmidt (*Haapsalu College, Tallinn University, Estonia*)
Brian Hudson (*University of Sussex, England*)
Nina Kilbrink (*Karlstad University, Sweden*)
Anna Lindqvist (*Umeå University, Sweden*)
Helle Plauborg (*Aarhus University, Denmark*)
Jens Rasmussen (*Aarhus University, Denmark*)
Vasileios Symeonidis (*University of Graz, Austria*)
Pavel Zgaga (*University of Ljubljana, Slovenia*)

VOLUME 2

The titles published in this series are listed at *brill.com/tepe*

Quality in Teaching and Teacher Education

International Perspectives from a Changing World

Edited by

Joanna Madalinska-Michalak

BRILL

LEIDEN | BOSTON

Cover illustration: iStock.com/155124586

All chapters in this book have undergone peer review.

Library of Congress Cataloging-in-Publication Data

Names: Madalinska-Michalak, Joanna, editor.
Title: Quality in teaching and teacher education : international perspectives from a changing world / edited by Joanna Madalinska-Michalak.
Description: Leiden ; Boston : Brill, [2023] | Series: Key issues in teacher education : policy, research and practice, 2772-5979 ; volume 2 | Includes bibliographical references and index.
Identifiers: LCCN 2022050930 (print) | LCCN 2022050931 (ebook) | ISBN 9789004536586 (Paperback : acid-free paper) | ISBN 9789004536593 (Hardback : acid-free paper) | ISBN 9789004536609 (eBook)
Subjects: LCSH: Teachers--Training of--Cross-cultural studies. | Teachers--Recruiting--Cross-cultural studies. | Education and state--Cross-cultural studies. | Teachers--Selection and appointment--Cross-cultural studies.
Classification: LCC LB2835 .Q35 2023 (print) | LCC LB2835 (ebook) | DDC 370.71/1--dc23/eng/20221110
LC record available at https://lccn.loc.gov/2022050930
LC ebook record available at https://lccn.loc.gov/2022050931

Typeface for the Latin, Greek, and Cyrillic scripts: "Brill". See and download: brill.com/brill-typeface.

ISSN 2772-5979
ISBN 978-90-04-53658-6 (paperback)
ISBN 978-90-04-53659-3 (hardback)
ISBN 978-90-04-53660-9 (e-book)

Copyright 2023 by Joanna Madalinska-Michalak. Published by Koninklijke Brill NV, Leiden, The Netherlands.
Koninklijke Brill NV incorporates the imprints Brill, Brill Nijhoff, Brill Hotei, Brill Schöningh, Brill Fink, Brill mentis, Vandenhoeck & Ruprecht, Böhlau, V&R unipress and Wageningen Academic.
Koninklijke Brill NV reserves the right to protect this publication against unauthorized use. Requests for re-use and/or translations must be addressed to Koninklijke Brill NV via brill.com or copyright.com.

This book is printed on acid-free paper and produced in a sustainable manner.

Printed by Printforce, United Kingdom

Contents

Preface   IX
List of Figures and Tables   XI
Notes on Contributors   XII

Introduction   1
   Joanna Madalinska-Michalak

PART 1
Towards the Nature of Quality in Teaching and Teacher Education

1   What Does Quality Teacher Education Mean and How Can the Preparation of Future Teachers Be Quality Assured?   11
   Kay Livingston

2   Unpacking Quality in Teacher Education   32
   Maria Assunção Flores

3   Teacher Quality Driven by Equity and Social Justice: Arguments for an Alternative Values-Centred Vision of Teacher Education   50
   Noel Purdy, Kathy Hall, Daria Khanolainen and Conor Galvin

4   Genealogy of the Ethics of Teacher Self-Evaluation: From Adherence to Norms to Self-Discipline through Self-Evaluation   72
   Hannele Pitkänen

5   Re-thinking the Concept of Classroom Management: Implications for Quality in Future Classroom Management Practices   98
   Helle Plauborg

PART 2
Quality Teaching and Teacher Education in Times of Crisis and Uncertainty

6   Teacher Experiences and Practices in the Time of COVID-19: Implications for Understanding Quality in Teaching   121
       Carol Hordatt Gentles, Sarah Younie, Marilyn Leask and Helen Caldwell

7   Developing Emancipatory Online Learning Environments in Quality Teacher Education   147
       Gisselle Tur Porres and Washington Ires Correa

8   Situational Support to Develop the Well-being of Future Teachers: Supporting Sustainable Development Goal 4   166
       Irma Eloff and Anna-Barbara du Plessis

9   Educating for Sustainability and Global Citizenship in Uncertain Times: A Case Study with In-service Teachers in Portugal   180
       Mónica Lourenço and Ana Isabel Andrade

10   Teacher Education in Conflict-Affected Societies: The Case of Mosul University after the Demise of the Islamic State   203
       Vasileios Symeonidis, Felix Senger, Heike Wendt, Amal Fatah Zedan, Saraa Salim Dawood and Fawzi Habeeb Jabrail

PART 3
Strengthening Quality Teaching and Teacher Education: Looking to the Future

11   Teacher Education for the 31st Century? Preparing Teachers for Unknown Futures   231
       A. Lin Goodwin

12   Developing Teachers: A Necessary Condition for Quality Retention   252
       Qing Gu

13   The Teacher, Teacher Careers and Teacher Education: Conditions for a Career Long Dedication and Passion   277
       Marco Snoek

14 Mobilising Policy to Reframe Teaching and Teacher Education in Europe: The European Commission's Emerging Role within the Teacher Quality Agenda   304
   Conor Galvin, Panagiotis Kampylis, Deirbhile Nic Craith, Joanna Madalinska-Michalak and Noel Purdy

15 Educating about and through Research: The Role of Research in Pre-service Teachers' Classroom Practices   329
   Stéphane Colognesi and Virginie März

16 Quality in Teaching and Teacher Education: Key Dilemmas and Implications for Research, Policy and Practice   352
   Joanna Madalinska-Michalak, Björn Åstrand and Marco Snoek

Index   377

Preface

The Teacher Education Policy in Europe (TEPE) Network is taking the initiative to publish a book series titled *Key Issues in Teacher Education: Policy, Research and Practice* with Brill. Through this series, issues regarding teacher education and discussions on its practice, policy and research are presented to inspire and facilitate needed dialogue on teacher education as an ongoing process of professional development within the continuum of the teaching profession, from initial teacher education, through induction and on to continuing professional development throughout teacher careers. This series includes specific topics on practice, policy and research concerning teacher education and provide a comparative European/international view that values diversity in perspectives and viewpoints, addresses the continuum of the teacher education, bridges research, practice and policies, and with regard to local, national and/or international policies, practices and research.

The TEPE Network, an academic network, brings together teacher educators, educational researchers, policy-makers, teachers and practitioners from Europe and beyond to discuss and identify key elements that contribute to strengthening teacher education and the quality and professionalism of teachers in schools. This network is dedicated to advancing research in and on Teacher Education that can influence policy making. It builds on previous European collaborative projects in the field of teacher education policy.

The editors of the TEPE book series brought together leading authors to create Volume 2, *Quality in Teaching and Teacher Education: International Perspectives from a Changing World*. The chapters presented in the book were selected through submissions elicited from 'a call for abstract submissions' to scholars concentrated around Teacher Education Policy in Europe Scientific Network (TEPE Network) and its annual conference which was organised during 16–18 May 2019 in Cracow, Poland, with Professor Joanna Madalinska-Michalak as Chair. The Conference theme was: *Quality Teachers and Quality Teacher Education: Research, Policy and Practice*.

The theme of the 2019 TEPE conference encouraged academics, teachers, teachers' educators and education officials to present their research and engage in discerning discussions about their work, their concerns and their visions for teachers and teacher education. The theme provoked to examine the elusive concept of quality teachers and quality (in) teacher education and required addressing several basic questions such as: What does it take to educate high quality teachers? What can be done to create such systems where every learner can have well-trained, qualified and motivated teachers

who promote inclusive and equitable quality education for all? How do working conditions for teachers influence teacher quality? What is high quality in teacher education? The following sub-themes were established to explore the general theme of the conference:
- Exploring international and European perspectives on quality in education and teacher education and their policy impact;
- Reforming teaching and teacher education: towards high quality education for all;
- Raising teacher quality: attracting, supporting and preparing a diverse student teacher population;
- Strengthening teacher education and teaching profession: conditions for quality teaching and learning;
- Developing cultures of sharing and collaboration as a means of supporting teachers' professional learning and development.

The editors of the Key Issues in Teacher Education: Policy, Research and Practice series welcome proposals for future volumes.

Figures and Tables

Figures

7.1 Emancipatory pedagogical approaches in online learning environments.   155
13.1 Six possible career paths for teachers (based on ET2020 Working Group Schools, 2020, p. 23).   287

Tables

4.1 Research frame.   81
4.2 From bureaucracy and planning economy to discursive practice of self-evaluation.   90
6.1 Five critical elements of pedagogy.   125
9.1 Categorisation matrix.   189
10.1 Annual budget of the ministries responsible for education and higher education since 2016 (figures in trillion IQD).   213
10.2 Annual salary for public servants in Iraq (Teaching sector, amounts in USD).   216
10.3 Percentage of knowledge domains addressed in teacher education at Mosul University.   220

Notes on Contributors

Ana Isabel Andrade
is Full Professor in the Department of Education and Psychology at the University of Aveiro, Portugal. She holds a PhD in Language Teaching and she teaches in masters' and doctoral programmes in the field of Education. Her current research interests include diversity and language education, plurilingual education, teacher education, and supervision of teaching practice.

Björn Åstrand
holds a PhD in history and he is senior lecturer in educational work at Umeå University. He has been visiting scholar at Stanford University and he has served as dean for teacher education and educational science at both Umeå and Karlstad University. He served at the Swedish School Commission 2015 and he has twice chaired governmental inquires; on the teaching profession (2016) and for improvement of equity in education (2018). Currently he focus on educational history, equity in education, democracy and values and teacher education.

Helen Caldwell
is Associate Professor at the University of Northampton. She is a specialist in educational technology, teacher education and online learning and an Apple Distinguished Educator. Her research interests include technology-enabled social online learning in teacher education, change-makers and social innovation education and the use of immersive technologies for teaching and learning.

Stéphane Colognesi
is Professor at the Faculty of Psychology and Educational Sciences of the University of Louvain, and co-director of the Interdisciplinary Research Group in Socialization, Education and Training (GIRSEF). His research interest focuses on learning and instruction in both primary and secondary school as well as in higher education. More specifically, Colognesi's research concentrates on Learning and Instruction (writing and oral), Teacher Education, and support for teachers.

Saraa Salim Dawood
works as a full professor in the Administration and Economics Department at University of Mosul, Iraq. Her research focus is on economic and public

finance and lately she works in the field of taxation, pollution taxes, budgeting in crisis situations and sovereign funds as well as financial crisis and public expenditure especially in the field of education.

Anna-Barbara du Plessis
is a contract researcher in the Department of Educational Psychology, University of Pretoria, South Africa. Her research interests include special needs education, resilience and well-being, which she approaches from a multi-systemic perspective. She is a registered educational psychologist.

Irma Eloff
is Professor of Educational Psychology at the University of Pretoria, South Africa. Her research foci include quality education and good health and well-being (Sustainable Development Goals 3 & 4). She uses phenomenological approaches – including vignette research – often in combination with quantitative methods.

Maria Assunção Flores
works at the University of Minho, Portugal. She received her PhD at the University of Nottingham, UK. Her research interests include teacher professionalism and identity, teacher education and professional development. She is currently editor of the *European Journal of Teacher Education* and Director of the Research Centre on Child Studies.

Conor Galvin
is the Director of Doctoral Programmes at UCD School of Education, Dublin, Ireland where he also lectures and researches. His academic interests include policy and policy networks, professional knowledge, and the impact of technology on learning and society. He has published on EU policy and policy networks and in the social history of the Belfast/Good Friday Agreement on the island of Ireland. Dr Galvin is a consultant to the European Commission and an adviser on the new Jean Monnet Schools Action.

A. Lin Goodwin
is Thomas More Brennan Chair of Education at Boston College. Previously she was Professor and Dean of the Faculty of Education at The University of Hong Kong, and is a past Vice President of the American Educational Research Association (AERA) – Division K: Teaching and Teacher Education (2013–2016). Her research focuses on teacher and teacher educator beliefs, identities and development; equitable education and powerful teaching for immigrant and

minoritised youth; international analyses/comparisons of teacher education practice and policy; and the particular issues facing Asian/Asian American teachers and students in U.S. Schools. She began her career as a special education teacher in secondary school.

Qing Gu
is Director of the UCL Centre for Educational Leadership and Professor of Leadership in Education. She is the Past Chair of the British Association of Comparative and International Education (BAICE), Co-Editor of Teachers and Teaching: Theory and Practice, Associate Editor of *International Journal of Educational Development*, a member of the Research Standing Committee of the World Council of Comparative Education Societies (WCCES), and a member of the Research Evidence and Impact Panel for the Leadership College for UK Government. She is a Senior Research Fellow at the Asia Pacific Centre for Leadership and Change (APCLC) and Honorary Professor in the Department of Education Policy and Leadership at the Education University of Hong Kong. In 2022 she was conferred the Award of Fellow of the Academy of Social Sciences (FAcSS). Her research focuses on the areas of teachers' work, lives and effectiveness, school improvement, and educational systemic change.

Kathy Hall
is Professor of Education at University College Cork, Ireland where she leads a Cohort PhD Programme and conducts research on teacher education, inclusion, assessment, and learning. She is interested in socio-cultural theory and its relevance for understanding human action especially in relation to education.

Carol Hordatt Gentles
is Senior Lecturer in Education at the University of the West Indies, Mona, Jamaica. Her research focuses on the use of critical pedagogy, effecting educational change, quality in teaching and teacher education, the work and practice of teacher educators and the pedagogy of qualitative research.

Washington Ires Correa
is an independent researcher, reflexologist (UK and European Qualifications Framework), therapist and musician affiliated to the 'Uruguayan Authors' General Society' (AGADU). He has worked in formal and non-formal education settings in the field of Vocational Education and Training, with teacher educators and student-teachers. His research interests focus on the topic of body awareness and corporal re-education.

Fawzi Habeeb Jabrail
is Full Professor and works at the Department of Chemistry (Science) at University of Mosul, Iraq. Professor Fawzi's main field of research is polymer chemistry. He is interested in hydrogels and their bio-applications, recycling of different polymers, biodegradation of synthetic polymers and controlled drug and agrochemical release.

Panagiotis Kampylis
is Senior Research Fellow at the National Research Council of Italy – Institute for Educational Technology. He holds a PhD in cognitive science from University of Jyväskylä, Finland. His research interests include creativity, innovation and digital transformation of education and training, education policy, computational thinking, and digital and entrepreneurship competences.

Daria Khanolainen
is a PhD candidate and an early stage researcher at the Department of Teacher Education, University of Jyväskylä, Finland. In her current research she primarily focuses on the longitudinal effects of parental difficulties and the home environment on children's reading and mathematical development. Her research interests also include both teachers' and students' perceptions of and responses to school bullying and conflicts.

Marilyn Leask
is Visiting Professor at De Montfort and Winchester Universities, UK, and is committed to supporting international collaboration between teachers and educational researchers for the benefit of learners everywhere. She initiated the Learning to Teach in the secondary school series of textbooks and is co-chair of the Education Futures Collaboration Charity which oversees the MESHGuides initiative.

Kay Livingston
is Professor of Educational Research, Policy and Practice at the School of Education, University of Glasgow. She works with policy-makers, researchers and practitioners at local, national and international levels. She was a member of the European Commission's ET2020 Working Group on Schools. Her main research interests include the professional development of teachers from initial teacher education, induction to career-long professional learning; mentors and mentoring of all teachers, innovative teachers, quality assurance, formative assessment, digital literacies, and inclusive education.

Mónica Lourenço
is a researcher at the University of Aveiro, Portugal. She has a PhD in Didactics and Teacher Education and experience teaching and supervising master's and PhD students in the field of Education. She is co-convenor of the Special Interest Group on Teacher Education of the Academic Network on Global Education and Learning (ANGEL). Her main research interests include global citizenship education, virtual communities of practice, internationalisation of the curriculum and education for linguistic and cultural diversity.

Joanna Madalinska-Michalak
is Full Professor at University of Warsaw and a Honorary Professor at Aarhus University. She is Vice-President of the World Education Research Association (WERA) and she is past Chair of TEPE Network (2016–2020), and a past President of Polish Educational Research Association (PERA) (2014–2019). She serves as an expert for European Commission. Her research interest include teacher education, teacher education policy, teacher professional development, and educational leadership.

Virginie März
is Professor at the Faculty of Psychology and Educational Sciences at UC Louvain and a member of the Interdisciplinary Research Group in Socialization, Education and Training (GIRSEF). Her research interests include the professional development of teachers (early career teachers, end-of-career teachers, second-career teachers), school development, and curriculum reform. As a methodological approach, she is particularly interested in qualitative research methods and social network analysis.

Deirbhile Nic Craith
is former Director of Education and Research with the Irish National Teachers' Organisation. She holds a PhD in policy for primary teacher education from University College Dublin. Her research interests include teacher education, professional development and learning, teacher professionalism, education policy, and her areas of work have also included curriculum, assessment and inclusive education.

Hannele Pitkänen
is a Finnish Academy funded postdoctoral researcher at the Department of Teacher Education, Faculty of Education and Psychology, University of Jyväskylä, Finland. Her research, spanning the fields of sociology and politics of education, history of education and curriculum studies, focuses on evaluation

and assessment in education and guidance as a form of governing education and the educated.

Helle Plauborg
is Associate Professor at the Danish School of Education, Aarhus University, Denmark. Her research interests include classroom management and learning theory – in recent years with particular interest in various posthuman approaches to learning. She is currently involved in a project exploring issues related to teachers and their choice to stay in the teaching profession (with teacher shortage a common problem in an increasing number of Danish municipalities).

Noel Purdy
is Director of Research and Scholarship and Head of Education Studies at Stranmillis University College, Belfast, Northern Ireland, where he is also Director of the Centre for Research in Educational Underachievement. His research interests include educational underachievement, pastoral care in education (particularly addressing bullying in schools) and special educational needs and inclusion.

Felix Senger
is a trained school educator and educational researcher formerly working at the Institute of school development research (Institut für Schulentwicklungsforschung, IFS) at TU Dortmund (Germany). He is now affiliated with the Faculty of Spatial Planning at TU Dortmund and serves as coordinator of the project Rethink Science and Education in Iraq, which is an interdisciplinary cooperation with University of Mosul (Iraq) and University of Graz (Austria). His research interest is internationalisation/transnationalisation in higher education with a focus on capacity building projects as well as higher education in post-conflict situations.

Marco Snoek
is Professor of Teacher Development and School Innovation at the Amsterdam University of Applied Sciences. His main area of interest is teachers' development throughout their working life. He is involved in the development of a career framework in the Netherlands and has been part of the EC's Working Groups on Schools.

Vasileios Symeonidis
is a postdoctoral researcher at the Institute of Education Research and Teacher Education at the University of Graz, Austria. He has previously worked as

a Marie Skłodowska-Curie fellow for the European Doctorate in Teacher Education (EDiTE) and is currently board member of TEPE and InFo-TED networks. His research interests include teacher education policy and practice, international and comparative education, and experiential dimensions of learning.

Gisselle Tur Porres
is Lecturer and Programme Director for the BA in Early Childhood Studies at Swansea University, United Kingdom. Her research interests include teachers'/practitioners' training with a focus on emancipatory pedagogical/educational practices, in the field. She is convenor of the International Research Network (IRN) of the World Education Research Association (WERA): Promoting and supporting children's agency and participation in Early Childhood Education and Care (during COVID-19 pandemic and beyond).

Heike Wendt
is Professor for Education Research at the University of Graz, Austria. She has for many years served as research coordinator in international comparative studies and higher education partnerships, publishing widely on education systems and issues of equity in education. Since 2015 she leads the higher education partnership between the Universities of Mosul, Dortmund and Graz which aims to strengthen academic reconstruction and reconciliation at Mosul university and the region.

Sarah Younie
is Professor of Education Innovation at De Montfort University in the UK. She has been involved in international research on technologies in education for UNESCO, EU, UK Government Agencies, Local Authorities, and educational charities and is the Editor-in-Chief for the *International Journal of Technology, Pedagogy and Education*. She is a trustee and founder member of the Education Futures Collaboration (EFC) charity and MESH (Mapping Education Specialist knowHow) project.

Amal Fatah Zedan
is Full Professor in the Department of Educational Science at University of Mosul. In her research she focusses on the impact of pedagogical interventions in teacher training and approaches to inclusive education in the Iraqi context.

Introduction

Joanna Madalinska-Michalak

In a world that is marked by complexity, uncertainty, and ambiguity, a world that has recently been witness to hitherto unknown threats and the acceleration of social, political, economic and cultural life, great hope is placed in education. Teachers who are willing and able to teach to their best ability and who have the necessary competencies to be able to face the challenges of today and tomorrow play a pivotal role in schooling/education.

Given the continuing concerns of governments worldwide about teacher quality and teaching quality, school development, student learning outcomes and student well-being, this book provides portraits of the contexts and conditions for understanding and enhancing quality in teaching and teacher education. The aim of the book is to bring together, disseminate and communicate original and influential international research which provides new knowledge, insights and experience about quality teaching, learning, and learning to teach in light of current challenges and future possibilities.

The theoretical investigations and the presentation of research results are preceded by a Preface, List of Figures and Tables, Notes on Contributors, and an Introduction. The main body of the book is categorised into three parts that form broad themes connected with searching for the nature of quality in teaching and teacher education, examining quality in teaching and teacher education in times of crises and uncertainty, and considerations on strengthening quality teaching and teacher education with recommendations for the future. There are five chapters in each part of the book. The chapters are written by researchers from such parts of the world as Europe, Asia, Africa, and North America.

The book concludes with a final chapter entitled 'Quality in Teaching and Teacher Education: Key Dilemmas and Implications for Research, Policy and Practice'. Joanna Madalinska-Michalak, Björn Åstrand and Marco Snoek, on the basis of their own analysis and discussion of the fifteen chapters collected in this book, provide a synthesis of their learnings on quality in teaching and teacher education and the implications for future research on quality in teaching and teacher education, policy and practice.

In Part 1, *Towards the Nature of Quality in Teaching and Teacher Education*, the authors of the first five chapters raise issues on the global, complex, problematic, contested and demanding nature of quality in teaching and teacher education. They indicate that different views of education and schooling, as well as the complexity of teaching and contrasting understandings of the teachers and their qualities in specific contexts, have an influence on interpretations of the concept of quality and its definitions, the nature of teaching and the roles required of a teacher. They look critically at the prioritisation of education for economic purposes that had led to attempts to solve key policy problems of teacher education through manipulating and defining how and where teachers should be prepared and through determining what their preparation should focus on. For the authors, teaching in today's globalised world is acknowledged as challenging and ever-changing.

In Chapter 1, Kay Livingston explores the concept of quality in teacher education, the understanding of what it means, and the priorities for the measurement of quality as well as the processes put in place to ensure quality. She indicates an increased focus on policy reforms to improve teacher and teaching quality. Her chapter draws on the perspectives of researchers, policy-makers, school leaders and teachers to look at what quality teacher education means. Livingston argues for new approaches to the quality assurance of teacher preparation that enrich rather than diminish the success and joy of teaching and learning.

Drawing on existing international literature, and taking the Portuguese legal framework as an example Maria Assunção Flores discusses how quality is understood and examines the question of what quality teacher education means (Chapter 2). Flores stresses that any analysis of quality as a dynamic and contested concept must, among other things, consider the voices of the various stakeholders and the broad political, social and cultural environment in which teacher education is situated. Her considerations show that quality should be problematised particularly in the context of teacher education reform and that attention needs to be given to a shared frame of reference as well as to specific features of national, regional and local settings.

In Chapter 3, Noel Purdy, Kathy Hall, Daria Khanolainen and Conor Galvin present arguments for a values-centred vision of teacher education. Purdy et al. indicate that teacher quality remains an issue of policy interest and the focus of considerable teacher education activity across Europe. They refer to the issue of ensuring quality in teacher education, which has become a fundamental concern of the European Commission in the context of establishing the European Education Area by 2025 and a constant focus of research among teacher educators. The authors of this chapter direct our attention to the emerging trend called the 'practice turn', which can be characterised by the re-emergence of simplified craft models of teaching, accompanied by the binary debates between proponents of school-based or university-based teacher education, and argue for the value of a teacher education that places equity & social justice at the heart of its mission.

Hannele Pitkänen (Chapter 4) leads us to think about quality evaluation and the ethics of teacher self-evaluation. Quality evaluation is acknowledged as a self-evident and necessary method of improving quality in education across education systems. Pitkänen indicates that along with the quality 'evaluation wave', schools and teachers have not only become objects of evaluation but have also, at the same time, been subjected to increasing demands to self-evaluate. Using a genealogical methodology, Pitkänen analyses the emergence and formation of the politics of school and teacher self-evaluation in Finnish schools. She argues that the ethics of this evaluation of teachers is closely entangled with and supports the governing of education through quality evaluation.

Helle Plauborg, in Chapter 5, discusses quality in classroom management practices. Drawing on agential realism, she shows how the distinction between management and instruction obstructs new insights into classroom management practices. In her analysis of the chosen case study – a Danish Year 6 class with a reputation among teachers, pupils and the school management team of being very difficult to teach – she proposes to re-think the concept of classroom management by integrating instruction and discusses the implications of this re-thinking for quality in future classroom management practices.

In Part 2, *Quality Teaching and Teacher Education in Times of Crisis and Uncertainty*, we find the chapters that contribute to knowledge in the fields of teaching, teacher education and teacher education policy in the context of improving the quality of teacher education in Europe and beyond. Times of crisis and uncertainty, times of natural disasters and times of wars in conflict-affected societies require our special attention and solidarity to create the best conditions for education for all and the proper conditions for teachers' work and for their professionalism. In crisis situations, education systems often fail to provide access to the quality of education that is arguably crucial for stabilisation and development. Challenges to educational provision in (post-)crisis situations and teacher education are presented by the authors of the collected chapters in this part of the book.

Carol Hordatt Gentles, Sarah Younie, Marilyn Leask and Helen Caldwell (Chapter 6) contest accustomed ways of understanding quality in teaching and propose some implications for informing policy-maker and stakeholder decision-making for future-proofing educational practices in times of crisis and normalcy. On the basis of their own findings from two international research projects, the authors highlight how in the process of transitioning to online delivery and finding creative, offline ways of reaching students, teachers at all levels of the system of education demonstrated their capacity to be innovative and to take ownership of accelerating changes in how they think and work. Hordatt Gentles et al. also consider the implications of this shift for new ways of thinking about quality in teaching.

In Chapter 7, Gisselle Tur Porres and Washington Ires Correa discuss the development of emancipatory online learning environments in quality teacher education, and raise questions about what quality teaching means in online learning environments. The authors argue that quality teaching in teacher education implies thinking about emancipatory pedagogical approaches in the development of learning environments. They explore emancipatory ways of understanding quality in online learning teacher education and advise teaching strategies to create online learning environments with a focus on emancipatory pedagogical approaches.

In their considerations of the ways in which well-being is supported within teacher training programmes for pre-service teachers, Irma Eloff and Anna-Barbara du Plessis explore the situational support available to pre-service teachers within their immediate learning environments (Chapter 8). They indicate that situational support factors embedded within learning environments are critical to subjective well-being. Their study also shows a cluster of situational support factors that support the development of the well-being of pre-service teachers: i) the campus environment and facilities, ii) pragmatic student support structures, iii) the quality of the academic experience and the vital role of lecturers in the learning experience of students, iv) feelings of safety, and v) opportunities for socialising outside of the formal academic programme.

In Chapter 9, Mónica Lourenço and Ana Isabel Andrade present a study on the impact of an online course on teachers' professional learning, changes related to their conceptualisations of education for sustainability and global citizenship (ESGC), their pedagogical repertoires, their understandings of the purposes of education and of the teacher's role in a globalised and uncertain world, and their motivations and commitment to teaching according to ESGC principles. Some implications of their research for quality teaching and teacher education in uncertain times are discussed.

Vasileios Symeonidis, Felix Senger, Heike Wendt, Amal Fatah Zedan, Saraa Salim Dawood and Fawzi Habeeb Jabrail focus on the critical role of teachers and the challenges of initial teacher education in conflict-affected societies and the quality of teaching in post-crisis contexts (Chapter 10). Their study provides an insight into teacher education structures in Iraq and the broader challenges presented by crisis contexts and leads to identifying the challenges of providing quality teaching and teacher education in crisis situations by studying the case of Mosul University in Iraq.

The collected research presented in the chapters in Part 3, entitled *Strengthening Quality Teaching and Teacher Education: Looking to the Future*, contributes to reflections on the complexities of teaching, learning to teach and the teaching profession. The presented research findings lead us to the question of meaningful and valuable ways to strengthen the quality of teaching and teacher education not only for today but also for the future.

A. Lin Goodwin, in her paper on future teachers' education, poses very significant questions on the required changes in teacher preparation and teachers' professional development to meet the needs of an unknown and constantly evolving future (Chapter 11). She is especially interested in the questions about the needed knowledge and/or competencies that are fundamental and enduring enough to serve society long beyond the 21st century and about the ways that these competencies, in turn, might influence and shape curricula and teaching for preparing young people for their tomorrow. She offers five domains of knowledge for teaching to help us think anew about teacher competencies and understandings with a focus on the teacher preparation curriculum, as well as some insights for continuing professional development and for teacher educator learning. Goodwin argues that these five knowledge domains can enable us to reimagine teaching and learning, and reform the teaching profession in ways that can support, nurture and sustain the professionals we need, not just for the 21st century but also for the 31st.

Qing Gu's considerations on developing teachers build upon but extend our current understanding of why the quality retention of teachers matters and the conditions for sustaining teacher quality through learning and development over the course of their professional lives (Chapter 12). Using a social-ecological perspective and grounded in a synthesis of empirical research from the last two decades, she explores variations in the needs of teachers' professional learning and development over the course of their professional lives. She also investigates the ways in which the increasingly complex and diverse landscape of teaching supports or hinders their capacity to teach to their best in different schools and in different phases of their professional lives.

In Chapter 13, Marco Snoek focuses on the role of career opportunities in keeping teachers passionate about and motivated by their profession and in contributing to teachers' growth, variations in teachers' professional development, and the recognition of their achievements. Snoek argues that career opportunities can both attract high-quality candidates to the profession and keep talented teachers in the profession for a longer time. His considerations, based on the analysis of six international reports on teachers' careers, lead us to his conclusions and the implications for teachers, school heads and teacher education. Snoek stresses the need for a wider and more dynamic view of the profession, the need for the development of career competencies for teachers, and the need for initial teacher education institutes to actively support teachers not only during their initial development but throughout the different stages of their career.

Chapter 14, written by Conor Galvin, Panagiotis Kampylis, Deirbhile Nic Craith, Joanna Madalinska-Michalak and Noel Purdy, focuses on unpacking the changing policy practices of the European Commission in pursuit of its teacher quality agenda over recent years. The authors detail and critique the move to a new policy method and consider its implications for teachers and teacher education, and specifically what it will likely mean for teacher education policy work in Europe in the near future. Galvin et al. consider how positive and proactive engagement with the new policy's working realities by the teacher education research community in Europe can help strengthen and deepen the pluralism and diversity of teachers and their education in ways that both the European Commission and teacher education professionals can readily value and share. Meaningful access to spaces of influence and the relevant policy fora to do so will need to be argued for and occupied.

In Chapter 15, Stéphane Colognesi and Virginie März explore the role of research in pre-service teachers' classroom practices and focus on the importance of educating about and through research. The authors focus on bridging the theory-to-practice gap within initial teacher training by educating student teachers about research through research. They present the findings of a study on the implementation of a research-training module in the final year of teacher training. The findings illustrate how participation in a collaborative research project can contribute to student teachers' research conceptions and reflexivity skills through the joint work of practitioners and researchers on questions that both consider to be relevant.

There are already several volumes connected with teachers, teacher education and teaching as a profession, however, this book focuses mainly on the issues of quality teaching and teacher education in the context of a changing word and on the contemporary and future challenges of teaching and teachers. The book explores the nature of quality, and addresses emerging and potentially redefining challenges for teaching, learning and teacher education for our times. At the centre of the discussion are the tenets of education, teaching profession, and a values-centred vision of Teacher Education.

It is shown in the book that teaching and teacher education, understood broadly as an ongoing process of professional development within the continuum of the teaching profession, are concerns for teacher educators, student teachers, teachers, school principals, school boards, leaders within education systems, those providing continuing professional development for teachers, and national and international policy-makers at different levels.

The book reveals certain tensions regarding education and its quality, and it recognises the possible consequences of these tensions for teacher education practice, policy and research. At the same time, it helps to identify the directions, questions and methods through which the explorations of the issue of quality in teaching and teacher education might be deepened and the education practice might be improved. The authors formulate recommendations for strengthening quality teaching and teacher education with a recognition of a turbulent and demanding world and a view to the future.

The presented international collection of studies problematises the category of quality in the field of teaching and teacher education, and it presents a broad view of the challenges facing teachers, teacher educators, researchers, school principals, school boards, policy-makers and society in making sense of the quality of education. The book provides a unique way of looking at education at different levels and teacher education, understood as a continuum with a focus not only on teachers' initial development but that is also maintained throughout the different stages of their careers. The implications for teachers, school principals and teacher education can be derived from the presented studies, including the need for a wider and more dynamic view of the teaching profession and the need for strong analyses to drive decisions on policy and practice in the fields of teaching and teacher education, thereby adding the significance of this book.

The volume indicates the complexity of the area under study, the diverse methods that different countries adopt to address the same challenges connected with the quality of education, and how essential it is to constantly engage in research on teachers, teaching and teacher education. This can help us to deepen our reflections on the value of teacher education research, explore the implications of teacher education research for policy and practice, and evaluate what meaningful research for teacher education practice is and how teacher education research can inform education policy.

The research presented in the book further develops the critical debate on quality teachers and teacher education that we need in Europe and beyond, and its focus on teachers and teacher education is related to the policy environment and to the wider social, cultural, political and economic contexts in which it is embedded. The research thus leads to the question: How do we see teachers, teaching and teacher education not just for the here and now but also for the unknown but inevitable future in our changing world?

This book is dedicated to researchers, policy-makers, teacher educators, teachers, teacher associations, head teachers, school principals and prospective teachers who share their concerns over the current and future conditions of education, students' learning and development, teachers' work and the teaching profession, teacher education, the teacher education research, policies and practice. It is hoped that the book will interest to a wider readership.

I owe a huge debt of gratitude to all the authors of the chapters that make up this book and to the publisher. Our cooperation on this book took place in the years 2020–2022. As we know now, this time turned out to be very complex and challenging. From the first half of 2020, we all started to operate in new, unexpected and unpredictable realities. The events related to the COVID-19 pandemic further exposed the strengths and weaknesses of the education systems around the world and, at the same time, the role of the teacher and the need for research focusing on the teacher's work, the reality in which teachers have to work and the situation concerning teachers and their profession, with reference to both the present and the future. I am extremely grateful to all my colleagues who accepted my invitation to contribute to this book for their dedication and passion and for focusing their energy in order to present their international perspectives on the quality of teaching and teacher education in a changing world, where schools and universities are under direct challenges from cultural, economic, political and social unrest.

PART 1

Towards the Nature of Quality in Teaching and Teacher Education

CHAPTER 1

What Does Quality Teacher Education Mean and How Can the Preparation of Future Teachers Be Quality Assured?

Kay Livingston

Abstract

The concept of quality in teacher education is complex. Different stakeholders have different understandings of what it means and the priorities for measurement of quality as well as the processes put in place to assure quality differ. Despite this conceptual ambiguity and a contested landscape there is an increased focus on policy reforms to improve teacher and teaching quality. This is accompanied by greater emphasis on quality assurance processes in teacher education, including the requirement in many countries for initial teacher education programmes to measure their graduates' ability to teach against a set of competencies or standards which set out what teachers should know and be able to do when they enter the teaching profession. At the same time, teaching in today's globalised world is acknowledged as challenging and ever-changing which highlights that teaching is more than prescribed knowledge to be delivered using a toolbox of teacher strategies. The dynamic nature of teaching and the many roles required of a teacher cannot be easily measured using a narrow checklist of quality indicators that do not take account of individual teacher and student differences, the relationships between them and the context in which education takes place. This chapter draws on perspectives of researchers, policy-makers school leaders and teachers to explore what quality teacher education means and argues for new approaches to quality assuring teacher preparation which enrich rather than diminish the success and joy of teaching and learning.

Keywords

quality teacher education – quality assurance – quality teachers – quality teaching – narratives – dialogue labs – multiple stakeholder collaboration

1   **Introduction**

Quality teachers and quality teacher education are enduring themes in education policy, practice and research discourses. Yet, the contested nature of the concepts, 'quality teacher' and 'quality assurance in teacher education', remain, as does the ambiguity in how they are understood and interpreted at policy and practice levels. Whilst identifying that the value of high-quality education systems and high-quality teachers is acknowledged, Niemi, Harford and Hudson (2012, p. 1) point out 'realizing this ideal has at best been problematic, with the gap between policy rhetoric and the reality of education settings often being unbridgeable'. While we hardly need any further evidence to demonstrate the complex, dynamic and contested nature of these concepts, the global pandemic has changed views for many teachers and teacher educators about what quality teaching and learning and teacher education means. The school closures and restrictions due to the pandemic starkly exposed the challenges for teachers in realising quality teaching and equity of access for all pupils, to learning and learning environments. Similarly, rapid changes were needed in teacher education, including re-thinking quality assurance systems (Moyo, 2020). At a personal level, I have been involved in teacher education for over 30 years and questions relating to quality teacher education and quality assurance have been part of my work throughout that time. I have experienced many reviews of teacher education and changes to how quality is framed, understood and assured during my involvement in teacher education. However, there has never been a more important time than now to reflect on what quality teacher education means when we are living through a period of uncertainty in all areas of our lives. I argue we have to think anew what quality teacher education is and how we assure that all teachers and pupils in our educations systems have access to quality learning opportunities and learning environments.

In this chapter I examine two main inter-related questions, What is quality teacher education? and How can the preparation of future teachers be quality assured? However, questions of quality in teacher education cannot be considered in isolation from questions of quality teachers and teaching, nor from the policy contexts in which teachers work. The chapter proceeds in five sections. In section two, I consider the policy context as a starting point for exploring different underpinning values and purposes for the pursuit of quality teachers and teacher education. In the next two sections I draw on literature to explore different understandings of quality teachers, the contested nature of the quality concepts and reflect on the different discourses of quality and the implications for teacher education. In the fifth section, I draw on empirical research studies in which I have been involved, including a policy experimentation project which engaged policy-makers, researchers and practitioners in dialogue about quality teaching and teacher education. In the final section, I argue for new approaches to quality assuring teacher education through collaboration and dialogue between policy-makers, researchers and practitioners. In conclusion, I propose that quality teacher education and how it is quality assured should be developed based on the principles of collaboration, humanistic purpose, dialogue, narrative with policy-makers, school leaders, teachers, student teachers and teacher educators working together as agents of change.

2   Policy Context

Publications by the European Commission, the Organization for Economic Cooperation and Development and the World Bank, particularly leading up to and at the start of the 2000s linked the importance of the education of a nation's citizens to the provision of knowledge and skills for a global knowledge society and to the nation's economic prosperity. This led to the production of many national policy documents setting goals to be the best performing education system by 2020 (and more recently by 2030) with a strong emphasis on improving the quality of teachers. As Linda Darling-Hammond (2000) put it, there was a growing consensus that teachers were a central factor in student achievement and therefore to the nation's workforce. This view of quality was predominantly underpinned by an economic instrumentalism that focused on preparing students for a globalised society. This continues to be the case with a European Commission guide on policies to improve initial teacher education (2015, p. 10) stating, 'Education systems all over the world are under constant pressure to adapt to the changing needs of society and the economy. (…) Therefore, the quality of how teachers are prepared for their role has become a focus for policy attention'. This highlights the connection of concepts of teacher quality to the quality of teacher education. The calls for quality teachers have been accompanied by a strong emphasis on systems and methods of quality assurance for the preparation of teachers. For example, 'Developing strong quality assurance systems is crucial to ensuring all students in schools throughout Europe receive a high-quality education' (European Commission, 2018, p. 1) and 'Quality assurance plays a key role in systematically gathering and deploying evidence in order to generate further improvement. Appropriate quality assurance policies are therefore vital to providing high-quality inclusive education in Europe' (European Commission, 2020, p. 4). The continuous stream of policy publications underlines the enduring attention given to quality teachers and teacher education for over two decades. Cochran-Smith (2021, p. 416) argues,

> ... teacher quality had become part of common parlance in the international discourse of education policy generally, and in particular, in discussions related to teaching standards, teacher evaluation policy and practice, teacher preparation practice and policy, and comparisons of education systems.

This intensity of policy activity in relation to teacher and teacher education quality is evident in the extensive number of reviews and reports. Clarke (2014, p. 588) sums up this intense policy focus saying, '... quality is one of the touchstones of modern education systems'. For example, Mayer and Reid (2016) highlight the focus on teacher quality across North America, Australasia, the United Kingdom and other European countries, as well as across Asia, Africa and South America, which in turn increases the focus on teacher education. They exemplify the Australian context saying that 'in the last decade alone there have been no fewer than 40 reports on various aspects of teacher education and since the late 1970s there have been more than 100 reviews' (Mayer & Reid, 2016, p. 461). In the UK, all four nations have all seen reviews of, and reports on teacher education in recent times. For example,
– Teaching Scotland's Future. Report of a review of teacher education in Scotland (Donaldson, 2011).
– A Review of Initial Teacher Training in Wales (Tabberer, 2013).
– *Report of an Inquiry into the role of research in teacher education* including a review of the international research evidence on high quality teacher education (BERA-RSA, 2014).
– Aspiring to Excellence. Report of the international review panel on the structure of initial teacher education in Northern Ireland (Department for Employment and Learning, 2014).
– *Carter Review of Initial Teacher Training* in England (Carter, 2015).
– Teaching Tomorrow's Teachers: Options for the future of initial teacher education in Wales (Furlong, 2015).

International comparison of education systems and their performance has also increased and resulted in greater policy attention to systems of quality assurance. This has been exacerbated by policy-makers' responses to the results from international assessment programmes, particularly the *Programme of International Student Assessment* (PISA), with increased teacher quality seen as a solution to problems of poor performance of students. Mockler (2013, p. 37) argues, '... embedded in the ensuing focus on teacher quality is a desire to narrowly measure and quantify teachers' work (usually represented simply in test scores), to standardise practice and attribute blame to teachers where their students fail to "measure up"'. Similarly, teacher educators are 'often explicitly or implicitly held accountable for teacher quality and frequently blamed when school students do not meet national or international expectations' (Cochran-Smith et al., 2020, p. 5). Clarke (2014, p. 588) argues that in contemporary neoliberal education systems 'quality is typically assumed to equate with improving test scores in high-stakes tests'. For Clarke, this begs the question, what are these tests capturing that is deemed to be of value? The concern is that quality education is reduced to improving test scores based on an assumption of a causal relationship between the quality of teacher education, the quality of the teacher, and students results in test scores. The emphasis on an outcomes conception of quality demonstrates the need to examine what is understood by 'quality', what is being measured in the name of quality, for what reasons, and what the conceptual underpinnings of various notions of quality are (Clarke, 2014).

Alongside the enduring policy emphasis on quality, research on quality teachers and quality teacher education has increased over the last two decades (Akiba & LeTendre, 2017). Despite the growing number of studies conducted, issues of quality remain ambiguous and highly contested. This is not all together unexpected as questions of quality are underscored by issues of values, beliefs, judgements and power which evoke strong emotions. Also, the assumption that teacher quality is directly linked to individual and national economic prosperity has been widely critiqued (e.g., Steadman & Ellis, 2021). In the context of this chapter, the questions, 'What is quality teacher education?' and 'How can the preparation of future teachers be quality assured?' cannot be considered in isolation from questions about 'What is a quality teacher?' and 'What is quality teaching?' This web of inter-dependent and multi-layered questions demonstrates the complexity of attempting to determine quality teacher education and how best it should be assured.

3   Different Understandings of What Is Meant by Quality Teachers and Quality Teacher Education

Akiba and LeTendre (2017), argue in their Introductory Chapter to *the International Handbook of Teacher Quality and Policy* that the whole concept of teacher quality has been contested. Defining teacher quality has been described as 'both problematic and elusive' (Liston et al., 2008, p. 111) and an 'ineffable term' (Bourke, Ryan, & Lloyd, 2016, p. 3). To complicate understandings about the nature of quality teachers, different terms are used synonymously in research studies. For example, Liston, Borko and Whitcomb (2008) identify three terms: highly qualified teacher; effective teacher; and good teacher. They point out, 'These focus on teacher characteristics or qualifications, teaching outcomes, and teaching practices, respectively' (Liston et at., 2008, p. 111). They suggest that none of these terms in themselves, adequately captures the complexity of teacher quality. Similarly, the terms 'teacher quality' and 'teaching quality' are often used interchangeably (Darling-Hammond et al., 2017; Mockler, 2013). However, there are distinctions between these two concepts. Darling-Hammond et al. (2017) explain teacher quality as the personal traits, skills, dispositions, attributes and understandings that an individual brings to teaching. They suggest this includes, strong content knowledge, pedagogical content knowledge, understanding of learners and their development and general abilities to organise and explain ideas, observe and think diagnostically and use adaptive expertise to make judgements in response to students' needs (Darling-Hammond et al., 2017, p. 17). They exemplify dispositions of quality teachers as a willingness to support all students' learning by adapting instruction, teach in a fair and unbiased manner, strive to continue to learn and improve and to collaborate with other professionals and parents for the benefit of the whole school. It is in relation to these personal qualities that attempts have been made to measure, standardise and quality assure the work of a teacher. The knowledge, skills and dispositions teachers require are increasingly set out in lists of competencies or professional standards by a growing number of governments/national agencies. Beginning teachers typically have to demonstrate their competence in relation to these requirements before they are recognised as qualified teachers. Tatto (2015, p. 173) argues,

> The main driving force in recent teacher education policy has been asking programmes to demonstrate that their graduates are qualified to teach against a set of norms or standards outlining what they should know and be able to do at the end of their preparation.

However, lists of competencies have been criticised for the use of opaque language in lists of decontextualised generic skills (Mayer & Reid, 2016). This means that the standards are open to subjective interpretation as to what they look like when they are enacted. The way they are understood depends on the values and assumptions held by those interpreting them. Lists of standards that measure only the personal performance of a teacher do not take into account the complexity of the multiple interactions within the social context of the school; for example, the interactions between the teacher and students and the curriculum area under study within the dynamic context of the classroom and school. Also, the nature of the interactions and relationships is constantly changing.

The complexity of attempts to measure the quality of teachers based only on their personal performance without consideration of the relationship between teaching and learning, is demonstrated by Fenstermacher and Richardson (2005). They refer to quality teaching arguing that it consists of both good teaching and successful teaching. By good teaching, they mean,

> ... the content taught accords with disciplinary standards of adequacy and completeness, and that the methods employed are age-appropriate, morally defensible, and undertaken with the intention of enhancing the learner's competence with respect to the content studied. (2005, p. 189)

Whereas they explain that successful teaching is dependent on the learner actually acquiring, 'to some reasonable and acceptable level of proficiency, what the teacher is engaged in teaching' (p. 189). This is an important distinction between good teaching and successful teaching which has not received enough attention in policy discussions concerning the role of teachers and teacher education in improving student learning. Fenstermacher and Richardson (2005) argue the presumption that improvement of teaching alone is a key element in improving student learning rests on a mistaken conception of a straight-forward causal connection between teaching and learning. Rather they emphasise that for a student to improve, good teaching needs to be joined with learners' willingness and effort to succeed, the social surround of family, community, and peer culture to support and assist them in their learning, and sufficient facilities, time and resources to accomplish the learning that is being sought. The complexity of these diverse conditions demonstrates that narrow measurement of student test results serves as a poor proxy for measurement of quality teachers. Teachers' work is embedded in historical, cultural and political contexts (Conway et al., 2009) and understandings of quality are influenced by different and often multiple factors – professional and personal. Multiple perspectives need to be considered and require sensitivity to the complexity inherent in every aspect of learning and teaching and school life.

4   Implications of Discourses of Quality and Quality Assurance for Teacher Education

The dynamic nature of teaching and learning and the extent of what a teacher does in undertaking their numerous roles, cannot be measured using a narrow checklist of standards that do not take account of individual teacher and student differences, the relationships between them and the context in which education takes place. As argued by Akiba and LeTendre (2017), there is emerging consensus among researchers that teacher quality is not simply about teachers' preparation, credentials and knowledge. Critique has come from researchers and practitioners in the education sector who are uncomfortable with policy borrowing from the world of business and industry, of inappropriate and meaningless approaches to quality assurance for the education context. Rizvi and Lingard (2010, p. 96), reflecting on the globalisation of education policy, argue that reform 'has been linked to reconstitution of education as a central arm of national economic policy'. For example, terms such as quality assurance, quality management and audit associated with business and industry have now been applied to education. For example, quality in a manufacturing context is understood and measured according to: perfection and consistency; fitness for purpose; and/or value for money. Processes and end product are linked in a linear way. Products that do not meet a specified and measured quality standard (perfect and consistent) can be rejected at point of manufacture or later returned as faulty or not fit for purpose by the user. These conceptualisations align with pre-established specifications and standards and quality assurance processes in relation to accountability, compliance and improvement. This prescribed production line to serve a specifically determined and consistent end product does not represent the complexity and individuality of learners, learning, teachers and teaching and the learning environment in which they work. Quality assurance mechanisms however (either mandated through legislation or proposed as policy guidance) have been put in place which aim to check the quality of processes or outcomes of teaching and teacher education through accrediting, measuring, auditing, controlling, monitoring and reviewing. The policy reforms have, in a linear way, linked the drive to improve student outcomes to teacher education in order to improve the preparation of quality teachers. In this way teacher education has been identified as the faulty process in the production line that needs to be fixed. This view has impacted on teacher education and teacher educators in different ways including shaping initial teacher education programmes approach according to a particular vision of the future teacher (Tatto, 2015).

Multiple discourses of quality interact resulting in different tensions impacting on teacher education. Following a review of a range of policies, relating to quality teachers and teaching, Churchward and Willis (2019) identified six discourses of quality that they suggest interrelate and impact on teacher education. They separated the discourses into three discourses that they argue are visible and three that are obscured. The visible discourses they identified are: readiness of beginning teachers to teach in school from day one following initial teacher education; performance measures used as quality indicators of attaining professional standards; and effectiveness linked to skills and attributes associated with quality teaching. They deemed these discourses visible as they found the terms readiness, standards and effectiveness were 'connected directly with the phrase quality' (Churchward & Willis, 2019, p. 254). The other three discourses responsiblisation, performativity and identity 'were obscured' (Churchward & Willis, 2019, p. 254), that they were implied rather than explicit in the policy documents they reviewed. They identified the responsibilisation discourse when responsibility for achieving success lies with individuals, rather than recognising other contributing factors; performativity related to judgements of individual and institutional performances based on the assumption that improved student performance is a measure of teacher quality; and identity with expectation that teacher education shapes student teachers' professional identity. Churchward and Willis argue that while numerous government reports specify the need to improve the quality of teachers the discourse of quality they refer to, and definition of quality are not clearly defined. They found the discourses of readiness, standards and effectiveness visibly impacting on teacher education programmes through course accreditation and measurement against standards.

> Yet to maintain these visible quality Discourses associated with readiness, standards, and effectiveness, the quality teacher must accede to the Discourse of performativity to establish and maintain their professional worth. While performativity is an obscured Discourse, it is a powerful current that runs beneath the surface of the more visible Discourses of quality. (Churchward & Willis, 2019, p. 259)

The powerful current of performance is increased when linked to the discourse of accountability adding further to the tension of quality assurance for teacher educators. The combining pressures of these visible and obscure discourses of quality alongside the negative portrayal of teachers and teacher education as the problem, contrasts sharply with views (e.g., in Finland) where emphasis is on creating a culture of trust (Sahlberg, 2010) which recognises that teachers and teacher educators are best placed to make decisions about what their students need to know and how to engage with them to improve their learning. Churchward and Willis (2019) emphasise the need for teachers and teacher educators to be aware of the quality discourses to enable them to be better positioned to move beyond the 'compliance cascade'.

While the emergence of the quality assurance movement in teacher education has been strongly critiqued, Tatto (2015) argues that it represents an opportunity to question the theories and practices that are used to prepare teachers. However, the challenge for many teachers and teacher educators, particularly those who have known only a working environment of accountability, performativity and narrow mechanisms of quality assurance, is that these discourses of quality are accepted as the norm. For others the complexity of the challenges of overcoming conceptual ambiguity and attempting to make meaning of what constitutes quality teachers and teacher education may leave teachers and teacher educators feeling overwhelmed and worn down. While 'there is no simple answer, no easy consensus, no secret formula'. (MacBeath et al., 2000, p. 87), the task is to look beyond narrow constraining definitions of quality teachers and teacher education and reductionist quality assurance measures and conceptualise anew approaches to quality in teacher education that are developed by, and meaningful and useful to, teachers and teacher educators.

5   Engaging Policy-Makers, Researchers and Practitioners in Dialogue about Quality Teaching and Teacher Education

In this section, I draw from the findings of three separate research projects that have informed my thinking about quality teachers and the need to reconceptualise approaches to understanding what quality means and quality assuring teacher education. The findings of the first project demonstrate the complexity of different stakeholder views about their expectations of teachers and highlight the challenge of preparing teachers for competing quality agendas. The findings of the second project demonstrate the importance of recognising teacher narratives about what is meaningful and of value for their pupils as a counter-narrative in performative times. The third project, a policy experimentation project, demonstrates the potential of discursive spaces for bringing policy-makers, researchers and practitioners together to share different views and understandings of approaches to teacher preparation.

In the sections above I discussed different views, understandings and priorities from policy-makers and researchers concerning quality teachers. Evidence of different stakeholders' views about expectations of teachers in the school context were collected during a project developing and researching a model of mentoring to strengthen career-long professional learning (Livingston & Shiach, 2014). The project was implemented through a partnership between two universities, two regional authorities and their associated schools. It involved a range of teachers (from beginning teachers to teachers with more than 30 years teaching experience) in primary and secondary schools. One of the tasks in the development process was understanding different views about what is expected of teachers as professionals. The teachers and school leaders engaged in dialogue and identified and shared their different expectations. For this chapter, I draw on the findings from one of the primary schools which extended the task to include parents. The following 3 short excerpts (Livingston & Di Nardo, 2016), illustrate responses from a selection of stakeholders (school leader, mentor teacher and a parent) when asked about their expectations of a beginning teacher (pseudonym has been used for the name of the teacher). Different conceptions of what is valued are evident.

Excerpt 1: School Leader
I expect Sam to evaluate herself, her learning about the context of the school, the primary stage and most importantly the pupils she is working with. It is important that she makes effective use of class planning to support her with her organisation and management of classroom learning and teaching. It is also essential that her daily preparation and organisation supports effective learning and teaching and promotes pupil independence. In the primary school stages, it is particularly important that she is able to work in partnership with the parents to get it right for each child and ensure that responsive and appropriate teaching and learning is taking place.

Excerpt 2: Mentor Teacher
Beginning teachers have to demonstrate that they are capable teachers and understand what being a professional means but they also need to show they are open to learning from others' experiences. I expect Sam to have her own views and ideas about what she is doing but at the same time be willing to find out how we function as a school and learn from working with colleagues. I have high expectations but these are all about caring for the pupils and ensuring they have the best possible start in their learning journey in the best possible learning environment.

Excerpt 3: Parent of a Child
The early years are so important for my child to feel safe and enjoy going to school. It is important that my daughter has strong foundations for her learning. I want her to be happy but I don't want her falling behind in her work.

The excerpts illustrate the different expectations of teachers, underpinned by different stakeholder agendas about what matters. The school leader's expectations provide an insight into quality values that aligned with the quality discourses identified by Churchward and Willis (2019). For example, there is an emphasis on the visible discourses of readiness and effectiveness linked to the language of standards. The mentor teacher has expectations linked to the standards to be achieved but also recognises the importance of ongoing development and enabling the beginning teacher to develop their own professional identity as a teacher. This suggests understanding that teacher quality is a dynamic concept, involving interaction between the teacher, pupils and the school context. The parent's expectations focus on what will be provided for their child by the teacher and the school. The parent's expectations of the teacher are implicit rather than explicit – what matters is the balance between facilitating learning while caring for their child. These different views demonstrate the challenges for beginning teachers, who may feel they are being pulled in different directions to suit competing agendas which impacts on the development of their professional identify. As Churchward and Willis (2019) point out, in relation to the obscured discourse of identity, experiences are important in the development of professional identity.

The challenge for teachers trying to suit competing agendas in performative times was also evident in the second project (Livingston & Doherty, 2020) I draw on. We argue that in regimes of performativity a common response, whether local, national or international, is to narrow the school curriculum to focus on just those elements that are tested with 'shrinking space for curricular and pedagogical innovation, creativity, or autonomy' (Crocco & Costigan, 2007, p. 516). As a counter-narrative, we investigated efforts to enrich the school curriculum, and how an enrichment programme might make itself relevant in the logic of performative times. We understand 'curriculum enrichment as the practice of intentionally adding more elements to the formal curriculum, above and beyond policy guidelines or mandated curriculum, to augment the learning made available to all students' (Livingston & Doherty, 2020, p. 668).

To answer the question, 'What impact do these curriculum enrichment programmes have?' We undertook a qualitative analysis of semi-structured interviews with school leaders and focus groups of teachers and students. For the purpose of this chapter, I draw particularly from our findings in two case schools, one secondary school and one primary school (CS1 and CS2). Both schools serve disadvantaged communities. Our findings showed how the school leaders and teachers in both schools work within and beyond the performative rhetoric of measurable outcomes to account for their impact. Both schools purposefully used enrichment programmes as a pedagogical tool to promote students' learning and enrich curricular outcomes while at the same time providing different opportunities and new experiences for their students.

When the school leaders and teachers in both schools were asked how they would account for the impact of the enrichment programmes, their immediate response was to reference measurable attainment in curricular subjects. However, our analysis of the findings traced two parallel narratives about the impact of the enrichment programme. The school leader in CS2 first emphasised the official policy imperatives of measurement then reverted to the less measurable criterion of students' affective engagement in learning experiences. Similarly, the school leader's view in CS1, was that her observations and professional judgement could provide a richer picture than any formal mode of assessment, although, she also offered an account of impact on subject grades. 'Efforts to formally measure the ineffable were considered to distort the object of the enrichment, or defeat the purpose of their more flexible, engaging invisible pedagogies' (Livingston & Doherty, 2020, p. 681). Our analysis showed the teachers in both schools are necessarily complying with measurement priorities in their focus on student attainment while at the same time, doing what they believe is important for their students in terms of enriching learning experiences. Importantly, the leaders in both schools emphasised how, for them, the opportunities afforded by curriculum enrichment offered the greatest potential to close the poverty-related attainment gap. The school leaders in both schools,

> ... are proactive in designing experiences that seek to be transformative by extending the students' capacity to do and be something, not just to know something, offering relatively disadvantaged students opportunities to extend their horizons and imagine a new future beyond their locale. While this made it hard to evidence their impact, all interviewees were in no doubt about the value of these programmes, and their particular relevance and power in disadvantaged communities to address their students' lack of opportunities. This is learning that is valued while not measurable using performative measures. (Livingston & Doherty, 2020, p. 682)

Livingston and Doherty argue that this counter-narrative of curricular enrichment in performative times is worth documenting. The interviewees expressed their professional judgement regarding the impact of access to experiences that otherwise would not be available to their students by drawing on their observations of student transformation through their engagement in the enrichment programmes. The findings of this empirical project illustrate the importance of listening to school leaders' and teachers' narratives as a way of moving beyond the use of only performative measures of quality.

We argue that there is a need to systematically collect teachers' professional judgement accounts and observations of student transformation through learning experiences as well as outcomes achieved.

The final project I draw on is TeachUP, a European policy experimentation project (2017–2020) coordinated by European Schoolnet, involving Ministries of Education/national education agencies from Austria; Greece; Estonia; Hungary; Lithuania; Malta; Portugal; Slovakia; Spain; and Turkey. The project involved an exploration of ways to provide online teacher education courses, focusing on a selection of areas for development (formative assessment, personalised learning and teaching, collaboration, and creative thinking). It involved a randomised-controlled trial using online courses as the experiment medium, involving 4,000 teachers in the 10 partner countries. The project also included a series of annual Dialogue Labs in each country that brought together policy-makers, teacher educators, teachers, researchers and other teacher education stakeholders (Livingston, 2020). I draw from the findings from the Dialogue Labs which were purposively designed to enable ongoing dialogue between multiple stakeholders (from policy, research and practice communities) about the development of teacher education for the future. The main aim was to enable a wide range of stakeholders to share their different perspectives to inform and improve the development, implementation and evaluation of the online courses for teachers' professional development (student teachers and in-service teachers engaged in the courses).

A day-long Dialogue Lab took place in each partner country in each of the three years of the TeachUP Project. They were designed as a connecting series to enable the participants to develop their thinking across the series of three Dialogue Labs. The same participants were encouraged to participate in all three Labs to develop a sense of community with the intention of forming a network of policy, research and practice stakeholders who could sustain knowledge sharing in teacher education beyond the lifetime of the policy experimentation. As an example of the number of stakeholders involved each year, across the 10 countries a total of 276 participants (policy-makers, Education Agency Officials, ITE and CPD educators, teachers, school leaders, student teachers, education experts/consultants, parents, and inspectors) participated in the 3rd Country Dialogue Labs. The design, implementation and evaluation of the series of three Dialogue Labs were guided by Dialogue Lab Guidelines (Livingston, 2017, 2018, 2019). The Guidelines set out the format for each Lab to ensure consistency in approach across the 10 countries and in the reflective questions that framed the dialogue.

Prior to the first Dialogue Lab taking place there were some reservations expressed by some of the partners about bringing together policy-makers with school leaders, teachers and student teachers to discuss policy development in teacher education, especially as the guidelines emphasised that there should be 'no speeches from the front'. Rather the emphasis was on mixed groups of stakeholders engaging in focused dialogue from the start of the Lab, to send a strong message that all voices mattered and should be heard to enable different perspectives to be discussed. After the first Dialogue Lab had been held there was unanimous praise for the structured format of the Labs that enabled discussion between all the stakeholders involved. The final evaluation comments after the 3rd Dialogue Lab showed that all the participants had found the dialogue process motivating and valuable. The experience of engaging in the Dialogue Labs was considered to be of great value due to the variety of profiles of the participants and highly recommended to be used for policy dialogue in teacher education nationally in future as they enable the exchange of participants' perspectives. The interdisciplinary composition of the Dialogue Labs was particularly highlighted as being an important feature. It was agreed that the process of the Labs had enabled a topic to be considered from the reality of different perspectives (e.g., perspectives of teachers, student teachers, school leaders, university researchers, teacher educators, consultants, inspectors and policy-makers). The importance of the involvement of practitioners in policy development was particularly acknowledged by the participants as, 'it makes it possible to take the reality of the school into account' (Livingston, 2020, p. 14). The diversity of the stakeholders participating in the Dialogue Labs was recognised as offering a positive way to network and as an opportunity for the professional development of all those involved, exemplified in the following participant comment, 'I think that these kinds of meetings that enrich and unite the educational ecosystem are very interesting and necessary' (Livingston, 2020, p. 14). Several countries have continued with Dialogue Labs beyond the TeachUP Project and others indicated they plan to do so.

As argued by Cochran-Smith et al. (2018), most reforms have 'positioned teachers, teacher educators, and teacher education institutions/programmes as the objects, rather than the agents, of reform' (Cochran-Smith et al., 2018, p. 572). However, the TeachUP policy experimentation project offers hope that teachers and teacher educators can be recognised as important in policy development processes. The Dialogue Labs were intentionally designed in an effort to make professional experiences visible and share knowledge, views and ideas between stakeholders. There was recognition of the importance of building trust between stakeholders as a foundation to understanding the development and implementation of policy reforms from different perspectives. The positive outcomes of the Dialogue Labs demonstrate that discursive spaces can be opened up between policy-makers, teachers and teacher educators to share their views about what quality teachers and teacher education means.

6 Re-conceptualisation of Quality: Looking to the Future

What can be learned from these three projects in relation to how, we as teacher educators, can help prepare teachers to navigate these different conceptions of quality and quality assurance without them feeling bound by them or diminishing the joy of teaching, or generally feeling they are being pulled in different directions to suit competing agendas? The findings from each of the projects highlight, in their own way, the importance and value of facilitated and open dialogue between policy-makers, researchers, teachers, students, parents and other relevant stakeholders about different meanings and understandings of quality teachers and approaches to quality assurance processes for teacher education. To speak back to the six discourses of quality portrayed by Churchward and Willis (2019) requires agentic teachers and teacher educators to be prominent in reforms of teacher education – teachers and teacher educators who are able through dialogue with other stakeholders to change the discourses of quality, particularly about what constitutes quality teachers and teacher education. The findings of the second project demonstrated the importance and value of listening to school leaders' and teachers' narratives, and the third project showed the possibility and the potential of stakeholder dialogue on teacher education. From sharing realities of the impact of current regimes of performativity, teachers and teacher educators can contribute to alternative discourses that demonstrate understanding of quality as transformation for everyone involved and quality assurance as a developmental approach rather than a judgemental one. The aim is to shift quality assurance discourses to focus on finding ways to enrich quality, based on understanding quality as multi-dimensional and dynamic (rather than a static concept) that cannot be decided by policy-makers without the voices of other stakeholders. This is an important step in counter-balancing the current focus on narrow standards and performance indicators and placing a renewed emphasis on values and dispositions as an essential element of teacher education. To make this possible the opening up of the territory of what quality teachers and quality teacher education mean and what the purpose of quality assurance mechanisms are, through collaboration and dialogue between different stakeholders at policy, research and practice levels is essential.

The COVID-19 pandemic changed the way schooling and teacher education were provided (in some cases almost overnight) and put the focus on what mattered most across all areas of life. The question of how teachers should be prepared for the future needs to include not only, what should teachers know and be able to do but also what should they care about? Hanlon (2015) asked the question: 'What should be the purpose of organised learning experiences in contemporary conditions?' She could not have predicted the scale and speed of the pandemic but in 2015 she answered her question by saying,

> Old narratives about economic competitiveness, or personal fulfilment are plainly inadequate. Today, learning has to be about saving our species on this planet, and in conditions which do justice to our aspirations for good lives. (Hanlon, 2015, p. 14)

In relation to teacher education, Hanlon's response underlines that looking to the future, the questions that need to be addressed are not only: 'What is quality teacher education?' and 'How can the preparation of future teachers be quality assured?' but also, 'What for?', 'For what purpose?' The search for answers should not be about making the programmes we have now better, or changing the structures of the model by moving teacher education so it is carried out in a different location, or with another provider or online. All three questions need to be addressed not by policy-makers, or researcher or practitioners alone in silos, but in collaboration through dialogue and narrative.

In response, to what Turvey (2019, p. 16) calls 'the cold climate of teacher education', he proposes humanising approaches to teacher education that prepare teachers as 'deliberative intellectuals'. Turvey characterises deliberative intellectuals as teachers who are able to theorise about practice through thoughtful critique, joint construction of local knowledge and through questioning of common assumptions. He proposes narrative as a humanising tool, describing it as meaningful and usable as it is constructed based on a rich provenance, just as the school leaders' and teachers' narratives in project two demonstrated. Turvey argues that narrative is central to 'establishment of care, dignity and dialogic consciousness raising' (2019, p. 16) as it

> offers some opportunity to hold the burgeoning of dehumanising forms of datafication in education and teacher education to account, and provide insights into the cultural impact of privileging certain kinds of evidence or misunderstanding the limitations of different kinds of evidence.

The findings from the Dialogue Labs in the third project discussed above demonstrated the power of collaborative dialogue between stakeholders and showed that school leaders, teachers, student teachers and teacher educators were able to act as 'deliberative intellectuals', willing and confident in sharing their narratives of reality. They were able to discuss, with policy-makers, researchers and other education stakeholders, potential solutions for alternative models of teacher education as well as the challenges of quality assurance approaches. The Dialogue Labs offered a starting point in policy experimentation, highlighting to the policy-makers involved the limitations of different kinds of evidence. The results showed that the randomised-control trial and the Dialogue Labs provided very different sorts of data and different insights. Also, the nature of the different agendas of the stakeholders regarding teacher education became clear. For example, the need to find a balance between autonomy and accountability is a significant and ongoing challenge for education systems generally, and in the context of this chapter teacher education specifically. In particular, there is an urgent need to explore the interaction between the different stakeholder agendas and internal and external quality assurance mechanisms impacting on schools and teacher education. The Dialogue Labs offered potential for discussion about some of the challenges in teacher education that arose during the intervention phase of the randomised-control trial. They enabled solutions to be discussed by the stakeholders and in some cases solutions to be implemented prior to the second and third year of the project. This demonstrated not only the value of dialogue between stakeholders but the value of multiple feedback loops between stakeholders, where the sharing of authentic narratives in a trusted discursive space enabled joint proposals for changes to the model of teacher education to be enacted.

The main points of each Lab were recorded by a Country-Coordinator in each of the 10 countries involved. These reports were analysed and a Cross-country Dialogue Lab Report (e.g., Livingston, 2020) provided feedback about the main points recorded to the stakeholders. The feedback from the previous Dialogue Lab became the first point of discussion at each subsequent Lab. This not only showed all the stakeholders that their views were being heard, they could also see how their suggestions for change had been enacted to enrich the model of teacher education being developed. This gave evidence to all involved that their participation was valued and of value, as were the feedback loops established between stakeholders and between the project data and practice. In this way the multiple stakeholders could be characterised as a professional learning community sharing views alongside consideration of evidence being collected during a policy experimentation project. They were agents of change within the project as suggestions for solving challenges or making improvements were enacted. I argue that the model of multiple stakeholder involvement in a series of one day Dialogue Labs, enabling structured dialogue focused on specific questions, such as how to better prepare teachers for the future and quality assure teacher education, is essential to recognise the inter-relationship of multiple perspectives and dignify the complexity inherent in considering issues of quality of teachers and teacher education. Difficult challenges cannot be addressed in one- or two-hour formal meetings of stakeholders where some voices are privileged over others. The Dialogue Lab model provides for plurality of views to come together in a space where challenges can be considered from multiple perspectives. The model also offers opportunities for a network of stakeholders, policy-makers, researchers, practitioners and other relevant education stakeholders to meet regularly to consider what matters and enrich the preparation of teachers for the changing contexts of teacher education.

References

Akiba, M., & LeTendre, G. (2017). Conceptualising teacher quality and policy in a global context. In M. Akiba & G. LeTendre (Eds.), *International handbook of teacher quality and policy* (1st ed., pp. 1–21). Taylor and Francis.

BERA-RSA. (2014). *Research and the teaching profession. Building the capacity for a self-improving education system.* Final report of the BERA-RSA Inquiry into the role of research in teacher education. British Educational Research Association.

Biesta, G. (2009). Good education in an age of measurement: On the need to reconnect with the question of purpose in education. *Educational Assessment, Evaluation and Accountability, 21*(1), 33–46.

Bourke, T., Ryan, M., & Lloyd, M. (2016). The discursive positioning of graduating teachers in accreditation of teacher education programs. *Teaching and Teacher Education. An International Journal of Research and Studies, 53*(1), 1–9.

Carter, A. (2015). *Carter review of initial teacher training.* Department of Education.

Churchward, P., & Willis, J. (2019). The pursuit of teacher quality: Identifying some of the multiple discourses of quality that impact the work of teacher educators. *Asia-Pacific Journal of Teacher Education, 47*(3), 251–264.

Clarke, M. (2014). The sublime objects of education policy: Quality, equity and ideology. *Discourse: Studies in the Cultural Politics of Education, 35*(4), 584–598.

Cochran-Smith, M. (2021). Exploring teacher quality: International perspectives. *European Journal of Teacher Education, 44*(3), 415–428.

Cochran-Smith, M., Grudnoff, L., Orland-Barak, L., & Smith, K. (2020). Educating teacher educators: International perspectives. *The New Educator, 16*(1), 5–24.

Cochran-Smith, M., Stringer Keefe, E., & Cummings Carney, M. (2018). Teacher educators as reformers: Competing agendas. *European Journal of Teacher Education, 41*(5), 572–590.

Conway, P., Murphy, R., Rath, A., & Hall, K. (2009). *Learning to teach: A nine country cross national study.* The Teaching Council.

Crocco, M., & Costigan, A. (2007). The narrowing of curriculum and pedagogy in the age of accountability. *Urban Education, 42*(6), 512–535.

Darling-Hammond, L. (2000). Teacher quality and student achievement: A review of state policy evidence. *Education Policy Analysis Archives, 8*(1). https://doi.org/10.14507/epaa.v8n1.2000

Darling-Hammond, L., Burns, D., Campbell, C., Goodwin, A. L., Hammerness, K., Low, E. L., & Zeichner, K. (2017). *Empowered educators: How high-performing systems shape teaching quality around the world*. Jossey-Bass.

Department for Employment and Learning. (2014). *Aspiring to excellence. Final report of the international review panel on the structure of initial teacher education in Northern Ireland*. Department for Employment and Learning.

Donaldson, G. (2011). *Teaching Scotland's future. Report of a review of teacher education in Scotland*. The Scottish Government.

European Commission. (2015). *Shaping career-long perspectives on teaching guide on policies to improve initial teacher education*. Education & Training – 2020, Schools Policy. European Commission.

European Commission. (2018). *Better learning for Europe's young people: Developing coherent quality assurance strategies for school education*. European Commission.

European Commission. (2020). *Supporting school self-evaluation and development through quality assurance policies: Key considerations for policy makers*. European Commission.

Fenstermacher, G. D., & Richardson, V. (2005). On making determinations of quality in teaching. *Teachers College Record, 107*(1), 186–213.

Furlong, J. (2015). *Teaching tomorrow's teachers*. Oxford University Press.

Hanlon, V. (2015). What is learning for? *European Journal of Education, 50*(1), 14–16.

Hanushek, E. (2011). The economic value of higher teacher quality. *Economics of Education Review, 30*(3), 466–479.

Liston, D., Borko, H., & Whitcomb, J. (2008). The teacher educator's role in enhancing teacher quality. *Journal of Teacher Education, 59*(2), 111–116.

Livingston, K. (2017). *Guidelines for country dialogue labs* (1st ed.). European Schoolnet.

Livingston, K. (2018). *Guidelines for country dialogue labs* (2nd ed.). European Schoolnet.

Livingston, K. (2019). *Guidelines for country dialogue labs* (3rd ed.). European Schoolnet.

Livingston, K. (2020). *Final cross-country dialogue lab report 2019–2020* (3rd ed.). European Schoolnet.

Livingston, K., & Di Nardo, P. (2016). Becoming a teacher. In D. Wyse & S. Rogers (Eds.), *Early years and primary teaching* (pp. 9–26). Sage Publication Ltd.

Livingston, K., & Doherty, C. (2020). A counter-narrative of curriculum enrichment in performative times. *The Curriculum Journal, 31*(4), 666–686.

Livingston, K., & Shiach, L. (2014). *Teaching Scotland's future: Further developing and sustaining a strengthened model of professional learning through mentoring processes in the context of career-long professional learning – Final report*. Education Scotland.

MacBeath, J., Schratz, M., Meuret, D., & Jakobsen, L. (2000). *Self-evaluation in European schools: A story of change*. Routledge.

Mayer, D., & Reid, J. A. (2016). Professionalising teacher education: Evolution of a changing knowledge and policy landscape. In J. Loughran & M. Hamilton (Eds.), *International handbook of teacher education* (pp. 453–486). Springer.

Mockler, N. (2013). Teacher professional learning in a neoliberal age: Audit, professionalism and identity. *Australian Journal of Teacher Education, 38*(10), 35–47.

Moyo, N. (2020). COVID-19 and the future of practicum in teacher education in Zimbabwe: Rethinking the 'new normal' in quality assurance for teacher certification. *Journal of Education for Teaching, 46*(4), 536–545.

Niemi, H., Harford, J., & Hudson, B. (2012). Introduction: From quality assurance to quality culture. In J. Harford, B. Hudson, & H. Niemi (Eds.), *Quality assurance and teacher education* (pp. 1–11). Peter Lang.

Rizvi, F., & Lingard, B. (2010). *Globalizing education policy*. Routledge.

Sahlberg, P. (2010). Rethinking accountability in a knowledge society. *Journal of Educational Change, 11*(1), 45–61.

Steadman, S., & Ellis, V. (2021). Teaching quality, social mobility and 'opportunity' in England: The case of the teaching and leadership innovation fund. *European Journal of Teacher Education, 44*(3), 399–414.

Tabberer, R. (2013). *A review of initial teacher training in Wales*. Welsh Government.

Tatto, M. T. (2015). The role of research in the policy and practice of quality teacher education: An international review. *Oxford Review of Education, 41*(2), 171–201.

Turvey, K. (2019). Humanising as innovation in a cold climate of [so called-evidence-based] teacher education. *Journal of Education for Teaching, 45*(1), 15–30.

CHAPTER 2

Unpacking Quality in Teacher Education

Maria Assunção Flores

Abstract

Quality teachers matter and quality teachers depend on the quality of their education. This chapter examines the question of what quality teacher education means. I draw on existing international literature, taking the Portuguese legal framework as an example to discuss how quality is understood. While there may be consensus about the key importance of quality teacher education, there is less agreement on what quality entails and how it is to be assessed. Therefore, any analysis of quality as a dynamic and contested concept must, among other things, consider the voices of the various stakeholders and the broad political, social and cultural environment in which teacher education is situated. It is argued that quality should be problematised, particularly in the context of teacher education reform, and that consideration needs to be given to a shared frame of reference as well as to specific features of the local settings.

Keywords

quality – teacher education – teacher quality – quality teacher education – policy – teaching

1 Introduction

The term quality has been widely used in policy and academic arenas to discuss (and justify) reforms within teacher education. However, while there may be consensus about the key importance of quality teacher education, there is less agreement on what quality entails and how it is to be assessed. As Russell and Martin (2016) assert, quality is an elusive concept and, as such, there is no single definition of quality that applies universally nor is there a single recipe for improving quality in initial teacher education programmes.

It is thus possible to identify distinct understandings of quality (Flores, 2016, 2019; Tatto & Pippin, 2017) which are used to frame different orientations and policies in the field of teacher education. Issues such as the globalisation of standards and the increased marketisation of education have led to a greater focus on the quality of teacher education, which meanwhile has become a prominent and contested field (Tatto & Pippin, 2017).

Quality teachers matter and quality teachers depend on the quality of their education. As Imig and Imig (2007, p. 107) argue, 'Everywhere there is the quest for greater quality in education – and, therefore, teacher education is the focal point for attention and concern'. Yet, it is also true that the discourse of quality has at times been accompanied by uncritical understandings and simplistic views of what counts as quality. For instance, Mayer (2014, p. 471) suggests that a 'naive view of teacher quality' has been associated with 'a linear relationship between policy and educational outcomes without accounting for school culture, resources and communities'. In a similar vein, Menter and Hulme (2011, p. 394) look at standards as 'part of the general move in the direction of accountability based on notions of performance (performativity) and [which] have been seen as unnecessarily restrictive'.

When examining discourses of quality in teacher education, features to be considered include the influence of transnational agencies, governmental intervention in the definition of standards and competencies to regulate teacher education, as well as the degree of involvement of the various stakeholders in defining a frame of reference for teacher education. Menter and Flores (2021) identify forces for convergence and divergence in policy development and discuss how teacher professionalism has been subject to processes of redefinition in a number of settings, especially through major changes in teacher education. They identify the influence of OECD exercises such as PISA and TALIS, leading to international comparisons and to policies trying to 'emulate those systems that are most "successful"' but also transnational agreements such as the Bologna process in Europe, with implications for 'new alignments between diverse systems of teacher education, for example in terms of course structures, durations and credit points' (Menter & Flores, 2021, p. 121). As for the forces of divergence, the same authors point to issues of national identity (e.g., distinctive approaches to languages and language education, cultural diversity and citizenship education).

It is, therefore, necessary to unpack what counts as quality in teacher education and how it has been shaped. As a matter of global concern (Cochran-Smith, 2021) quality is seen as a multifaceted concept that should be examined in terms of who defines it and how. This chapter aims to discuss quality in teacher education by drawing on existing literature with particular consideration given to Portuguese policy documents.

2 Problematising Teacher Quality

Although there is no single definition of quality, the concept is sometimes used as if it is universally understood in a straightforward and similar way. Its problematic and contested nature arises from different views of education but also from the complexity of teaching and contrasting understandings of the kinds of teachers that are to be educated in specific contexts. In short, quality is viewed according to different perspectives of teacher professionalism. It entails questions about what teachers need to know and be able to do, but also how their role is understood. Thus, there are considerable variations in how teacher quality is defined and enacted in different contexts. As Ell (2021, p. 115) argues,

> Definitions of teacher quality are highly significant to ITE [initial teacher education] providers, because they define the types of graduate that the system is asking for, which in turn determines the people who will be selected for teacher education, the experience teacher candidates need as part of their teacher education programme and the outcomes that they need to achieve. At times quality teachers are defined as teachers with sound content knowledge and high grades, at other times as teachers who can set and maintain behavioural standards.

Looking at how teacher professionalism is enacted in teacher education policy in Belgium (Flanders), Vanassche, Bruneel and Christiaens (2021) describe it as a technical quality possessed and performed by individual teachers that can be mapped and checked. The authors stress that the normative discourse about what it means to be a teacher emphasises questions about 'what works/does not work' and focuses on individual knowledge, skills and attitudes.

Examining the OECD documents, which are internationally seen as essential in discussions of teacher quality (OECD, 2005, 2018), Singh, Hoyte, Heimans and Exley (2021) conclude that quality is associated more with the individual teacher rather than with teaching. The authors state that there is no clear definition of what quality means but they identify over fifty attributes associated with quality teachers that revolve around issues of effectiveness, competencies, and qualifications. Nevertheless, effectiveness is a prevalent term linked to students' achievement and used almost interchangeably with quality.

It is, therefore, possible to find different expressions using the term quality: teacher quality, quality education, quality teaching and quality teacher education, to name but a few. For instance, Darling-Hammond (2010, p. 200) draws a distinction between 'the related but distinct ideas' of teacher quality and teaching quality. While teacher quality is associated with the 'bundle of personal traits, skills, and understandings an individual brings to teaching, including dispositions to behave in certain ways', teaching quality 'has to do with strong instruction that enables a wide range of students to learn' in order to meet 'the demands of the discipline, the goals of instruction, and the needs of the students in a particular context' (Darling-Hammond, 2010, p. 200). The same author argues that 'teaching quality is in part a function of teacher quality – teachers' knowledge, skills and dispositions – but it is also strongly influenced by the context of instruction' (Darling-Hammond, 2010, p. 200). In turn, Cochran-Smith identifies the emergence of teacher quality as a global concept which has been subject to shifts in its meaning. She argues that 'despite the global nature of teacher quality, what this concept means and how reforms are designed and implemented in particular countries vary considerably' (Cochran-Smith, 2021, p. 415).

Based on the Dutch context, Snoek (2021) analyses how definitions of teacher quality were associated with claims from different stakeholders such as the government, teacher education institutes, teachers, teachers' employers, etc. The author argues that what emerged was confusion and debate rather than a shared understanding. Snoek (2021) highlights a lack of a common language and the existence of different perspectives from the part of different stakeholders. He advocates for a more dynamic view of teacher quality but also recognises its complexity and demanding nature.

Drawing on the context of high-performing countries, such as Australia (New South Wales and Victoria), Canada (Alberta and Ontario), Finland, China (Shangai), and Singapore, Darling-Hammond (2021, p. 296) argues that frameworks for defining teacher quality have expanded to include 'increasingly evidence- and inquiry-based conceptions of practice' focusing on a child-centred curriculum and instruction and on quality and multicultural issues. In a similar vein, Goodwin and Low (2021) discuss how ideas about teacher quality in Hong-Kong and Singapore have focused on views of teachers as professionals who are able to reflect and adapt to meet students' holistic development.

Notions of quality vary and have to be understood in light of particular views of education and curriculum but also on given understandings of the kinds of professionals that are to be educated.

3   Conceptualising Quality Teacher Education

Quality teachers depend on quality teacher education programmes and, thus, attention has been paid worldwide to how definitions of quality have influenced given orientations in the field. For instance, Singh, Hoyte, Heimans and Exley (2021, p. 5) argue that 'there is a shift in teacher education effected by the teacher quality agenda, with its unrelenting focus on student learning attainment and outcomes'. They go on to say that 'This agenda narrows the curriculum (what is taught), pedagogy (how it is taught), and evaluation (assessment and measurement instruments) of teacher education programmes in Australia to constitute instrumentalist, technical notions of teaching'. This view is in line with existing literature which points to standards-driven education systems 'as a means of improving the quality of education provided and to increase student achievements' (Townsend, 2011, p. 488). A 'deficit discourse' has been prevalent in which teacher education is seen as a 'problem to be solved' (Mayer, Goodwin, & Mockler, 2021, p. 211). Brooks (2021) argues that quality indicators for initial teacher education tend to focus on standards rather than seeing quality as educational transformation.

There is no universal framework for examining the quality of teacher education. Kennedy, Adams and Carver (2021, p. 166) recognise that quality in initial teacher education is 'complex, permeating national, institutional, programme, and individual levels'. Imig, Wiseman, Wiseman and Imig (2016, p. 80) also assert that 'there remains a multitude of interpretations about how teacher education programmes are evaluated for quality'. Taking into account the USA context, they identify the following features (Imig et al., 2016, p. 81): i) to assess the knowledge and skills of graduates; ii) to use the system of voluntary professional accreditation to verify if the graduates meet national standards and are qualified to be licensed or certified; iii) to garner credibility through various reputational studies of the programme and of the faculty that teach in such programmes; iv) to provide a rigorous measure of candidate progress and proficiency during the teacher education programme. In general, a normative and performative discourse associated with narrow measures of what counts as quality teaching and quality teacher education has been identified (Mayer, Goodwin, & Mockler, 2021).

Existing literature points to different rationales and frameworks to evaluate teacher education programmes. As Feuer, Floden, Chudowsky, and Ahn (2013, pp. 1–2) assert, the evaluation of teacher education programmes draws on 'various types of evidence – each with its particular strengths and limitations – to make inferences about the quality of the preparation experience and its role in producing employable, high-quality teachers'. The authors identify six attributes related to initial teacher education quality and the commonly used evidence to measure them: (i) admissions and recruitment criteria; (ii) quality and substance of instruction; (iii) quality of student teaching experience; (iv) faculty qualifications; (v) effectiveness in preparing new teachers who are employable and stay in the field, and (vi) success in preparing high-quality

teachers. Feuer et al. (2013) argue that for an evaluation system to be coherent, a number of questions need to be asked regarding whether it serves its intended purposes and whether it leads to valid inferences about the quality of the programmes:
- What is the primary purpose of the initial teacher evaluation system?
- Which aspects of initial teacher education matter most?
- What sources of evidence will provide the most accurate and useful information about the aspects of teacher preparation that are of primary interest?
- How will the measures be analysed and combined to make a judgment about programme quality?
- What are the intended and potentially unintended consequences of the evaluation system for initial teacher education and education more broadly?
- How will transparency be achieved? What steps will be taken to help users understand how to interpret the results and use them appropriately?
- How will the evaluation system be monitored?

Advocating for a dynamic and adaptable framework, Kennedy, Adams and Carver (2021) 'Scotified' the six categories identified by Feuer et al. (2013) and included two more categories that the authors considered to be relevant to the Scottish context: i) partnership; ii) admissions; recruitment; and retention; iii) programme design; iv) practicum/fieldwork; v) teacher educators; vi) initial destinations; vii) post-registrations; and viii) institutional context.

Menter and Flores (2021, p. 123) argue for a connection to be made between teaching, teacher professionalism, teacher education and educational research stating that 'these relationships can provide key indicators for the evaluation of the condition of teaching and teacher education in any particular context'. They also suggest a series of questions that may serve as the basis for such an evaluation:
- How is teacher professionalism defined and by whom?
- What is the nature of the relationships between the respective communities of policy, practice and research?
- To what extent is an enquiry approach embedded within, respectively, initial teacher education, teacher induction, continuing professional development?
- In pursuing opportunities for positions in educational leadership (senior posts in schools or local management) are candidates' experience and skills in educational research taken into account?
- Who undertakes research into teaching and teacher education and what is its nature? Is a broad range of research methodologies employed? Is there evidence of independence and criticality in the research undertaken? How is such research disseminated and made use of?

What is clear from the above examples is that conceptualisations of quality in teacher education need to go beyond simplistic understandings that do not take into account its multiple layers, protagonists and dynamics. As Mayer (2021, p. 3) highlights, 'Various policy initiatives exhibit aspects of marketisation, free-market competition and accountability mechanisms using measurement of graduating teachers' readiness for teaching and graduating teachers' impact on school students' learning outcomes'. Meijer (2021), in the Dutch context, examines how policies deal with issues of quantity and quality within a trend to oversimplify teaching which includes issues such as lowering the threshold for entering teacher education, allowing for short and stackable tracks and lowering the standards to solve the shortage of teachers. She argues that there is a need to invest in quality in teacher education programmes to counteract quick fixes and to consider the complex and dynamic nature of the process of learning to teach. In the USA, Darling-Hammond (2006, p. 41) identified seven common elements in high quality teacher education programmes: (i) a common, clear vision of good teaching that permeates all course-work and clinical experiences; (ii) well-defined standards of professional practice and performance that are used to guide and evaluate course work and clinical work; (iii) a curriculum grounded in knowledge of child and adolescent development, learning, social-contexts, and subject matter pedagogy, taught in the context of practice; (iv) extended clinical experiences that are carefully developed to support the ideas and practices presented in simultaneous, closely interwoven course work; (v) explicit strategies that help students confront their own deep-seated beliefs and assumptions about learning and students, and learn about the experiences of people different than themselves; (vi) strong relationships, common knowledge, and shared beliefs link school-based and university-based faculty; and (vii) case study methods, teacher research, performance assessments, and portfolio evaluation that apply learning to real problems of practice.

As Menter (2022) asserts, the concept of quality in teacher education is complex and has many dimensions at various levels, including the system, the institutional and the individual. As such it is necessary to question what counts as quality in teacher education, particularly in contexts of reform, and to critically discuss the notion of evidence by asking 'evidence of what, generated by whom, and for what purpose' (Mayer, Goodwin, & Mockler, 2021, p. 217).

4 The Portuguese Legal Framework for Teacher Education: Exploring Its Meaning

In this section, I examine the Portuguese legal framework for teacher education issued after the forced implementation of the Bologna process, which represented a turning point in the restructuring process of all teacher education programmes. A master's degree in teaching has become the required qualification for all entrants into teaching (from pre-school to secondary school). A consecutive model was adopted (Decree-Law No. 43/2007). It involves a two-stage process which includes a first three-year degree (*Licenciatura*) in a specific subject (e.g. Mathematics, History) followed by a master's degree in teaching (usually a two-year degree), combining subject-based instruction with educational and pedagogical components, including practicum. In the case of pre-school and primary school, student teachers complete a first degree in Basic Education followed by a master's degree in Teaching. The condensed two-year programme at master's level has led to the need to reorganise both the content and structure of the courses and their modules. The former legal framework published in 2007 (Decree-Law No. 43/2007) was replaced by the legislative text issued in 2014, which is currently in place (Decree-Law No. 79/2014) and which will be examined with respect to the following questions: Is the term quality used in the legal framework? If so, how is quality defined? What counts as quality in teacher education? What are the implications of the framework for teacher professionalism?

4.1 *The Discourse of Quality as the Rationale for Change*

The new legal framework for teacher education issued in 2014 is justified by the need to enhance the quality of the education system. Reference to multiple international studies, in particular OECD and Eurydice, is put forward to emphasise the necessity to overhaul teacher education. The case of Finland is used for justifying the need to 'reinforce the qualification of teachers, especially in subject knowledge, didactics and initiation to professional practice' (Decree-Law No. 79/2014) through an increase in the duration of the master's degree and changes to the weighting of each curriculum component (higher in the case of subject knowledge and didactics). The word 'quality' is identified 13 times in the document to reinforce the idea that teacher education matters and is a key element in fostering the quality of education and of student learning. The need for teachers to possess deep content knowledge is advocated as is the notion that initial teacher education cannot be replaced by in-service education. Thus, the rationale for replacing the former legal framework (Decree-Law 43/2007) with the new one (Decree-Law No. 79/2014) was associated with the need to enhance teacher education 'particularly in subject knowledge and didactics' which implicitly translates as what quality means in this particular context.

4.2 *The Lack of an Explicit Definition of Quality*

Even though the policy document throughout reiterates the word quality, it does not provide an explicit definition and nor does it clearly refer to what quality teacher education entails. In fact, the document includes phrases such as quality of education, quality of the education system, quality teacher education, teaching quality, quality of activities related to initiation to professional practice, or quality of the study cycle. However, there is no identification of what counts as quality in this context. What is clear is the focus and direction of the change introduced in the new legal framework by stating that initial teacher education needs to be demanding, particularly as far as content knowledge and didactic knowledge is concerned. The same document stresses that 'the preparation of teachers needs to be done in a rigorous manner in such a way that it highlights the teacher's role' (see the Preamble of Decree-Law 79/2014). Therefore, notions of what and how to teach are reinforced in order to provide schools with teachers who are the 'most well prepared, most well trained, with the greatest vocation and the most motivated to undertake the noble and demanding task of teaching' (sic) (see the Preamble of Decree-Law 79/2014). Such a view emphasises the mastery of knowledge and skills for classroom teaching and the need to foster the key importance of initial teacher education to educate the best teachers. As Moreira (2017, p. 311) states that [t]he 'good' teacher knows a lot of fundamental subjects 'like mathematics and language, dominates the required techniques to teach the average student, and knows how to design reliable, objective assessment tests, tests that will replicate the external exams, so that the student-consumer can be satisfied, schools can be ranked, and the market better served'.

4.3   *The Content of Initial Teacher Education: A Focus on Didactics and Professional Practice*

Initial teacher education in Portugal is strictly regulated by the Ministry of Education, which stipulates, among other things, teaching profiles, length of programmes, curriculum components and the corresponding number of credits, resources, and conditions for teaching practice. It is up to the institutions to design and implement such programmes in accordance with the national legal framework. The legislative text currently in place (Decree-Law No. 79/2014) stipulates five mandatory components for the initial teacher education curriculum: (i) subject knowledge, (ii) general education, (iii) specific didactics, (iv) ethical, social and cultural dimensions, and (v) initiation to professional practice. Secondary school teachers (ISCED 2 and 3) and teachers qualifying for two education/schooling levels (ISCED 0 and 1) must complete a 120-credit programme, while kindergarten (ISCED 0) or primary teachers (ISCED 1) only need to complete 90 credits.

In general, emphasis is placed on specific didactics and professional practice. For instance, for secondary school (master's degree in Teaching with 120 credits in total) the initial teacher education programme includes the following credits: subject matter (minimum of 18 credits); general education (minimum 18 credits); specific didactics (minimum 30 credits); and, initiation to professional practice (minimum 42 credits). The component dealing with ethical, social and cultural dimensions receives no credits and is to be developed within the context of the other components in the programme.

The subject knowledge component aims to consolidate and further student teachers' knowledge and academic training in the field in which they are going to teach. General education includes knowledge, skills and aptitudes required of teachers and which are relevant to their work in schools and classrooms. It includes developmental psychology; cognitive psychology, namely elementary mathematics and reading; curriculum and assessment; the school as an educational organisation; special educational needs; and classroom organisation and management. Specific didactics relates to the pedagogy of a given subject and level of teaching. As for professional practice, it includes classroom observation, collaboration in teaching under supervision, planning, teaching and evaluation from the perspective of student teachers' professional development. The component dealing with cultural, social and ethical dimensions is intended to 'raise awareness of the main problems of the contemporary world, including key values of the Constitution of the Portuguese Republic such as freedom of speech and religion, respect for ethnic minorities, and gender equality' (Decree-Law No. 79/2014). It also includes scientific culture, arts, and humanities, research methods (data collection and critical analysis of data, hypotheses, and theories) and an awareness of the ethical and civic dimensions of the teaching profession.

4.4 *The Role of Practice and the Research Component: Teacher as a Technician or as a Professional?*

As discussed earlier, initiation to professional practice is seen as a key component of initial teacher education according to the legislative text. This practical component often results in an overemphasis on the technical analyses and prescriptions to guide teachers' work (Moreira, 2017, 2020). Such a view is seen in the reduction of so-called general education, particularly the foundational courses such as Philosophy of Education, History of Education, and Sociology of Education.

In addition, within the new legal framework issued in 2014, the research dimension is no longer a compulsory component of the initial teacher education curriculum. In the former legislative text issued in 2007 (Decree-Law No. 43/2007), the research dimension was explicitly identified as a compulsory component of the initial teacher education curriculum, although no specific credits were allocated for it. It aimed at 'enabling prospective teachers to adopt a research stance in their professional performance in specific contexts, on the basis of an understanding and critical analysis of relevant educational research' (Decree-Law No. 43/2007). Research methods in educational research were deemed relevant due to the need to see the job of teacher 'less as an employee or technician and more and more as a professional capable of adapting to the characteristics and singular challenges of each situation in accordance with the specific features of students and with the social and school contexts' (the Preamble of Decree-Law No. 43/2007).

The new Decree-Law issued in 2014 (Decree-Law No. 79/2014) no longer stipulates that research is a compulsory component of the curriculum of initial teacher education. The new legal framework thus represents a regressive step as far as the development of an inquiry-based approach is concerned. However, it has been argued that it should constitute a key element in the practicum experience in most institutions, even though it may assume a variety of formats. As initial teacher education occurs at the second cycle level (master's degree), the research component (Flores, 2018; Flores et al., 2016; Vieira et al., 2019, 2021) was tacitly assumed by institutions and encouraged by external assessments (Flores et al., 2016). Despite the separation of subject-matter knowledge (first degree) from educational and pedagogical components (master's degree) as well as a reduction in time spent in schools, the model implemented as a result of the Bologna process has led to a number of interesting and somewhat innovative features, with respect to the research component, an example being the practicum model at my institution, Institute of Education at the University of Minho (Flores, 2018; Vieira et al., 2021).

During their practicum student teachers are asked to develop a small-scale, learner-centred pedagogical project to combine teaching and research within a praxeological epistemology (Vieira et al., 2019). The main goal is to link teaching and research within practicum whereby research is at the service of pedagogy under a transformative view of education based on humanistic and democratic values (Flores et al., 2016; Vieira et al., 2019). A three-dimensional professional profile of the teachers-to-be is advocated, which involves a conceptual dimension (the theoretical framework of professional practice), a strategic dimension (the methodological framework of professional practice), and an axiological dimension (the values of professional practice including the ethical and political values that underpin educational action) (Flores, 2018; Vieira et al., 2019).

The design and development of the pedagogical project draws upon a set of principles that include the following features: a humanistic and democratic view of schooling; the adequacy of interventions within the contexts of practice and their educational value with regard to teacher and learner experience; the use of data collection to support the understanding and renewal of pedagogy; and the enhancement of professional development based on reflectivity, self-direction, collaboration, creativity, and innovation. Such a practicum model aims at developing student teachers' research literacy in order to make informed decisions about their practices. The development of these pedagogical projects is documented in a portfolio, to be compiled during practicum, and in the final report which is to be defended in a public examination. Flores et al. (2016) stressed that the integration of research into the practicum faced a number of challenges. These are related to time and resources since 'condensing professional development in two-year master's programmes led to a reduction of time allocated to school-based practice, with potential negative effects upon students' preparation and opportunity to engage in pedagogical inquiry' (Flores, 2016, p. 112).

A recent study of the 10 years since implementation of the new practicum model (Vieira, Flores, & Almeida, 2020; Vieira, Silva, & Vilaça 2020; Vieira et al., 2021) has concluded that supervisors, cooperating teachers and student teachers' perceptions (perceived quality) and evidence from practicum reports (inferred quality) are, in general, aligned with the model's rationale (intended quality). The model promotes inquiry competencies, multifaceted professional knowledge, and a transformative vision of education. Nevertheless, some critical aspects were also identified. Classroom inquiry represents an increase in student teachers' workload and more sophisticated and expansive supervision roles, and cooperating teachers show concerns about their ability to meet the requirements and demands of an inquiry-based approach (Vieira et al., 2019).

5 Concluding Remarks

Quality in teacher education remains a key concern at a global scale. As a dynamic and multifaceted concept, the term quality implies the analysis of different layers (e.g. policies, organisational models, curriculum content and form) and voices (e.g. student teachers, teacher educators, mentors) which need to be understood in context. As such, there is no recipe to enhance quality in teacher education nor is there a set of standards or criteria that apply universally. Analysing the concept of teacher quality, Cochran-Smith (2021, pp. 415–416) asserts that there are variations related to:

> the conceptually ambiguous nature of teacher quality as a policy concept and on differences in history and cultural values, geopolitical context,

current socioeconomic status, the size of the teaching workforce and the status of teaching as an occupation, organisational governance and oversight, and the problems and promises of local environments.

There is a need, therefore, to examine how quality is defined and by whom in a given context. Highlighting the inextricability of teacher quality and teacher preparation, Olsen (2021) identified the importance of a clear, shared framework for teacher quality, but also the existence of a useful tension between centralisation and decentralisation and between universality and situatedness. In order to discuss quality in teacher education, some common general criteria could be considered, such as the coherence and relevance of a programme's components; the status and qualification of teacher educators and existing opportunities for their professional learning; the recruitment and role of student teachers; consistency between guidelines for teacher education and existing practices; and the articulation of collaborative work between universities and schools as sites of professional learning.

Yet, attention must also be given to context specific features which are dependent on such issues as teacher recruitment policies and teacher education priorities, the voices of the stakeholders, modes of government intervention, the status of the teaching profession, institutional and organisational priorities and ways of enacting given policies. As Menter (2022) argues, maintaining quality in teacher education is a contemporary challenge that requires the continuing maintenance of quality research as well as the need to research policy and practice and to deploy a wide range of disciplinary methods.

5.1 Uncertain Times, Critical Scenarios

The future of initial teacher education in Portugal is uncertain and uncertainty calls into question issues of quality. At the time of writing initial teacher education occurs at master's degree level for all entrants into teaching from pre-school to secondary school. However, the prospect of introducing an on-the-job training orientation in order to deal with the shortage of teachers is seen as a critical move in initial teacher education. The profession is currently faced with the ageing of the teaching workforce (51.9% of the teachers are 50 years or above and only 1.6% are younger than 30 years of age) (CNE, 2021). According to the official statistics, there will be a need to recruit more than 34,000 teachers by 2030/2031 (on average 3,450 per year) due to retirement (DGEEC, 2021). This situation has clear implications for teacher recruitment and for teacher education. The decrease in the number of teacher candidates over the years along with the perceived lack of attractiveness of the teaching career add more complexity into the equation. Such a scenario might lead to emergency teacher education solutions which alongside initiatives such as Teach for Portugal call into question the issue of quality in teacher education.

Teaching is a complex and demanding profession which does not correspond with narrow, pragmatic and simplistic orientations for teacher education. As Loughran, Keast, and Cooper (2016, p. 416) suggest, teacher education is not 'about training, it should be an educative process that develops thoughtful, informed and highly able professionals'. Such a view calls for a broad understanding of teacher professionalism considering teaching as a knowledge-based profession with a clear intellectual, research and university-based dimension (Nóvoa, 2017). This approach implies a solid and academic-based education which not only recognises the technical dimension of teaching but also its problematic, dynamic, complex and sophisticated nature (Loughran & Menter, 2019) as well as its intellectual, cultural and contextual features (Cochran-Smith, 2004). As Menter and Flores (2021, p. 124) argue,

> Teaching is after all a profession concerned not only with knowledge and cognition, crucial though these are, but also with values and morality. It is challenges such as these that require a full recognition of the need to imbued teaching – and teacher education – with a sustainable inquiry orientation, indeed a base in education research.

If current initial teacher education programmes in the Portuguese context are to be improved, such re-evaluation must not be undertaken by reducing their key components, such as the general education component, nor through a quick and rushed move of teacher education to schools at the expense of quality. On the contrary, there is a need to invest in high quality initial teacher education which needs to be seen as a space of transformation based on a research-based approach along with the ethical, social, cultural and political dimension of teaching (Flores, 2021). In addition, the voice of the stakeholders, namely teacher education institutions and teacher educators, must be taken into consideration to find the best solutions for a crisis in the teaching profession that has been announced for some time and which has not attracted governmental attention. If quality teachers depend on the quality of their education, then there is a need to invest in initial teacher education and to build on existing consolidated knowledge in the field to establish red-lines and to avoid quick-fixes that menace the quality of teacher education.

References

Brooks, C. (2021). The quality conundrum in initial teacher education. *Teachers and Teaching: Theory and Practice, 27*(1–4), 131–146.

CNE. (2021). *Estado da Educação 2020*. CNE.

Cochran-Smith, M. (2004). Editorial. The problem of teacher education. *Journal of Teacher Education, 55*(4), 295–299.

Cochran-Smith, M. (2021). Exploring teacher quality: International perspectives. *European Journal of Teacher Education, 44*(3), 415–428.

Darling-Hammond, L. (2006). *Powerful teacher education: Lessons learned from exemplary programs*. Jossey-Bass.

Darling-Hammond, L. (2010). Reconhecer e potenciar a eficácia docente: Guia para decisores politicos. In M. A. Flores (Ed.), *A Avaliação de professores numa perspetiva internacional: Sentidos e implicações* (pp. 197–235). Areal Editores.

Darling-Hammond, L. (2021). Defining teaching quality around the world. *European Journal of Teacher Education, 44*(3), 295–308.

Decree-Law No. 43/2007. Diário da República no. 38/2007, Series I from 2007-02-22, 1320–1328. https://data.dre.pt/eli/dec-lei/43/2007/02/22/p/dre/pt/html

Decree-Law No. 79/2014. Diário da República no. 92/2007, Series I from 2014-05-14, 2819–2828. https://data.dre.pt/eli/dec-lei/79/2014/05/14/p/dre/pt/html

DGEEC. (2021). *Estudo de diagnóstico de necessidades docentes de 2021 a 2030*. Direção-Geral de Estatísticas da Educação e Ciência.

Ell, F. (2021). Teacher education policy in Aotearoa New Zealand: Global trends meet local imperatives. In D. Mayer (Ed.), *Teacher education policy and research. Global perspectives* (pp. 113–128). Springer.

Feuer, M. J., Floden, R. E., Chudowsky, N., & Ahn, J. (2013). *Evaluation of teacher preparation programs: Purposes, methods, and policy options*. National Academy of Education.

Flores, M. A. (2016). Teacher education curriculum. In J. Loughran & M. L. Hamilton (Eds.), *International handbook of teacher education* (pp. 187–230). Springer.

Flores, M. A. (2018). Linking teaching and research in initial teacher education: Knowledge mobilisation and research-informed practice. *Journal of Education for Teaching, 44*(5), 621–636.

Flores, M. A. (2019). Unpacking teacher quality: Key issues for early career teachers. In A. Sullivan, J. Johnson, & M. Simmons (Eds.), *Attracting and keeping the best teachers* (pp. 15–38). Springer.

Flores, M. A. (2021). Educating teachers in the post-Bologna context in Portugal: Lessons learned and remaining challenges. In D. Mayer (Ed.), *Teacher education policy and research. Global perspectives* (pp. 141–157). Springer.

Flores, M. A., Vieira, F., Silva, J. L., & Almeida, J. (2016). Integrating research into the practicum: Inquiring into inquiry-based professional development in post-Bologna initial teacher education in Portugal. In M. A. Flores & T. Al-Barwani (Eds.), *Redefining teacher education for the post-2015 era: Global challenges and best practice* (pp. 109–124). Nova Science Publisher.

Goodwin, L., & Low, E. L. (2021). Rethinking conceptualisations of teacher quality in Singapore and Hong-Kong: A comparative analysis. *European Journal of Teacher Education, 44*(3), 365–382.

Imig, D., & Imig, S. R. (2007). Quality in teacher education: Seeking a common definition. In T. Townsend & R. Bates (Eds.), *Handbook of teacher education. Globalization, standards and professionalism in times of change* (pp. 95–112). Springer.

Imig, D., Wiseman, D. L., Wiseman, A., & Imig, S. R. (2016). What is high quality teacher education? In J. C. Lee & C. Day (Eds.), *Quality and change in teacher education* (pp. 95–112). Springer.

Kennedy, A., Adams, P., & Carver, M. (2021). Measuring quality in initial teacher education in Scotland: A context-specific endeavour. In D. Mayer (Ed.), *Teacher education policy and research. Global perspectives* (pp. 159–176). Springer.

Loughran, J., Keast, S., & Cooper, R. (2016). Pedagogical reasoning in teacher education. In J. Loughran & M. L. Hamilton (Eds.), *International handbook of teacher education* (pp. 387–421). Springer.

Loughran, J., & Menter, I. (2019). The essence of being a teacher educator and why it matters. *Asia-Pacific Journal of Teacher Education, 47*(3), 216–229.

Mayer, D. (2014). Forty years of teacher education in Australia: 1974–2014. *Journal of Education for Teaching, 40*(5), 461–473.

Mayer, D. (2021). Teacher education policy and research: An introduction. In D. Mayer (Ed.), *Teacher education policy and research. Global perspectives* (pp. 1–10). Springer.

Mayer, D., Goodwin, L., & Mockler, N. (2021). Teacher education policy: Future research, teaching in contexts of super-diversity and early career teaching. In D. Mayer (Ed.), *Teacher education policy and research. Global perspectives* (pp. 209–223). Springer.

Meijer, P. (2021). Quality under pressure in Dutch teacher education. In D. Mayer (Ed.), *Teacher education policy and research. Global perspectives* (pp. 101–111). Springer.

Menter, I. (2022). Maintaining quality in teacher education: A contemporary global challenge? *Child Studies, 1*, 87–105.

Menter, I., & Flores, M. A. (2021). Connecting research and professionalism in teacher education. *European Journal of Teacher Education, 44*(1), 115–127.

Menter, I., & Hulme, M. (2011). Teacher education reform in Scotland: National and global influences. *Journal of Education for Teaching, 37*(4), 387–397.

Moreira, M. A. (2017). Challenges and possibilities of teacher education in Portugal in neoliberal times. *Teacher Education and Practice, 30*(2), 310–313.

Moreira, M. A. (2020). Profesores: Un escenario preocupante en la formación inicial del profesorado [Teachers: A troublesome scenario in initial teacher education]. In R. Espinosa Lolas & J. F. Angulo Rasco (Eds.), *Conceptos para dissolver la educación capitalista [Concepts to dissolve a capitalist education]* (pp. 391–399). Terra Ignota Ediciones.

Nóvoa, A. (2017). Firmar a posição como Professor, afirmar a profissão Docente. *Cadernos de Pesquisa, 47*(116), 1106–1133.

OECD. (2005). *Teachers mater: Policies for attracting, developing and retaining effective teachers.* OECD Publishing.

OECD. (2018). *Effective teacher policies: Insights from PISA.* OECD Publishing.

Olsen, B. (2021). Teacher quality around the world: What's currently happening and how can the present inform the future? *European Journal of Teacher Education, 44*(3), 293–294.

Russell, T., & Martin, A. K. (2016). Exploring the complex concept of quality in teacher education. In J. Loughran & M. L. Hamilton (Eds.), *International handbook of teacher education* (pp. 143–180). Springer.

Singh, P., Hoyte, F., Heimans, S., & Exley, B. (2021). Teacher quality ad teacher education: A critical policy analysis of international and Australian policies. *Australian Journal of Teacher Education, 46*(4), 1–15.

Snoek, M. (2021). Educating quality teachers: How teacher quality is understood in the Netherlands and its implications for teacher education. *European Journal of Teacher Education, 44*(3), 309–327.

Tatto, M. T., & Pippin, J. (2017). The quest for quality and the rise of accountability systems in teacher education. In D. J. Clandinin & J. Husu (Eds.), *The Sage handbook on teacher education* (pp. 68–89). Sage.

Townsend, T. (2011). Searching high and searching low, searching east and searching west: Looking for trust in teacher education. *Journal of Education for Teaching, 37*(4), 483–500.

Vanassche, E., Bruneel, S., & Christiaens, L. (2021). A critical examination of the conception of teacher professionalism enacted in current teacher education policy in Flanders (Belgium). In D. Mayer (Ed.), *Teacher education policy and research. Global perspectives* (pp. 27–41). Springer.

Vieira, F., Flores, M. A., & Almeida, M. J. (2020). Avaliando o modelo de estágio dos mestrados em ensino da Universidade do Minho: Entre a qualidade desejada e a qualidade percebida [Evaluating the practicum modelo f the masters' in teaching of the University of Minho: Between the desired quality and the perceived quality]. *Instrumento: Revista Estudos e Pesquisa em Educação, 22*(2), 231–247.

Vieira, F., Flores, M. A., Silva, J. L., & Almeida, J. (2019). Understanding and enhancing change in post-Bologna pre-service teacher education: Lessons from experience and research in Portugal. In T. Al Barwani, M. A. Flores, & D. Imig (Eds.), *Leading change in teacher education. Lessons from countries and education leaders around the globe* (pp. 41–57). Routledge.

Vieira, F., Flores, M. A., Silva, J. L. C., Almeida, M. J., & Vilaça, T. (2021). Inquiry-based professional learning in the practicum: Potential and shortcomings. *Teaching and Teacher Education, 105*(103429).

Vieira, F., Silva, J. L., & Vilaça, M. T. M. (2020). Formação de professores baseada na investigação pedagógica: Um estudo sobre o estágio nos mestrados em ensino [Teacher education based on pedagogical inquiry: A study on the practicum of masters' in teaching]. *Educação em Perspectiva, 11*, 1–17.

CHAPTER 3

Teacher Quality Driven by Equity and Social Justice

Arguments for an Alternative Values-Centred Vision of Teacher Education

Noel Purdy, Kathy Hall, Daria Khanolainen and Conor Galvin

Abstract

Teacher Quality remains an issue of enduring policy interest and the focus of considerable debate and activity within the teacher education community across Europe. Indeed, ensuring quality in teacher education has become a fundamental European Commission concern in the context of establishing the European Education Area by 2025 and a constant focus of research among teacher educators. Over the past decade in particular, and using comparative data drawn from international studies, arguments have been made to justify what has been described as the 'practice turn' (Reid, 2011) characterised by the re-emergence of simplified craft models of teaching, where 'trainees' learn in an apprenticeship model in the school, leading in turn to binary debates between proponents of school-based or university-based teacher education. Additionally, it has become common for education to be viewed as an engine for economic growth, facilitating a nation to compete against global competitors – with all the econometric baggage and policy expectation this engenders. This has led to attempts to solve key policy problems of teacher education through manipulating and defining *how* and *where* teachers should be prepared (e.g. in training schools rather than in universities or colleges) and through determining what exactly their preparation should focus on (e.g. practical classroom teaching skills rather than educational principles situated in sociology, psychology, history or philosophy of education), while seeking to ensure compliance and consistency through ever tighter regulation and accountability. There is, we suggest, another and more equitable way to meet this deep-seated challenge. This chapter explores that proposition in a deliberative manner and uses examples and instances from ongoing and recent research in various Europe contexts and beyond to elaborate on our claim and to argue for the value of a teacher education that places equity and social justice at the heart of its mission.

Keywords

quality teacher education – equity – social justice – European Education Area – values-centred teacher education

1   **Introduction**

Teacher quality remains an issue of considerable policy interest and of teacher education community activity across Europe. Indeed, ensuring 'quality' in teacher education is viewed as a fundamental European Commission policy concern in the context of establishing the European Education Area (EEA) by 2025 (European Commission, 2020) and represents a constant focus of research and discussion among teacher educators in Europe and beyond. Conceptualisations of teacher quality run from the avowedly econometric (e.g., Hanushek, 2011) to the much richer, multi-layered view encapsulated in Cochran-Smith's positioning of teacher quality as a product of 'differences in history and cultural values, geopolitical context, current socioeconomic status, the size of the teaching force and the status of teaching as an occupation, organisational governance and oversight, and the problems and promises of local environments' (2021b, pp. 415–416). It includes concerns for the nature and possibilities of teacher education at both initial teacher education (Flores, 2016) and in-career development (Clarke et al., 2020), and regularly touches on the need to attract, support and retain quality entrants (Sullivan et al., 2019), often through innovations such as 'career crafting' for professional growth (Snoek et al., 2019). *Teachers and Trainers* are named as one of the six underpinned dimensions of the EEA framework:

> The vision for the education profession within the European Education Area is one of highly competent and motivated educators who can benefit from a range of support and professional development opportunities throughout their varied careers. Within the European Education Area, teaching and training should be valued professions. (European Commission, 2020, p. 9)

By placing teachers at the heart of the EEA agenda in this way, the European Commission has effectively declared a policy intent based on a particular reading of teacher quality that we will see play out in terms of ambitious actions and programmes in the immediate future. The recent Jean Monnet – Teacher Action and the ERASMUS+ Teacher Academies Call represents the first of these. Both were launched in the spring of 2021, with second calls planned for the late autumn.

This chapter raises a number of issues regarding the nature of teacher quality at the heart of this emerging European Commission policy work. It also proposes an alternative values-centred vision of teacher education rooted in concerns for equity and social justice.

2   Context

It has been argued that teacher education over the past half-century has been conceptualised first as training (the replication and mastery of a set of teaching skills); then as professional learning (with a focus on pedagogic content knowledge and reflective practice); and finally as a policy problem needing a solution (Cochran-Smith & Fries, 2005; Mayer, 2021). Over the past decade in particular and using comparative data drawn from international studies such as PISA and TALIS, evidence was cited to justify what has been described as the 'practice turn' (Reid, 2011), characterised by the re-emergence of simplified craft models of teaching, where trainees learn in an apprenticeship model in the school, leading in turn to binary debates between proponents of school-based or university-based teacher education. Parts of Europe are more deeply affected by this ideologically underpinned discourse than others but notions of clinical placement and policy support and advocacy for teacher education frameworks purporting to be standards-based and competencies-centred have regularly featured in Commission rhetoric and policy actions.

Education policy work in the context of European integration has now increased to the point where, arguably, the European Commission has become a major policy player in education (Lawn & Lingard, 2002) particularly since the launch of the Lisbon Strategy in 2000 (Pépin, 2007). Antunes (2006, p. 43) described this growth in cooperation as a maturing of the 'Europeification' process which was slowly gestating in the decades before the Lisbon Strategy and has since evolved into the fully-articulated competency frameworks that now characterise teacher education throughout most of Europe. Much of the tone and direction of this was set in the seminal Commission document *Common European principles for teacher competences and qualifications* (2005) and the work of a subsequent EC Peer Learning Cluster dedicated to Teachers & Trainers whose remit, according to Snoek (2006), was to stimulate the exchange of good practices in teacher policy between EU Member States. The idea of individual *teacher competency* also featured centrally in the EU TUNING project on education sciences for initial teacher education – a Phase One TUNING project that ran 2000–2004. However, it was the publication by the Commission of the *Rethinking Education* (European Commission, 2012a) framework and a series of related reports and supporting documents that positioned defined sets of career stage competencies at the core of all teacher development and education. These included *Supporting the teaching professions for better learning outcomes* (European Commission, 2012b) which detailed the approach in depth, and *Supporting teacher competence development for better learning outcomes* (2013) which sought to link teaching activity directly to student attainment (Manso & Sánchez-Tarazaga, 2018).

Associated with competency in this vein are of course the policy concerns for standards and improvement and the machinery for monitoring and evaluation that inevitably follow: these remain at the heart of EU thinking on the matter of teacher quality and relevant teacher education. As a result, in Europe, as elsewhere, recent developments in teacher education policy have been characterised by increased accountability measures, introduced as a powerful tool to drive forward improvement. This has been realised through the introduction of new competency-framed standards, monitoring systems, accreditation criteria and quality assurance processes for Initial Teacher Education providers (Cochran-Smith, 2021a). Indeed, according to Telling and Serapioni (2019, p. 388) the emergence and prosecution by the Commission of its 'competence strategy' should be counted among the most significant developments to date, with respect to the consolidation of a European educational discourse. This is only likely to increase as the EC drives towards its goal of achieving the European Education Area by 2025. Consequently, any analysis of teacher education policy is highly revealing of that society's dominant values, as those in power seek to shape the world as they see fit for their future citizens (Menter, 2016). In such a context, it has become common for education to be viewed as an engine for economic growth, allowing a nation to compete against global competitors – with all the econometric baggage and policy expectation this engenders (Agasisti et al., 2019): teacher education has, almost inevitably, been co-opted into this mission also (Krejsler, 2018). As Mayer (2021) has claimed, this prioritisation of education for economic purposes had led to attempts to solve the policy problem of teacher education through manipulating and defining how and where teachers should be prepared (e.g., in training schools rather than in universities or colleges) and through determining what exactly their preparation should focus on (e.g., practical classroom teaching skills rather than sociology, psychology, history or philosophy of education), while seeking to ensure compliance and consistency through ever tighter regulation and accountability.

The tension between differing conceptualisations of teacher education has been highlighted most recently in the UK following the publication in July 2021 of the *Initial Teacher Training (ITT) Market Review Report* (Bauckham et al., 2021). This Market Review Report sets out a plan to ensure consistency of ITT provision in line with the 2019 *ITT Core Content Framework* through a new accreditation process for new and existing providers, but already there are concerns that such reforms could lead to a significant reduction in the number of accredited providers and could discourage existing providers from continuing their involvement in ITT because of the increased and restrictive prescription of content. There are also concerns that this increase in prescribed content will make it more difficult to prepare questioning, research-informed professionals willing and capable of contextualising and critiquing practice (Noble-Rogers, 2021).

Increased regulation has focused almost entirely on easily measurable elements such as standards of entry to teacher education, levels of literacy and numeracy, and the assessment of teachers' capability measured against agreed standards. On a macro-level the short-term nature of political cycles has meant that quick-fix solutions to teacher education (e.g. focusing on entry standards) become more attractive than the introduction of, for instance, longer-term changes (which fail to produce tangible results within a parliamentary term); changes which don't lend themselves readily to quantifiable measurement (e.g. a focus on values or ethos); and those which are place-based, localised, non-generalisable and 'messy' (e.g. acknowledging that effective teacher education is highly contextualised). As a result, teacher competence has increasingly prioritised the mastery of a set of technical skills at the expense of a focus on values. In this, it reflects the observation by Telling and Serapioni (2019, p. 388) that competence has been and remains a core aspect of the EU's increasingly interconnected educational, economic and social policy. Teacher quality in a particular competence-laden specification also features in this retreat from other values such as equity, social justice, participatory democracy and community solidarity. Symeonidis (2018, p. 23) notes the implications for ITE and CPD institutions in terms of institutional policies and procedures of the *Standards and guidelines for quality assurance in the European Higher Education Area* (ESG). These were presented as a contribution 'to a common understanding of quality assurance for learning and teaching across borders and among all stakeholders' (ESG, 2015, p. 6) but seem to serve principally to promote a narrow, efficient workforce view of teachers and teaching and to increase the Commission's capacity to influence Member States' educational developments – including teacher education.

There is, we suggest, another and more equitable way to meet the deep-seated challenges of a view on teaching and teacher education bound inextricably to regulated uniformity, measurability and utilitarian and/or economic ends.

3   An Alternative Values-Centred Vision of Teaching and Teacher Education

If, however, those in power were to place a value on the role of teacher education in addressing issues of equity or social justice, then a quite different focus would be required which would aim to promote teachers' criticality, autonomy and agency, placing them quite at odds with heavily regulated systems focused on measurable outcomes against agreed universal standards or competencies (Hulme et al., 2015; Tatto, 2021). By contrast, much of the Commission's current policy positioning regarding teachers and teacher education and most education systems which seek to hold teacher education to account are explicit in terms of classroom-based standards, but have little to say in relation to broader social purposes:

> The emphasis on developing teachers' criticality through investment in processes, resources, time and collective dialogue, which would promote teacher autonomy and agency and are the basis for teaching for social justice, is at odds with the dominant requirement that programmes be evaluated on their outcomes and that they conform to and comply with the requirements for accreditation as prescribed. It is difficult to assess the latent potential of student teachers for social justice; in an era of increased managerialism and accountability, standards prioritise knowledge that is measurable and relevant, while they are frequently silent on the fundamental issues of equality and equity, social justice and citizenship. (Hulme et al., 2015, p. 224)

Few have specifically addressed the potential to transform teacher education and to give greater prominence to equity issues. Beyond Europe, Nieto (2000a) highlights the largely monocultural and monolingual approach to teacher education and the corresponding lack of diversity among teacher education faculty in the United States. In response, Nieto argues that teacher education programmes need to take a stand on social justice and equity; to make social justice 'ubiquitous' in teacher education, rather than a narrow specialism for a chosen few; and, to promote teaching as a life-long journey of transformation. Nieto calls for teacher education programmes to put their 'lofty statements' and 'grandiose statements' (Nieto, 2000a, p. 183) about the purposes of education in a democratic society into practice by preparing their students to teach in a diverse, pluralistic and fast-changing society.

More recently, Tatto (2021) has critiqued UNESCO's *Sustainable Development Goal 4* (which pursues inclusive and equitable quality education and lifelong learning for all) for insisting on narrow and technical indicators to measure progress, and for identifying 'Equity' as a separate target rather than as a crosscutting target relating to *every* aspect of education:

Conceived in this way equity is not only about access to education for all but rather a way of living and relating in education institutions. Teachers at all levels of education are to be considered as essential in the pursuit of equitable access to education and as active agents in the activation/moderation of implementation strategies (Tatto, 2021, p. 31).

Where too often in the past teacher education policy work has fallen victim to the dominant accountability and measurement models and remained silent on issues surrounding equity and social justice, the current COVID-19 pandemic offers an unprecedented opportunity to revisit our values and priorities for education and teacher education at a local, national and international level. In so doing, we must work towards realising the potential of teacher education to move beyond silence or tokenism to address issues related to equity and social justice in a new and meaningful way.

3.1 *A Nuanced Perspective on Learning and Pedagogy*

In working towards such a goal, we wish to argue that a most urgent need in teacher education today is to focus closely on a perspective on learning and pedagogy that emanates from socio-cultural theory which we believe has profound implications for the way we understand and foster learning, assess achievement, and value and define subject matter. It is a perspective on pedagogy that is subtle and complex but which has enormous explanatory power and high relevance in the context of equity and social justice. In this we are particularly influenced by the original, ground-breaking work of scholars such as Jean Lave (1988), Etienne Wenger (1998) and Barbara Rogoff (2003).

The first key point here is that learning should not be understood merely as an epistemological matter simply about, say, learning outcomes and the acquisition and possession of knowledge and skills – the dominant way of thinking about learning and teaching, especially in official policy documents. Rather, learning needs to be thought of as always a feature of human living and interaction. It is potentially everywhere. From a socio-cultural perspective there is no distinction then between learning in school and learning in everyday life, which are seen as just different opportunities for learning. The everydayness of learning, the application of learning, the appreciation and understanding of its value and usefulness in the here and now of students' lives is what is so central. If learning is central to any practice and is potentially all round us, how people take up and resist the opportunities to learn that are extended to them should be of major interest to student teachers and teachers. It is therefore of key importance for student teachers, teachers and their educators to try to understand and appreciate how circumstances, histories and institutions operate to enable and constrain different ways of living and being.

Important and rich, inter-related questions pertaining to pedagogy in any given context then become:
- What learning is made available and desirable, and to whom?
- Who is being supported to learn, who is enabled to participate in the valued practice? Who is being marginalised? Who is denied access?

- What is it possible to learn in particular circumstances with particular people?
- What are the mechanisms and practices that do the enabling and the constraining?

Such questions shift us away from mere epistemological matters such as what is to be known and to what extent has it been achieved, towards historical and cultural analyses of a given situation. From the point of view of student teachers and their educators it should focus close attention on observations of moment-by-moment interactions and actions in classrooms and 'unofficial' spaces like playgrounds to see what assumptions and meanings people are making together about what is valued, their own representations of the way to be, and their expectations about how others may perceive them. Slices of classroom life become important for analysis, for it is the focus on the specificity of the moment in action, the engagement on a specific task, that renders visible what is often invisible. But this requires conceptual tools for thinking, such as identity, agency, context, and relationality (see Hall, 2008; Hall et al., 2008, 2014; Nind et al., 2016).

Identities are never fixed but are always in flux and emergent through the opportunities and openings on offer and through the constraints that are also part of practice in any given moment in time. The classroom setting provides differentiated spaces, possibilities for action that learners will interpret differently depending on what they bring to the task in question. Greater attention needs to be given to student teachers to study how practice in the moment-by-moment of classroom life can open up or close down learning opportunities for individuals. By attending to the sometimes hidden messages that are enshrined in classroom action and interaction, student teachers and teachers can be helped to notice the invisible yet consequential messages associated with their own pedagogy for the shaping of identity of their learners.

A person's learning varies according to setting and within a given context because learning is understood not (just) in terms of what people can and can't do or even do, but crucially, in terms of what it is possible to do in particular situations with particular people. As Ivinson and Murphy (2007) demonstrate in their study of single sex schooling, while actions in classrooms have significance and consequences for the actors involved, moments of classroom life can be viewed as 'semi-public' affairs that others in the setting interpret. As Ivinson and Murphy note, while the action disappears, a trace of the participation remains in the form of changed identities either in the form of a movement away from the periphery towards a more central position in the community of that practice or it could be a movement towards marginality. How learners are moved from the periphery to the centre of a practice depends on the identities being performed and the agency extended or denied through the practice engaged in by all concerned.

That learning happens in school is unproblematic – it will happen for everyone – but what is available to be learned is complexly problematic in a sociocultural take on learning and pedagogy. Learning is never alone activity. One cannot be literate, numerate, educated, popular, cool, expert etc. (and their opposites). Other people, procedures and settings are part of the production of one's identity which happens in moment-by-moment interaction and through one's access to and desire for particular ways of being (Hall, 2008; McDermott, 1996). Yet, and importantly, practice is never inevitable and there is always the space for agency within a social context. Since individuals come with their different histories, experiences and agendas, there is always an element of unpredictability in social contexts including a classroom setting such that identities are in process, emergent and performed as opposed to fixed and determined. The extent to which learning of an aspect of a school subject is enabled is a function of the people in the setting and their relationality to each other and to the subject matter in hand.

The notion of the relational self would make us attend more closely to the historical as well as the present, the historical self (one's history of participation in various communities of practice) and the momentary self which is being positioned in different ways within the variety of social contexts in which we live. We need to look at the nature of people's participation in activities in schools; we need to look at the ways in which there is continuity and change in people's participation changes. To understand learning from this perspective, attention has to be shift from individual to collective learning, powerfully summed up by McDermott (1996, p. 277) as follows:

> It probably makes more sense to talk about how learning acquires people more than it makes sense to talk about how people acquire learning. Individually we may spend our time trying to learn things, but this phenomenon pales before the fact that, however hard we try, we can only learn what is around to be learned.

The notion of pedagogy endorsed in this chapter is fundamentally concerned with what people perceive to be meaningful and relevant as they engage in activity and develop competence in a practice. Since we cannot assume what is meaningful to people as they engage in tasks, we have to reflect on the way experience is organised and authorised, produced, reproduced and transformed in settings. A quarter of a century ago Jerome Bruner (1996, p. 63) explained how 'a choice of pedagogy inevitably communicates a conception of the learning process and the learner'. 'Pedagogy', he argued, 'is never innocent. It is a medium that carries its own message' (Bruner, 1996, p. 63).

In contrast to this socio-cultural perspective on pedagogy, the contemporary and dominant take on pedagogy can be summed up in the phrase 'what works'. The idea of 'what works' is seductive given policy concerns with measurable outcomes as indicators of the success of educational systems. Furthermore, it would be hard to argue against the call for a closer connection between research, policy and practice, which is clearly important and desirable.

However, it matters what is judged as research and in terms of education, particularly pedagogy, and so a 'what works' stance is too simplistic. This is because of the view of learning it brings with it – it assumes neutrality on the part of the people involved in the 'treatment', the teaching method – where all the participants can be assumed to stand outside the phenomena under investigation. This assumption leads to the privileging of the programme or method over the agents, the teacher and the learner – a move, which makes the agent invisible. The assumption is that there is no need for a process of meaning making and any deficits are located in learners which can be controlled for by the random allocation of learners to 'treatment' (in the case of research studies usually based on randomised control trials).

This view of pedagogy assumes that the intentions and beliefs of different teachers about the teaching approach they were assigned to would not influence the way they applied the teaching methods in question. The assumption of impartiality on the part of enactors of pedagogy in the 'what works' way of thinking about effectiveness has been heavily criticised, not just in education, but in other aspects of social life as well (e.g. Biesta, 2007; Hollway, 2001).

People have to implement policy directives about pedagogy and associated curriculum programmes (e.g. the teaching of early reading in England). But those people, as agents, always have views, perspectives and beliefs about the world and what works in their context with their learners. Furthermore, assuming that one programme can be equally effective with all learners, ignores learners' different histories of participation, as in this view of pedagogy and related view of learning, social and cultural influences do not impact on learning. Measures used to determine outcomes like pedagogic methods are also treated as unproblematic, neutral, techniques.

A socio-cultural view of learning challenges the neutrality and stability of tasks and would therefore challenge the very evidence base that is claimed for in a 'what works' approach to pedagogy and, by extension, to teacher education. Such studies can provide important illumination but cannot ever deliver a person-proof pedagogy. In a socio-cultural perspective, participants (learners, teachers/mentors) act and negotiate their meanings in the course of engaging with particular tasks within particular sets of relations, roles, interests and expectations, and broader institutional practices and imperatives. This makes a universal notion of pedagogy untenable and challenges the assumed direct connection between specified, prescribed or so-called effective teaching methods.

Dominant perspectives on learning tend to blame the marginalised for being marginal. We have argued the need to look at the person in the context of the surround and the surround is not just the physical environment but is a social context that is replete with expectations, assumptions and agendas that have consequences for what is available to be learned and by whom. A socio-cultural perspective on learning and pedagogy directs attention to the extent to which people feel empowered to participate fully in their learning (agency) and directs attention to how best to extend the agency of learners based on knowledge of their understanding of the relevance and meaningfulness of the learning in question. Crucially socio-cultural theory provides us with valuable conceptual tools for understanding and enhancing participation of learners who may be disaffected, marginalised and dis-identifying with school learning. It constitutes a set of powerful ideas that, if understood by student teachers and their educators, would, we believe, offer a challenge to the dominant model of learning and pedagogy that has emerged in recent European Commission policy and would challenge practices in ways that would enhance equity and social justice.

3.2   *Multicultural Teacher Education*

A further priority of teacher education for social justice must be to embrace the potential of critical multiculturalism. In view of rapid demographic changes towards increased heterogeneity taking place across the world, multicultural education has been steadily gaining recognition as an important cross-national policy agenda. Indeed, educational policy-makers in many countries see multicultural competence as a key to success in the global economy (Cha & Ham, 2014). Thus, teachers are expected to prepare the new effective workforce while accommodating diverse needs within their classrooms. However, this shift towards business-driven (or corporate) multiculturalism in educational systems reinforces growing social and economic inequalities as high-quality multicultural education is being delivered only to the privileged (Resnik, 2009). Moreover, corporate multiculturalism supports the depoliticised version of multicultural education that does not question unjust systems but rather reproduces the status quo (Gorski, 2006; Carr et al., 2016).

Standing in opposition to this is critical multiculturalism. Notably, the critical lens played the integral role in the initial conceptualisation of multicultural education as it was created to promote pluralism and challenge all forms of discrimination in educational settings through ongoing critique of educational policies and structures they create (Banks, 2004; Nieto, 2000b; Sleeter & McLaren, 1995). To maintain commitment to the authentic vision for multicultural education it is important for teachers and teacher educators to be aware of their essential role in promoting social justice and equity (Carr et al., 2016), but most education systems are a long way away from realising that. When asking about the goals of multicultural education Gorski (2006) discovered that most multicultural educators see its main purpose as learning about and celebrating diversity. This limited understanding of multicultural education translates into the organisation of cultural festivals, dances, and food fairs rather than critical reflection about the socio-political context around us and our place within it. The first step to change this is through recognising what stands in the way of critical thinking.

International research reveals that within many education systems minority students are taught by teachers who come from dominant groups (Magos, 2007; Sales et al., 2011; Tatar & Horenczyk, 2003; Zembylas et al., 2011). The main problem with this is that majority teachers often do not understand the obstacles their minority students are facing (Cochran-Smith, 2004; Gay & Kirkland, 2003). It is also not uncommon for them to hold stereotypical beliefs about minorities (Kumar & Hamer, 2013) and to lack 'critical awareness of themselves as cultural or linguistic beings' (Haddix, 2008, p. 260). Evidence shows that teachers themselves report being unprepared to work in diverse settings and feel uncomfortable when facing the topics of privilege, discrimination, and injustice (Bravo-Moreno, 2009; Tandon et al., 2017; Villegas et al., 2018). Indeed, these topics are often skirted around by teachers in conversations with other teachers as well as with students because most teacher education programmes leave these topics out of formative discussions (Carter Andrews et al., 2019; Chang-Bacon, 2021). Sometimes student teachers report touching on these topics in their programmes but their institutions 'spoke of social justice but didn't actually implement it' (Tolbert & Eichelberger, 2016). Essentially, teachers enter the workforce too often unprepared to recognise and acknowledge discrimination, let alone tackle it in educational settings (Daniels & Varghese, 2019; Matias & Mackey, 2016).

Even when teacher education programmes do include components/courses that focus on race, ethnicity, and social justice, more often than not they are simply 'treated as obligatory check-boxes' producing passive non-engagement (Moore, 2021) or even resistance (LaDuke, 2009; Shim, 2018). Moreover, simply gaining theoretical knowledge is not enough as many teachers don't know how to connect multiculturalism theory with practice (Almarza, 2005; Gorski,

2006). Overcoming this is possible if teacher educators develop their programmes placing the multicultural component at the core. It is also important to introduce multiculturalism early on in teacher education as research suggests that junior students are more likely to grow culturally sensitive and are less likely to be set in their ways compared to their senior/graduate counterparts (Brown, 2004). Resistance can also be reduced using 'a pedagogy of discomfort' (Boler, 1999) that allows teachers' intense emotions to be brought into the conversation instead of sweeping them under the carpet (Cutri & Whiting, 2015). Moreover, seeing positive examples can be transformative so teacher educators need to model critical thinking as well as self-reflection and self-inquiry (McCarthy, 2018). For instance Gracie (2018) has identified challenges but also the opportunities for education and teacher education on both sides of the Irish border as a result of an increasingly multi-cultural society and school population. Among her recommendations for teacher education are the compulsory incorporation of training in English as an Additional Language, more bilingual resources, teaching around racism and racist bullying and an encouragement for student teachers to 'look with new eyes' (Gracie, 2018, p. 406) at the classroom to ensure it is truly welcoming for pupils of any country, religion or ethnicity.

Another important issue/barrier to multiculturalism is that very few teacher education programmes prepare bilingual teachers, even in contexts where these teachers are most needed. For example, mother-tongue medium bilingual education is especially important for Indigenous communities as it is known to benefit Indigenous learners more than any other forms of education (Magga et al., 2005; McIvor & McCarty, 2017). In addition, bilingual programmes offer pedagogical advantages to all students and lead to better academic achievement (Adesope et al., 2010; Petitto, 2009; Reljić et al., 2015; Thomas & Collier, 2002). Nevertheless, many Western European governments, despite their continuous rhetoric in support of multicultural education, still adhere to the one-nation one-language dogma (Rego & Nieto, 2000; Sierens & Van Avermaet, 2017). Even the countries that are officially bilingual/multilingual often practise double standards – they value competence in high-prestige European languages and discourage the use of low-status minority languages (Sierens & Van Avermaet, 2017). With such a low value being assigned to minority languages it is not surprising that teachers (even those coming from minority backgrounds) are rarely bilingual. Becoming proficient in an additional language while preparing to be a teacher requires a great deal of commitment. In view of this, teacher education programmes need to offer real incentives to their students to help them stay motivated while acquiring new language skills and deeper multicultural competence that comes with it (Nieto, 2000b).

Teacher education also has the potential transformative power to overcome not just barriers to learning within classrooms and surrounding communities but also barriers to mutual understanding across national borders too. The development of the Standing Conference on Teacher Education North and South, SCoTENS, across the island of Ireland highlights how, in the spirit of the 1998 Belfast (Good Friday) Agreement, teacher educators and student teachers have been facilitated to come together across a contested border. Using a Wenger-Trayner value-creation framework, Clarke et al. (2021) recount how this unique cross-border teacher education network has provided opportunities for professional development for student teachers and teacher educators, but perhaps more significantly how participants were able to develop personally in terms of their understanding of the 'other', spending time together in a safe space. There are lessons here for an increasingly fractious Europe, and particularly perhaps for the possibilities of working towards a more expansive vision of European teacher education that reflects values of inclusion and social justice.

4   Future Prospects for Values-Led Teacher Education

Too often however attention to issues of social justice in teacher education have been more in name than in substance, with many empty claims made within programme specifications and little focus given to issues beyond the individual classroom (Zeichner, 2006). It has also been argued that there remains conceptual confusion as to the meaning of social justice in relation to teacher education, and a lack of empirical research that examines the classroom practice of teachers who claim to work towards social justice and/or who were trained in programmes which claim to have social justice as their conceptual orientation (Grant & Agosto, 2008). Furthermore, in the policy arena of teacher capacity, there is continued emphasis on easily taught and measured classroom-based teaching skills and an enduring silence around the more complex but immensely valuable notion and purpose of social justice. If we truly believe that teachers should become agents for social change, then teacher education must enable prospective teachers to 'think deeply about and deliberately claim the role of educator as well as activist based on political consciousness and ideological commitment to combating… inequities' (Cochran-Smith, 2001, p. 3). In terms of its commitment to social justice and to a fairer, more equitable society, it is time for teacher education to find its voice and policy-makers to support this.

We have argued in this chapter that the current predominant focus in many countries and reflected in recent European Commission policy work is on the creation of an increasingly uniform, measurability-oriented, accountability-driven model of teacher education characterised by ever increasing regulation. We argue that this push towards a competency-centred 'Europeification' of teacher education is ideologically opposed to and threatens the promotion of a more nuanced, place-based/contextually relevant, values-centred model of teacher education in which socio-cultural tools can help us understand learners, learning and learning contexts, and in which equity and social justice really matter. These should be among the proper concerns of European Commission teacher education policy work if the European Education Area is to be a substantive factor in realising the strong social Europe advocated in the recent European Pillar of Social Rights (2021).

There are however some grounds for hope, albeit now outside the territory of the EU. In Northern Ireland, an Expert Panel established by the Education Minister recently published its Final Report and Action Plan to advise government how to address persistent educational underachievement linked to social disadvantage (Purdy et al., 2021). Building on the work of many other commentators (e.g. Cochran-Smith, 2001; Demie, 2019; Ellis, 2017; Forlin, 2012) the expert panel recommended that Initial Teacher Education should include more focus on addressing educational underachievement and seek to ensure all students gain relevant practical experience as part of their teaching placements insisting that all teachers have first-hand knowledge of effective practice in addressing educational underachievement in socially disadvantaged communities, helping to build understanding and break down prejudice. The Action Plan also calls on government departments to work with ITE providers and other stakeholders to consider ways in which to encourage a more diverse teaching profession including strategies to attract more males into the teaching profession. At the time of writing, this significant report has received endorsement from all major political parties in the Northern Ireland Executive and a high-level implementation board has been established to monitor and evaluate the delivery of the costed actions. While still in the early days of its implementation, this example demonstrates that teacher education, teacher quality, equity and social justice are not mutually exclusive and can in fact rhyme, as the report authors conclude:

> In commending this Action Plan to the Northern Ireland Executive, we fully recognise the magnitude of the challenge in addressing the underlying causes of social disadvantage, the intractability of many of the issues facing families living in disadvantaged circumstances and the need for systemic change in education… but we are also convinced that the impact of the actions proposed in this Action Plan will be significant,

promoting equity, fostering greater collaboration between schools, families and communities, closing the achievement gap, and giving all of our children and young people 'A Fair Start'. (Purdy et al., 2021, p. v)

References

Adesope, O. O., Lavin, T., Thompson, T., & Ungerleider, C. (2010). A systematic review and meta-analysis of the cognitive correlates of bilingualism. *Review of Educational Research, 80*(2), 207–245.

Agasisti, T., Munda, G., & Hippe, R. (2019). Measuring the efficiency of European education systems by combining data envelopment analysis and multiple-criteria evaluation. *Journal of Productivity Analysis, 51*(2), 105–124.

Aleksić, I. (2019). *The evolving education 'mandate' of the EU – A long-term impact of the Lisbon 2000 reform*. DebatEU Jean Monnet Paper, 2019/02.

Almarza, D. J. (2005). Connecting multicultural education theories with practice: A case study of an intervention course using the realistic approach in teacher education. *Bilingual Research Journal, 29*(3), 527–539.

Antunes, F. (2006). Globalisation and Europeification of education policies: Routes, processes and metamorphoses. *European Educational Research Journal, 5*(1), 38–55.

Banks, J. (2004). Multicultural education: Characteristics and goals. In J. Banks & C. Banks (Eds.), *Multicultural education: Issues and perspectives* (pp. 3–30). Jossey-Bass.

Bauckham, I., Blake, J., Gill, R., Moore, R., & Twiselton, S. (2021). *Initial Teacher Training (ITT) market review report*. https://assets.publishing.service.gov.uk/government/uploads/system/uploads/attachment_data/file/999621/ITT_market_review_report.pdf

Biesta, G. (2007). Why 'what works won't work: Evidence-based practice and the democratic deficit in educational research. *Educational Theory, 57*(1), 1–22.

Boler, M. (1999). *Feeling power: Emotions and education*. Routledge.

Bravo, M. A., Mosqueda, E., Solís, J. L., & Stoddart, T. (2014). Possibilities and limits of integrating science and diversity education in preservice elementary teacher preparation. *Journal of Science Teacher Education, 25*(5), 601–619.

Brown, E. L. (2004). The relationship of self-concepts to changes in cultural diversity awareness: Implications for urban teacher educators. *The Urban Review, 36*(2), 119–146.

Bruner, J. (1996). *The culture of education*. Harvard University Press.

Carr, P. R., Pluim, G., & Thésée, G. (2016). The dimensions of, and connections between, multicultural social justice education and education for democracy: What are the roles and perspectives of future educators? *Citizenship Education Research Journal/Revue de recherche sur l'éducation à la citoyenneté, 6*(1), 3–23.

Carter Andrews, D. J., Brown, T., Castillo, B. M., Jackson, D., & Vellanki, V. (2019). Beyond damage-centered teacher education: Humanizing pedagogy for teacher educators and preservice teachers. *Teachers College Record, 121*(6), 1–28.

Cha, Y. K., & Ham, S. H. (2014). The institutionalization of multicultural education as a global policy agenda. *The Asia-Pacific Education Researcher, 23*(1), 83–91.

Chang-Bacon, C. K. (2022). 'We sort of dance around the race thing': Race-evasiveness in teacher education. *Journal of Teacher Education, 73*(1), 8–22.

Clarke, L., Galvin, C., Campbell, M., Cowan, P., Hall, K., Magennis, G., O'Doherty, T., Purdy, N., & Abbott, L. (2021). Assessing the value of SCOTENS as a cross-border professional learning network in Ireland using the Wenger–Trayner value-creation framework. *Oxford Review of Education, 47*(1), 79–97.

Cochran-Smith, M. (2001). Learning to teach against the (new) grain. *Journal of Teacher Education, 52*(1), 3–4.

Cochran-Smith, M. (2004). Blind vision: Unlearning racism in teacher education. In S. Anderson, P. Attwood, & L. Howard (Eds.), *Facing racism in education* (pp. 277–304). Harvard Educational Review Reprint Series.

Cochran-Smith, M. (2021a). Rethinking teacher education: The trouble with accountability. *Oxford Review of Education, 47*(1), 8–24.

Cochran-Smith, M. (2021b). Exploring teacher quality: International perspectives. *European Journal of Teacher Education, 44*(3), 415–428.

Cochran-Smith, M., & Fries, K. (2005). Researching teacher education in changing times: Politics and paradigms. In M. Cochran-Smith & K. Zeichner (Eds.), *Studying teacher education: The report of the AERA panel on research and teacher education* (pp. 69–109). Lawrence Erlbaum Publishers.

Cutri, R. M., & Whiting, E. F. (2015). The emotional work of discomfort and vulnerability in multicultural teacher education. *Teachers and Teaching, 21*(8), 1010–1025.

Daniels, J. R., & Varghese, M. (2019). Troubling practice: Exploring the relationship between whiteness and practice-based teacher education in considering a raciolinguicized teacher subjectivity. *Educational Researcher, 49*(1), 56–63.

Demie, F. (2019). *Educational inequality – Closing the gap*. UCL Press.

Ellis, S. (2017). The Strathclyde literacy clinic: Developing student teacher values, knowledge and identity as inclusive practitioners. In M. Peters, B. Cowie, & I. Menter (Eds.), *A companion to research in teacher education* (pp. 121–133). Springer.

European Commission. (2012a). *Communication from the Commission to the European Parliament, the Council, the European Economic and Social Committee and the Committee of the regions rethinking education: Investing in skills for better socio-economic outcomes.* 20.11.2012 SWD(2012) 374 final.

European Commission. (2012b). *Supporting the teaching professions for better learning outcomes.* European Commission.

European Commission. (2013). *Supporting teacher competence development for better learning outcomes*. European Commission.
European Commission. (2017). *Communication from the Commission to the European Parliament, the Council, the European Economic and Social Committee and the committee of the regions: School development and excellent teaching for a great start in life*. COM/2017/0248 final. European Commission.
European Commission. (2020). *Communication from the Commission to the European Parliament, the Council, the European Economic and Social Committee and the committee of the regions on achieving the European Education Area by 2025*. 30.9.2020 COM 625 final. European Commission.
European Parliament & European Council. (2006). *Recommendation of the European Parliament and of the council of 18 December 2006 on key competences for lifelong learning* (2006/962/EC). https://eur-lex.europa.eu/legal-content/EN/AUTO/?uri=celex:32006H0962
Farrell, R. (2021). The school-university nexus and degrees of partnership in initial teacher education. *Irish Educational Studies*, 40(2), 1–18.
Flores, M. A. (2016). Teacher education curriculum. In J. Loughran & M. Hamilton (Eds.), *International handbook of teacher education* (pp. 187–230). Springer.
Gay, G., & Kirkland, K. (2003). Developing cultural critical consciousness and self-reflection in pre-service teacher education. *Theory into Practice*, 42(2), 181–187.
Gorski, P. C. (2006). Complicity with conservatism: The de-politicizing of multicultural and intercultural education. *Intercultural Education*, 17(2), 163–177.
Gracie, A. (2018). Moving to multi-cultural classrooms. In M. Attard Tonna & J. Madalińska-Michalak (Eds.), *Teacher education policy and practice – International perspectives and inspirations* (pp. 124–146). Foundation for the Development of the Education System.
Grant, C., & Agosto, V. (2008). Teacher capacity and social justice in teacher education. In M. Cochran-Smith, S. Feiman-Nemser, D. J. McIntyre, & K. Demers (Eds.), *Handbook of research on teacher education* (pp. 175–200). Routledge.
Haddix, M. (2008). Beyond sociolinguistics: Towards a critical approach to cultural and linguistic diversity in teacher education. *Language and Education*, 22(5), 254–270.
Hall, K. (2008). Leaving middle childhood and moving into teenhood: Small stories revealing agency and identity. In K. Hall (Eds.), *Pedagogy and practice: Culture and identities* (pp. 87–104). Sage.
Hall, K., Curtin, A., & Rutherford, V. (2014). *Networks of mind: Learning, culture and neuroscience*. Routledge.
Hall, K., Murphy, P., & Soler, J. (Eds.). (2008). *Pedagogy and practice: Culture and identities*. Sage.

Hanushek, E. A. (2011). The economic value of higher teacher quality. *Economics of Education Review, 30*(3), 466–479.

Hollway, W. (2001). The psycho-social subject in 'evidence-based practice'. *Journal of Social Work Practice, 15*(1), 9–22.

Hulme, M., Menter, I., Murray, J., & O'Doherty, T. (2015). Thirteen insights from the five nations and implications for the future. In G. Beauchamp, L. Clarke, M. Hulme, M. Jephcote, A. Kennedy, G. Magennis, I. Menter, J. Murray, T. Mutton, T. O'Doherty, & G. Peiser (Eds.), *Teacher education in times of change* (pp. 219–234). Policy Press.

Ivinson, G., & Murphy, P. (2007). *Rethinking single-sex teaching*. Open University Press.

Krejsler, J. B. (2018). EuroVisions in school policy and the knowledge economy: A genealogy of the transnational turn in European school and teacher education policy. In N. Hobbel & B. L. Bales (Eds.), *Navigating the common good in teacher education policy* (pp. 180–194). Routledge.

Kumar, R., & Hamer, L. (2013). Preservice teachers' attitudes and beliefs toward student diversity and proposed instructional practices: A sequential design study. *Journal of Teacher Education, 64*(2), 162–177.

LaDuke, A. E. (2009). Resistance and renegotiation: Preservice teacher interactions with and reactions to multicultural education course content. *Multicultural Education, 16*(3), 37–44.

Lave, J. (1988). *Cognition in practice: Mind, mathematics and culture in everyday life*. Cambridge University Press.

Lawn, M., & Lingard, B. (2002). Constructing a European policy space in educational governance: The role of transnational policy actors. *European Educational Research Journal, 1*(2), 290–307.

Magga, O. H., Nicolaisen, I., Trask, M., Dunbar, R., & Skutnabb-Kangas, T. (2005). *Indigenous children's education and indigenous languages* [Expert paper]. The United Nations Permanent Forum on Indigenous Issues.

Magos, K. (2007). The contribution of action-research to training teachers in intercultural education: A research in the field of Greek minority education. *Teaching and Teacher Education, 23*, 1102–1112.

Manso, J., & Sánchez-Tarazaga, L. (2018). Competency frameworks for teachers: A contribution from the European education policy. In M. Attard Tonna & J. Madalińska-Michalak (Eds.), *Teacher education policy and practice – International perspectives and inspirations* (pp. 80–101). Foundation for the Development of the Education System.

Matias, C. E., & Mackey, J. (2016). Breakin' down whiteness in antiracist teaching: Introducing critical whiteness pedagogy. *The Urban Review, 48*(1), 32–50.

Mayer, D. (2021). The connections and disconnections between teacher education policy and research: Reframing evidence. *Oxford Review of Education, 47*(1), 120–134.

McCarthy, M. D. (2018). Critically teaching criticality? Modeling social and pedagogical inquiry with literary texts. *Studying Teacher Education, 14*(2), 174–193.

McDermott, R. (1996). The acquisition of a child by a learning difficulty. In S. Chalkin & J. Lave (Eds.), *Understanding practice: Perspectives on activity and context* (pp. 269–305). Cambridge University Press.

McIvor, O., & McCarty, T. L. (2017). Indigenous bilingual and revitalization-immersion education in Canada and the USA. In S. May, O. Garcia, & A. M. Lin (Eds.), *Encyclopedia of language and education: Bilingual and multilingual education* (pp. 422–438). Springer International Publishing AG.

Menter, I. (2016). Introduction. In The Teacher Education Group (Eds.), *Teacher education in times of change* (pp. 119–233). Policy Press.

Moore, A. E. (2021). 'My job is to unsettle folks': Perspectives on a praxis toward racial justice. *Teaching and Teacher Education, 102,* Article 103336.

Nieto, S. (2000a). Placing equity front and center – Some thoughts on transforming teacher education for a new century. *Journal of Teacher Education, 51*(3), 180–187.

Nieto, S. (2000b). *Affirming diversity: The sociopolitical context of multicultural education.* Longman.

Nind, M., Curtin, A., & Hall, K. (2016). *Researching pedagogy.* Bloomsbury.

Noble-Rogers, J. (2021). *UCET Research & International Forum: ITE market review.* UCET.

Pantić, N., & Florian, L. (2015). Developing teachers as agents of inclusion and social justice. *Education Inquiry, 6*(3), 333–351.

Pépin, L. (2007). The history of EU cooperation in the field of education and training: How lifelong learning became a strategic objective. *European Journal of Education, 42*(1), 121–132.

Petitto, L. A. (2009). New discoveries from the bilingual brain and mind across the life span: Implications for education. *Mind, Brain, and Education, 3*(4), 185–197.

Purdy, N., Logue, J., Montgomery, M., O'Hare, K., & Redpath, J. (2021). *A fair start: Final report and action plan.* Expert Panel on Educational Underachievement.

Rego, M. A. S., & Nieto, S. (2000). Multicultural/intercultural teacher education in two contexts: Lessons from the United States and Spain. *Teaching and Teacher Education, 16*(4), 413–427.

Reid, J. (2011). A practice turn for teacher education. *Asia Pacific Journal of Teacher Education, 39*(3), 293–310.

Reljić, G., Ferring, D., & Martin, R. (2015). A meta-analysis on the effectiveness of bilingual programs in Europe. *Review of Educational Research, 85*(1), 92–128.

Resnik, J. (2009). Multicultural education–good for business but not for the state? The IB curriculum and global capitalism. *British Journal of Educational Studies, 57*(3), 217–44.

Rogoff, B. (2003). *The cultural nature of human development.* Oxford University Press.

Sales, A., Traver, J. A., & García, R. (2011). Action research as a school-based strategy in intercultural professional development for teachers. *Teaching and Teacher Education, 27*, 911–919.

Shim, J. M. (2018). Working through resistance to resistance in anti-racist teacher education. *Journal of Philosophy of Education, 52*(2), 262–283.

Sierens, S., & Van Avermaet, P. (2017). Bilingual education in migrant languages in Western Europe. In O. García, A. Lin, & S. May (Eds.), *Bilingual and multilingual education. Encyclopedia of language and education* (3rd ed.). Springer.

Sleeter, C., & McLaren, P. (1995). Exploring connections to build a critical multiculturalism. In C. Sleeter & P. L. McLaren (Eds.), *Multicultural education, critical pedagogy, and the politics of difference* (pp. 5–32). State University of New York Press.

Snoek, M. (2006). Educating change agents. Teacher competences in an era of change. *Proceedings ATEE, 31*(2006), 35–48.

Snoek, M., Dengerink, J., & de Wit, B. (2019). Reframing the teacher profession as a dynamic multifaceted profession: A wider perspective on teacher quality and teacher competence frameworks. *European Journal of Education, 54*(3), 413–425.

Sullivan A., Johnson B., & Simons M. (Eds.). (2019). *Attracting and keeping the best teachers. Professional learning and development in schools and higher education.* Springer.

Symeonidis, V. (2018). Revisiting the European teacher education area: The transformation of teacher education policies and practices in Europe. *CEPS Journal, 8*(3), 13–34.

Tatar, M., & Horenczyk, G. (2003). Diversity-related burnout among teachers. *Teaching and Teacher Education, 19*, 397–408.

Tatto, M. T. (2021). Comparative research on teachers and teacher education: Global perspectives to inform UNESCO's SDG 4 agenda. *Oxford Review of Education, 47*(1), 25–44.

Telling, K., & Serapioni, M. (2019). The rise and change of the competence strategy: Reflections on twenty-five years of skills policies in the EU. *European Educational Research Journal, 18*(4), 387–406.

Thomas, W. P., & Collier, V. (2002). *A national study of school effectiveness for language minority students' long-term academic achievement.* Center for Research on Education, Diversity & Excellence.

Tolbert, S., & Eichelberger, S. (2016). Surviving teacher education: A community cultural capital framework of persistence. *Race, Ethnicity and Education, 19*(5), 1025–1042.

Villegas, A. M., La Mora, K., Martin, A., & Mills, T. (2018). Preparing future mainstream teachers to teach English language learners: A review of the empirical literature. *The Educational Forum, 82*(2), 138–155.

Wenger, E. (1998). *Communities of practice: Learning, meaning and identity.* Cambridge University Press.

Zeichner, K. M. (2006). Reflection of a university-based teacher educator on the future of college- and university-based teacher education. *Journal of Teacher Education, 57*(3), 326–340.

Zembylas, M., Charalambous, C., Charalambous, P., & Kendeou, P. (2011). Promoting peaceful coexistence in conflict-ridden Cyprus: Teachers' difficulties and emotions toward a new policy initiative. *Teaching and Teacher Education, 27*, 332–341.

CHAPTER 4

Genealogy of the Ethics of Teacher Self-Evaluation
From Adherence to Norms to Self-Discipline through Self-Evaluation

Hannele Pitkänen

Abstract

Quality evaluation (QE) has assumed major importance in governing education. QE is acknowledged as a self-evident and necessary method of improving quality in education across education systems. Along with the quality 'evaluation wave', schools and teachers have not only become objects of evaluation, but have also been subjected to increasing demands to self-evaluate. Using genealogical methodology, this chapter analyses the emergence and formation of the politics of school and teacher self-evaluation and also the power and subjectivities invoked through it in the case of Finnish comprehensive education. The research material includes curricular, legislative and education policy texts and national guidelines and textbooks on school and teacher self-evaluation in the period 1970–2014.

The chapter demonstrates how, along with these changes in policy, the ethics of the necessity for self-evaluation in Finnish basic education emerges. It shows how teachers and schools traditionally strictly governed by rules and norms and subjectified as obedient to norms have since the early 1980s transformed into the self-developing and self-evaluative teacher and school. Becoming entangled with the long histories of teachers as reflectors on their own work, these changes enabled the formation of self-evaluation as a normal and self-evident everyday practice of teachers and schools to evolve, and along with this, the related ethics of the necessity for self-evaluation to emerge. This ethics is closely entangled with and supports the governing of education through quality evaluation.

Keywords

archaeology of knowledge – discourse – ethics – genealogy – governing – quality evaluation – teacher self-evaluation

1   Introduction

Throughout the history of formal education, educational institutions, schools and teachers have been under external evaluative control and surveillance (Alarcón López & Lawn, 2019; Pitkänen, 2019). For example, in Europe, school inspection – the monitoring and supervision of schools and teachers by official school inspectors – has been practised since the emergence of modern mass education around the mid-nineteenth century (Evertsson, 2015; James & Davies, 2009; Knudsen, 2016; Varjo et al., 2016). Recent decades have witnessed a global rise and spread of large-scale assessments and test-based accountabilities (Verger et al., 2018; Sahlberg, 2016; Smith, 2016) and the related politics of quality (Kauko et al., 2018), cultures of audit (Kipnis, 2008) and quality evaluation (Ozga et al., 2011) focusing on performance and quality of education, school and teachers (Ball, 2003; Holloway & Brass, 2018). Through these changes, teachers and schools have increasingly become the objects of intensified external evaluative control and surveillance, increasingly implemented in the name of quality of education in pursuit of global competitiveness between nations (European Commission/EACEA/Eurydice, 2015).

Concurrently, there is also a long history of teachers reflecting and evaluating themselves, putting their selves and their pedagogical activities under the control and surveillance of themselves. In her article, 'Teacher reflection in a hall of mirrors: Historical influences and political reverberations', Lynn Fendler (2003) traces the descent of the well-established idea of reflexive teacher and reflection in teacher education from the emergence of Cartesian rationality perceiving self-awareness as a source of knowledge. Whereas in the Cartesian scheme, reflectivity refers to the enactment of self-awareness, where the self is simultaneously 'the subject-who-reflects' and 'the object-who-is-reflected', John Dewey (1933), according to Fendler (2003), raised reflection as a pedagogical aim in his *How we think: A restatement of the relation of reflective thinking to the educative process*. For Dewey, reflection represented the prevailing of reason and science over instinct or impulse (Fendler, 2003), as it 'converts action that is merely appetitive, blind, and impulsive into intelligent action' (Dewey, 1933, as cited in Fendler, 2003, p. 18). Since Dewey, reflection has come into focus in the teacher education literature and in the discipline itself, but especially since Donald Schön's (1983) *Reflective practitioner: How professionals think in action*, reflection has found its way to the core of teachers' professionalism (Fejes, 2011; Fendler, 2003). Through these different notions of reflection and 'how they work together historically' as Fendler (2003, p. 17) puts it, reflection has come to be seen as a pedagogical ideal to improve the quality of pedagogical practices (Fejes & Dahlstedt, 2012, p. 23), teachers' professionalism and effectiveness as educators (Fox et al., 2019, p. 369). It has become a 'conspicuous part of education' (Fejes, 2011) and perceived as natural in teacher education and professionalism discourses (Fendler, 2003; Sitomaniemi-San, 2015) as encapsulated in Ken Zeichner's (1996, as cited in Fendler, 2003) maxim 'there is no such thing as an unreflective teacher'. Thus, the idea of teacher as 'reflective practitioner' has become 'normalized within the discourse of a "good teacher"' (Perryman et al., 2017, p. 748).

This chapter focuses on how this well-established notion of teacher as a reflective practitioner engages with the more recent trend towards the global advent of quality evaluation in education described above. These have given rise to the notion that it should not only be individual teachers reflecting on themselves and their pedagogical activities, but practising self-evaluation as part of the normal and everyday practices of school communities (Kauko et al., 2020; Pitkänen, 2019), taking the form often referred to as an internal or school self-evaluation.

Like quality evaluation and assurance in general, at the level of policy, school self-evaluation has been offered as a solution to the challenges of the quality, equality and efficiency of school education (OECD, 2013). Along with increased reliance on data received from external evaluations, such as large-scale student achievement testing, school inspection or performance measurements and indicators, a marked tendency towards school and teacher self-evaluation has become apparent. The requirements or recommendations regarding self-evaluation have been included in European policy (European Commission/EACEA/Eurydice, 2015; European Commission, 2020; European Parliament and Council, 2001) and promoted by influential transnational organisations such as the OECD through their policy recommendations or comparisons (e.g., OECD, 2013, 2020). For example, in Europe, in 2001, the European Parliament and Council (2001/166/EC) indicated that quality evaluation should be perceived as one of the means of achieving its objective of quality education in Europe and as part of making a recommendation 'to encourage school self-evaluation as a method of creating learning and improving schools, within a balanced framework of school self-evaluation and any external evaluations'. By 2014 school self-evaluation, conceptualised as a 'process initiated and carried out by schools themselves to evaluate the quality of the education they provide' in general education had been made compulsory or recommended in the majority of European countries (European Commission/EACEA/Eurydice, 2015, pp. 41–42). Recently, the development of 'a culture of self-reflection and self-evaluation which are fundamental for improving all children's and young people's learning and well-being' has been acknowledged to be of great political importance and deserving of support from national and regional policy-makers (European Commission, 2020, p. 3). This tendency can be called the emergence of the politics of self-evaluation. Consequently, it can be argued that the self-evaluation conducted in schools, mostly by school personnel such as teachers and head-teachers (European Commission/EACEA/Eurydice, 2015) as an integral part of the quality assurance and evaluation procedures, has become a fundamental element in governing education.

The aim of this chapter is to explore the socio-historical emergence and formation of the current policies and practices of teacher and school self-evaluation. Thus, the chapter is concerned with the question of how it has become commonplace to think about schools and teachers as self-evaluators within the normal and everyday practices of the school community, and increasingly as part of the politics of quality evaluation in education. Importantly, as Holloway and Brass (2018, p. 361) following Ball (2003, pp. 215–217) acknowledge, these policies, practices or 'technologies of reform not only work to govern education systems – but to produce new kinds of teacher subjects'. In consequence of these notions, the chapter aims to analyse the related mobilisations of teacher subjectivities within changing practices of governing through the politics of quality evaluation as well. This chapter presents a one-case analysis of the issue, focusing on the case of Finnish quality evaluation policy discourse in comprehensive education. It asks: (1) How has the politics of teacher and school self-evaluation been socio-historically mobilised? (2) What is the teacher subjectivity raised within the politics in question?

2   The Finnish Case

Finnish comprehensive school, lasting nine years and compulsory for all children, was established in the early 1970s replacing the previous dual-track compulsory school system consisting of elementary school and selective grammar-school. Comprehensive school is mainly publicly organised, financed and free of cost to pupils. Since the success of Finnish schools in the PISA assessment in the early 2000s, Finnish comprehensive education has become internationally acknowledged as a positive reference society (Takayama et al., 2013; Waldow, 2017), an education system to be seen as a model and learned from.

Compared to other education systems, the Finnish education system and, accordingly, the system of quality evaluation, has remained quite unreceptive to global impacts (Kauko et al., 2020; Simola, 2015; Simola et al., 2009), or as Pasi Sahlberg (2007, 2016) calls it the 'global education reform movement' (GERM). By GERM he refers to a globally disseminated package of policy reforms often including the adoption of market-based and managerial solutions such as school choice, school autonomy and highlighting the mechanism of competition in raising standards and improving the quality of education (Sahlberg, 2016, pp. 185–188). At the core of GERM Sahlberg (2016, p. 188) also raises an 'adoption of *test-based accountability policies*' holding teachers and schools to accountable for pupils' performance, especially through 'the processes of evaluating, inspecting, and rewarding or punishing schools and teachers'.

Even though similar processes, for example, decentralisation and increased school autonomy (Simola et al., 2009) and increased opportunities for school choice (Kosunen, 2016), have taken place in Finland, too, as argued elsewhere, Finland has rather being swimming against the global mainstream (Kauko et al., 2020; Simola, 2015), especially when it comes to quality evaluation policy. For example, since the early 1990s there has been no school inspection system. Additionally, Finland has no student achievement testing of the entire pupil population, thus there is no means of establishing and publishing school rankings. Instead, the Finnish evaluation system relies heavily on the combination of national sample-based testing of pupil performance and the local self-evaluation legally required of schools and local education providers. Sample-based testing and other external evaluations are used only for developing the education system, not for controlling or sanctioning schools and teachers. This purpose of evaluation as development is enshrined in the educational legislation (Kauko et al., 2020; Pitkänen, 2019; Simola et al., 2009; Wallenius, 2019). Additionally, there prevails a firm trust in university-educated (master's level) teachers and in the school institution in general (Simola, 2015, pp. 211–212).

The combination of these Finnish peculiarities; comparatively high quality of comprehensive education without a high-stakes evaluation system relying rather on sample-based and local evaluations and university-educated teachers' professionalism, makes the Finnish case an interesting one for analysis. Earlier research on quality evaluation and assurance, especially in the fields of sociology and politics of education, has analysed the power, governance and subject formation enacted through the policies and practices of external evaluation, especially in contexts where the stakes have been high (Ball, 2003; Holloway & Brass, 2018; Perryman et al., 2017). This chapter raises these issues in self-evaluation taking place in the national context, where the external stakes are lower and trust in teachers providing high-quality education is high. However, this does not imply an absence of evaluative control and governance. Rather, as I argue here, the governing increasingly rests on the mechanism of self-governance by autonomous teachers, as they are persuaded to impose internalised control through the emerging ethics of necessity for teacher self-evaluation.

3 Quality Evaluation as a Technique of Power and the Self

Theoretically, quality evaluation, including evaluation at all levels of education and education systems, such as school and teacher self-evaluation, can be approached as a technique of governing education, the educated and society (Ball, 2013; Holloway & Brass; Ozga et al., 2011; Pitkänen, 2019). The concept and idea of governing has been applied in many and various ways, e.g., in the fields of social and political sciences or sociology and in the politics of education, studying changes in the governance of and in societies. A discussion around what has been called the analytics of government (Dean, 1999; Rose, 1999; Rose & Miller, 2010), building on Michel Foucault's discussion of governmentality, subject and power (Foucault, 1982, 2000), deserves for closer attention. The perspective of the analytics of government serves to emphasise the nature of governing as socio-historically changing, and thus requiring analysis rather than fixed theories or conceptual definitions of power and governance (Foucault, 1982, p. 778).

Government as one of the main concepts in the analytics of government can be perceived in a very general way as any kind of deliberate attempt to shape human behaviour in accordance with a particular set of norms and ends (Dean, 1999, pp. 11–12). As a 'conduct of the conduct' Mitchell Dean (1999, p. 11) determines the government further as follows:

> Government is any more or less calculated and rational activity, undertaken by a multiplicity of authorities and agencies, employing a variety of techniques and forms of knowledge, that seeks to shape conduct by working through our desires, aspirations, interests and beliefs, for definite but shifting ends and with a diverse set of relatively unpredictable consequences, effects and outcomes.

Government, thus, does not only relate to the power and rules exercised by state authority but to a network of governing agencies, to a mixture of techniques utilised based on specific forms of knowledge and rationalities, and supporting and reinforcing specific forms of individual and collective ethos (Rose, 1999; Rose & Miller, 2010). The government then operates with the support of diverse socio-historically changing techniques of governing and power, supported by a specific set of knowledge and related ways of rationalising, and by operating on people's subjectivities. In this sense, government is operationalised at the point of contact between the techniques of power and the techniques of self (Foucault, 1988; Rose & Miller, 2010).

Thus, the power of government in present-day liberal societies does not rest mainly on the force of the sovereign or the power of discipline, but is elementarily also practised more gently through persuading, caring, guiding but also individualising ways of pastoral power (Fejes & Dahlstedt, 2012; Foucault, 1982), which shapes people's aspirations, beliefs and conduct (Dean, 1999). It shapes their subjectivities, thus embedding a subjectifying power. It is 'a form of power which makes individuals subjects', both in the sense of subjugating and making subject to (Foucault, 1982, p. 781). These diverse forms of power operate together, or as Perryman et al. (2017, p. 746) put it, they 'interweave, overlap and compound one another'.

In light of these notions, the practices of present quality evaluation are approached here as techniques of governing education – enacted at a distance and put into effect at 'thousands of microlocales', as articulated by Rose (1999, p. 260). This technique and its imposition on the practices of education is not only technical or methodical apparatus or matter, but a technique through which new kinds of subjectivities are called for, and through which the self of the teachers using the technique is constituted. It operates as a technique of the constitution of the teachers' selves complying the rule of the ethics of the necessity for self-evaluation.

4 Genealogical Methodology

Aligning with the theoretical frame, the research reported employs genealogical methodology (Anderson, 2015; Christensen, 2016; Foucault, 1977; Tamboukou, 1999) – the history of present – in analysing the emergence and formation of the politics of Finnish school and teacher self-evaluation, with a special focus on the relations of power, governance and the subjectivities.

Gerd Christensen (2016, p. 765) describes genealogical methodology as the writing of 'the history of the becoming of the contemporary subject'. Generally, genealogy investigates the descent of some contemporary phenomenon, idea or practice taken-for-granted and deemed self-evident, something very normal and ahistorical (Anderson, 2015; Christensen, 2016), and in Foucault's (1977, 1991) terms, truth, and more precisely, the regime of truth. Genealogy aims at studying the socio-historical emergence, mobilisation and formation – not the singular origin, essence, logical-linear constitution or rational evolution – of that truth. It focuses on a series of continuations, interruptions, breaks, transformations e.g., in the constitution of current ideas, practices or phenomena (Foucault, 1977; Popkewitz, 2013; Tamboukou, 1999). Thus, it analyses the socio-historically formulated conditions for the possibility of the current 'truth', which determines the limits of what is thinkable, sayable and practicable.

In their reading of the work of Foucault, Bacchi and Bonham (2014, p. 177) raise discursive practice as the main analytical category in studying those 'practices that install regimes of truths'. Following this notion, genealogical reading is conducted by deploying Foucault's idea of discursive practices, which he refers to as the practices of discourse (Foucault, 1969/2013). In this way he raises the materiality of a discourse. Thus, discourse refers not to language or language use, but to a specific socio-historically constituted formation of knowledge, which contributes to the organising and shaping of the conduct and way of thinking of people in a specific society in its specific time and space.

In the research presented, school self-evaluation is studied as a discursive practice, and the focus is on its emergence and constitution. The subject of the research concentrates on how through and within this practice, teachers are constituted and mobilised as self-evaluative subjects as part of education governance. Thus, the genealogical focus of the research can be specified as the study of the history of the teacher becoming a self-evaluative subject in the discursive practice of school self-evaluation.

In his *Archaeology of Knowledge*, Foucault (2013) suggests a variety of possible lines in analysing discursive practices, which can be analysed as being constituted of statements reciprocally referring to each other (Foucault, 2013; Krejsler, 2011, p. 2), and contributing to the formation of discursive practice as its own specific system for reasoning education and its governance. Through statements peculiar to the discourse the specific object, the positions for the subject of the discourse as well as concepts and strategies (Foucault, 2013) usable and rational from the point of view of intrinsic logic of the discursive practice are construed.

These analytical categories facilitate the analysis of the object constituted in the discursive practice analysed (self-evaluation as an object of a discursive practice) and the subject constituted as ideal in that practice (self-evaluative and reformist teacher).

The research data consists of a sample from a larger dataset which collected to address the socio-historical constitution of the Finnish quality evaluation discourse (Pitkänen, 2019). It includes more than 400 texts on quality evaluation in education, consisting of national education policy and government documents such as curricula, legislation, white and green papers, policy recommendations and documents in which these policies were put into operation in the form of guidelines and textbooks in the period 1970–2014. The texts were published by national authorities with authority or interest in educational evaluation in comprehensive education such as the Finnish National Board of Education (FNBE) established in 1991, currently called the Finnish National Agency for Education (EDUFI), its antecedent the National Board of General Education (NBGE) (1869–1990), the Ministry of Education (MoE) renamed the Ministry of Education and Culture (MinEdu) in 2010, and the Finnish Education Evaluation Council (FEEC) established in 2003, preceding the current national evaluation agency called the Finnish Education Evaluation Centre (FINEEC), the Association of Finnish Local and Regional Authorities (AFLRA) or other expert bodies on education evaluation. The data includes both hortatory and non-binding texts. Regarding the theoretical frame of the chapter, the data represents the operations of governing as they engage in shaping the conduct of teachers by stipulating the orders and regulations but also indirectly, by appealing to the minds, aspirations and beliefs of teachers, by operating on the free will of the subject and at same time, disciplining the self (e.g., Dean, 1999; Rose, 1999). Thus, the material does not appear in the analysis as cautioned by Popkewitz (2000, p. 1783) as a neutral presentation of school reform but should be read as a site where the governing of teachers and education, ordering the opportunities for action and self-reflection, has been put into operation. Based on close reading of the whole dataset, a selected sample of these texts will be focused on with the aim of illustrating the emergence and formation of teacher self-evaluation as a discursive practice and the site of governance. The sample of these texts includes all curricular documents, main legislative and policy texts concerning teacher and school self-evaluation as well as examples of texts where politics was operationalised through guidelines, textbooks and recommendations during the research period. The focus is on texts showing the break with earlier policy discourse or when new kinds of statements merged into it.

The analysis was conducted first by identifying and collecting all statements concerning quality evaluation in comprehensive education. These statements were collected into a separate document, which included over 1,000 pages of text and mainly those statements referring to the idea of teacher and school self-evaluation were taken into consideration. For the analysis the analytical categories of object, concept, strategy and subject formation, which intertwine in the constitution of a specific discursive practice were used.

The main focus here is on how school and teacher self-evaluation emerge and take shape as a discursive practice around the objects, subjects, concepts and strategies specific to it, and how it operates in the governing of teachers and education. The overall research frame is presented in Table 4.1.

TABLE 4.1   Research frame

Research questions	1. How has the politics of teacher and school self-evaluation been socio-historically mobilised in Finnish comprehensive education?
	2. What is the teacher subjectivity raised within the politics in question?
Data	Sample of policy texts representing the Finnish politics of teacher and school self-evaluation.
Genealogical focus	The history of teachers becoming a self-evaluative subject in the discursive practice of school self-evaluation and in the practices of educational governance.
Analysis of the discursive practice	Object Concept Strategies Subject

5   The Making of a Reflexive But Obedient and Compliant Teacher

The research data constitutes evaluation as intrinsic and natural to the educational institutions and teachers' professionalism (Granö-Suomalainen, 2002, p. 6; Korkeakoski & Tynjälä, 2010, p. 9; Lehtinen, 1995, p. 9; Lyytinen, 1993, p. 72). It is fundamentally taken as something like an ahistorical constant within the practices of teaching and education. Teacher self-evaluation is approached in the same way:

> There is nothing new in self-evaluation. Some kind of self-evaluation has always belonged essentially to teaching. It has been a central part of the process of teachers' professional development, if not consciously and systematically, but at least it has belonged as a natural part of the planning work of the teacher. (Lyytinen, 1993, p. 72)

The first curriculum of the Finnish comprehensive school (Committee for the Comprehensive School Curriculum [CCSC], 1970), and at same time, the earliest document of this study, raises the idea of teacher self-evaluation. However, it is only marginally discussed, as in evaluation the focus is mainly on guiding teachers to evaluate pupils – using multitudes of ways and techniques of pupil assessment. However, pupil assessment is also acknowledged as a point of reference for teachers to evaluate themselves. Teachers are expected to observe the results of their own work by examining pupils' results and performance, thereby assessing the effectiveness of the teaching methods used.

> The variation in the results of schoolwork may result from the effectiveness of diverse teaching practices and methods. By examining the pupils' school achievement teachers gain knowledge of how they have managed to achieve their aims by using specific methods. (CCSC, 1970, p. 158)

In the early years of the comprehensive school system, the idea of the self-reflective teacher is also articulated in the textbooks on evaluation at school (Heinonen & Viljanen, 1978, p. 41; Heinonen & Viljanen, 1980, p. 54). Whereas in the curriculum (CCSC, 1970, p. 158) the idea of teacher self-evaluation was expressed using the concepts of examination and observation, the textbook introduces the concept of self-evaluation. In the textbook, self-evaluation is constituted as a form of self-knowledge, which, unlike in the curriculum (CCSC, 1970), not only focuses on the teachers' own teaching practices or methods, but especially on the teachers' inner selves. According to the textbook it is fundamental to self-knowledge that teachers should contemplate and analyse themselves so as to lay bare and bring everything to the surface. The concepts used in this textbook resemble the conceptual field of psychoanalysis.

> At the foundation of teacher self-knowledge lies the principle that one should not repress any individual deficiencies, but each of these should be revealed and analysed. Thus, teachers should carefully examine their own backgrounds, the environment where they grew up and discover those factors which explain their conduct. (Heinonen & Viljanen, 1978, p. 41)

It is characteristic of these early ideas of teacher self-evaluation in the research data is that they appear in a very specific socio-historical context, in which teachers are mainly subjected to rather strict governmental and legal orders and rules. For example, the 1970 curriculum has been considered by earlier research to be in the nature of a handbook or manual of school keeping (Simola et al., 2009), which should concern, direct and guide all the elements of school education (CCSC, 1970, pp. 56–57). In line with the egalitarian rationale and prevailing technique of the so-called planning economy, the main elements in building the Finnish welfare state at the time (Ahonen, 2003) the idea of a strict and very detailed curriculum was to ensure an equal level of quality of education for all pupils, regardless of the school and the teacher. Even though the curriculum allowed teachers methodological autonomy, on the other hand, it was rather sceptical about the ability of the 'ordinary teacher' to provide an equal level of education and equal opportunities for pupils to learn unless the curriculum provided them with sufficient strict guidance.

> One should start from thinking realistically what an ordinary teacher having completed basic teacher education is able to achieve in a classroom. It is not enough that in some schools pupils can receive very enthusiastic teaching by extraordinarily diverse and inventive teachers. Instead, teacher education should ensure that all pupils attend classes where they have good opportunities to learn. This cannot be guaranteed by teacher education unless the curriculum states what teachers by themselves should know and master. (CCSC, 1970, p. 59)

Accordingly, the curriculum is full of prescriptive statements telling teachers what to do and how to be: 'it is necessary for the teacher', 'the teacher must show', 'the teacher must use' and 'the teacher is obliged' (CCSC, 1970, pp. 44, 52, 228). Importantly, these statements were not only guidelines and orders directed towards individual teachers themselves. They also counted as frames against which teachers were positioned as objects to be monitored, evaluated and then supervised, gently but firmly, especially by head-teachers or the school inspectorate. In this sense, the curriculum can be interpreted as an authoritative statement concerning teaching and being a good teacher in comprehensive school, which teachers should learn through the gentle supervision, or pastoral power as Foucault (1982) calls it, of the head teacher.

> It is indispensable for a head-teacher to monitor the teaching a lot. The negotiation after monitoring, however, is much more important when it comes to pedagogical supervision. The head-teacher should discreetly but emphatically guide the teaching sufficiently and especially the treatment of pupils. In this task head teachers will achieve results if they can indicate that their intention really is to help and support the teacher, not to pass judgement in a negative sense. (CCSC, 1970, p. 231)

In line with the curriculum, teachers were firmly governed through the education legislation (Decree, 443/1970; Decree, 718/1984). A *Decree on Establishing Comprehensive Education* (443/1970) imposed a hierarchical system of control on teachers and teaching in schools at municipal level. For example, following and monitoring teaching as well as instructing and advising both school and/or teachers, was stipulated as a task for a municipal school board (53§), a school council (56§), a chief education officer or municipal inspector (59§) and finally the head teacher (109§). In addition, the educational district administration was tasked with monitoring and inspecting teachers but so also were municipal education administrators and officials and with checking how they performed the official duties assigned to them (185§). Additionally, the educational legislation stipulated numerous tasks imposing duties on teachers. The legislation stated, for example, that teachers should prepare their lessons carefully and perform their teaching tasks conscientiously, use and develop teaching methods suitable for different kinds of teaching situations and to obey the directions given by the head-teacher, the curriculum and the regulations of the school. The education legislation also assigned the task of pupil assessment to teachers (Decree, 443/1970, 108§; Decree, 718/1984, 108§). However, the legislation made no references to teacher self-evaluation as currently understood.

In sum, an early and still very tentative idea about teacher self-evaluation was already manifest in the curricular documents and textbooks during the first decades of the comprehensive school system. At that time, teachers were governed primarily through the notion of official duties and detailed sets of tasks and rules to be implemented in teaching and other school activities. In these frames, teacher and school are mostly seen as the object of evaluation and inspection of multi-layered educational government in relation to the official duties prescribed by the legislation and the curriculum. The position of teachers and schools was externally inspected and monitored as well as strictly governed through legislation, curriculum and other kinds of governmental guides relates to the context of the planning economy and the egalitarian ideal of providing equal quality of education for all pupils regardless of the teacher or the school, (and more generally regardless of the socio-economic background or gender of the pupil). As a result, the compliant and conforming teacher was construed as ideal to achieve these ends.

6 The Rising Practice of Self-Evaluation and the Mobilisation of the Self-Evaluative Teacher

Since the turn of the 1980s new kinds of statements appear in the discourse, bringing self-evaluation into focus and making it an object of discourse. In the research data, mounting doubts regarding bureaucratically and centrally led school development and governance are articulated (e.g. NBGE, 1982). Teachers and schools are still governed through the notion of official duties and practices of multi-layered monitoring (Decree, 718/1984). However, there arises an idea of and a tendency towards local and school-based development of comprehensive education. Additionally, a gradually increasing emphasis on teachers' professional sense of duty and responsibility at least partly replaces the notion of official duty and the related notion of a teacher compliant with the norms.

Increasingly since the late 1970s, it appears in the research data that the development of schooling/education should arise more and more from the active, pedagogically oriented inputs of individual teachers and schools (NBGE, 1978, 1982, 1986a, 1986b; Lyytinen et al., 1989). Alongside national level reforms imposed from above, which was the main model of school improvement in the 1970s, professionally inspired school-based development is perceived as a prerequisite for more permanent and far-reaching changes in comprehensive education (NBGE, 1978, pp. 22–23, 56–58; NBGE, 1982, p. 1). The practices of educational development based on professionally inspired individual schools and teachers was raised as an important issue and discursively normalised as a natural and indispensable part of the day-to-day practices of teaching and education. It was, for example, determined that 'development should be involved as a natural part of teaching and education' (NBGE, 1982, p. 13). These ideas were promoted both in policy texts (NBGE, 1982, pp. 29–30; NBGE, 1985, p. 18; NBGE, 1986b; MoE, 1982, 1983) and the professional literature and textbooks (Hämäläinen & Lonkila, 1985; Holopainen et al., 1982).

> In the development of school/ing emphasis should be placed on the importance of developmental activity originating from the school itself. Reducing the problems in schoolwork and the development of school by the active input of the school personnel often brings about more permanent and far-reaching effects than development demands imposed from outside the school. (NBGE, 1978, p. 56)

The development of teaching, school and schooling at school level is conceptualised as activities and operations pursuing the socially determined goals assigned to education. The goals and targets of education concerned not only learning outcomes but also those things assumed to impact on good learning achievement. In addition to emphasising enhancing knowledge and skills, education was expected to contribute positively to pupils' personality development and attitudes (NBGE, 1986a, p. 3). In response to these demands and to improve the performance of the whole comprehensive school system, school level development was argued to be necessary.

> Regarding school improvement, it is not reasonable to focus on and pay attention only to learning outcomes but also to those activities at school which are apparently conducive to the achievement of good learning results in a wider sense. (NBGE, 1986b, p. 20)

In these changing frames of thinking of education and education governance, the idea of evaluating one's own and especially the school's activity was mobilised explicitly and systematically in the Finnish policy discourse.

Self-evaluation came to be seen as a necessary activity in developing the school community and teachers and also as part of that educational community. It was raised as an elementary and normal part of developing education at the level of the school. It was specifically the teacher and school-level self-evaluation in relation to educational targets set in the legislation and curriculum which was deemed necessary. Ultimately, this was expected to impact the improvement of comprehensive education as a whole (Hämäläinen & Lonkila, 1985; NBGE, 1982, pp. 1, 29–30; NBGE, 1985, p. 18). For example, it was stated:

> The independent task of the school is to continuously evaluate the appropriateness of the operations of the school unit in relation to the achievement of the educational aims and, based on these, to make changes in the operations of the school. (NBGE 1982, pp. 29–30)

The idea of continuous and development-oriented self-evaluation at the level of the school community originating in the early 1980s was absorbed into the Finnish comprehensive education policy discourse by the 1994 curriculum. This took place during the larger reforms in education and in the Finnish administration in general, including a marked decentralisation and deregulation coupled with the reforms in school funding policy and the introduction of the quality evaluation system (Basic Education Act 628/1998; FNBE, 1995), which were conducted in line with the doctrine of New Public Management during the 1990s (Simola et al., 2009).

> Continuous evaluation is an essential part of the activities of the developing school community. Alongside student evaluation, the evaluation of the entire school community becomes more and more important. [...] The school's self-evaluation is part of the continuous development of the curriculum. It is a necessary tool in the work done in the school which knows its aims and which wishes to produce results. (FNBE 1994, p. 26)

Since the 1990s, the idea of school self-evaluation as a fundamental part of school development has remained in the focus of curricula (FNBE, 1994, 2004, 2014) and education policy (e.g. MinEdu, 2012). Further, it has been promoted by a vast body of literature addressed to the teachers and schools to guide them in self-evaluation and foster the 'quality evaluation culture' in schools (Hämäläinen et al., 1993; Kilpinen et al., 1995; Korkeakoski et al., 2000; Laukkanen et al., 1992; Nikkanen & Lyytinen, 1996). Additionally, specific models and techniques for self-evaluation have been widely published (FNBE, 1995; Oppi ja laatu -hanke, 2003; Räisänen & Rönnholm, 2006).

As part of the local-level quality evaluation, school self-evaluation was made a legal obligation in the Basic Education Act of 1998 requiring an education provider to 'evaluate the education it provides and its impact and take part in external evaluations of its operations' (Basic Education Act 628/1998, 21§) with the purpose of developing the education offered. Even if the Act itself does not explicate the school self-evaluation, the preparatory act (SiVm 3/1998, p. 17) declared it an elementary part of local evaluation together with the municipal-level quality evaluation. The idea is also embedded in the current curriculum (FNBE, 2014, pp. 11, 47) and in the quality criteria for basic education (MinEdu, 2012, p. 21), which highlights self-evaluation both at the level of the individual teacher and the school community:

> The most important task of the teacher is to guide and support the learning process of the pupil. Teachers evaluate the learning of the pupils, but should also evaluate their own actions and participate in the evaluation of the entire school organization.

In the theoretical frame of the chapter it was argued that the introduction of self-evaluation is not only a matter of a neutral or apolitical technique of education governance. Rather, it mobilises and constitutes teachers as specific subjects. Accordingly, it is argued here that through the emergence and construction of a discursive practice of self-evaluation analysed above, teachers become increasingly positioned as reformist and self-evaluating, as active members of the self-developing school, striving for the continuous improvement of the school system. Along with the emergence of the practice of self-evaluation, teachers are not primarily subjectified as compliant and conforming implementers of strict and detailed rules, but increasingly as active developers of the school system and of Finnish schooling. The early notions of these can be found at the turn of the 1980s:

> In general, teachers' self-confidence concerning their own abilities and the importance of their own work needs to be fostered and the importance of the idea that in every school it is possible to develop operations through one's own efforts. (NBGE, 1978, p. 67)

> School development requires persevering and systematic efforts. It also requires continuing efforts on the part of the respective educators towards better solutions. New solutions need to be developed by the school itself. These cannot be transposed unrefined from one school to another. However, it is possible to learn from planning. This means

that teachers must work through their own processes of school reform. (Holopainen et al., 1982, pp. 106–107)

The mobilisation of teachers as reforming and self-evaluative professionals does not emerge at one specific point in time. Rather, the position of reforming and self-evaluative teachers emerges gradually in the discourse in which the position of a compliant and conforming teacher continues to be more or less present. For example, the second national core curriculum (NBGE, 1985) includes elements of both of these subject positions for teachers. Schools and teachers are required to assume a more active and responsible role than before in improving and evaluating themselves. Therefore, they are given 'a certain level of self-directiveness' (NBGE, 1985, p. 18). Second, the limits of this area of self-directiveness are still fairly tight strict, and nationally co-ordinated development continues to be important. In this sense, teachers and schools are given a position from which to implement these centrally led reforms.

After the turn of the 1990s the texts appeal increasingly to the teachers' professional and moral sentiments, to the professional sense of duty and responsibility of teachers instead of the official duties as they discuss evaluation. For example, the following quote about being a good and responsible teacher requires absorbing the subjectivity of continuous self-evaluator in the area of pedagogy and teaching. The activity based on evaluation is contrasted with random activity. Self-evaluation practised by teachers represents the commitment and will to advance their professional development and also to promote school improvement.

> Through self-evaluation teachers can identify their own professional needs and develop strategies through which to process them and thereby improve their own professional actions. This means that teachers are responsible for their own professional development. (Lyytinen et al., 1989, p. 5)

This also applies at the level of the school organisation.

> School-level evaluation has been found to be conducive to the professional growth of teachers. [...] First of all, evaluation has been found to be an essential part of the activities of a performative school. Randomness does not then form the base for activities; instead, self-evaluation develops the self-awareness of the school community. (Lyytinen et al., 1989, p. 8)

In the 1990s school and teacher self-evaluation become increasingly construed as a necessary activity of a good, regenerative or high-quality and performing school. Also, these statements did not primarily appeal to the official duties of teachers but to the teachers' sense of professional obligation, or even morality. Thus, government of teachers and schools relied on subjectifying techniques in addition to direct regulation through the law, official duties and rules. These statements persuade teachers and schools to practise self-evaluation, for example, by making self-evaluation a natural element of self-reforming school instead of directly stipulating what teachers and schools are required to do. For example, it is stated that 'assuming that the school takes care of its regeneration it cannot neglect self-evaluation' (Lyytinen et al., 1989, p. 12).

> Teachers are considered to be professional and conscientious people who want to develop themselves and their professional practices. Teachers are expected to observe problems in the operations of the school and to present questions as well as solutions concerning the pedagogical development of the school. (Kangasniemi, 1993, p. 119)

> It has been accepted that the evaluation of one's own work is a prerequisite for improving quality. Each individual is the right person to evaluate the results of their own work. At the same time account must be taken of the evaluations made by others. (Hämäläinen et al., 1993, pp. 5–6)

As noted in the quote above, teachers constituted as the ideal subjects of the discourse, the regime of truth, are not only willing to self-evaluate or to evaluate the school community of which they are a part, but are also willing to be evaluated by others. These two aspects together constitute the emerging ethics of the necessity for self-evaluation in line with the requirements imposed in the policy discourse of quality evaluation, and more widely in the realms of the evaluation society (Dahler-Larsen, 2011), governed through the technologies of evaluation (e.g. Ozga et al., 2011).

7   Final Remarks

By taking a Foucauldian genealogical approach, this chapter explored the socio-historical emergence and formation of the current policies and practices of teacher and school self-evaluation in the case of Finnish comprehensive education. The analysis presented made visible those lines of thought and practices according to which it has eventually become somewhat natural to think about schools and teachers as self-evaluators as a core assumption in transnational and national policies of education governance. In this way, the analysis not only addressed the question of how these practices have emerged evolved into a policy discourse, but also the history of teachers mobilised as self-evaluative subjects. It was shown how these techniques and subjectivities have become possible in the wider contexts of changing education governance from a centralised planning economy to decentralised education governance relying increasingly on data provided through diverse forms of quality evaluation. The results of the analysis are summarised in Table 4.2. In the table, discursive formations identified in the analysis are presented (columns) and specified in Foucauldian genealogical analytical axes of techniques of governing and subjectivities invoked in that governing (rows).

Through the emerging discursive practice of self-evaluation identified in the analysis, self-evaluation is constituted as an indispensable and normal activity of teachers and schools. It also enables and raises the position for self-reforming and evaluative teachers practising self-evaluation individually and as part of the school community, instead of the former subjectivity of compliant teachers which was the ideal in the context of centralised governance and the bureaucratic planning economy.

The analysis showed that during the research period teachers complying with norms and rules gradually became self-evaluative, not only conforming to the official rules but rather constituted as active developers of their own work and that of the school community by practising self-evaluation

TABLE 4.2   From bureaucracy and planning economy to discursive practice of self-evaluation

	Discursive practice of bureaucracy and planning economy	Discursive practice of self-evaluation
Techniques of governing	Duty and rule-based discipline through strict and detailed laws and curricula, inspection, and references to official obligations	Teacher self-disciplined through professional sense of duty, appealing to the rationality and moral sentiments of teacher, normalising self-evaluation
Subjectivities invoked in governing	Compliant and conforming teacher, teacher as object of multi-layered governance	Reforming, evaluative teacher, a responsible teacher willing to evaluate and to be evaluated

and internalising this demand as part of their professional sense of duty. To become a professional, one must not only internalise the demand for continuous self-evaluation but also be willing to be evaluated by others. This is what is suggested here as constituting the emergence of the imperative of internalising the ethics of teacher self-evaluation. This continues to be crucial in the context of the current evaluation society (Dahler-Larsen, 2011).

The self-evaluative teacher is constituted in the discursive practice of self-evaluation, which is ruled by the principle of the ethics of the necessity for self-evaluation. The term ethics is used here to refer, to Michel Foucault's (1982, 1988) idea of practices of the self, and under what conditions people might think of and constitute themselves as ethical actors. This chapter claims that the discursive practice of self-evaluation constitutes the limits for teachers to see themselves as decent professionals only if they obey this rule constructed in discourse and in the practices of governing and power. It prescribes the conditions under which they can recognise themselves and be recognised by others as decent professionals.

Even if the discourses on evaluation are continuously changing and new statements and ways of reasoning emerge, I argue that the discursive turn described in this chapter has relevance from the point of view of the evaluation society. The considerations presented also make it possible to focus on discourses as sites where socio-political power is operationalised by determining subjectivities. Thus, as suggested by many researchers in the field (e.g. Ball, 2003; Holloway & Brass, 2018), the discourses are approached not as neutral but rather as being involved in shaping and organising the conduct of individuals as well as collectives by outlining and defining the field of possibility, for example, of rational reasoning and action as well as through subject positioning or, as Foucault calls it, disciplining the self.

This chapter examined documents on the politics of teacher and school self-evaluation from the perspective of genealogy, also known as critical history. Not enough is known about how the politics of teacher and school self-evaluation are experienced by teachers themselves, and how they live with the ethics of the necessity for self-evaluation raised in the analysis. Yet it is sure that the technology of self-evaluation is not apolitical, nor separate from power relations and governance of society (e.g., Pitkänen, 2022). It would be important to examine how this power is operationalised in the everyday routines of schools, and with what effects. The current globally disseminated discourse constitutes self-evaluation as a technique for improving the quality, performance and equality of education (OECD, 2013) in a very uncontextualised manner, ignoring the diverse educational and societal contexts of self-evaluation. This is why it would be desirable to scrutinise what actually takes place as the politics of self-evaluation is enacted in 'thousands of micro locales' and contexts and influencing innumerable individual teachers and schools conducting self-evaluation in these very specific locales.

Acknowledgement

This work was supported by the Academy of Finland under Grant 332155.

References

Ahonen, S. (2003). *Yhteinen koulu. Tasa-arvoa vai tasapäisyyttä? Koulutuksellinen tasa-arvo Suomessa Snellmanista tähän päivään.* [*Common school for all. Equality or levelling? Educational equality in Finland from Snellman today*]. Vastapaino.

Alarcón López, C., & Lawn, M. (Eds.). (2019). *Assessment cultures: Historical perspectives.* Peter Lang Verlag.

Anderson, A. (2015). The critical purchase of genealogy: Critiquing student participation projects. *Discourse: Studies in the Cultural Politics of Education, 36*(1), 42–52.

Bacchi, C., & Bonham, J. (2014). Reclaiming discursive practices as an analytic focus: Political implications. *Foucault Studies, 17*, 173–192.

Ball, S. J. (2003). The teacher's soul and the terrors of performativity. *Journal of Education Policy, 18*(2), 215–228.

Basic Education Act 628/1998 with amendments up to 1136/2010.

Christensen, G. (2016). Genealogy and educational research. *International Journal of Qualitative Studies in Education, 29*(6), 763–776.

CCSC. (1970). *Peruskoulun opetussuunnitelmakomitean mietintö I. Opetussuunnitelman perusteet.* Valtion Painatuskeskus.

Dahler-Larsen, P. (2011). *The evaluation society.* Stanford University Press.

Dean, M. (1999). *Governmentality. Power and rule in modern society.* Sage.

Decree of 12 October 1984, *Peruskouluasetus,* 718/1984 [Decree on Comprehensive Education].

Decree of 26 June 1970, *Peruskouluasetus,* 443/1970 [Decree establishing comprehensive education].

European Commission. (2020). *Supporting school self-evaluation and development through quality assurance policies: Key considerations for policy makers.* Report by ET2020 Working Group Schools May 2020. Education and training. European Commission.

European Commission/EACEA/Eurydice. (2015). *Assuring quality in education: Policies and approaches to school evaluation in Europe.* Eurydice Report. Publications Office of the European Union.

European Parliament and Council. (2001). *Recommendation of the European Parliament and of the council of 12 February 2001 on European cooperation in quality evaluation in school education* (2001/166/EC).

Evertsson, J. (2015). History, nation and school inspection: The introduction of citizenship education in elementary schools in late nineteenth-century Sweden. *History of Education, 44*(3), 259–273.

Fejes, A. (2011). Confession, in-service training and reflective practices. *British Educational Research Journal, 37*(5), 797–812.

Fejes, A., & Dahlstedt, M. (2012). *The confessing society: Foucault, confession and practices of lifelong learning*. Routledge.

Fendler, L. (2003). Teacher reflection in a hall of mirrors: Historical influences and political reverberations. *Educational Researcher, 32*(3), 16–25.

FNBE. (1994). *Peruskoulun opetussuunnitelman perusteet* [*Framework curriculum for the comprehensive school*]. National Board of Education.

FNBE. (1995). *Koulutuksen tuloksellisuuden arviointimalli* [*The framework for evaluating educational outcomes*]. National Board of Education.

FNBE. (1998). *Koulutuksen tuloksellisuuden arviointimalli* [*The framework for evaluating educational outcomes*]. National Board of Education.

FNBE. (2004). *Perusopetuksen opetussuunnitelman perusteet* [*National core curriculum for basic education*]. National Board of Education.

FNBE. (2014). *Perusopetuksen opetussuunnitelman perusteet* [*National core curriculum for basic education*]. National Board of Education.

Foucault, M. (1977). Nietzsche, genealogy, history. In D. F. Bouchard (Ed.), *Language, counter-memory, practice: Selected essays and interviews* (pp. 139–164). Cornell University Press.

Foucault, M. (1982). The subject and power. *Critical Inquiry, 8*(4), 777–795.

Foucault, M. (1988). Technologies of the self. In L. H. Martin, H. Gutman, & P. H. Hutton (Eds.), *Technologies of the self. A seminar with Michel Foucault* (pp. 16–49). The University of Massachusetts Press.

Foucault, M. (1991). *Discipline and punish: The birth of the prison*. Penguin Books. (Original work published 1975)

Foucault, M. (2000). Governmentality. In J. D. Faubion (Ed.), *Power. Essential works of Foucault 1954–1984* (pp. 201–222). The New Press.

Foucault, M. (2013) *Archaeology of knowledge* (A. M. Sheridan Smith, Trans.). Routledge. (Original work published 1969)

Fox, R. K., Dodman, S., & Holincheck, N. (2019). Moving beyond reflection in a hall of mirrors: Developing critical reflective capacity in teachers and teacher educators. *Reflective Practice, 20*(3), 367–382.

Granö-Suomalainen, V. (2002). Johdanto [Introduction]. In V. Granö-Suomalainen & M. Lovio (Eds.), *Mihin me pyrimme? Miksi arvioida kunnan koulutus- ja kirjastopalveluja?* (pp. 6–8). Association of Finnish Local and Regional Authorities.

Hämäläinen, K., & Lonkila, T. (1985). *Koulun sisäinen kehittäminen* [*Internal development of schools*]. Kunnallispaino.

Hämäläinen, K., Laukkanen, R., & Mikkola, A. (Eds.). (1993). *Koulun tuloksellisuuden arviointi* [*Evaluating the effectiveness of schools*]. Opetushallitus & Helsingin yliopiston Vantaan täydennyskoulutuslaitos.

Heinonen, V., & Viljanen, E. (1978). *Evaluaatio koulussa* [*Evaluation at school*]. Jyväskylän ylipisto.

Heinonen, V., & Viljanen, E. (1980). *Evaluaatio koulussa* [*Evaluation at school*]. Otava.

Holloway, J., & Brass, J. (2018). Making accountable teachers: The terrors and pleasures of performativity. *Journal of Education Policy, 33*(3), 361–382.

Holopainen, P., Laukkanen, R., Lepistö, V., & Pyykkönen, M.-L. (1982). *Kohti itseuudistuvaa koulua* [*Towards a self-reforming school*]. Kunnallispaino.

James, D. C., & Davies, B. (2009). The genesis of school inspection in South East Wales 1839–1843: Issues of social control and accountability. *History of Education, 38*(5), 667–680.

Kangasniemi, E. (1993). Arviointi koulun kehittämisen väline [Evaluation as a means of school improvement]. In K. Salmio (Ed.), *Tuloksellisuuden arviointi koulun kehittämisen välineenä* (pp. 119–126). National Board of Education.

Kauko, J., Rinne, R., & Takala, T. (Eds.). (2018). *Politics of quality in education: A comparative study of Brazil, China, and Russia*. Routledge.

Kilpinen, B., Salmio, K., Vainio, L., & Vanne, A. (Eds.). (1995). *Itsearvioinnin teoriaa ja käytäntöä* [*Theory and practice of self-evaluation*]. National Board of Education.

Kipnis, A. B. (2008). Audit cultures: Neoliberal governmentality, socialist legacy, or technologies of governing? *American Ethnologist, 35*(2), 275–289.

Knudsen, A. T. (2016). Profession, 'performance', and policy: Teachers, examinations, and the state in England and Wales, 1846–1862. *Paedagogica Historica, 52*(5), 507–524.

Korkeakoski, E., Niemi, K., Arra, O., Lindroos, K., & Säilä, E. (Eds.). (2000). *Kuntien ja koulujen itsearviointikäytäntöjä* [*Self-evaluation practices in schools and municipalities*]. National Board of Education.

Korkeakoski, E., & Tynjälä, P. (2010). Johdanto [Introduction]. In E. Korkeakoski & P. Tynjälä (Eds.), *Hyötyä ja vaikuttavuutta arvioinnista* (pp. 9–17). Finnish Education Evaluation Council.

Kosunen, S. (2016). *Families and the social space of school choice in urban Finland*. Studies in Educational Sciences 267. University of Helsinki, Institute of Behavioural Sciences.

Krejsler, J. B. (2011). What works in education and social welfare? A mapping of the evidence discourse and reflections upon consequences for professionals. *Scandinavian Journal of Educational Research, 57*(1), 16–32.

Laukkanen, R., Salmio, K., & Svedlin, R. (Eds.). (1992). *Koulun itsearviointi* [*School self-evaluation*]. Valtion painatuskeskus.

Lehtinen, J. (1995). *Itsearviointi evaluoinnin osana* [*Self-evaluation as part of evaluation*]. Kirjallisuuskatsaus. National Board of Education.

Lyytinen, H. K. (1993). *Itsearvioinnin kehitysnäkymiä* [*Development prospects in self-evaluation*]. In K. Salmio (Ed.), *Tuloksellisuuden arviointi koulun kehittämisen välineenä* (pp. 71–89). National Board of Education.

Lyytinen, H. K., Jokinen, H., & Rask, S. (1989). *Koulun työkäytäntöjen arviointi* [*Evaluating the work practices of schools*]. Prosessiarvioinnin näkökulma. National Board of General Education.

MinEdu. (2012). *Perusopetuksen laatukriteerit: Perusopetuksen, perusopetuksen aamu- ja iltapäivätoiminnan sekä koulun kerhotoiminnan laatukriteerit* [*Quality criteria for basic education: Quality criteria for basic education, morning and afternoon activities, and school's club activities*]. Ministry of Education and Culture.

MoE. (1982). *Opetussuunnitelmien laatimiseen ja hyväksymiseen liittyvät uudistukset. Opetusministeriön kirje Kouluhallitukselle, 23.6.1982, n:o 8271/27/82* [*Administrative letter from the Ministry of Education to the National Board of General Education on curricular development*]. Ministry of Education.

MoE. (1983). *Peruskoulun kehittäminen* [*Development of basic education*]. Opetusministeriön vastauskirje 24.3.1983, n:o 8271/27/82 Kouluhallituksen kirjeeseen 30.11.1982 [A rejoinder from the Ministry of Education to the National Board of General Education on developing basic education]. Ministry of Education.

NBGE. (1978). *Peruskoulun opetuksen kehittämisohjelma 1979–1984.* [*Development plan for teaching in comprehensive education 1979–1984*]. National Board of General Education.

NBGE. (1982). *Peruskoulun kehittämisohjelma 1980-luvulle. Kouluhallituksen ehdotus opetusministeriölle 30.11.1982* [*Development plan for comprehensive education in the 1980s. Proposal by the National Board of General Education to the Ministry of Education*]. National Board of General Education.

NBGE. (1985). *Peruskoulun opetussuunnitelman perusteet* [*Framework curriculum for comprehensive school*]. National Board of General Education.

NBGE. (1986a). *Peruskoulun ja lukion tuloksellisuus* [*Performance of comprehensive and upper secondary schools*]. Ehdotus tuloksellisuuden arviointijärjestelmäksi Kouluhallituksessa sekä peruskoulun tilannekartoitus vuodelta 1986. National Board of General Education.

NBGE. (1986b). *Koulutuksen tuloksellisuuden prosessiarviointi* [*Process evaluation of performance in education*]. Muistio Kouluhallitukselle 15.12.1986. National Board of General Education.

Nikkanen, P., & Lyytinen, H. K. (1996). *Oppiva koulu ja itsearviointi* [*The learning school and self-evaluation*]. Koulutuksen tutkimuslaitos.

OECD. (2013). *Synergies for better learning. An international perspective on evaluation and assessment*. OECD Reviews of Evaluation and Assessment in Education. OECD: Secretary-General of the OECD.

OECD. (2020). *Education policy outlook Finland 2020*. https://www.oecd.org/education/policy-outlook/country-profile-Finland-2020.pdf

Oppi ja laatu -hanke. (2003). *Opetustoimen laadun arviointiperusteet* [*The framework for evaluating quality in the education sector*]. Efektia oy.

Ozga, J., Dahler-Larsen, P., Segerholm C., & Simola, H. (Eds.). (2011). *Fabricating quality in education. Data and governance in Europe*. Routledge.

Perryman, J., Ball, S. J., Braun, A., & Maguire, M. (2017). Translating policy: Governmentality and the reflective teacher. *Journal of Education Policy, 32*(6), 745–756.

Pitkänen, H. (2019). *Arviointi, tieto ja hallinta. Peruskoulun paikallisen arvioinnin genealogia* [*Evaluation, knowledge and power: Genealogy of local quality evaluation in the field of comprehensive education*]. University of Helsinki.

Pitkänen, H. (2022). The politics of pupil self-evaluation: A case of Finnish assessment policy discourse. *Journal of Curriculum Studies*. doi:10.1080/00220272.2022.2040596

Popkewitz, T. S. (2000). Rethinking decentralization and state/civil society distinctions: The state as a problematic of governing. In S. J. Ball (Eds.), *Sociology of education* (pp. 1780–1812). Routledge.

Popkewitz, T. S. (2013). *Rethinking the history of education. Transnational perspectives on its questions, methods, and knowledge*. Palgrave Macmillan.

Räisänen, A., & Rönnholm, H. (2006). *Itsearviointi kouluyhteisöä kehittäväksi. EFQM-arviointimalli yleissivistävässä koulutuksessa* [*Self-evaluation in developing the school community: The EFQM evaluation model in general education*]. Finnish Education Evaluation Council.

Rose, N. (1999). *Powers of freedom. Reframing political thought*. Cambridge University Press.

Rose, N., & Miller, P. (2010). Political power beyond the state: Problematics of government. *The British Journal of Sociology, 61*(1), 271–303.

Sahlberg, P. (2007). Education policies for raising student learning: The Finnish approach. *Journal of Education Policy, 22*(2), 147–171.

Sahlberg, P. (2016). The global educational reform movement and its impact on schooling. In K. Mundy, A. Green, B. Lingard, & A. Verger (Eds.), *The handbook of global education policy* (pp. 128–144). Wiley-Blackwell.

Simola, H. (2015). *The Finnish education mystery: Historical and sociological essays on schooling in Finland*. Routledge.

Simola, H., Rinne, R., Varjo, J., Pitkänen, H., & Kauko, J. (2009). Quality Assurance and Evaluation (QAE) in Finnish compulsory schooling: A national model or just unintended effects of radical decentralisation? *Journal of Education Policy, 24*(2), 163–172.

Sitomaniemi-San, J. (2015). *Fabricating the teacher as researcher. A genealogy of academic teacher education in Finland.* University of Oulu.

SiVM 3/1998vp/26.5.1998. *Sivistysvaliokunnan mietintö. Hallituksen esitys koulutusta koskevaksi lainsäädännöksi* [*Government proposal for legislation in education*] Government of Finland.

Smith, W. C. (Ed.). (2016). *The global testing culture shaping education policy, perceptions, and practices.* Symposium Books Ltd.

Takayama, K., Waldow, F., & Sung, Y.-K. (2013). Finland has it all? Examining the media accentuation of 'Finnish education' in Australia, Germany and South Korea. *Research in Comparative and International Education, 8*(3), 307–325.

Tamboukou, M. (1999). Writing genealogies: An exploration of Foucault's strategies for doing research. *Discourse: Studies in the Cultural Politics of Education, 20*(2), 201–217.

Varjo, J., Simola, H. & Rinne, R. (2016). *Arvioida ja hallita: Perään katsomisesta informaatio-ohjaukseen suomalaisessa koulupolitiikassa* [*To evaluate and govern – From 'looking after' to management by data in Finnish education politics*]. Suomen Kasvatustieteellinen Seura.

Verger, A., Parcerisa, L., & Fontdevila, C. (2018). The growth and spread of large-scale assessments and test-based accountabilities: A political sociology of global education reforms. *Educational Review, 71*(1), 5–30.

Waldow, F. (2017). Projecting images of the 'good' and the 'bad school': Top scorers in educational large-scale assessments as reference societies. *Compare: A Journal of Comparative and International Education, 47*(5), 647–664.

Wallenius, T. (2020). *Schools, performance and publicity: Contrasting the policy on publicising school performance indicators in Finland with the other Nordic countries.* University of Helsinki.

CHAPTER 5

Re-thinking the Concept of Classroom Management

Implications for Quality in Future Classroom Management Practices

Helle Plauborg

Abstract

Setting out to challenge widespread distinctions between instruction and management and between the academic and the social, this chapter discusses quality in classroom management practices. I present a case study produced in the City Class – a Danish Year 6 class with a reputation among teachers, pupils and the school management team for being very difficult to teach. I draw on agential realism, a theoretical approach that seeks to understand the world as deeply entangled and offers a foundation for grasping the interplay between instruction and management and between the academic and the social. This allows me to show how the distinction between management and instruction obstructs new insights into classroom management practices, including how classroom management can unite the academic and the social. Based on the case study, the concept of classroom management is re-thought by integrating instruction. The implications of this re-thinking for quality in future classroom management practices are discussed.

Keywords

classroom management – instruction – management – the academic – the social – case study – quality

1 Introduction

In this chapter, I discuss the quality of teachers' classroom management practices by challenging two widespread and often taken for granted distinctions – namely, a distinction between the academic and the social, and a distinction between instruction and management. The distinction between the academic and the social is often expressed by school professionals in statements such as 'Pupils need to feel at ease before they can learn anything' or 'We must not only focus on the academic side of things. The pupils also need a positive social environment'. Such statements indicate a separation of the academic and the social: in the first case, well-being is a prerequisite for academic attainment; in the second case, it is suggested that prioritising academic work hinders the development of well-functioning classroom cultures. However, it is not only school professionals that operationalise this distinction. The same distinction between and separation of the two is echoed in public discourse and in many political texts. There are likewise numerous examples of such a distinction within the research literature, influencing the focus and findings of the studies in question. Meanwhile, there is also a substantial body of research identifying links between academic attainment and sociality: several studies suggest that schools with a high academic level also have a greater prevalence of prosocial behaviour (e.g. Caprara et al., 2000; Luiselli et al., 2005). Other studies indicate that so-called effective learning environments have direct and positive effects on pupils' academic performance and prosocial behaviour (McEvoy & Welker, 2000, p. 136).

The chapter builds on a case study conducted in a Danish school class (the City Class), the purpose of which was to qualify understandings of the interplay between the academic and the social (Plauborg, 2015). I will focus on two excerpts from field notes produced in two lessons during the same school day – a math lesson and Danish lesson.

The birth of research on classroom management is often dated back to the 1950s (Brophy, 2006). Over the course of the following 70 years, an increasingly broader and more complex understanding of the concept has developed. Evertson and Weinstein (2006, p. 4) argue that classroom management should be understood:

> [...] as the actions teachers take to create an environment that supports and facilitates both academic and social-emotional learning. In other words, classroom management has two distinct purposes: It not only seeks to establish and sustain an orderly environment so students can engage in meaningful academic learning, it also aims to enhance students' social and moral growth.

As such, classroom management is understood as creating an environment for teaching. However, this understanding also isolates classroom management from other aspects of teaching. This division between classroom management and teaching is reinforced by a strong tendency to distinguish between management and instruction within the, primarily American, literature on the subject.[1] The point is that this distinction between management and instruction has the effect that classroom management becomes associated with management, while instruction is seen as related to, but either not included in or conferred only a peripheral role in, the understanding of classroom management. For example, Brophy (2006, p. 17) writes:

> [...] classroom management refers to actions taken to create and maintain a learning environment conducive to successful instruction (arranging the physical environment, establishing rules and procedures, maintaining students' attention to lessons and engagement in activities).

The aim of classroom management practices is thus to support instruction, whereby Brophy also points out that management and instruction influence each other. This is a point he shares with other leading scholars within the field, e.g. Jones (1996) who points out that instruction can help minimise inappropriate behaviour and classroom management be exercised more effectively when adapted to instruction and Doyle (1985) who argues that management and instruction must be exercised in ways that support each other. Nevertheless, the distinction is maintained.

The point I want to make is that this distinction reduces classroom management practices to a question of teachers' efforts to create a foundation for teaching. The literature in the field has a reputation for focusing on discipline and behavioural control in order to establish such a foundation[2] (see e.g. Evertson & Weinstein, 2006). Classroom management becomes a matter of organising a foundation for teaching, often referred to as the learning environment, but the reflections and actions involved in the preparation, implementation and evaluation of teaching, including questions regarding the what, how and why of teaching, are for the most part not considered part of classroom management. Thus, the ways in which the academic is performed are also not part of classroom management. Put differently, the concept of classroom management is de-academicised and the Didactic is filtered out.[3]

In this chapter, I will challenge these two distinctions through analysis of a case study I conducted in the City Class – a Danish Year 6 class with a reputation among teachers, pupils and the school management team for being very difficult to teach. I draw on agential realism, a theoretical approach that seeks to understand the world as deeply entangled and offers a foundation for grasping the interplay between instruction and management and between the academic and the social. This approach allows me to show how the distinction between management and instruction obstructs new insights into classroom management practices, including how classroom management can unite the academic and the social. Based on the case study, I develop an alternative to dominant conceptions of classroom management by integrating instruction. The implications of this re-thinking for quality in classroom management practices are discussed in light of the case study.

2 Agential Realism

The chapter's theoretical foundation is agential realism, as developed by the American physicist and feminist Karen Barad (2007). I will not detail my understanding of agential realism here as I have done so elsewhere (e.g. Juelskjær et al., 2020; Plauborg, 2018). However, I will explain two agential realist concepts that I draw on in the analysis: entanglement and intra-action.

In relation to entanglement, Barad explains: 'To be entangled is not simply to be intertwined with another, as in the joining of separate entities, but to lack an independent, self-contained existence. Existence is not an individual affair' (Barad, 2007, p. IX). Entanglement thus emphasises the relational ontology agential realism is based on and breaks with any kind of thinking in terms of separate entities, individuation, fixity and giveness (Juelskjær et al., 2020). Instead, the research interest centres on examining the world (in this case classroom management practices) in all its connectivity. This break also involves our everyday understanding of time and space as passive context – an understanding that is troubled in agential realism as entanglement is to be understood as quantum entanglement, implying that many scales (of which I will focus on time and space) are mutually folded into each other (Barad, 2010; Juelskjær et al., 2020). In relation to the analysis of the case from the City Class, this means, among other things, that attention is paid to how different agencies (of which I will give examples in the following section) are related and intra-act across time and space, which, as mentioned, are seen as ungiven.

The concepts of entanglement and intra-action are closely related as entanglement is the premise for the development and definition of all agential realist concepts (Juelskjær et al., 2020). The concept of intra-action can therefore also help to unfold the implications of quantum entanglement. Intra-action offers an alternative to the concept of interaction. While interaction, according to Barad, presupposes the existence of individualised and distinct entities prior to a given interaction, at the core of the concept of intra-action is the idea that such entities do not exist a priori but come into being iteratively and in and through intra-action. As such, entities only ever exist as already relating to other entities (Barad, 2007; Juelskjær et al., 2020; Plauborg, 2018). Further, Barad argues that the concept of interaction relies on a classical understanding of time and space, whereas a dynamic understanding of time, space, agency, cause and effect underpins agential realism, as will be apparent in the analysis below. I regard the interplay between the academic and the social and between instruction and management as examples of intra-action. As such, no pure form of the academic and the social or of instruction and management exists prior to intra-action; rather, they come into being because of intra-action. Moreover, in the intra-active movements, the academic and the social have an active and mutually transformative effect on 'each other',[4] and the same goes for instruction and management. This also means that intra-actions enact. Something is created and changed as a result of intra-action, and the intra-activity is always ongoing. In this chapter, the deconstruction of these distinctions consists in seeking insights into how they intra-act and discussing the implications in relation to quality in classroom management practices.

3   The City Class

Multiple agencies contributed to the establishment of the complex teaching situations through which intra-actions between the academic and the social and between management and instruction were enacted in the City Class. The following is not an exhaustive list but examples of some of the agencies that seemed to influence these intra-actions.

The City Class's reputation for being difficult to teach was reflected in numerous ways: the year before, some of the boys' criminal extracurricular activities had led to collaboration between the local community street team, their teachers and school, the social services and the police in order to get the boys 'on the right track'. Monthly meetings were arranged between the boys' teachers and parents. The City Class also faced a number of other challenges, including a lack of parental resources and the school's location in an area characterised by widespread social problems. This reputation for being difficult to teach had not escaped the attention of the pupils. As Mustafa whispered to me: 'We are one of those classes that makes a lot of noise and where things have gone a bit wrong'. However, it was also a class where many pupils were inquisitive and interested in learning and getting good grades, and where 12 of the total 24 pupils were described by their teachers as 'nice girls', while 8 boys were described as 'disruptive and impudent' (Fahid, Anders, Hakan, Mads and Adika were particularly highlighted). The remaining 4 pupils (both boys and girls) were rarely mentioned in the teachers' narratives about the class.

In the interviews I conducted with pupils from the class, they highlighted a special unity in the class, with pupils making a virtue out of helping each other when something was academically challenging or when a classmate had forgotten school supplies. However, it also emerged from the interviews that they perceived the class as very divided and that there was a pronounced fear of being excluded from the class community. This fear was also part of the teachers' narratives about the class. Through the interviews, it emerged that there was another characteristic of this unity; namely a kind of code familiar from the Mafia and other criminal organisations. This was based partly on a principle of standing by one's responsibility and not telling teachers when criminal activities took place, partly based on a fear of reprisals and beatings.[5]

The City Class was taught by a total of 6 teachers. Within this group, there was disagreement regarding 'what worked' in terms of tackling the issues in the class. This disagreement concerned whether the problems were best solved through authoritarian management strategies such as threats and sarcasm or whether they could be tackled using appropriate instructional strategies. Structure and involvement were proposed strategies in relation to the latter. It was also characteristic of the City Class that many lessons were marked by disruption, noise and admonishment.

The study at the heart of the original exploration of the interplay of the academic and the social was based on three case studies, of which the City Class was one. Each of these case studies consisted of: four periods of teaching observation spread over a school year; informal conversations with pupils, teachers and the school management team; interviews with 6–10 pupils from each class a total of three times during the school year; excerpts from teaching materials; interviews with teachers; and minutes from meetings in a working group affiliated with the project. The empirical material upon which the study was based thus comprised a total of 63 interviews with pupils, 4 interviews with teachers, approximately 100 pages of observation notes and minutes from 3 meetings in the working group (Plauborg, 2015, 2016).

3.1 *A Maths Lesson*

The first excerpt is from a maths class where the pupils have just received the results of a test in arithmetic.

> 'Be quiet now'. Jan is trying to make himself heard – again. 'We are about to embark on a completely new subject'. 'Oh, no', the pupils exclaim unanimously. 'Stop commenting on everything. Sit down Mads. Can any of you explain what scales are? What do you know about scales?' No response. Jan presents a few examples by way of a map of the world that he displays on the smartboard while explaining, 'Before the colon is the drawing, after is reality'. He then draws two squares and asks, 'What can you say about these two?' The pupils are still mumbling about their marks in the arithmetic test. Jan explains that the figures are congruent.

Then he draws another two squares, one twice the size of the other. He writes similar figures above the drawing and explains, 'They are the same shape but one is bigger than the other. This is what we'll be working on. Similar figures. In similar figures, the angles don't change. Only the sides do'. He hands out a piece of paper. 'What you have to do here is simply to draw similar figures'. The pupils are still more concerned with questions such as, 'How many did you get wrong?', 'Are you happy with your mark?', 'Did he correct this in yours? He didn't in mine'. Jan says, 'Right, now you will work with the paper I have given you. You work independently. You work on your own, and you stay seated. If you have questions about the test, I'll come and help you'. The pupils appear to find the assignment difficult. Two pupils try to work on it together and repeat Jan's words to each other, 'The drawing should be on the left side of the colon and reality on the right side', after which one of them adds, 'But if the drawing is to be enlarged, there isn't enough space on this paper'. Noise levels are high. Jan is angry and raises his voice, 'Now listen up 6V. I will not listen to your continued shouting'. Aamira walks over to Emilie's desk to borrow a rubber and to offer Emilie help. Emilie is having problems solving the assignment and she is one of the pupils shouting. Aamira is told to sit back down, which she does, except she immediately gets up again and walks back over to Emilie. Fahid picks up additional assignments and tells me while doing so that he finds maths easy. Several pupils help each other out. Aamira has now walked up to the smartboard, on which she writes, 'Hello 6V. I think our class is really nice'. Jan asks her to stop, but as soon as he turns his back, she continues. Adika is trying to get Hakan's attention. Blerim walks over to Adika to borrow a ruler. Jan gets angry, asks Blerim to sit down and says, 'I will have no more of this roaming around. Things just get out of control'. Aamira is now standing by the window at the back of the classroom. 'It's snowing', she says aloud. There is a clattering of chairs as most of the pupils stand up to look out the window. It is not snowing. Jan shakes his head despairingly. Aamira turns to Hakan, 'Hakan, how do you say 'hi' in your language?' Then she turns to Sufia, 'Sufia, how do you say 'how are you' in your language?' And then she turns to Mariam, 'You're wearing your small shoes today'. Jan finishes up the lesson with a look of exasperation on his face, 'Sit down, would you. Don't keep interrupting me, Hakan. Both assignments are homework, and now you can get your lunch boxes out'.

In the maths lesson, the pupils are primarily preoccupied with the results of the arithmetic test, as is apparent from their conversations. Jan, on the other hand, is busy introducing a new topic: similar figures. Despite the pupils' preoccupation with the test results, they also focused on this new topic, although not in the way Jan had wanted them to (i.e. working independently at their desks). Instead, they moved around the classroom, borrowing or lending rubbers and rulers or offering academic assistance. Nevertheless, they tried to solve the assigned task, but this proved impossible with the available materials due to insufficient space on the paper they have been given to enlarge the original figure. The Swedish researcher in classroom management Kjell Granström (2006) points out that, for pupils, the classroom is not only a space for academic activities but also an arena for building friendships and belongingness. As such, there may be other reasons for the pupils' constant 'roaming around' than giving and receiving academic assistance or borrowing and lending various school supplies; it may also be an expression of the pupils' attempts and need to establish and maintain contact with their classmates. The academic and the social were mutually folded into each other by the pupils' attempts to be in contact with each other through the provision of and requests for academic assistance and the borrowing and lending of school supplies. Jan, on the other hand, tried to separate the academic from the social by asking pupils to work independently – a request the pupils, however, largely failed to answer.

In his introduction to the assignment, Jan asks the pupils a number of questions about scale and congruent figures. However, they did not answer, either because they could not or due to their preoccupation with the test results. Jan therefore briefly answered his own questions, after which he handed out a sheet with the assignment. Once again, the academic and the social seemed to be entangled in that Jan seemingly did not register or chose not to take note of the pupils' need to review Jan's corrections and marks in the arithmetic test, which prevented a shared academic focus on the new topic of similar figures. While working on the assignment, there was a distinct and conspicuous sense of restlessness in the class. This seemed to be related to confusion over the unsolvable task, which fostered the pupils' practices of offering and seeking each other's help – practices which Jan registered as the pupils 'roaming around' and which led to his increasing irritation and anger. The academic and the social were not distinct entities, but were co-created in and of – not prior to – each other; hence, they intra-acted.

In my interview with Jan, he mentioned Aamira as a pupil who did not focus on the academic content of the lesson (which, from Jan's perspective, was similar figures). The question is how Aamira saw the situation. Immediately after Jan's angry outburst regarding the noise level in the classroom, Aamira walks over to Emilie, offering academic assistance. Emilie is one of the pupils who had been crying out for help. Aamira is told to sit down, but she gets up again, writing on the board that she thinks 6V is a nice class, proclaiming that it is snowing outside, turning to Hakan to ask how to say hello in his language, asking Sufia how to say 'How are you?' in her language and telling Mariam that she is wearing her small shoes today. Aamira is admittedly not focused on similar figures, but seems to be preoccupied with something else. Granström (2006, p. 1145) points out:

> Students' socially shared processes also have an important function as a relief from anxiety, tension, and anger. Students may sometimes perceive the social or academic situation, with its ambiguous demands as frightening. In such a situation their need for relief and to give vent to their feelings is hard to control. Teachers thus face a number of challenges as a consequence of group processes in the classroom. Without knowledge of such processes, the teacher may easily regard a number of 'misbehaving' students as provocative, rather than viewing their behavior as being an indication of a basic need for security.

Aamira's 'roaming around' can thus be understood as an indication that she is busy trying to recontextualise the classroom. She uses the smartboard and her positive statement to alleviate the effect of Jan's irritation and anger and invents snow in an attempt to promote joy and thus relieve the strained atmosphere in the classroom. Such an interpretation aligns with Aamira's stories of her fear of being scolded during the interviews; a fear she shared with many of her classmates. The academic and the social were thus jointly created and transformed through complex dynamics – Aamira's fear of being scolded and her need to change the atmosphere in the classroom led to her various interactions with classmates, which Jan considered disruptive. However, she was also concerned with providing academic assistance to Emilie, who had been having difficulty with the task. Based on the interviews, this fear appeared to be a key part of the explanation for why school life in the City Class was sometimes hard. One interesting point that the case from the City Class can shed light on is that it was not only the boys categorised as trouble-makers who were affected by the teachers' scolding and anger. In fact, in the interviews, teachers' anger seemed to be more of a concern among the pupils who were seldom on the receiving end. In other words, the teachers' ways of relating to certain individual pupils had a contagious effect on all pupils. This is a point that is confirmed in other studies.

> Hughes, Cavell, and Willson (2001) reported that classmates' perceptions of the quality of the relationship between their teacher and a selected

child in the classroom were related to their own perceptions of the quality of their relationship with the teacher. [...] Relatedly, White and Kistner (1992) examined relations between teacher feedback and children's peer preferences in early elementary students, finding that teachers' negatively-toned feedback toward selected children was related negatively to classmates' preferences for these children. (Pianta, 2006, p. 695)

Pupils thus take stock of a teacher's relationships with the other pupils in the class, and pupils' perceptions of the quality of these relationships are related to their experience of the quality of their own relationship with the teacher. Furthermore, relations between teachers and pupils influence how pupils relate to each other. In the City Class, relational practices between teachers and pupils and the ways in which the academic work was organised co-constituted how the pupils related to one another. The case from the City Class thus sheds light on these practices as dynamic and intra-acting – also with the Didactic.

3.2   *A Danish Lesson*
The second excerpt is from a Danish lesson later that day.

> 'Right, we're ready. Or rather, I'm ready; are you ready? Fahid, you keep interrupting with all sorts of things that have nothing do to with this. Can I start now?' Fahid nods. 'Yesterday was a little confusing because half of you were here and the other half weren't [because they participated in a volleyball competition, HP]. Yesterday, the class discussed that it would be nice if you were better at working outside your normal group constellations. I have tried to make a plan that will accommodate this. And so, in a minute, I'll tell you what you'll be doing and whom you'll be doing it with, but first I'll explain what it is you have to do. Those of you who were here yesterday, we'll call you number ones. The number ones will teach the number twos. And what will you be teaching the number twos?' The pupils summarise yesterday's lesson. Marie asks clarifying questions such as: 'What did you do yesterday? What must you remember to tell the number twos? You were also given information before you started'. She continues, 'In assignment three, you have to use quotation marks. What do you need to explain for them to understand the assignment? What did I tell you yesterday? In assignment four, you have to rewrite the sentences, placing the quoted passage at the beginning. And that is why you have to tell your partner about quotations. Once you have helped your partner get started, you continue from where you left off yesterday. It's important that you make yourself attractive as a partner in the work

you are about to carry out. What do you consider an attractive partner? Attractive means popular, someone you'd like to work with again. What is it you do when you're at your best?' The pupils offer suggestions that Marie writes on the smartboard: 'Do not complain about the partner you have been assigned', 'must be helpful, calm and friendly', 'do not provide answers, but explanations', 'concentrate on the assignment'. 'I think you have mentioned some really good elements here. Now I'll let you know who'll be working with whom and where you'll be sitting. You all know what to do now?' The pupils start working. Hakan is helping Sarah. He gives her examples and explains how to use quotation marks. Maysaa is helping Anders. Marie walks around to each pair asking questions: 'What did you explain about direct speech?' 'What were you told about quotations?' Golriz is helping Aamira. Mads is helping Adika. Ciprian is helping Dejan. All pupils are concentrated on their tasks. Fahid is helping Ejona. They identify subjects, verbs, commas, colons, full stops, capital letters and quotation marks within the sentences. The number ones appear to be taking their teaching responsibility seriously. Marie is walking around, giving the pupils encouraging remarks: 'Two minutes left. Give it all you've got while I write your homework on the board'. As the lesson is summed up, Marie returns to the notion of the attractive partner and asks the pupils to evaluate their partners from the criteria they had set out. On his way out of the door, Adika turns to me: 'Mads was an attractive partner today. Did you notice that I was too?'

In the Danish lesson, there was a common focus on what the pupils were supposed to learn and the pupils seemed to relate positively to each other through the work with the academic content and activities. The academic and the social were mutually and positively co-created through complexly entangled elements: Marie introduced the assignment thoroughly, involving the pupils who participated as number ones and asking them to give examples so that those who were number twos could engage in the lesson. She made sure that all pupils knew what they were expected to do and asked what information the number twos had received. At the same time, Marie was responsive to the pupils' desire to collaborate across usual group constellations and had taken this into account in her preparation of the lesson. Marie thus also related positively to the pupils through the ways in which she instructed the academic work that the pupils were to embark on, taking their wishes into consideration and showing through her instruction that she had prepared their work process thoroughly. Other studies also address these relationships between instruction and teacher-pupil relationships as relational phenomena (e.g., Brophy, 2004;

Howes & Ritchie, 2002; Pressley et al., 2003). These relationships are usually examined in ways that focus on how instruction and relationships mutually influence each other. However, I will try to highlight the complex, permeable, unbounded and infiltrated nature of these dynamics. For the same reason, my interest is not centred on mutual influence but on mutual transformation, which is why the instruction and execution of academic work in the City Class cannot be separated as non-relational. Marie related to the pupils through the ways in which she instructed the academic work, and these ways of instructing and conducting the academic work and relating to the pupils intra-acted; they were mutually shaped and transformed.

Marie also trained the pupils in the practice of well-functioning collaboration and took responsibility for deciding who should collaborate with whom. This is consistent with other studies. Granström (2006) points out, for example, that it is naive to believe that pupils can cooperate as a matter of course; there is a need for an explanation of what such collaboration entails. The case from the City Class shows that explanation is not enough – collaboration must also be based on academic content that the pupils find meaningful. By providing such meaning, Marie tried to govern the pupils' ways of relating to each other.

Furthermore, Marie gave the pupils opportunities to make a fresh start, as she called it. This seemed to have a great impact on the group of boys who were often referred to as the main trouble-makers in the City Class. This was the case, for example, with Adika, who, with great satisfaction, asked me if I had noticed that he had been an attractive partner – reading between the lines, he thereby revealed that it was important for him to be an attractive partner. This impact was also clear from Fahid's commitment to explaining punctuation and quotation marks to Ejona. Marie thus succeeded in repositioning the pupils as interesting to each other through the ways in which she presented the academic work. These repositionings contributed to the academic and the social not becoming competing endeavours (as was the case in the mathematics class), but instead constituting mutual preconditions. With the remark 'Two minutes left. Give it all you've got while I write your homework on the board', Marie emphasised that the academic was an important and attractive matter, and that the time should therefore be used to the full – an emphasis that can be contrasted with the unsolvable task of enlarging similar figures in the maths lesson.

3.3   *Entangled Co-constitutions of Instruction and Management*
From the empirical examples, it is not easy to determine what can be traced back to instruction and what can be traced back to management as they were always already entangled co-constitutions. In the mathematics class,

no foundation had been established for focusing on similar figures due to the pupils' preoccupation with their test results. In addition, the atmosphere in the classroom was marked by Jan's irritation and, as the lesson went on, anger. Towards the end of the lesson, this seemed to have morphed into a sense of resignation, with Jan remarking that both tasks were homework and that the pupils should get out their packed lunches. This framing of the lesson, where the teacher and pupils were focused on different things and the atmosphere was marked by irritation, resulted in somewhat brief explanations of the concepts of scale, congruence and similar figures, after which the pupils were asked to work on what turned out to be an unsolvable task. As such, instruction and management affected and transformed each other negatively.

In the Danish class, Marie exercised management through instruction by making it clear to the pupils how they could do well in the specific teaching situation. She did this, among other things, by thoroughly explaining the assignment and through her questions (e.g., what did you do yesterday? What must you remember to tell the number twos?) – questions that both summed up the previous day's lesson, signalled that the academic content and execution of the task were taken seriously and marked an expectation that the number ones would take a similar approach when instructing the number twos. This was supplemented by specifying what it means to collaborate and a subsequent evaluation of this collaboration. It was also supported by the fact that Marie directed the repositioning of pupils through considerations of who should collaborate with whom, and where. Thus, instruction and management were not separate processes, but intra-actively entangled and co-constitutive. Therefore, it makes no sense to try to isolate management from instruction – or vice versa. In the Danish lesson, this inseparability was practised in ways that seemed to be coherent, which is probably part of the explanation as to why it seemed easy for the pupils to navigate this teaching situation.

These intra-actively entangled co-constitutions of instruction and management did not only depend on the specific situation and context in which the teaching unfolded. Asked what they considered good teaching, the pupils highlighted the way Marie explained tasks, which meant 'understanding them the first time they were explained'. Thus, pupils also brought experiences from the times and spaces of previous lessons into the lesson where quotation marks were on the agenda, and these experiences were (quantumly) entangled in the jumble of agencies that intra-acted in the lesson. Similarly, multiple times and spaces figured in the maths lesson, where (Jan's) focus was on similar figures. Teacher/pupil relations thus seemed to be related and come into being across time and space, involving other situations, contexts, times, spaces and life stories. Applying an agential realist approach, Marie and Jan can therefore not be regarded as isolated, delimited and self-dependent individuals. On the contrary, they were enacted subjects, which is why the (respectively positive and negative) outcomes of the Danish lesson and the maths lesson do not unambiguously reflect on Marie and Jan, respectively, but a complex apparatus. This apparatus includes, for instance, the pupils' experiences from previous Danish and mathematics lessons, the difficult conditions for teaching in the City Class, including the lack of parental participation in school activities, and the fact that the positive assessments of Marie's explanations were made in comparison to the class's other teachers, including Jan. Future spaces also figured in the two lessons. For example, during interviews, many of the pupils said that they attached great importance to getting an education, which may be one of the reasons why their focus on the topic of similar figures seemed to be limited: the pupils were more concerned with their results from the arithmetic test – results they regarded as important for their further education.

3.4 Classroom Management Re-thought

Why are these distinctions so problematic? One of many effects of the distinctions between management and instruction and between the academic and the social is that they encourage a belief that for example management and instruction are separate matters and can be practised as such. In this way, teachers can practise management and instructional strategies that are incompatible, even detrimental to one another, despite their entangled co-constitution. McCaslin and Good point out that in many classrooms in the United States, there is a mismatch between the ways in which teaching is executed (instruction) and the ways of trying to control pupils' behaviour (management):

> Educators have created an oxymoron: a curriculum that urges problem solving and critical thinking and a management system that requires compliance and narrow obedience. The management system at least dilutes, if not obstructs, the potential power of the curriculum for many of our students. Students are asked to think and understand, but in too many classrooms they are asked to think noiselessly, without peer communication or social exchange. (McCaslin & Good, 1998, p. 173)

McCaslin and Good thus address a problem with the distinction between management and instruction, which can easily result in a mismatch between instructional practices based on theories of learning, where pupils exchange knowledge and experiences with each other, and management practices that are aimed at ensuring pupils' compliance and obedience (McCaslin & Good, 1992; Evertson & Poole, 2008). With the distinction between instruction and management that is maintained in the vast majority of the classroom management literature, the risk of this mismatch increases – often with the consequence that it is left to the pupils to find a coherence that is not immediately apparent from the performance of the teaching situation.

This distinction between management and instruction also has consequences for knowledge production in the field of classroom management. Emmer and Sabornie write that 'Both constructs [i.e. behaviour and instruction, HP] are related, and they interact in classrooms at all levels, but understanding the exact characteristics of the bond between the two factors awaits future research' (2015, p. 7). Management and instruction are usually examined either as separate entities or as aspects of teaching that interact, leaving the impression that there are clear boundaries between the two. However, the analysis of the case from the City Class testifies to the fact that teaching situations materialise in other ways – as comprehensive apparatuses characterised by multiple intra-acting agencies, of which the academic and the social, instruction and management are central elements. Emmer and Sabornie (2015) also reveal another effect of the distinction, pointing out that we have become no wiser regarding the bond between management and instruction despite the fact that the literature on classroom management recognises that management and instruction must support each other and can make each other more efficient. In this literature, management and instruction are seen as entities that are related to each other, with interest centred on their mutual influence; meanwhile, in agential realist thinking they are inseparable. It therefore becomes possible to spot the complex and infiltrated nature of the dynamics embedded in teaching situations. This is important because, with the interest in mutual influence and the understanding of the concepts as separate entities, a tendency to approach management and instruction in different ways is easily reinforced. The point I want to make is thus that if they are interpreted as separate and distinct, it becomes all too easy to practise them as such; however, even when practised as separate, they are connected through their separation, whereby it can become contradictory and difficult for pupils to orient themselves in teaching practice.

With the distinctions between the academic and the social, instruction and management, there is a separation of a whole that, as becomes apparent when viewed through the lens of agential realism, is inextricably linked; a whole that simply does not exist as isolated or discrete entities is nonetheless studied as discrete entities. The distinction is therefore not just a harmless separation of two aspects of teaching, which is not consistent with an agential realist understanding of reality. It becomes an obstacle preventing us from seeing the entanglements, and therefore also an obstacle preventing us from learning more about how classroom management is constituted, including the prerequisites for successful classroom management and how classroom management can be practised in such a way that the academic and the social come into being positively through intra-action. Thus, the arguments for why it is necessary to re-think the concept of classroom management are: (1) that the dominants understanding of classroom management splits into discrete entities something that is indivisible, whereby (2) it becomes difficult to gain insights into how classroom management is constituted and to produce knowledge about how successful classroom management is operationalised and (3) there is a greater risk that practice will be characterised by different kinds of thinking about instruction and management, the academic and the social; however, (4) whether these aspects of teaching are practised based on different ways of thinking or not, they are intra-actively entangled, which is why it is important to think and practise them as such.

Re-thinking the concept of classroom management entails integrating instruction, and thus the Didactic questions of the what, how, why and where of teaching, as well as its preparation, implementation and evaluation. Because, as the analysis of the case from the City Class testifies, Didactics is deeply entangled with management and crucial to the successful operationalisation of classroom management.

This re-thinking also involves incorporating the social into the concept of classroom management, which, it can be argued, it has been all along (or at least since the 1950s). However, when focusing on the social in existing classroom management literature, there has been (and still is) a widespread tendency to focus on behavioural problems. Inspired by Long (2015),[6] the understanding of the social I propose goes beyond relational practices between teachers and pupils and certainly does not reduce these practices to an interest in behavioural problems alone. It also involves relationships between pupils, temporality and spatiality. An example of temporality is that teachers and pupils had prior assumptions about each other (Aamira as a pupil with a short attention span, the boys who were categorised as trouble-makers, teachers with a reputation among pupils for being angry or for being good at explaining tasks). Spatiality, meanwhile, refers to how the social materialised in the class*room*, exemplified by Aamira's inquiries to her classmates, whereby she simultaneously breaks the hierarchy of the classroom in an attempt to set a different agenda. Furthermore, the social was also influenced by agencies outside the specific classroom as seen, for instance, in Marie's frequent attempts to repair a bad atmosphere in the City Class carried over from previous lessons.

The academic and the social, instruction and management are completely entangled elements of classroom management in the re-thinking of the concept that I advocate. Therefore, classroom management cannot be separated from teaching. Classroom management is not just the foundation for teaching, and classroom management is not just about organising a learning environment that establishes order and makes it possible to provide learning opportunities for pupils. The distinction between, on the one hand, creating a foundation for teaching and, on the other hand, teaching itself is broken, and thus also the distinction between management and instruction. Classroom management is intra-activity of the academic and the social, instruction and management. Another aspect of the re-thinking of the concept of classroom management emphasises the complexity embedded in, and therefore constituting a basic condition of, classroom management practices. It is a comprehensive apparatus, characterised by multiple intra-acting agencies that create specific teaching situations. As such, there is no recipe and no quick fix. For the same reason, this analysis has sought to offer insights into a complex intra-acting reality with many different outcomes and effects.

3.5 *Quality in Future Classroom Management Practices*

The presented re-thinking of the concept of classroom management has several implications when assessing the quality of classroom management practices: quality becomes associated with understanding the academic and the social, as well as instruction and management, as coming into being through each other, thus emphasising their coherence. This is not an easy task in that the tendency to divide teaching situations into separate aspects such as the academic and the social, instruction and management is widespread. Moreover, quality is also associated with an ongoing questioning of one's own classroom management practices, paying particular attention to the mismatches that may emerge due to these distinctions. To help teachers with this task, there is a need for further research on classroom management practices where the starting point is not fixed in a distinction between management and instruction but rather in a co-thinking hereof.

Studies on teacher quality often focus on the teacher as the most important factor influencing the quality of education in schools (e.g. Darling-Hammond, 1999; Hattie, 2009). The research in the field points back to an individual (the teacher) and the quality of his/her practice (cause) as correlating with pupils' learning outcomes (effect). However, as the case from the City Class showed, the teacher is not a self-contained individual but an enacted subject. In parts of the research literature, there is also a tendency to isolate individual elements of teaching practice and explore them as delimited entities through effect studies with the ambition of identifying universal quality indicators in teacher practices (e.g. Hattie, 2009).

With the analyses in this chapter, I have sought to illustrate how teaching is characterised by inseparable dynamics in which quality indicators do not unfold in versions that make it possible to bracket everything else and designate their unambiguous effects. Therefore, it is also not possible to pinpoint cause and effect in the jumble of agencies in the City Class; cause and effect were constantly and specifically co-constituted. The quality of classroom management practices is part of related, dynamic entanglements and must intra-act positively with a range of agencies in the teaching apparatus if they are to have positive effects.

Notes

1. There are also researchers in the field who distinguish between behavioural management and instructional management and understand them as 'two sets of beliefs [that] frame the nature of teachers' actions and underlie two components of classroom management' (Martin et al., 2016, p. 46; Emmer & Sabornie, 2006). In this understanding, instruction is thus included in the concept of classroom management and an inverse relationship between the two is argued, but the distinction is maintained.
2. This reputation is probably related to the most common understanding of management: 'Look in any classroom today (or talk to teachers and children) and you will see "management" conceptualised and operationalised in terms of rules, reinforcers, and structure (e.g. Walker et al., 1998). Although broader views of management might include management of time and transitions, for the most part management takes form in discrete techniques and practices for the purposes of increasing desirable and decreasing undesirable behaviors' (Pianta, 2006, p. 687).
3. While the concept of the Didactic has retained an association with moral instruction in the English-speaking world, often implying a somewhat patronizing tone, I use the term here without such negative connotations to refer to the science or art of teaching. This understanding of the Didactic is found throughout Scandinavia, as well as in other European countries – Germany in particular. In Scandinavian research, Didactics encompasses grounds and conditions for every important decision in relation to the planning, performance and evaluation of teaching. Therefore, the Didactic is a value-neutral concept. It is this understanding of the concept that lies at the heart of this chapter. In the hope of reminding the reader of this understanding throughout the chapter, I have chosen to write it with a capital D.
4. In quotation marks as 'each other' could indicate separateness, which is not in line with agential realist thinking.
5. Mustafa experienced this Mafia-like code first-hand. In an interview, he told me that the boys in his class committed crimes in the form of violence and theft, and that he found it difficult not to get involved. He also said he felt compelled to talk to his mother, who worked at the school, about the problems, but at the same time, he feared reprisals. In another interview, Dejan told me that Mustafa was and always would be on the periphery of the group of boys in the class because he snitched. A few weeks later, Mustafa changed school. Prior to this, he had been assaulted. According to his parents, the assault was 'ordered'. According to Jan, the attack was due to Mustafa having 'sung'.
6. Nicholas Long argues that sociality cannot and should not be reduced to human relationality or affectivity (Long & Moore, 2013, p. 3). The subject is not just a product of social relations

and/or social interaction; the non-human is also involved in and transforms human processes of becoming. Long (2015) also argues for keeping the concept of sociality as open as possible and designates sociality as a dynamic relational matrix through which humans come into existence.

References

Barad, K. (2007). *Meeting the universe halfway. Quantum physics and the entanglement of matter and meaning.* Duke University Press.

Barad, K. (2010). Quantum entanglements and hauntological relations of inheritance: Dis/continuities, SpaceTime enfoldings, and justice-to-come. *Derrida Today, 3*(2), 240–268.

Biggs, B. K., Vernberg, E. M., Twemlow, S. W., Fonagy, P., & Dill, E. J. (2008). Teacher adherence and its relation to teacher attitudes and student outcomes in an elementary school-based violence prevention program. *School Psychology Review, 37*(4), 533–549.

Brophy, J. E. (2004). *Teaching* (Educational Practices Series, Vol. 1). International Academy of Education, International Bureau of Education.

Brophy, J. E. (2006). History of research on classroom management. In C. M. Evertson & C. S. Weinstein (Eds.), *Handbook of classroom management. Research, practice and contemporary issues* (pp. 17–43). Lawrence Earlbaum Associates.

Caprara, G. V., Barbanelli, C., Pastorelli, C., Bandura, A., & Zimbardo, P. (2000). Prosocial foundations of children's academic achievement. *Psychological Science, 11*(4), 302–306.

Darling-Hammond, L. (1999). *Teacher quality and student achievement: A review of state policy evidence.* Center for the Study of Teaching and Policy, University of Washington.

Doyle, W. (1985). Recent research on classroom management: Implications for teacher preparation. *Journal of Teacher Education, 36*(3), 31–35.

Emmer, E. T., & Sabornie, E. J. (2015). *Handbook of classroom management.* Taylor & Francis Group.

Evertson, C. M., & Poole, I. R. (2008). Proactive classroom management. In T. Good (Ed.), *21st century education: A reference handbook* (pp. 131–139). Sage Publications.

Evertson, C. M., & Weinstein, C. (2006). Classroom management as a field of inquiry. In C. M. Evertson & C. S. Weinstein (Eds.), *Handbook of classroom management: Research, practice and contemporary issues* (pp. 3–15). Lawrence Earlbaum Associates.

Granström, K. (2006). Group phenomena and classroom management in Sweden. In C. M. Evertson & C. S. Weinstein (Eds.), *Handbook of classroom management: Research, practice, and contemporary issues* (pp. 1141–1159). Lawrence Erlbaum Associated.

Hattie, J. (2009). *Visible learning: A synthesis of meta-analyses relating to achievement*. Routledge.

Howes, C., & Ritchie, S. (2002). *A matter of trust: Connecting teachers and learners in the early childhood classrooms*. Teachers College Press.

Hughes, J., Cavell, T., & Wilson, V. (2001). Further support for the developmental significance of the quality of the teacher-student relationship. *Journal of School Psychology, 39*(4), 289–302.

Jones, V. (1996). Classroom management. In J. Sikula, T. J. Buttery, & E. Guyton (Eds.), *Handbook of research on teacher education* (2nd ed., pp. 503–521). Macmillan Library.

Juelskjær, M., Plauborg, H., & Adrian, S. W. (2020). *Dialogues on agential realism. Engaging in worldings through research practice*. Routledge.

Long, N. J. (2015). Sociality in anthropology. In J. D. Wright (Ed.), *International encyclopedia of the social and behavioral sciences* (2nd ed., Vol. 22, pp. 854–860). Elsevier.

Long, N. J., & Moore, H. L. (2013). *Sociality: New directions*. Berghahn Books.

Luiselli, J. K., Putnam, R. F., Handler, M., & Feinberg, A. B. (2005). Whole-school positive behaviour support: Effects on student discipline problems and academic performance. *Educational Psychology, 25*(2–3), 183–198.

Martin, N. K., Schafer, N. J., McClowry, S., Emmer, E. T., Brekelmans, M., Mainhard, T., & Wubbels, T. (2016). Expanding the definition of classroom management: Recurring themes and new conceptualization. *Journal of Classroom Interaction, 51*(1), 31–41.

McCaslin, M., & Good, T. L. (1992). Compliant cognition: The Misalliance of management and instructional goals in current school reform. *Educational Researcher, 21*(3), 4–17.

McCaslin, M., & Good, T. L. (1998). Moving beyond management as sheer compliance: Helping student to develop goal coordination strategies. *Educational Horizons, 76*, 169–176.

McEvoy, A., & Welker, R. (2000). Antisocial behavior, academic failure, and school climate: A critical review. *Journal of Emotional & Behavioral Disorders, 8*(3), 130–140.

Pianta, R. C. (2006). Classroom management and relationships between children and teachers: Implications for research and practice. In C. M. Evertson & C. S. Weinstein (Eds.), *Handbook of classroom management: Research, practice, and contemporary Issues* (pp. 685–709). Lawrence Erlbaum Associated.

Plauborg, H. (2015). *Intra-aktivitet af didaktik, faglighed og socialitet og udvikling af en tænkning om læring og didaktik – analyser af tre eksperimentelle casestudier* [PhD dissertation]. Aarhus University.

Plauborg, H. (2016). *Klasseledelse gentænkt*. Hans Reitzels Forlag.

Plauborg, H. (2018). Towards an agential realist concept of learning. *Subjectivity, 11*(4), 322–338.

Pressley, M., Roehrig, A., Raphael, L., Dolezal, S., Bohn, C., Mohan, L., Wharton-McDonald, R., Bogner, K., & Hogan, K. (2003). Teaching processes in elementary and secondary education. In W. Reynolds & G. Miller (Eds.), *Handbook of psychology: Educational psychology* (Vol. 7, pp. 153–176). John Wiley.

Walker, H. M., Stiller, B., Severson, H. H., Feil, E. G., & Golly, A. (1998). First step to success: Intervening at the point of school entry to prevent antisocial behavior patterns. *Psychology in the Schools, 35,* 259–269.

White, K., & Kistner, J. (1992). The influence of teacher feedback on young children's peer preferences and perceptions. *Developmental Psychology, 28*(5), 933–940.

PART 2

Quality Teaching and Teacher Education in Times of Crisis and Uncertainty

CHAPTER 6

Teacher Experiences and Practices in the Time of COVID-19

Implications for Understanding Quality in Teaching

Carol Hordatt Gentles, Sarah Younie, Marilyn Leask and Helen Caldwell

Abstract

The experiences and practices of teachers during the COVID-19 pandemic, appear to have changed how stakeholders think about the work of teachers and their professionalism. Drawing on findings from two research projects, the ICET/MESHGuides international research on Teachers Experiences during COVID-19 (ICET/MESHGuides, 2021), the Northampton University Active Distance Learning (ADL) research and development project (Caldwell et al., 2021), and the eye witness records of the pandemic's impact on education in Leask and Younie (2021), we highlight how in the process of transitioning to online delivery and finding creative, offline ways of reaching students, teachers at all levels demonstrated their capacity to be innovative and to take ownership of accelerating changes in how they think and work. They showed their willingness to practice agency and autonomy in developing the pedagogic skills, collaborative practices, knowledge, and competencies they considered most appropriate for teaching and learning during the pandemic. In this chapter we consider the implications of this shift for new ways of thinking about what quality in teaching means. This work is significant because it contests accustomed ways of understanding quality in teaching. We contend this is a critical departure that must inform policy-maker and stakeholder decision making for future proofing educational practices in times of crisis and normalcy.

Keywords

teacher education – teaching quality – online learning – pedagogy – teacher voice – teacher experience – COVID-19 pandemic – active distance learning – teacher professionalism

1 Introduction

The concept of quality in teaching and how to accomplish it is a contested notion. This is because it is stakeholder, time, and context relative (Akiba & LeTendre, 2017; OECD, 2005). In this chapter we compare teaching practices adopted during COVID-19 with established criteria for good pedagogic practice. We discuss teacher professionalism as tested and demonstrated throughout the pandemic when schools were closed, and teachers had to find other means of teaching. Our research (ICET/MESHGuides, 2021; Hordatt Gentles & Leask, 2020; Caldwell et al., 2021; Leask & Younie, 2021) suggests that during the pandemic many teachers have demonstrated tremendous capacity for leadership of learning and innovation. They have shown willingness and capacity to change their mindsets, upskill, acquire the knowledge and instructional competencies they thought necessary for managing rapidly changing teaching and learning contexts. They have collaborated with each other and parents in different and meaningful ways.

Consequently, the narrative about teachers and what they can do has shifted. This is evident in reports from global organisations who have described the response of teachers during the pandemic as heroic and praiseworthy. At the International Summit on the Teaching Profession hosted by Education International (EI, 2020) in June 2020, Ministers of Education from across the globe praised:

> The leadership of educators during the crisis, the ways in which they came together as a community to share ideas, knowledge, and experience to support their students. One minister referred to the mobilisation of educators as the *precious silver lining of the crisis*. (Theme 3)

The Ministers further described teachers as essential, frontline workers who had shown, 'leadership, resilience, adaptability, creativity, and dedication to their students' by taking on the role of 'navigating this crisis, overcoming challenges, and ensuring educational continuity for students' (EI, 2020, para. 2). These statements and data reported in Leask and Younie (2021) suggests that along with this recognition came the realisation that teachers just might have something to contribute to policy making for managing the pandemic. This has implications for how we should think about quality in teaching now and in the future.

2 Literature Review

The literature informing this chapter highlights how we understand quality in teaching and what is needed to facilitate this. The literature defines quality in teaching as bringing about quality learning and learner agency, through learners' active engagement in *both* face to face and online environments. This is best achieved if teachers enjoy agency and autonomy in their decision-making about what, when, why and how to organise their teaching.

2.1 Quality in Teaching

Defining the concept of quality in teaching is difficult because what it means changes according to time, context, and culture. Much attention has been paid to identifying exactly what constitutes quality teaching. It seems there are a myriad of ways to think about the concept which raises numerous questions. Does quality in teaching refer to what teachers do in the classroom – how they teach to bring about student learning? Is it their personal characteristics – their morals, beliefs, attitudes, and values? Is it their capacity for providing psychological and emotional support to their students? Is it their willingness to deliver the types of student learning outcomes set out by curricula or is it their attempts to teach independently? Is it their commitment and dispositions to use their practice to build a better society or to contribute to building a stronger profession? Is it a combination of some or all of these?

Berliner (2005) suggests quality in teaching combines both good teaching and successful or effective teaching. Good teaching has to do with how well teachers enact the pedagogical competencies, personal qualities, content knowledge, knowledge of student learning and psychology, and moral dispositions that facilitate quality learning and learner agency (Darling-Hammond, 2010; Wechsler & Shields, 2008). As Loughran (2010, p. 61) contends, 'Good teaching is about creating real opportunities for students to begin to determine for themselves how their knowledge needs to be structured and reconstructed to enhance the quality of their learning'. Teaching is considered successful or effective when this type of student learning has taken place.

Hidson and Leask (2022) also suggest that quality in teaching is dependent on strong connections between quality pedagogy, teacher professionalism, learner agency and quality learning. As they explain,

> Pedagogy can be thought of as an umbrella term that helps us to think about teaching and learning, and all the various processes that together make up the work of the professional teacher. Under the umbrella term *pedagogy*, we can identify *essential categories* [such as this cited above] *underpinned by theories* that shape our understanding of how learning occurs. *Theories of learning* fall into three broad groups broadly as behaviourism, cognitivism, and constructivism (Ertmer & Newby, 2013), aligning with what learners are *doing, thinking, and creating.* (Hidson & Leask, 2022)

How teaching is undertaken and structured is dependent on the personality and knowledge of the teacher and the expectations of learners and their communities. Thus, teaching which leads to learning is complex and individual and so resistant to dictat. The ICET/MESHGuides research (Hordatt Gentles & Leask, 2020; ICET/MESHGuides, 2021) found that during the COVID-19 pandemic, while some governments worked with teachers to find solutions to ensuring continuity of learning, others tried to dictate how teaching would be undertaken. The research findings suggest that the flexibility and context-dependent professional judgement required of teachers in adapting models of teaching meant that this level of control was not supportive of continuity of learning during the crisis.

Hidson and Leask (2022) define four areas constraining and shaping an individual teacher's approach to teaching any single lesson and these are included here as we suggest this makes the importance of teachers' professional judgement in 'in the moment' decisions transparent. Given local variations of context, controlling quality in teaching through dictat during crises is simply not possible. Instead, they suggest we should be cognizant that:

1. Teachers work with the mind and so should be experts in the *learning sciences:* how the brain works, cognition, motivation, behaviour, and development of positive attitudes are all relevant.
2. Part of teaching is *craft* – constructing positive learning environments and learning materials.
3. *Performance in the classroom* contributes to creating a teachers' unique pedagogical style. This includes the ways they capture the attention of a group, explain, question, model and demonstrate, use language effectively to convey meaning and the ways they respond to learners, their gestures, ways of moving, and dress.
4. *Processes* also shape teaching: the structure of the school day, term, and year, whether classes are mixed ability or streamed, the length of the lesson, the space between lessons used for giving immediate post-lesson support and individual guidance, the assessment structures applied to subjects and classes.

Hidson and Leask also point to a study (Entz, 2006) from the Center for Research on Education, Diversity and Excellence (CREDE) which suggests five principles of effective pedagogy for all learners. These seem to include a focus on 'what learners are *doing, thinking and creating*' which are identified as important foci for pedagogy from the learning theories mentioned above. For this chapter we use these five principles and the four elements listed above to provide a useful framework for thinking about quality in teaching. Table 6.1

TABLE 6.1   Five critical elements of pedagogy

CREDE's critical element	What this looks like in practice
Joint productive activity	Teacher and students producing together
Language development	Developing language and literacy across the curriculum.
Contextualisation	Making meaning connecting schools to students' lives.
Challenging activities	Teaching complex thinking
Instructional conversation	Teaching through conversation

SOURCE: ADAPTED FROM CREDE'S FIVE CRITICAL ELEMENTS OF PEDAGOGY (ENTZ, 2006)

lists CREDE's five critical elements of pedagogy (Entz, 2006) and examples of practice which exemplify these. Later in this chapter these principles and elements are applied to teacher reported practices during the COVID-19 times, to illustrate how quality in teaching was achieved in the circumstances created when schools were closed.

These understandings, of what constitutes quality in teaching in normal times, provide an initial framework for analysing the quality of teaching approaches developed by teachers to support ongoing learning once schools were closed. In many countries, governments required teachers to switch to online learning (even though this excluded learners and teachers without access to the internet or personal devices).

The next section therefore takes this discussion on pedagogy further by establishing criteria for quality in online pedagogy and outlining a model supporting deep learning using online tools developed and tested at the University of Northampton (UK) – the Active Distance Learning (ADL) model.

2.2   *Quality in Online Pedagogies – An Emerging Active Distance Learning Model*

In exploring what makes good online teaching and learning we can draw from a range of theoretical underpinnings. Theories of learning relevant to our digital age plot a journey from constructivism to social constructivism, with connectivism and constructionism acknowledging the central role of technologies. From constructivism we can take an emphasis on learners' active engagement with constructing knowledge (Cummings et al., 2017) and the link between social interaction and learning (Vygotsky, 1978). There is also the notion of communities of practice with shared goals (Wenger, 1998), which many educators seek to nurture in online environments. Social online communities make it possible for students to 'join in' and 'apply to practice' at the same time, blending talking and doing, or 'participation and reification', to use Wenger's terms (1998). Goggins et al. (2011, p. 210) describe this as,

> Participation involves acting and interacting, and reification involves producing artefacts (such as tools, words, symbols, rules, documents, concepts, theories, and so on) around which the negotiation of meaning is organized.

Areas in need of further consideration, they suggest, are 'the functions and uses of the technological tools that most effectively support and mediate a community's social and intellectual engagement' (Goggins et al., 2011, p. 224). This sits well with the idea that posted comments, media, images, and digital artefacts help articulate pedagogy and practice, and can act as anchors for the evolution of ideas within online communities (Caldwell et al., 2020). Related to this are constructionist theories that suggest that digital environments create ripe conditions for active knowledge building through the creation and sharing of digital artefacts (Harel & Papert, 1991). When constructionist ideas are applied to communities of practice 'making' refers to the articulation of ideas, and might take a physical or digital form, consisting of articulation and externalisation of an idea or an example from practice in a form that someone can respond to. The to-and-fro between articulations and responses is essential to the knowledge building process within a learning community (Caldwell et al., 2020, 2021).

Connectivism also recognises the role of technology in learning, namely the integration of networked communication into collaborative learning environments and a suggestion that the nature of knowledge shifts as connections are formed and reformed (Downes, 2010; Siemens, 2005). This emphasises the links between people and resources, and the fact that knowledge can be encoded in digital artefacts (Nilmanat, 2011; Siemens, 2005; Young & Tseng, 2008). The tacit knowledge that can be encoded in an image can span several dimensions that would be difficult to explain in words, such as attitudes, motivations, and experiences, and can mediate the sharing of experiences (Burnett, 2016; Nilmanat, 2011). These findings are in line with connectivist theories of learning that emphasise the links between people and resources (Siemens, 2005), and the making of personal choices within an environment mediated by technology (Saadatmand & Kumpulainen, 2014).

The learning frameworks described in the section above highlight action, collaboration, and reflection as key aspects of online learning (Bonk & Zhang, 2006; Godlewska et al., 2019). They also highlight the role of teachers working actively and collaboratively with students to build learner agency. A case study that illustrates how these aspects came together for practice is highlighted below, and can be seen in action at the University of Northampton, UK, where a pedagogical model of *Active Blended Learning* (ABL) has been implemented across the institution since 2014. Its goal is to enhance student engagement through a digitally rich learning environment in which students interact with content, peers, and tutors (Armellini et al., 2021; Palmer et al., 2017; Rodriguez & Armellini, 2021). The ABL precedent meant that lecturers were well placed to make the transition to *Active Distance Learning* (ADL) in response to the demand for remote learning when the COVID-19 pandemic began (Caldwell et al., 2021). Through ADL learners make sense of ideas using digital tools to demonstrate their understanding, and then build upon them through social online learning. Collective knowledge construction is mediated by technology tools, the exchange of tangible outputs, and synchronous and asynchronous interactions (Caldwell et al., 2020, 2021).

In many ways the online environment has advantages over a face-to-face setting. There is also much to be learned from the theory and practice of quality online pedagogy that can be adopted to improve the quality of face-to-face teaching. For example, in their discussion of 'seamless flipped learning', Hwang et al. (2015, p. 1) suggest that technology can facilitate across learning contexts, times, and social settings. They note that the use of media makes it easier to engage with, revise and share content. Similarly, Royle et al. (2014) draw attention to the opportunities for more agile learning using technology and the speed with which connections can be made and experiences shared across contexts. We can conclude that online environments can provide opportunities to develop shared understandings based on captured events, forming a bridge between informal and formal learning, and combining synchronous interaction with the creation of digital artefacts around which shared understandings evolve. In this way, the online community of practice amplifies the learning of individuals as the collective learning potential of the crowd exceeds that of the individual (Hung, 2002; Johnson, 2001; Richardson, 2010). Conditions can be created for online learners to have agency and voice online by designing and nurturing community spaces that cut across formal hierarchies and cultivate trust and reciprocity.

3 Teacher Professionalism – Agency and Teacher Voice

Any discussion of quality in teaching must include concepts of teacher professionalism because these reflect societal perceptions of teaching and the value of teacher work. Doucet et al. (2020) in their report titled *Thinking about pedagogy in an unfolding pandemic*, argue, 'This is not the time for unilateral, top-down only approaches to education. Teachers can and should lead in many ways and use their professional judgement to make the best decisions for their students' (2020, p. 2). They contend that 'A multilateral collaborative partnership across sectors is needed when approaching education during a pandemic with institutionalized dialogues that ensure teacher voices as a major part of the solution' (2020, p. 2). These views reflect a view of teachers' work and teacher professionalism that values Teacher Voice, Teacher Autonomy and Teacher Agency as critical parts of quality in teaching.

These challenge the dominance of a 'managerial professionalism' which according to Stevenson and Gilliland (2016, p. 113) 'relates to the ways in which teachers' professional knowledge has often been ignored as particular pedagogical practices have been imposed on teachers, whilst in other cases professional development has been used crudely to promote national initiatives or organisational objectives'. The conditions that have been shaping the teaching profession for the previous decade concern public accountability, which prioritises external performance measures. Increased regimes of accountability and audit are meant to improve public trust in education, which are implemented through standards regimes. These political conditions confronting the teaching profession are becoming more universal,

> The strong and sustained push for accountability required by governments... ensures the external control of the teaching profession. Regulatory frameworks serve to constrain teachers' practices and to emphasise a conservative and reactive form of teacher professionalism. (Sachs, 2003, p. 9)

We find the idea of 'democratic professionalism' useful for conceptualising quality in teaching driven by teacher confidence in their capacity and competence to shape and control their own practice and pedagogy. This is 'based on fundamental values of social justice and democracy, [and] emphasises teacher control and influence in relation to three domains of professional agency – shaping learning and teaching conditions, developing, and enacting policy and enhancing pedagogical knowledge and professional learning' (Stevenson & Gilliland, 2016, p. 113). Teachers who practice democratic professionalism can exercise their Teacher Voice and agency. Borrowing from the theoretical discourse of Critical Pedagogy, Pennycook (2001, p. 130) defines 'Voice' as 'far more than just speaking; rather, it is a broader understanding of developing the possibilities to articulate alternative realities. And since it has to do with gaining the agency to express one's life, it is less about the medium of voice (speaking, writing, etc.) and more about finding possibilities of articulation'. 'Democratic professionalism' places an obligation on the teacher to draw on their professional knowledge including what they know about local communities, conditions and research when reaching professional judgements about appropriate pedagogies.

In contrast, Strathern (2000) identifies 'emerging universalism' through an audit culture of professional competencies. Strathern argues that a tendency towards universalism can be found at a national and international level, where definitive lists of competencies for teachers are published. This indicates a move to a situation in which the work of professionals is 'managed' by an external specification of competencies, which are measured by the 'language of indicators' (Strathern, 2000, p. 314). This drive towards universalism appears to be led by policy makers rather than teacher professionals and the value and merit of such measurability remains open to debate. Stronach et al. (2001), refer to such quantitative performance measures as 'economy of performance', which require universal criteria in order that standardised comparisons can be made locally and nationally, or even internationally. This supports the research of Day et al. (2000, p.116), who recognised an 'emerging international consensus' concerning the need to identify 'quality in teaching' as determined by a set of acquired competencies rather than as a professional act requiring judgement and deep knowledge.

The ICET/MESHGuides (2021) research findings reported below indicate that during the COVID-19 pandemic crisis standardised practices designed to assure quality in teaching had limited value. Some teachers were clearly able to operate as autonomous professionals arguably working within a 'democratic professionalism' paradigm and taking independent action to overcome barriers to learning. Others reported they were operating in a more dependent nonprofessional mode – waiting for central government leadership.

The shift to online learning required teachers to enact digital pedagogies. However, we know from prior research (Atkins, 2018; Younie, 2007) that knowledge about effective digital pedagogies was not widely shared, due to insufficient focus in education systems on the opportunities for technology to support learning. Given that schooling for most children is normally based on a face-to-face pedagogic model it is perhaps not surprising that teachers were unprepared for remote learning with technology, although those schools that had invested in technology and training (infrastructure *with* teacher skills via CPD) were much better placed in the pandemic to transition to Active Distance Learning when school closures were announced by governments. The research we have undertaken shows a strong connection between the principles for effective pedagogies in face-to-face classroom settings and those

3.1 The Just-In-Time (JIT) Teacher Professional Development Model

The 'just-in-time learning' (JIT) model for teacher professional development has been identified in prior research into the adoption of education technologies by teachers (Atkins, 2018; Younie, 2007) as the most effective way for teachers to upskill themselves, via a self-driven identification of their own needs and identifying which aspects of technology the teachers needed to learn for their professional/pedagogic practice. This research showed that not only urgent emerging needs for new knowledge can be met through more knowledgeable others (colleagues & IT experts known to the teacher), who provide 'community of practice' networks i.e., through – social constructivism –, but that collaboration fostered by these networks which allows teachers from dispersed locations to construct new pedagogical knowledge, when there are no 'experts' – together providing JIT learning when needed. This way of learning is conceptualised as 'communal constructivism', whereby 'teachers learn *with* and *for* each other' (Younie & Leask, 2001, 2013). Communal constructivism was identified as an early affordance of *online* communities of practice. Research showing the power of 'communal constructivism' – where there is no knowledgeable other than only a professional group exploring the unknown – was undertaken across Europe as part of the 1998 EU funded MM1010 online European SchoolNet initiative[1] (Leask & Younie, 2001) and the adoption of internet-based technologies in schools (Younie, 2007). The COVID-19 pandemic when teachers were faced with urgent professional learning needs with respect to shifting to online pedagogies highlights the need to move from a 'one-size-fits-all' model of CPD training to providing opportunities for teachers to continually update their knowledge and skills ('just-in-time learning', JIT).

4 Methodology

The data gathered during the COVID-19 pandemic in 2020 and used for this chapter came from:
1. the ICET and MESHGuides research project gathering data on teachers' experiences during COVID-19 using ICET and MESHGuides international networks[2] (reported in ICET/MESHGuides, 2021), and
2. the research and development work of the Tech for ADL research group at the University of Northampton UK (reported in Caldwell et al., 2021).

For the ICET and MESHGuides research project, data were gathered during the period of June to December 2020, by ICET and MESHGuide network members from over 550 teachers from 47 countries through a series of qualitative group interviews and from discussions held in two international symposia on 8th and 15th October 2020.

The aim of the project was to provide a space in which to document the voices of teachers as they shared their experience during the first six months of the pandemic. The following questions were posed to educators in focus groups, in individual interviews and in break out room discussions during the symposia:

1. How has your job changed since the pandemic?
2. What new strategies/practices did you develop?
3. What strategies/practices do you want to continue using?
4. What do you see yourself doing differently in the future?
5. What do you see as challenges for sustaining education during times of crisis?

There was also the opportunity for educators to speak about other issues they thought to be important. What was gathered was seen as snapshots of educators' experiences – classroom teachers, teachers in training and teacher educators. For the purposes of analysis, the data were collated around the themes which emerged from the data collected. The transcribed data were coded manually, categorised, and collated around emergent themes by the two lead researchers. The findings were then shared with co-researchers for feedback. This allowed for peer debriefing and member checking as they read through the emerging results to verify the findings. The researchers complied with the ethical requirements for research in their contexts.

The Tech for ADL research group developed the concept of Active Distance Learning for university teaching during COVID-19 through building on research and development work on Active Blended Learning undertaken at the university (Armellini et al., 2021; Palmer et al., 2017; Wareing, 2021). The ADL model was developed through drawing on the learning theories mentioned above and the analyses of learning in online environments including the role of *dialogue*, *digital making* and *online posting* in the construction and sharing of knowledge in online environments. The Tech for ADL research group created and implemented a model for ADL prior to COVID-19 pandemic. Student evaluations confirmed the power of the model in enhancing learning. The advent of COVID-19 led to the development of and testing of the Active Distance Learning model with students (Caldwell et al., 2020). In addition, the Just-In-Time professional development model was developed from EU funded projects when the internet was being introduced into schools (Leask & Younie, 2001) and the integration of educational technologies in schools (Younie, 2007). Desk research for the quality in pedagogy section was undertaken for the pedagogy chapter in the *Learning to teach in the Secondary School* (Capel et al., 2022).

5   Findings

The section below offers a summary of what was learned from educators across the globe, about their experiences during the early part of the COVID-19 pandemic. It illustrates and discusses how these led to new mindsets and shifts in thinking about the benefits and challenges of online teaching and learning.

5.1   *ICET/MESHGuides Global Report – Summarising Findings*

The findings from the ICET/MESHGuides research are drawn from what teachers shared about their experiences, challenges, and successes during the first six months of the pandemic (see ICET/MESHGuides, 2021 for a fuller report). Examples are provided below. They paint a picture of teaching in which examples of teacher agency and professional autonomy are evident and strong. Across all 47 countries, the closure of schools created fear, anxiety, and uncertainty. It was an unprecedented situation for which no one was adequately prepared. Yet, teachers rapidly adopted remote teaching using online technologies where possible. This change of role required teachers to adapt their professional practice, in some cases, literally overnight. Their deep commitment was testament to their professionalism, highlighting their ethic of care and dedication to continue to deliver schooling, even without classrooms. However, it should be noted that there were significant challenges thrown up by the pandemic. The analysis here is intended to reflect and record these so we can learn lessons and build a more robust future which considers the role of quality in teaching and defining it to 'future proof' education against major disruptions.

The specific challenges for teachers when schools and classrooms were closed was to provide alternative and remote ways of delivering education that allowed for continuity of learning. The challenges were multiple and involved utilising educational technologies. Teachers reported that to survive and manage in virtual spaces, they made changes to their pedagogy. In many instances (at least initially) they had to do this with non-existent or limited government support. Many reported they found that online delivery made their teaching more student centreed and they needed to be more mindful of practising differentiation. Teachers reported that the paradigm shifts they had been resisting for so long took place with respect to integrating digital technologies into pedagogic practice. There were numerous ways in which pedagogy changed.

As one teacher described it, 'Previously technology was used as a side dish – now digital tools are the main dish'. Teachers became more creative. As another teacher shared 'my teaching improved'. 'I had to think about moving from pen and paper assessments'. She felt empowered to 'actually cater to all the different learning needs of my students'. Teachers reported they changed ways of providing feedback to students and parents, ways of record keeping, ways of recording memories of teaching and learning since actual snapshots and recordings were now possible and now allowed and they developed techniques for engaging students. Increased independent learning also took place. One teacher said,

> I have begun to engage my students increasingly into self-exploration and independent learning. Before the pandemic 60% of my classes were used in information input through lecture. Today, information input in the form of lecture is almost 0%.

Another said,

> The pandemic demanded a new methodology and teaching practices to support the students on a large scale.

The abrupt change in pedagogic practice to online delivery was not without its challenges though. Teachers did report that the shift to virtual classrooms created a major challenge of reaching and identifying students who needed assistance – *often you have no way of knowing if a child has grasped a concept or not.* With online teaching the teachers struggled to be able to monitor the participation of learners in the lesson, especially where cameras were not permitted to be activated due to safeguarding concerns in some schools. Consequently, keeping all students engaged was reported as difficult to achieve consistently. Also, there was a decentring of power relations as teachers moved from a central role to a facilitating role, which demanded more autonomous self-directed learning from the students. However, not all students had the capacities or facilities to make the shift to home-centreed learning. Teachers reported that learning equity and access were universal concerns,

> One of the biggest challenges for teachers was to 'keep students on board'. Children's home situations do not always allow them to participate in lessons or the other educational activities offered by schools. Even though it was possible to observe a good deal of achievement in provision of distance education in schools, teachers noticed that some parents are not

in a position to be able to support their children's learning effectively, especially those with insufficient digital skills and not having access to the Internet at home. Therefore, disadvantaged students were struggling to adapt to pandemic times reality, with less access to learning material, access to online platforms, and less parental support.

In addressing these challenges, teachers responded by developing several strategies. For example, with engagement, teachers used a strategy to continuously pull students into the lesson with probing questions. Rather than present passively they directed questions at students, encouraging the use of the 'chat box' function for all students to respond. This was effective where cameras were switched off. Similarly, the use of 'breakaway rooms', available across many types of digital platforms, enabled student-led group work.

Teachers also recommended the use of 'flipped classroom teaching' as a useful strategy. This involves sending students off to research a topic offline. Students would have to collaborate offline and then present live and online and encourage feedback and constructive criticism from peers. Providing students with recorded lectures, presentations and other multimedia materials were also found to be useful. The teachers pointed out that the students who did not want to speak during the traditional classes often spoke out during online classes. Therefore, teachers appreciated the creation of online discussions using virtual forums and bulletin boards for this purpose, which improved communication with students. Some teachers pointed out that creating tasks, quizzes, and tests online was also helpful in verifying students' knowledge. Overall, teachers experienced steep learning curves as they tried to identify, learn, and manage technology. As one summarised, 'The bar of competences required for teachers to function was raised'.

5.2 Adopting a New Mindset and Paradigm Shift

Teachers for the most part, reported that their teaching would be different in the future even if there was a return to the 'old normal'. There is now widespread knowledge across the profession of digital technology tools, which teachers had to learn about very quickly and which they wish to continue to use both for personalising learning, extending the subject matter available and improving communications with students and families. Teachers said they will incorporate the methods they used during the pandemic in future teaching to provide varieties of learning opportunities beside the traditional chalk and talk method that they practiced before the pandemic. The pandemic changed their mind set and they are willing to explore other teaching methods and new digital applications for teaching now. The following quotation provides an example of a positive outcome of the pandemic which is that there has been a shift in teachers' pedagogical use of educational technologies which is likely to have long-term impact on classroom practices. 'COVID-19 has been a push to get teachers to use [online] interactive whiteboards and become expert users'.

Teachers said they want to capitalise on their experience of getting past their resistance to the use of technology and taking ownership of improving their professional capacity for virtual teaching and learning. The pandemic experience motivated them to feel confident about leaving comfort zones of traditional practices. In particular, teachers reported on their desire to capitalise on changes in their mindset around: (i) seeing the value of using technology; (ii) taking more ownership of their own professional learning; (iii) teaching in more student-centreed ways.

> There has been a more valuable and more marked transformation and evaluation. Other ways to learn to participate, that teachers receive the training and are protagonists, leaders, of their own training. This is the scenario in the future.

5.3 *Benefits of Online Learning – Teachers Experiences during COVID-19*

Although online learning was missing many of the opportunities that make schools great learning environments – social interaction, community activities and face-to-face creative collaborative work across subjects, benefits of online learning emerged from the data including:

1. Seeing the home of the student through a virtual lens gave new insights to other needs impacting students.
2. Children with special needs who found school an uncomfortably challenging and competitive space found it a relief to be taught online.
3. Some quiet students engaged more online than normally in the classroom through using the chat function to pose questions.
4. Using online platforms to showcase students' work; to also gauge the progress of students' work, increase accessibility and make it more open to all.
5. Teachers encouraged more independent learning among students.
6. Multimodal approaches to teaching were used: more video clips, PowerPoints, multimedia resources.

Teachers often stated that they wanted to continue with some forms of remote learning, especially those ones that allow as much direct contact with students as possible. Teachers appreciated the possibility of providing students with lecture recordings and presentations and sharing them. Similarly, students reported liking recorded lectures because they could play them back repeatedly to learn more difficult material at their own pace. Teachers also reported that they also want to keep building the improved relationships with parents and community and capitalise on parents' involvement with supporting teachers' work. Overall, teachers positively testified to the unintended professional development that the pandemic created:

> COVID has provided us with many opportunities for developing ourselves which we did not do before.

Teachers want to maintain taking ownership over their own professional learning by continuing to train themselves and improve their capacity to teach online.

5.4   *Reaching Students without Online Access*

Our research also showed that for many teachers, it was difficult to reach their students online. Their responses demonstrated dedication, creativity, and innovation in working without online tools. More specifically, issues with poor wi-fi access, limited connectivity, limited devices, and limited funding to buy data severely hampered their ability to establish and maintain contact with their students. One teacher, for example, reported he had seen only 10% of his students in four months. The data gathered demonstrated that to overcome this problem teachers had to be innovative and creative. Teachers worked to involve their communities in reaching students. Some relied on social media such as Whatsapp to communicate with students and parents. Others had to rely on producing packages of paper worksheets to distribute for children to collect, complete and return for marking. In one country, teachers used the egg vendor to distribute materials. Others approached store owners to be collection spots. In another country, a teacher came up with a plan to paint community blackboards on shop walls which she and some colleagues wrote lessons and activities for children in the area to copy and work on. Others utilised technologies like solar-powered radios (provided by charities) to link with their students. These findings from the ICET/MESHGuides (2021) global report speak to teachers demonstrating quality in teaching through their motivation and determination to meet the learning needs of their students despite the challenges arising from the pandemic. They showed their willingness to navigate and manage dramatically changed educational landscapes with professional agency and autonomy. The strategies they used, and their changing mindsets suggest a shift to ways of teaching that reflect the CREDE critical elements of quality pedagogy identified earlier (Table 6.1). This is evident, for example, in teacher reports of being willing to engage in 'joint productive activity' by sharing power in the online classroom, and collaborating with teacher colleagues, parents and students to build knowledge of what worked. Teachers facilitated meaningful conversations with their students that extended beyond the set curriculum. They contextualised learning by devising strategies to connect the new learning environments (both on and offline) to students' 'new' lives in the pandemic. The experiences and practices of teachers during COVID-19 also conveyed heightened awareness of the value of online pedagogy for stimulating quality in teaching. This is evident in findings of the Technology for ADL group at the University of Northampton.

5.5 Tech for ADL Research Group Findings

From the literature review, drawing on the key theories of constructionism (Harel & Papert, 1991), connectivism (Downes, 2010; Siemens, 2005), and communal constructivism (Leask & Younie, 2001), we provide examples below of ADL practice that embody key principles of effective teaching for online learning as mentioned earlier namely *dialogue*, *digital making* and *online posting* in the construction and sharing of knowledge in online environments. The four examples of active online pedagogy which follow demonstrate the application of the Active Distance Learning pedagogy model in higher education teaching developed at the University of Northampton during COVID-19. These illustrate models of quality in teaching online which maximise the affordances of online teaching technologies.

Example 1 demonstrates the use of the Padlet tool for facilitating collaborative construction of knowledge.

Example 1: Remixing and Remaking Digital Artefacts

A padlet is a digital noticeboard. Teachers and students can use it collaboratively online. Students can remake and reclaim a Padlet by following the teacher's list of directions/instructions to edit the posts to generate a new Padlet on a theme of their choice that demonstrates their understanding of the tool. In engaging in this activity, they are articulating their ideas and then sharing them with their group. The remade Padlets are posted in a 'Padlet of Padlets' and the group is invited to respond to the new set of posts.

Example 2 demonstrates group collaboration.

Example 2: Group Collaboration within a Community of Practice

A Jamboard is a digital interactive whiteboard developed by Google. Here it is used for an interactive slide presentation on the impact of COVID-19 on children and families. Students begin by using the tools Kahoot and Mentimeter to explore and compare their personal reflections at the start of the teaching session. They are shown some theoretical frameworks. They then split into breakout groups to discuss the impact on an imaginary child in relation to her bedroom, her home, city, and the world. Each group uses sticky notes within Jamboard to record their responses and then they come back together to present their ideas and recommend some solutions as a whole group. This demonstrates how technology can facilitate the process of collective knowledge building within a learning community.

Example 3 demonstrates the using of technologies to bridge formal and informal learning.

Example 3: Technology Bridging Formal and Informal Learning

In this example, students are invited to post an image and a reflection on what educational research means to them as a pre-session task. The resulting set of images then provides a hook for a discussion in a virtual space bringing together the synchronous and asynchronous activities. The use of images makes powerful steppingstones for the group to use to develop shared understandings, increasing the pace of the online teaching. In this way, technology can make for a more seamless link between learning that takes place before and after an online teaching session.

Example 4 addresses inclusion issues.

Example 4: Inclusive Learning Environments Mediated by Technology

In this example several digital platforms and artefacts are combined to create a visually rich environment that allows for the evolution of ideas. The teaching session is structured and presented through the medium of a flip

> book using Book Creator. Within the pages are links to a collection of complementary tools: a blog for the assignment, a Padlet summarising progress across the module, and Adobe Spark and Powtoon for the session task of poster making on the theme of online safety. These tools combine to create a learning space that accommodates individual learning differences by offering flexibility and choice in the ways students access material, engage with it and demonstrate what they know, in line the Universal Design for Learning framework suggested by CAST (CAST, 2018).

In summary, these four examples illustrate ways in which the online environment can provide an Active Distance Learning experience (ADL). Data gathered from students on ADL courses during COVID-19, indicate that carefully chosen combinations of collaborative tools can engender a feeling of belonging to a community that engages in social online learning and can offer choices that promote inclusivity for a diverse range of learners. They found it helped them feel as if,

> The social aspect of university-level study was present, meaning that opportunities for networking and peer-support still existed regardless of our geographical separation.

Students expressed satisfaction saying,

> I find that the UON experience is supportive, encouraging, and motivational.

> The online option was perfect for me and my situation.

> The course itself is highly engaging.

> Studying online allowed me to hear from peers from all walks of life.

> The University of Northampton's education department is research-led and conducts specific research projects looking into online teaching and learning. This means that their practice is up-to-the-minute and continually developing, rather than clinging to outdated teaching styles.

The Tech for ADL research group concluded that an ADL approach can:
1. Facilitate sensemaking through digital making.
2. Enable virtual placements and debates.
3. Punctuate online sessions with creative digital activities.

4. Improve the pace and activity in online sessions.
5. Capture and share online collaborations.
6. Offer opportunities for assessment and reflection.
7. Increase accessibility and inclusivity.
8. Sustain a sense of community.

It is interesting that these examples of quality online teaching also reflect the five elements of effective pedagogies identified in Table 6.1.

6   Summary and Concluding Remarks

In considering our findings, there is much to be learned from what has happened during the COVID-19 pandemic, about that which constitutes quality in teaching. This is discussed below.

6.1   *Positive Outcomes for Teaching Quality – What We Take Forward*

Using the criteria for effective pedagogies and effective online pedagogies summarised in the literature review the findings provided above show that during COVID-19, teachers demonstrated quality in teaching in how they navigated unexpected new contexts for teaching and learning in courageous ways working within the constraints (C1, 2, 3, 4) set out in Table 6.1: using their knowledge of learning, to construct new learning environments (C2), changing their ways of performing in the classroom (C3) and developing new processes shaping their teaching environment (C4). They took on online pedagogy in exemplary ways and changed their mindsets about student centeredness, rebalancing power and authority by engaging with learners in a more egalitarian way that encouraged learner agency demonstrating the five elements of pedagogy critical to effective learning identified in Table 6.1. They also demonstrated caring, resilience, responsibility, and agency. As teachers supported students and parents in managing the crises of fear, uncertainty, well-being, around loss of learning and simply surviving the pandemic, they rose to the challenge of learning how to teach online, and how to be innovative in reaching their students. For many teachers, they did this despite a lack of clear leadership and directives from policy-makers – especially in the first few months of school closures. There is evidence that many took ownership over reconfiguring curricula, upskilling, devising new ways of planning, delivering, and assessing content. What seems to have motivated teachers most was their concern and caring for their students. They wanted to ensure continuity of student learning despite the many challenges they faced.

Another explanation for teachers' practices during COVID-19 can be found in the research of Moore, Edwards, Halpin and George (2002) who discovered that teachers reposition themselves in the face of rapid and extensive educational change. Moore et al. (2002) interviews with teachers indicated that responses to public policy were prompting teachers to become increasingly pragmatic in their practice. One form of pragmatism identified was *contingent* pragmatism, adopted by teachers as reactions to change that take on the function of a survival strategy. We argue it is particularly important to understand this professional positioning in response to the pandemic, in particular the rapidity of the disruption that school closures brought to the profession during COVID-19 pandemic. The multiple demands of teachers in their situated professional practice, between external pressures (government policy edits), local contextual pressures (school culture and region/community) and teachers' preferred practice, leads us to consider how teachers came to rework their professional commitments during the pandemic: as an external pressure impacted on their preferred practice and they suddenly needed to move their pedagogy online.

6.2 *Lessons Learnt and Future Proofing*

Throughout this chapter we have identified key principles and practices that underscore quality in teaching in both face to face and online environments. These include contingent pragmatism, connectivism, just-in-time learning through communities of practice, communal constructivism, care and concern. Taken together these create possibilities for a model for the type of democratic teacher professionalism needed for teachers and learners to feel competent, confident, and capable of practising agency and autonomy. Our research suggests that teachers' practices during the pandemic show that teachers can reject the prioritisation of performativity cultures and regimes of accountability and adopt practices of agency and autonomy. They showed their capacity for professional decision making – decisional capital 'the ability to make discretionary judgements' (Hargreaves & Fullan, 2012, p. 93). By managing the rapidly changing contexts of teaching in a pandemic they were engaging in quality in teaching, as Loughran (2010, p. 82) states,

> Quality in teaching is when activities, procedures, and strategies are developed and used by teachers to encourage selection, attending and processing. ... Quality in teaching is not about using a teaching procedure just to break up the normal classroom routine; it is about using a particular teaching approach for a particular reason.

6.3 Questions about Future Practices

In closing, we suggest we have identified what teachers' experiences during COVID-19 can teach us about maintaining quality in teaching for the future if learners are able to access educational technologies and in all the countries in our research, there were young people denied continuity of their education through lack of access to these tools. As we start to see a possible end to the pandemic, we must ensure that governments take action to ensure all learners can learn remotely and that the shift in narrative about teachers and teacher professionalism does not revert to one in which teachers',

> professional knowledge has often been ignored as particular pedagogical practices have been imposed on teachers, whilst in other cases professional development has been used crudely to promote national initiatives or organisational objectives. These initiatives are often geared to meeting externally imposed targets, rather than being driven by the professional needs of the teacher. (Stevenson & Gilliland, 2016, p. 113)

The lessons we have learnt with respect to how teachers responded to providing continuity of learning during the pandemic provides important insights into how we can future proof educational practices to ensure quality in teaching is maintained. Given that future crises are inevitable, whether through natural disasters, pandemics or human made conflicts, we can plan to future proof against disruptions to schooling. We now know what is possible with educational technologies to fill the gap when teachers are removed from children, and how learning can be supported; with access to the internet and technology devices, online content repositories to support the curriculum and teachers' digital competencies for online pedagogies. The lessons learnt enable teachers to have 'emergency planning toolkits' in place, ready to go should such circumstances arise again.

Acknowledgements

We would like to thank our colleagues who shared examples from practice from the University of Northampton, senior lecturers: Jean Edwards, David Meechan, Joanne Barrow.

We also acknowledge our co researchers for the ICET/MESHGuides project listed in the publication (ICET/MESHGuides, 2021).

Notes

1 www.eun.org
2 www.icet4u.org and www.meshguides.org

References

Akiba, M., & LeTendre, G. (2017). Conceptualising teacher quality and policy in a global context. In M. Akiba & G. LeTendre (Eds.), *International handbook of teacher quality and policy* (pp. 1–21). Routledge.

Armellini, A., Teixeira Antunes, V., & Howe, R. (2021). Student perspectives on learning experiences in a higher education active blended learning context. *Techtrends, 65*, 433–443.

Atkins, L. (2018). *Exploring teachers' professional development and digital literacy: A grounded theory study* [Unpublished PhD thesis]. De Montfort University.

Berliner, D. C. (2005). The near impossibility of testing for teacher quality. *Journal of Teacher Education, 56*, 205–213.

Bonk, C. J., & Zhang, K. (2006). Introducing the R2D2 model: Online learning for the diverse learners of this world. *Distance Education, 27*(2), 249–264.

Burnett, C. (2016). *The digital age and its implications for learning and teaching in the primary school.* Cambridge Primary Review Trust.

Caldwell, H., Whewell, E., Devecchi, C., Quirke, M., & McGukin, C. (2021). Towards a digital pedagogy of inclusive active distance learning. In S. Studente, S. Ellis, & B. Desai (Eds.), *The impact of COVID-19 on teaching and learning in higher education* (pp. 23–51). Nova Science Publishers, Inc.

Caldwell, H., Whewell, E., & Heaton, R. (2020). The impact of visual posts on creative thinking and knowledge building in an online community of educators. *Thinking Skills and Creativity, 36*, 100647. https://doi.org/10.1016/j.tsc.2020.100647

Capel, S., Leask, M., & Younie, S. (Eds.). (2022). *Learning to teach in the secondary school: A companion to school experience.* Routledge.

Cope, B., & Kalantzis, M. (2009). Ubiquitous learning: An agenda for educational transformation. In V. Hodgson, C. Jones, T. Kargidis, D. McConnell, S. Retalis, D. Stamatis, & M. Zenios (Eds.), *Proceedings of the 6th international conference on networked learning 2008* (pp. 576–582). Lancaster University.

CREDE. (2021). *The CREDE five standards for effective pedagogy and learning.* https://manoa.hawaii.edu/coe/credenational/the-crede-five-standards-for-effective-pedagogy-and-learning/

Cummings, C., Mason, D., Shelton, K., & Baur, K. (2017). Active learning strategies for online and blended learning environments. In Information Resources Management

Association, IRMA (Ed.), *Flipped instruction: Breakthroughs in research and practice* (pp. 88–114). IGI Global.

Darling-Hammond, L. (2010). *Evaluating teacher effectiveness. How teacher performance assessments can measure and improve teaching.* Center for American Progress.

Downes, S. (2010). New technology supporting informal learning. *Journal of Emerging Technologies in Web Intelligence*, 2(1), 27–33.

Entz, S. (2006). *Why pedagogy matters: The importance of teaching in a standards-based environment.* Forum on Public Policy and The Center for Research on Education, Diversity and Excellence (CREDE).

Ertmer, P. A., & Newby, T. J. (2013). Behaviorism, cognitivism, constructivism: Comparing critical features from an instructional design perspective. *Performance Improvement Quarterly*, 26(2), 43–71.

Godlewska, A., Beyer, W., Whetstone, S., Schaefli, L., Rose, J., Talan, B., Kamin-Patterson, S., Lamb, C., & Forcione, M., (2019). Converting a large lecture class to an active blended learning class: Why, how, and what we learned. *Journal of Geography in Higher Education*, 43(1), 96–115.

Goggins, S. P., Laffey, J., & Gallagher, M. (2011). Completely online group formation and development: Small groups as socio-technical systems. *Information Technology & People*, 24(2), 104–133.

Harel, I. E., & Papert, S. E. (1991). *Constructionism*. Ablex.

Hargreaves, A., & Fullan, M. (2012). *Professional capital. Transforming teaching in every school.* Teachers College Press.

Hidson, E., & Leask, M. (2022). *Pedagogy*. In S. Capel, E. Hidson, J. Lawrence, M. Leask, & S. Younie (Eds.), *Learning to teach in the secondary school: A companion to school experience.* Routledge.

Hordatt Gentles, C., & Leask, M. (2020). ICET/MESHGuides. *Teacher experiences and practices during COVID-19.* Interim Report.

Hung, D. (2002). Situated cognition and problem-based learning: implications for learning and instruction with technology. *Journal of Interactive Learning Research*, 13(4), 393–415.

Hwang, G. J., Lai, C. L., & Wang, S. Y. (2015). Seamless flipped learning: A mobile technology-enhanced flipped classroom with effective learning strategies. *Journal of Computers in Education*, 2(4), 449–473.

ICET/MESHGuides. (2021). *Teacher experiences and practices during COVID-19. A global report.* https://www.icet4u.org/docs/ICET_MESH_REPORT_AUGUST_2021.pdf

Johnson, C. M. (2001). A survey of current research on online communities of practice. *The Internet and Higher Education*, 4(1), 45–60.

Loughran, J. J. (2010). *What expert teachers do: Enhancing professional knowledge for classroom practice.* Allen & Unwin.

Leask, M., & Younie, S. (2001). Communal constructivist theory: Pedagogy of information and communications technology & internationalisation of the curriculum. *Journal of Information Technology for Teacher Education*, *10*(1/2), 117–134.

Leask, M., & Younie, S. (2021). *Education for all in times of crisis: Lessons from Covid-19*. Routledge.

Moore, A., Edwards, G., Halpin, D., & George, R. (2002). Compliance, resistance and pragmatism: The (re)construction of schoolteacher identities in a period of intensive educational reform. *British Educational Research Journal*, *28*(4), 551–565.

Nilmanat, R. (2011). Investigating image usage and tacit knowledge sharing in online communities. *International Journal of Innovation and Learning*, *10*(4), 350–364.

OECD. (2005). *Teachers matter: Attracting, developing and retaining effective teachers*. OECD Publishing.

Palmer, E., Lomer, S., & Bashliyska, I. (2017). *Overcoming barriers to student engagement in active blended learning*. University of Northampton. https://www.northampton.ac.uk/ilt/wp-content/uploads/sites/2/2017/10/Student-Engagement-with-ABL-Interim-Report-v3-October-2017.pdf

Pennycook, A. (2001). The politics of pedagogy. In A. Pennycook (Ed.), *Critical applied linguistics: A critical introduction* (pp. 114–140). Lawrence Erlbaum Associates.

Richardson, W. (2010). *Blogs, wikis, podcasts and other powerful web tools for classrooms*. Corwin.

Royle, K., Stager, S., & Traxler, J. (2014). Teacher development with mobiles: Comparative critical factors. *Prospects*, *44*(1), 29–42.

Saadatmand, M., & Kumpulainen, K. (2014). Participants' perceptions of learning and networking in connectivist MOOCs. *MERLOT Journal of Online Learning and Teaching*, *10*(1), 16–30.

Sachs, J. (2003). *The activist teaching profession*. Open University Press.

Siemens, G. (2005). Connectivism: A learning theory for the digital age. *International Journal of Instructional Technology and Distance Learning*, *2*(1), 3–10.

Stevenson, H., & Gilliland, A. (2016). The teachers voice: Teacher Unions at the heart of a new democratic professionalism. In J. Evers & R. Kneyber (Eds.), *Flip the system. Changing education from the ground up* (pp. 108–119). Routledge.

Stronach, I., Corbin, B., McNamara, O., Stark, S., & Warne, T. (2001). *Towards an uncertain politics of professionalism: Teacher and nurse identities in flux*. Manchester Metropolitan University.

UNESCO. (2020). *Teacher Task Force calls to support 63 million teachers touched by the COVID-19 crisis*. https://en.unesco.org/news/teacher-task-force-calls-support-63-million-teachers-touched-covid-19-crisis

Vygotsky, L. S. (1978). *Mind in society: The development of higher psychological processes*. Harvard University Press.

Wareing, S. (2021). Measuring the success of active blended learning. In B. C. Padilla Rodriguez & C. A. Armellini (Eds.), *Cases on active blended learning in higher education* (pp. 291–302). IGI Global.

Wechsler, M. E., & Shields, P. M. (2008). *Teaching quality in California: A new perspective to guide policy*. The Center for the Future of Teaching and Learning.

Wenger, E. (1998). *Communities of practice: Learning, meaning and identity*. Cambridge University Press.

Young, M. L., & Tseng, F. C. (2008). Interplay between physical and virtual settings for online interpersonal trust formation in knowledge-sharing practice. *Cyberpsychology & Behavior*, *11*(1), 55–64.

Younie, S. (2007). *Integrating ICT into teachers professional practice: The cultural dynamics of change* [PhD thesis]. De Montfort University.

Younie, S., & Leask, M. (2013). *Teaching with technologies: The essential guide*. Open University Press.

CHAPTER 7

Developing Emancipatory Online Learning Environments in Quality Teacher Education

Gisselle Tur Porres and Washington Ires Correa

Abstract

The chapter discusses the development of emancipatory online learning environments in quality teacher education. Under the uncertainty of a changing world caused by COVID-19 pandemic, teachers were required to adapt their teaching to online learning environments. Additionally, they had to learn how to design interactive and quality online learning environments. Against this backdrop, it is necessary to raise new questions about what quality teaching means in online learning environments. Discourses on quality teaching are commonly associated with teacher effectiveness. We argue, however, that quality teaching in teacher education also implies thinking about emancipatory pedagogical approaches in the development of (online) learning environments. In this sense, we explore emancipatory ways of understanding quality in online learning teacher education. First, we elaborate on quality debates in teacher education. Second, we focus on a specific dimension of quality teaching, that is, the development of (online) learning environments in teacher education. Third, we explore critical perspectives and emancipatory pedagogical approaches in teacher education. Last, we advise teaching strategies to create online learning environments with a focus on emancipatory pedagogical approaches. As a result, teaching strategies are suggested to connect quality online learning environments to emancipatory pedagogical approaches.

Keywords

quality teaching – teacher education – pedagogy – emancipation – online learning environment – COVID-19

© GISSELLE TUR PORRES AND WASHINGTON IRES CORREA, 2023
DOI:10.1163/9789004536609_008

1   Introduction

In times of crisis, under the uncertainty of a changing world, teacher educators have been required to adapt their teaching from face-to-face to online learning environments. This shift has been a tendency around the globe caused by COVID-19 pandemic. Teacher educators not only have faced the need to learn how to design quality online learning environments, but also most of them have had to learn how to work and to integrate technologies to their educational practices (Arroyo et al., 2018; Tur Porres & Ires Correa, 2020). Furthermore, this shift has also implied a challenge for students, regarding connectivity, internet access and electronic devices to be used during lectures. For instance, some families must share one computer with various family members and students access lectures with their cell-phones.

In this chapter, we tackle the issue of developing emancipatory online learning environments in quality teacher education. Taking this on board, this chapter raises questions about what quality teaching means in online learning environments and what are potential implications for teacher education. We claim that online teaching is not only about learning how to use Information and Communication Technologies (ICT) tools, virtual platforms, among other resources, and adapting teaching strategies to online learning environments, but it is also about thinking education in new emancipatory ways. To address this issue, quality debates in teacher education, and more particularly, quality online learning environments in teacher education are elaborated. Then, critical perspectives and emancipatory pedagogical approaches with a focus on quality teacher education are discussed. Last, we share some teaching strategies to inspire emancipatory pedagogical approaches within (quality) online learning environments.

2   Quality in Teacher Education

Quality in teacher education is a concept that can be understood from different traditions and debates; it can be related to evaluation, effectiveness, among other standpoints. For instance, debates on quality teaching are commonly associated with teacher effectiveness (Borich, 2000; Hénard & Roseveare, 2012; Ko & Sammons, 2012; Mincu, 2015; Lampert et al., 2018; Rice, 2003; Sakarneh, 2011). Nonetheless, we argue that quality teacher education also implies thinking about pedagogical approaches that enhance the emancipatory potential of both face-to-face and online learning environments. Hence, we explore ways of understanding quality teaching in online learning teacher education along with critical perspectives and emancipatory pedagogical approaches in education.

With regards to quality in teacher education, Hénard and Roseveare (2012, p. 7) have paid considerable attention to the dimensions of quality teaching,

> including the effective design of curriculum and course content, a variety of learning contexts (including guided independent study, project-based learning, collaborative learning, experimentation, etc.), soliciting and using feedback, and effective assessment of learning outcomes. It also involves well-adapted learning environments and student support services.

In their contribution, the authors highlighted a multilevel interdependent approach to understand quality teaching at institutional, programme, and individual levels. At institutional level, the authors gave substantial attention to 'projects such as policy design, and support to organisation and internal quality assurance systems' (Hénard & Roseveare, 2012, p. 7). With respect to programme level, they elaborated on actions for measuring, enhancing the design, content and delivery of the programmes within a department or a school. Finally, the authors discussed the individual level, including

> initiatives that help teachers achieve their mission, encouraging them to innovate and to support improvements to student learning and adopt a learner oriented focus. These three levels are essential and interdependent. However, supporting quality teaching at the programme level is key so as to ensure improvement in quality teaching at the discipline level and across the institution. (Hénard & Roseveare, 2012, p. 7)

According to Wang et al. (2011, p. 333) quality teaching in teacher education is not only a matter of applying cognitive resources, but rather of 'changing prospective teachers' beliefs through engaging them in reflections about their own learning and teaching experiences and challenging them with alternative ideas and models of teaching'. Similar findings emerged from Loughran (2017) who reflected on the context wherein teacher educators work and how quality teaching and learning environments can be promoted. This approach indicates that quality teaching implies thinking about specific teaching and learning contexts. In common with Greene (1988), quality suggests a link between teaching, thinking, and transforming the reality.

In following this argument, quality debates that prescribe outcomes in teacher education, based on dominant discourses of effectiveness, 'marks the end of diversity, movement and experimentation (…), fixing it in perpetuity to a tried, proven and unchanging formula' (Dahlberg et al., 2013, p. VIII). This 'unchanging formula' in an uncertain world does not work. Moreover, a contextualised research is needed to face with rapid changes; what works in a particular context, may not work in another one. In this light, there are no 'universal' answers for good/quality practices, rather, there are local practices that may teach us what works in local contexts and perhaps can be transferred to other contexts as lessons learned. To some extent, these studies challenge our understanding of quality teaching in different local contexts and the required transition from 'in-person' to 'online' teaching contexts.

2.1   What Is Quality about in Online Learning Environments?

First, it is necessary to define what online learning is about; it refers to teaching and learning processes that are mediated by virtual learning environments. In contrast with traditional classroom contexts, interactions can occur at different times and places through the web platform (Bernard et al., 2014; Chigeza & Halbert, 2014; Northey et al., 2015; Pellas & Kazanidis, 2015; UNESCO, 2002).

To discuss about quality in online learning, we must address the distinction between online education and remote teaching. Interesting discussion on this issue one might find in the work: *Reimagining the new pedagogical possibilities for universities post-Covid-19* (see Peters et al., 2020).

With regards to learning environments, even if it is generally agreed that are a relevant dimension in quality teaching, quality online learning environments need to be studied further in COVID-19 pandemic and post-pandemic contexts. Interestingly, the design of collaborative and challenging online learning environments become significant to support students (Bransford et al., 2000; Brindley et al., 2009; Capdeferro & Romero, 2012; Kumi-Yeboah, 2018).

Quality discourses on prescriptive solutions about technology applied to education practices should be challenged to the context and the local needs (Biesta, 2009, 2016; Dahlberg et al., 2013; Snoek et al., 2012). Despite the use we can make of open educational resources platform, cultural diversity required a thoughtful design of online learning practices.

In line with this, it is relevant to discuss what will happen after COVID-19 pandemic and what will be the place of school and face-to-face learning against online education. König et al. (2020, pp. 168–169) pointed out that

> … school remains the obligatory environment for student learning with teachers responsible for providing structured learning opportunities (…) [S]chools should develop their concepts towards blended learning, that is, a strategic combination of presence at school and structured approaches to student learning at home.

Against this background, a crucial question is 'what makes an online learning environment good in COVID-19 times? Studies about learning environments have suggested that interactive environments may support quality and meaningful students' learning (Bascia, 2014). Accordingly, we argue that quality online environments may support learning when reflective practices play a role (Schön, 1983, 1990). An environment, therefore, that engages teachers and students with reflective practices and action, with clear purposes and challenges, will have an impact in the learning experience. Like Reggio Emilia schools' approach, the environment may become a 'third teacher' that 'opens' the doors for participation and culture (Ceppi & Zini, 1998; Tur Porres, 2020). The concept used in Reggio Emilia schools of the environment as third teacher was elaborated by Malaguzzi (2001). Also, Hoyuelos (2005) pointed out that learning environments should be collectively designed to motivate participation of all stakeholders within education contexts; that is, the teacher, the students, the community. Moreover, Rinaldi (2009) highlighted the flexibility of learning environments to collect personal and group stories documented through dialogue. We agree that the design of learning environments is also important in online learning and it can transform the experience of teachers and students to engage with the content. A central issue in developing a contextualised online learning environments is to consider culture relevant content and to encourage participation and critical reflection. Accordingly, integrating interactive tools to motivate the discussion, the content appraisal and critical reflection among participants is central to promote change in education during COVID-19 times.

3 Emancipatory Pedagogical Approaches in Teacher Education

The tension between autonomy and adapation to the status quo is a core process to understand emancipation in education (Adorno, 1998). Interestingly, the concept of emancipation has different roots, according to political, philosophical, economic, social, and educational perspectives. (Biesta, 2008; Bingham & Biesta, 2010). For instance, in the critical theory tradition, emancipation is acknowledged as an act of liberation of oppressive circumstances. This central notion of autonomy and liberation can be identified in Freire's well-known book, *Pedagogy of the oppressed* (Freire, 2014) that develops a pedagogical approach to think liberatory and emancipatory education opportunities through critical dialogue, conscientisation and change, for individual and social transformation.

With regards to emancipatory pedagogies, we agree with Nouri and *Sajjadi* (2014, p. 78) that they involve a way of thinking about, negotiating, and transforming the relationships in classroom teaching, the production of knowledge, the institutional structures of the school, and the social and material relations of the wider community, society, and nation-state.

In this work, emancipatory pedagogical approaches are understood as a critical dimension that challenges and transforms pedagogical relations among the teacher, the students, the content, and the online learning environment. This approach is related to the work of Freire (2014) wherein emancipation emerges in the pedagogical relation through critical dialogue and conscientisation, that ultimately leads to action upon individual and social transformation.

The ideas developed by Freire (2014) with regards to education as a means of liberation for the oppressed population, gained a relevant place in social, political, and educational movements of resistance towards oppressive structures. Freire's problem-posing education helped teachers and students engaging with processes of inquiry and critical thinking to overcome oppression and to achieve equality. For Freire (2014), the world is the object of reflection and action for change. Thus, social and cultural reality matters in education for emancipation and change. In this regard, a critical reading and dialogue of the world may lead to become aware of power relations and possible mechanisms of oppression operating in society.

Moreover, for Freire (2014) by reading the 'word' we could read the 'world', and hence, we could decode and transform reality. A pedagogical approach used for decoding the word and the world was the 'culture circles' that enabled participants to read the world in meaningful ways. (Tur Porres et al., 2014). In this way, Freire's pedagogical approach involved political engagement within educational practices and emancipatory processes that lead to individual and social transformation. As a result, through education individuals may become emancipated and orient their actions towards broader social struggles to achieve social emancipation.

Consequently, Freire (2014) believed that through education we could change existing conditions of inequality (oppressed/oppressors) through a three-step process:
- naming the world (Word),
- reflecting on it (Work), and
- acting upon reality towards social change (Praxis).

In common with Freire's view (2014), we argue that bringing the world into 'virtual' classrooms may contribute to promote critical dialogue, conscientisation and action towards thinking and transforming the world surrounding us. Furthermore, reading the world, within COVID-19 pandemic, may provide teachers and students the opportunity of acting upon the transformation of pedagogical approaches and relations mediated by technology and online interactions.

Likewise, Peters et al. (2020, p. 2) we agree that 'the COVID-19 pandemic offers us the opportunity to rethink not only new digital, online, and pedagogical possibilities but also the basic purposes of education, and how renewed vision of education might be harnessed to develop more democratic and just societies'.

Following from the above, we argue that online teaching in COVID-19 pandemic should not be framed as a simple adaptation from in-person teaching to online learning with the use of ICT tools. Instead, we state that creating emancipatory online learning environments is a renewed way of understanding education.

4 Method

This study used a review on the move from face-to-face pedagogical approaches to virtual learning environments that teacher educators have faced with the emergency of COVID-19 pandemic. Therefore, the review and conceptual framework were oriented to relevant published scholarly works on three domains: (a) quality in teacher education, (b) online learning environments and (c) emancipatory pedagogical approaches. This method helped us gaining understanding of quality and online learning environments in teacher education, to suggest teaching strategies that motivate quality online learning environments with a focus on emancipatory pedagogical approaches.

5 Rethinking Online (Emancipatory) Learning Environments: A Call for Quality in Teacher Education

Designing quality and emancipatory online learning environments implies a contextualised exploration of good practices required in the transition from 'in-person' to 'online' teaching contexts. With 'good practices' we refer to consider local needs and cultural diversity towards the development of online contents and learning environments. In this light, we argue that an emancipatory approach to online learning includes considering environments that respond to the emergency of COVID-19 and reflect on new ways of understanding education.

Following from the above, the design of emancipatory online learning environments may allow us – in agreement with Freire (2014) – to bring the 'world' into discussion in 'virtual classrooms'. Online learning as well as face-to-face teaching may contribute to promote critical dialogue and conscientisation towards individual and social change. Thus, emancipatory online learning environments need to create conditions for participation in meaningful ways. A collaborative approach must be supported, to share opinions with respect and an in-depth level of understanding.

In common with Simons and Masschelein (2008) who elaborated on learning environments that redefined teachers as designers, we argue that teachers' pedagogical approach is not to become a 'designer' of virtual environments; however, the development of reflective and inquiry-based environments may help supporting emancipatory pedagogical approaches in online learning teacher education. Furthermore, likewise Masschelein and Simons (2015, p. 93) we agree that

> ICT may have a unique potential to create attentiveness (indeed, the screen has the ability to attract our attention in an unprecedented way) and to present and unlock the world – at least when ICT is freed from the many attempts to privatise, regulate and market it. (…) but the challenge is whether and how it can truly bring something to life, generate interest, bring about the experience of sharing (gathering around a 'common good') and enable one to renew the world. In this sense, making information, knowledge and expertise available is not the same as making something public. Screens – just as a black board – might have a tremendous ability to attract attention, exact concentration and gather people around something, but the challenge is to explore how screens help to create a (common) presence and enable study and practice.

Against this background, online learning environments that support the attention of students and teachers towards 'a thing in common' may also create opportunities for emancipation with a Rancièrean's (1991) perspective. Thus, 'directing the students' attention to observe, to think, to verify and to translate for themselves' (Tur Porres et al., 2020, p. 30) represents a challenge to connect online learning with emancipatory learning environments.

Equally important to direct students' attention towards a thing in common is to transform online learning environments in communities that construct knowledge in own creative ways. This includes becoming familiar and directing one's own attention to ICT tools, virtual platforms and interactive resources that embrace diversity for action.

5.1 Teaching Strategies with a Focus on Emancipatory Pedagogical Approaches

The conceptual framework has been oriented to review and analyse relevant published scholarly works concerning quality in teacher education and (emancipatory) online learning environments during COVID-19 pandemic and beyond. This qualitative analysis of scholarly works on quality teacher education and online learning environments is accompanied by some teaching strategies proposals in view of emancipatory pedagogical approaches.

A model that includes an emancipatory pedagogical approach in the pedagogical relation among the teachers, the students, the content, and the online learning environments is used (see Figure 7.1).

In this model,
- The educational setting matters, hence, the online learning environment becomes a source for emancipatory pedagogical approaches.
- The emancipatory pedagogical approaches are situated in the pedagogical relation among the teacher, the students, the content, and the online learning environment.

FIGURE 7.1 Emancipatory pedagogical approaches in online learning environments

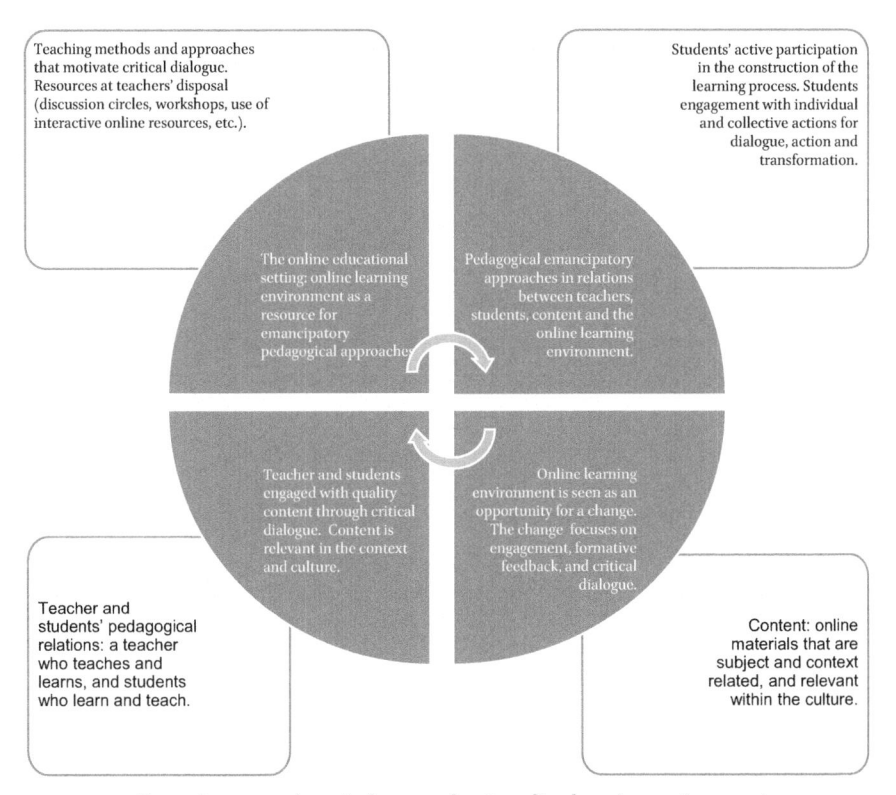

- The teachers and students engage with opportunities for dialogue, discussion groups/boards, pre-session and live session talks, activities, challenges, projects.

Against this background, it is worth mentioning that we do not aim at designing online tools or websites to work with students; rather, we elaborate on the need of creating conditions for critical dialogue, reflection, and action. In this sense, at mentoring teaching approach in online classes is important, thus, the number of students per group is also significant to achieve an emancipatory pedagogical approach, and to reconnect quality in teacher education with online learning. Also, formative assessment and feedback is needed in this approach. In doing so, the use of 'breakout rooms' with a purpose for discussion are useful to help students actively engaging in the discussion. It is also interesting to have a spokesperson per group that shares the opinion of the small group to motivate the discussion in the broad group. Additionally, the way we interact in the broad group can be adapted to the group needs; for instance, students' opinion can be shared through a *Padlet*, the interactive whiteboard annotation tool of *Zoom*, among other options. These tools are a way of facilitating dialogue, but they do not replace the content and conversation that emerge within the group. This is a significant point of departure to create quality online learning environments, the interactive tools are not the aim and outcome of online learning, rather they are ways of facilitating education. Moreover, a model that develops quality online learning environments needs to be advanced on inclusive and intercultural perspectives to fulfil the potential of all participants.

5.1.1   Examples of Emancipatory Practices

To illustrate the proposed model, below we describe two examples that are directly connected with the model and ways of putting it into practice.

5.1.1.1   *Example 1*

In this example,
- The educational setting is online; it considers asynchronous activities (pre-live session tasks) and synchronous activities (during the live session).
- The emancipatory pedagogical approach emerged in the pedagogical relation among the teacher, the students, the content, and the online learning environment through the creation of online 'discussion circles'.
- The teachers and students engage with opportunities for critical dialogue through 'discussion circles'. It is significant to consider that the selected text for discussion must accomplish the prerequisite of being inclusive, context related and hence relevant within the culture.

The example of practice to integrate emancipatory approaches in line with Freire's view is to include 'discussion circles' (similar to Freire's 'culture circles') during live (online) sessions. Discussion circles' can also be adapted from 'Dialogic Literacy Circles' for sharing readings and creation of meanings (Martínez-Valdivia et al., 2021). In doing so, first, students should read a suggested text assigned for the pre-task session. Then, students are asked to highlight the ideas and/or concepts that call their attention. These ideas and/or concepts can include statements that students agree with or not, statements that they do not completely understand and they want to share with the group and open the discussion of the 'circle' during the live session. It is advisable that the selected texts are relevant for the context, culture, subject matter. And furthermore, it is important that the text reflects the students' world and includes 'power relations', current challenges and constraints that engage teachers and students with action and change.

Once in the live session, the teacher or students will facilitate dialogue within 'discussion circle'. Critical dialogue must emerge in a safe and secure place to express opinions, to listen, and to show respect with the opinion of others. Thus, critical thinking is encouraged as well as an effective use of the language. Like in learning communities, it is necessary that the person who facilitates the dialogue, asks participants to register on a list for sharing their opinions. A list that is flexibly constructed with the purpose of facilitating dialogue.

In this manner, the first participant on the list will share with the group the idea, concept and/or paragraph selected. The person shall mention the page number of the highlighted paragraph to help participants directing their attention to that part of the text and discussion. The person will read the concept and/or paragraph; after reading they will share with the circle why they have decided to select and share that idea; what have called their attention; what kind of agreement and/or disagreement, concepts and/or paragraph imply.

Once the discussion is opened, all participants are asked to comment and give their opinions in relation to the idea, concept, and/or paragraph discussed. The person who facilitates the discussion shall ask to other participants if they have chosen the same concept or idea and why. Then, the second participant on the spokesperson list will be asked to share the idea and/or concept selected and will follow the same process for the discussion.

It is important to stimulate the discussion with open-ended questions that the facilitator will wrap-up with main ideas and/or concepts discussed during the 'discussion circle' in action.

Following from the above, the suggested 'discussion circle' is a practice that can be implemented for the active participation of teachers and students in the construction of learning. Also, it allows participants to questioning and constructing own knowledge whilst learning from others. This practice, in line with Freire's pedagogical approach supports pedagogical relations that abolish the position of the teacher 'who knows everything' and students 'who know nothing'.

In this light, the 'discussion circle' proposal for online learning environments is closed related to Freire's 'culture circles' (Freire, 2014) whereas the selected ideas and/or concepts that are context related become Freire's 'thematic universe'. Additionally, the selection of words and themes that belong to familiar contexts of the participants may be identified as Freirean' generative words and themes' because they will enable students to generate other words and themes to read the world. Last, the decoding process of becoming conscious of possible social, political and/or economic oppressive conditions and/or power relations take place to act upon change. Becoming conscious of oppressive conditions is the first step towards individual emancipation (or individual liberation) and social emancipation (liberation of the collective towards social change).

Informed by Freire's view, we suggest that online learning environments that support collective interests and actions for social change show new ways of understanding education with a focus on emancipation. Moreover, the attempt to encourage critical dialogue through different texts, contexts and situations may lead to 'naming the word and the world' whilst acting upon change. In addition, students must be addressed as competent citizens in raising critical awareness. Conscientisation is not straightforward; however, critical dialogue can be constructed within online learning environments in different times and places, for instance, in live sessions; discussion boards; videos; pre-(live)session tasks.

Online learning environments that promote a student-teacher relation of questioning and critical reflection, create opportunities of emancipatory discussion towards the design of virtual (emancipatory) pedagogical approaches and relations. In addition, COVID-19 pandemic may become a topic of reflection on unequal living conditions among students; lack of connectivity and/or access to technological devices; lack of space to work comfortably during live sessions. In this light, Freire's claim that education should lead to social change becomes possible, and hence, it is possible to understand that living conditions are potentially open to transformation.

5.1.1.2   *Example 2*
In this example,
– The educational setting is online; it considers asynchronous activities (pre-live session tasks) and synchronous activities (during the live session).

- The emancipatory pedagogical approach emerged in the pedagogical relation among the teacher and the students that integrates body self-awareness and metacognition practices ('thinking about the learning experience') in the online learning environment.
- The teachers and students engage with opportunities of metacognition and body awareness' exercises in the online pedagogical relation. Despite the pedagogical relation is mediated by online learning settings (and devices), the 'physical' experience of our bodies matters.

Thus far, this example contributes to emancipatory approaches in online learning environments with the inclusion of body awareness and metacognition activities in this new way of framing pedagogical relations. Providing tools for body awareness in online learning environments suggests 'an integral process of metacognition of the body, culture, education, and emotions, which poses a challenge for an autonomous work based on research and self-education ...' (Tur Porres & Ires Correa, 2020, p. 84). In this sense, it is suggested to integrate teaching and learning practices that include techniques for integrating our body in teacher education, in both face-to-face and online learning environments.

One common concern among teachers is the lack of connection with students' body language and non-verbal communication that help teachers 'reading' or 'interpreting' e.g. if students are engaged with a suggested activity or discussion. In addition, there are ongoing discussions about the need of turning cameras on/off during live sessions to create a lively experience and/or to simulate 'in person teaching'. This mainly depends on the group needs and/or agreements made between students and teachers. For example, in the Ecuadorian context (where we used to work) it was difficult to ask students to turn the cameras on during live sessions because most students had connection issues and the 'video on' fast consumed the internet data. Other situations that may prevent students to turning their cameras on are related to privacy issues.

In new online learning contexts with live sessions by turning their cameras off students preserve their privacy. For instance, in the Welsh context (where we currently work) many students share rooms and accommodations to alleviate university expenses, and for the majority of students finding a place to connect, in private, without disruptions have become a challenge.

Following from the above, in this example, we do not aim at requiring students to turn the videos on to become aware of the 'body experience' and engaged with the online (live) sessions; they can decide whether turning their cameras on/off according to their own living conditions and situations. Rather, we invite re-thinking ways of engaging with each other, of integrating the body in this pedagogical encounter mediated by online learning environments. Thus, we invite teachers and students to think about new ways of relating to each other in online sessions, and to explore emancipatory pedagogical approaches 'in terms of self-knowledge, self-education, and body metacognition' (Tur Porres & Ires Correa, 2020, p. 84). In this sense, inspiring body awareness' experiences in virtual environments will allow teacher and students to create emancipatory opportunities mediated by ICT 'without having to redeem the body in such a process-and provoking critical reflection' (Tur Porres & Ires Correa, 2020, p. 85).

A sequence of activities can be suggested for asynchronous or synchronous tasks that, e.g. include rhythm, movement, expression, and communication. For instance, we can suggest students some exercises, e.g. Tai-Chi, meditation in movement practices to go for a 'conscious' walk outdoors. Accordingly, we can invite students to write, recall and capture their memories on a diary of self-conscious learning experiences during the COVID-19 pandemic. For instance, students can reflect on their own learning experience during the pandemic: How and where they feel more comfortable reading texts for pre-session tasks: outdoors or indoors? Do their concentration and attention span change if they start studying after a 'conscious' walk? Do they feel that integrating the body experience to online learning have an impact on their well-being? Some experiences of these self-knowledge diaries can be shared at different moments of the online modules, e.g. at the beginning, middle and end of term, to encourage a process of meta-cognition (to think about their own learning experience). The reflections will help teacher and students engaging with learning in meaningful ways; understanding education in online learning environments in emancipatory ways; and critically reflecting on self-education processes that include ways of being in the virtual classroom, whilst respecting students' learning pace, style and rhythm.

This diary practice helps students critically reflecting on online learning experiences beyond the specific subject content. It engages students to address their own concerns, strengths, and weakness of online learning during COVID-19 and post-pandemic. In this chapter, our focus is on teacher education, thus, this practice also serves for the purpose of students' reflecting on their own teaching practices and re-thinking their future as teachers. Likewise, the diary practice can be included in our teaching strategies as a pedagogical documentation tool to document the online learning experience with the use of written narratives, photographs, screenshots, among other ways of capturing the reflective practice (Tur Porres, 2020).

Integrating narratives of self-learning experiences, in both face-to-face and online learning environments, encourage critical thinking in the pedagogical relationship among the teacher, the students, and the online learning environment. Thus, critical dialogue may emerge within the pedagogical relation of the virtual classroom, 'that offered not only a theoretical debate about the link between body and corporality, but also generated a rich (…) encounter through the practice of conscious body exercises proposed by the instructor' (Tur Porres & Ires Correa, 2020, p. 88).

In this light, the pedagogical approach is to 'become conscious of the importance of integrating the body in their own pedagogical practices (…) and to increase critical and autonomous reflection, for example, through forums' (Tur Porres & Ires Correa, 2020, p. 89). Likewise, in person teaching, online learning environments may include asynchronous and/or synchronous activities that allow participants to develop a metacognition process of their own learning experience.

Consequently, the suggested diary and digital narrative is coherent with Freire's emancipatory and liberatory education claim of 'reading the word and the world' to transform our living conditions. This pedagogical approach allows participants to critically reflect on online learning experiences during the pandemic and to stimulate actions of change to fulfil the best of individual and collective capacities.

6 Conclusion: Designing Online Learning Environments That Foster Emancipatory Pedagogical Approaches

In this chapter, the need to re-think what good teaching means in online learning environments has been stressed. Massively, during COVID-19 pandemic, face-to-face teaching has been translated to virtual classrooms. Despite the transition to online learning has been part of adaptation and mitigation strategies, we acknowledge that online teaching is not only about adapting teaching strategies to online learning environments, but it is also about thinking education in new emancipatory ways. Thus, online learning environments need to be thought as synchronous and asynchronous spaces that embrace current needs of integrating emancipatory pedagogical approaches in both face-to-face and online learning, in classrooms and online environments. Furthermore, we need to critically reflect on new ways of engaging in online learning environments without redeeming the body experience in the pedagogical relation (Tur Porres & Ires Correa, 2020).

Moreover, in online learning environments local needs and culture matter. Thus, it is necessary to reflect on own ways of doing, saying and thinking about online learning, that include emancipatory pedagogical approaches in the relation among the teachers, the students, the content, and the online learning environment in teacher education. We have argued that Freire's emancipatory approach (2002, 2014) contributes to raise awareness to changing living conditions. More, in COVID-19 times re-thinking online learning environments from a Freirean perspective that helps teachers and students creating conditions for conscientisation and social transformation should be noted. This includes re-thinking self-knowledge and self-education experiences in view of emancipatory pedagogical approaches, to gain new understandings of online education and learning.

As a result, the inclusion of teaching strategies that connect quality online learning environments to emancipatory pedagogical approaches, focuses on a type of online education that is not a translation of in-person teaching experiences to online platforms caused by COVID-19 pandemic. Instead, this new way of understanding education requires teachers and students to engage with each other (individually and collectively), the content, and the online learning environment in critical and emancipatory ways. In this light, designing quality and emancipatory online learning environments in teacher education implies leaving behind 'universal' answers for 'best practices'. Instead, it invites thinking about quality in context, with inclusive and cultural perspectives that create conditions for meaningful and self-constructed ways of learning, doing and saying in online pedagogical relations.

References

Adorno, T. W. (1998). Educación para la emancipación. In G. Kadelbach (Ed.). *Conferencias y conversaciones con Hellmut Becker (1959–1969)*. Ediciones Morata, S.L.

Arroyo Vera, Z., Fernández Prieto, S. F., Barreto Zambrano, L. B., & Paz Enrique, L. E. (2018). Entornos virtuales de aprendizaje en comunidades de práctica de docentes universitarios del Ecuador. *Revista Ensayos Pedagógicos, 13*(2), 185–200.

Bascia, N. (2014). *The school context model: How school environments shape students' opportunities to learn*. People for Education, Measuring What Matters.

Bernard, M. B., Borokhovski, E., Schmid, R. F., Tamim, R. M., & Abrami, P. C. (2014). A meta-analysis of blended learning and technology use in higher education: From the general to the applied. *Journal of Computing in Higher Education, 26*(1), 87–122.

Biesta, G. J. J. (2008). Toward a new 'logic' of emancipation: Foucault and Rancière. In N. C. Burbules (Ed.), *Philosophy of Education Society* (pp. 169–177). Philosophy of Education Society.

Biesta, G. J. J. (2009). Good education in an age of measurement: On the need to reconnect with the question of purpose in education. *Educational Assessment, Evaluation and Accountability, 21*(1), 33–46.

Biesta, G. J. J. (2016). *Good education in an age of measurement: Ethics, politics, democracy.* Routledge.

Bingham, C., & Biesta, G. (2010). *Jacques Rancière: Education, truth, emancipation.* Continuum International Publishing Group.

Borich, G. D. (2000). *Effective teaching methods* (4th ed.). Merrill.

Bransford, J. D., Brown, A. L., & Cocking, R. R. (Eds.). (2000). *How people learn: Brain, mind, experience, and school.* National Academy Press.

Brindley, J., Blaschke, L. M., & Walti, C. (2009). Creating effective collaborative learning groups in an online environment. *The International Review of Research in Open and Distance Learning, 10*(3), 1–18.

Capdeferro, N., & Romero, M. (2012). Are online learners frustrated with collaborative learning experiences? *The International Review of Research in Open and Distance Learning, 13*(2), 26–44.

Ceppi, G., & Zini, M. (Eds.). (1998). *Children, spaces, relations. Metaproject for an environment for young children.* Reggio Children and Reggio Emilia, Domus Academy Research Center.

Chigeza, P., & Halbert, K. (2014). Navigating e-learning and blended learning for preservice teachers: Redesigning for engagement, access and efficiency. *Australian Journal of Teacher Education, 39*(11), 133–146.

Dahlberg, G., Moss, P., & Pence, A. (2013). *Beyond quality in early childhood education and care. Languages of evaluation.* Routledge.

Freire, P. (2002). *Education for critical consciousness.* Continuum International Publishing.

Freire, P. (2014). *Pedagogy of the oppressed: 30th anniversary edition.* Bloomsbury.

Greene, M. (1988). Quality in teacher education. *Educational Policy, 2*(3), 235–250.

Hénard, F., & Roseveare, D. (2012). *Fostering quality teaching in higher education. An IMHE guide for higher education institutions.* OECD. http://www.oecd.org/education/imhe/

Hoyuelos, A. (2005). La escuela como ámbito estético educativo. In I. Cabanellas & C. Eslava (Eds.), *Territorios de la Infancia. Diálogos entre la arquitectura y pedagogía* (pp. 166–175). Graó.

Ko, J., & Sammons, P. (2012). *Effective teaching: A review of research. Executive summary report prepared for CfBT.* University of Oxford, Department of Education.

König, J., Jäger-Biela, D. J., & Glutsch, N. (2020). Adapting to online teaching during COVID-19 school closure: Teacher education and teacher competence effects among early career teachers in Germany. *European Journal of Teacher Education, 43*(4), 608–622.

Kumi-Yeboah, A. (2018). Designing a cross-cultural collaborative online learning framework for online instructors. *Online Learning, 22*(4), 181–201.

Lampert, J., Burnett, B., Comber, B., Ferguson, A., & Barnes, N. (2018). Quality teaching discourses. A contested terrain. In S. Gannon, R. Hattam, & W. Sawyer (Eds.), *Resisting educational inequality: Reframing policy and practice in schools serving vulnerable communities* (pp. 150–158). Routledge.

Loughran, J. (2017). Quality in teacher education: Challenging assumptions, building understanding through foundation principles. In X. Zhu, A. L. Goodwin, & H. Zhang (Eds.), *Quality of teacher education and learning. Theory and practice* (pp. 69–84). Springer.

Malaguzzi, L. (2001). *La educación infantil en Reggio Emilia*. Octaedro, S.L.

Martínez-Valdivia, E., Pegalajar-Palomino, M. C., & Higueras-Rodríguez, M. L. (2021). Dialogic literary circles as a methodological strategy for the training of students in early childhood education degree. *International Journal of Instruction, 14*(3), 255–270.

Masschelein, J., & Simons, M. (2015). Education in times of fast learning: The future of the school. *Ethics and Education, 10*(1), 84–95.

Mincu, M. E. (2015). Teacher quality and school improvement: What is the role of research? *Oxford Review of Education, 41*(2), 253–269.

Northey, G., Bucic, T., Chylinski, M., & Govind, R. (2015). Increasing student engagement using asynchronous learning. *Journal of Marketing Education, 37*(3), 171–180.

Nouri, A., & Sajjadi, S. M. (2014). Emancipatory pedagogy in practice: Aims, principles and curriculum orientation. *International Journal of Critical Pedagogy, 5*(2), 76–87.

Pellas, N., & Kazandis, I. (2015). On the value of second life for students' engagement in blended and online courses: A comparative study from the higher education in Greece. *Education and Information Technologies, 20*(3), 445–466.

Peters, M. A., Rizvi, F., McCulloch, G., Gibbs, P., Gorur, R., Yoonjung Hwang, M. H., Zipin, L., Brennan, M., Robertson, S. Quay, J., Malbon, J., Taglietti, D., Barnett, R., Chengbing, W., McLaren, P., Apple, R., Papastephanou, M., Burbules, N., ... Misiaszek, L. (2020). Reimagining the new pedagogical possibilities for universities post-Covid-19. *Educational Philosophy and Theory*, 1–45. https://doi.org/10.1080/00131857.2020.1777655

Rancière, J. (1991). *The ignorant schoolmaster. Five lessons in intellectual emancipation*. Stanford University Press.

Rice, K. J. (2003). *Teacher quality. Understanding the effectiveness of teacher attributes*. Economic Policy Institute.

Rinaldi, C. (2009). El ambiente de la Infancia. In Reggio Children and Domus Academy Research Centre (Ed.), *Niños, Espacios y Relaciones: Metaproyecto de ambientes para la Infancia* (pp. 114–120). Red Solare. School of Art and Communication.

Sakarneh, M. (2011). A Literature review on concepts and implications of quality teaching. *Journal of Education and Practice, 2*(5), 83–96.

Schön, D. A. (1983). *The reflective practitioner: How professionals think in action.* Basic Books.

Schön, D. A. (1990). *Educating the reflective practitioner: Toward a new design for teaching and learning in the professions.* Jossey-Bass.

Simons, M., & Masschelein, J. (2008). From schools to learning environments: The dark side of being exceptional. *Journal of Philosophy of Education, 42*(3–4), 687–704. https://doi.org/10.1111/j.1467-9752.2008.00641.x

Snoek, M., Spil, S., van den Berg, E., & Suasso de Lima de Prado, E. (2012). In search of teacher excellence: Honours programmes and the recognition of teacher excellence in the Netherlands. *Reflecting Education, 8*(2), 72–87.

Tur-Porres, G. (2020). Designing provocative education environments for teacher training emancipatory practices. In J. Madalińska-Michalak (Ed.), *Studies on quality teachers and quality initial teacher education* (pp. 220–241). FRSE Publishing House.

Tur Porres, G., & Ires Correa, W. (2020). Body re-education in teacher continuing education. *Forum Oświatowe 31, 2*(62), 83–93.

Tur Porres, G., Wildemeersch, D., & Simons, M. (2014). Reflections on the emancipatory potential of vocational education and training practices: Freire and Rancière in dialogue. *Studies in Continuing Education Journal, 36*(3), 275–289.

Tur Porres, G., Wildemeersch, D., & Simons, M. (2020). Revisiting Rancière's concept of intellectual emancipation in vocational educational and training practices. *Sisyphus – Journal of Education, 8*(3), 23–40.

UNESCO. (2002). *Open and distance learning. Trends, policy and strategy considerations.* UNESCO.

Wang, J., Lin, E., Spalding, E., Klecka, C. L., & Odell, S. J. (2011). Quality teaching and teacher education: A kaleidoscope of notions. *Journal of Teacher Education 62*(4), 331–338.

CHAPTER 8

Situational Support to Develop the Well-being of Future Teachers

Supporting Sustainable Development Goal 4

Irma Eloff and Anna-Barbara du Plessis

Abstract

This chapter investigates the ways in which well-being is supported within teacher training programmes for pre-service teachers. The study explores the situational support available to pre-service teachers within their immediate learning environments. Well-being studies increasingly suggest that situational support factors embedded within learning environments are critical to subjective well-being and hence they require a deeper understanding. For this study, data were collected in interviews (n = 209) and focus group discussions with pre-service teachers at a large, residential university in South Africa where all participants were enrolled for teacher education programmes. Interviews were conducted in a rapid, face-to-face format on campus and consisted of a single question, i.e. 'What supports your well-being at university?' The focus group was also conducted on site, via a semi-structured interview protocol that utilised the PERMA theoretical framework as structural organiser. Data were analysed through interpretive phenomenological analysis (IPA). The study indicates a cluster of situational support factors that support the well-being of the pre-service teachers: (i) the campus environment and facilities, (ii) pragmatic student support structures, (iii) the quality of the academic experience and the vital role of lecturers in the learning experience of students, (iv) feelings of safety, and (v) opportunities for socialisation outside of the formal academic programme. The chapter concludes with the implications for teacher well-being and teacher education programmes.

Keywords

teacher well-being – well-being – quality education – teacher workforce – SDG 4 – SDG 3 – situation support – situational support

1   Introduction

The importance of teacher well-being is well established in the literature (Cefai & Cooper, 2017; Jian, 2021). In terms of global sustainable development, teacher well-being connects to several sustainable development goals, most prominently Sustainable Development Goal 3 (Good health & well-being) and Goal 4 (Quality education). It can be argued that, in the long term, investments in teacher well-being may have a positive impact on teacher retention rates at the systemic level (Van der Vyver et al., 2020) and on the quality of learning outcomes on a classroom and individual level (Turner & Thielking, 2019).

It is proposed here that improved teacher well-being at the pre-service level may affect the number of teacher education graduates entering the profession and the quality of education that they will provide in the future. Concerns about teacher education graduates not even entering the profession, or leaving it early (De Stercke et al., 2015) have been raised in several contexts around the world. Teacher attrition rates (See et al., 2020) influence the quality of education and undermine long-term education planning processes. The current study found that improvements in pre-service teacher well-being have the potential not only to contribute towards reduced teacher attrition rates, but also to provide additional positive outcomes for individual teachers.

Primarily, the implicit agency for improving well-being is positioned within the human capacity to adapt and adjust (Eloff & Graham, 2020; Wissing et al., 2020). While the resources for improving well-being are frequently highlighted in studies on well-being (Ebersöhn, 2020), the *agency for well-being* most frequently resides in the human capital. The implicit assumption is that it is people who need to support and improve well-being.

The current study probed the question whether the environment within which people (i.e. pre-service teachers) find themselves, can potentially affect their well-being (in this instance, teacher well-being), thereby creating an additional dimension of 'agency' for well-being. The study sought to explore the interactions between pre-service teachers and their physical learning environments in order to explain the dynamics of teacher well-being within the broad career trajectories of teachers.

The notion of 'situation support' (Santos, 2018) suggests that the situations in which human beings find themselves affect them in implicit and explicit ways and impact their well-being. For instance, at the individual level, nutrition and behaviour studies have shown that when food pantries are re-organised to ascertain the (healthy) food choices of participants, leveraging principles of choice architecture and behavioural economics has implications for healthier food selection in pantry settings for the most at risk populations (Wansik,

Bhana, Qureshi, & Cadenhead, 2016). There seems to be implicit, yet under-investigated, connections between physical environments and the subjective well-being of human beings. It is, hypothesised that behavioural science strategies such as adjusting convenience levels or altering attractiveness in the food industry, could potentially change eating patterns in scalable and affordable ways (Wansink, Bhana, Cadenhead, & Qureshi, 2016). If eating patterns can be affected by changing aspects of an environment, to what extent can well-being behaviour be influenced by environments?

More specifically, this study explored the ways in which the environments for pre-service teachers in an African context can be structured to support their well-being. We know that individual behaviour can be affected by adjusting the visibility and convenience levels of certain aspects within an environment (Painter et al., 2002). But what do we know about the interactions between student teachers and the environment within which they are becoming teachers? As such, the interactions between individuals and their environments need deeper investigation, especially as far as well-being is concerned. For future teachers, an in-depth understanding of the dynamics between their own well-being, their environments, and the situational support within those environments, may potentially yield insights that can positively impact their identities as teachers and perhaps also their entry into, and retention within, the profession.

2   Background to the Study

The current study investigated the situational factors that support the well-being of undergraduate education students, i.e. future teachers. The research question that guided the study was: What are the situational factors that support the well-being of pre-service teachers in an African context?

The rationale for the study was threefold. First, the study assumed that a deeper understanding of the well-being of pre-service teachers may potentially support the sustainable development goals on good health and well-being (SDG 3) as well as quality education (SDG 4), and therefore it may potentially contribute to Agenda 2030. Second, the study departed from an assumption that 'situational support' may play an integral role in the well-being of pre-service teachers, thereby expanding agency for well-being beyond the individual and personal levels. Third, the study subscribed to the assumption that investment in the well-being of pre-service teachers may impact entrance to the profession, teacher retention and long-term career satisfaction. Thus, the study sought to fully comprehend the situational support aspects that contribute to the well-being of pre-service teachers.

2.1 Setting

The study was conducted at a tertiary institution in South Africa. According to the 2019 School Realities Report (Department of Basic Education, 2020), 13,041,198 students attended 24,998 public and private schools in South Africa and were served by 444,857 teachers. Furthermore, most teacher education programmes in the country are delivered through universities – some through distance education, while others offer residential programmes. Prospective teachers can complete a four-year integrated degree programme or a three-year degree programme with a postgraduate one-year teaching certificate. Work-integrated learning is a statutory requirement for teacher education qualifications in the country.

The study took place at a large public residential university in South Africa that is one of the primary providers of teachers in the country. Education degree programmes are offered across the whole developmental spectrum, from early childhood education programmes to adult education, as well as in a wide variety of fields, e.g. languages, history, physical sciences, life sciences, technology, mathematics, music, arts, geography, business management, engineering graphics and design, economics and management sciences, and heritage and cultural tourism.

Ethics clearance to conduct the study was provided by the Ethics Committee of the Faculty of Humanities at the institution (GW0180232H). The data collected from participants was kept confidential and anonymous. All participants were allocated numerical codes for purposes of analysis.

2.2 Data Collection

The study was conducted by means of rapid face-to-face interviews and a focus group to collect qualitative data on situational support for student well-being. The face-to-face interviews were conducted by student fieldworkers over a two-week period during the first semester of the academic year. Data for the interviews was collected in four-hour time blocks at varying time points, on all the days of the week, in order to ensure diverse participation. Participants were approached on campus, provided with a short description of the project and invited to participate. Interested participants were provided with a consent form and they then completed the interview with the field worker. Fieldworkers captured responses on paper, after which data capturers transferred the written responses onto an electronic, collective document.

The semi-structured focus group was facilitated by a registered educational psychologist. The focus group questions were guided by the PERMA framework (Seligman, 2011) and included questions such as, 'What is the first factor that you think of when I ask you what contributes to your well-being?' and 'Do you have, or do you feel that you have meaning in your life?' The focus group was audio-recorded and transcribed verbatim.

2.3 *Participants*

The study was conducted with undergraduate students enrolled for a teaching qualification at the university where the study took place. All data were collected on campus. For the interviews, study participants were selected via random sampling by fieldworkers who approached potential participants on campus, outside lecture halls. For the focus group, participants were selected via convenience sampling by the focus group facilitator. All students in her undergraduate class at the time, were invited during a lecture to provide their contact details afterwards, if they were interested to participate.

The face-to-face interview participants (n = 209) were enrolled in various four-year BEd-degree programmes, e.g., BEd Foundation Phase, BEd Intermediate Phase, BEd Senior Phase, BEd Further Education and Training, and BEd Natural Sciences. Their ages ranged from 19 to 27 years. All participants except one ('other African') were South African citizens. The male – female ratio was approximately at 1:2 with a total of 143 participants being female and 66 male. Home languages included IsiXhosa, IsiZulu, Afrikaans, English, Setswana, IsiNdebele, Sesotho, Sepedi, Xitsonga, and Siswati. Five participants indicated 'other' as their home language.

The focus group participants (n = 7) were also enrolled in four-year Bed degrees (Senior phase and Further Education and Training) and their ages ranged from 20 to 35 years old. All of them were South African citizens, and their home languages included English, Afrikaans and isiZulu. Two participants were male, and five were female.

2.4 *Data Analysis*

Data were analysed by means of interpretive phenomenological analysis (IPA). Initially, one researcher comprehensively engaged with the data set and identified four preliminary themes. A second researcher then fully immersed herself in the data set, read it repeatedly and marked recurring words and phrases. Similar constructs were grouped together to form sub-themes. These were subsequently reconsidered and again grouped to constitute five main themes. These five themes were compared with the initial four themes, the wording of the themes was refined and five final main themes were established. The IPA only considered aspects from the data that related to situational support. A small number of data segments were not included due to inaudibility of the audio-recording or illegibility of the fieldworker's handwriting.

3 Findings of the Study

The following themes emerged as situational support factors that contribute to the well-being of undergraduate pre-service teachers:
– The campus environment and facilities.
– Pragmatic student support structures.
– The quality of the academic experience and the vital role of lecturers in the learning experience of students.
– Feelings of safety.
– Opportunities for socialisation outside of the formal academic programme.

3.1 *The Campus Environment and Facilities*

The campus environment and the facilities available on campus emerged as a dominant theme in supporting the well-being of the pre-service teachers in this study. Participants appreciated that the campus created spaces for socialising, eating and studying between lectures, which contributed to their well-being. Some participants mentioned that the setting of the campus – with its well-kept gardens, large trees and shrubs, open spaces, greenery, a large dam with ducks and other small wildlife – contributed to their positive state of mind and well-being. The campus environment also offered a range of exercise and sports opportunities, including enough space for safe jogging (the theme of safety to be discussed later), a variety of competitive and non-competitive sports, and a gymnasium that greatly facilitated self-care.

The availability of more than one facility to purchase food and snacks also emerged as a factor contributing to self-care. For some participants who hailed from low-resourced rural areas, the mere availability of food contributed to a feeling of well-being, as one study participant (Student, F, BEd Intermediate phase) mentioned: 'what contributes to my well-being as a student at the university […] is going to class with a full stomach'. For other students, the availability of more than one facility from which to buy food (thus allowing them the freedom to exercise choice) contributed to a feeling of well-being. The availability of water in drinking fountains and in the taps was also mentioned as situational contributors to well-being: 'water in the taps around the campus' (Student, F, BEd Senior FET).

Neat, modern and warm lecture halls situated in close proximity to one another and clearly marked, also furthered feelings of well-being. The on-campus library, which allows access to an extensive array of resources and provides a sterling academic support service, was also noted as an important aspect contributing to well-being: 'Utilising the library – being able to attain information using the free wifi and library catalogue' (Student, F, BEd Foundation Phase). Clean bathrooms, computer laboratories, access to printing services and the availability of dustbins were also highlighted. Free Wi-Fi was repeatedly mentioned as beneficial, not only for academic purposes, but also for communication with family and friends. The availability of transport in the form of buses running along a predetermined route and schedule between campuses was also commented upon, as well as the easily available parking at the education campus. The residences, as other campus structures, were also noted with appreciation (see the role of residences elsewhere in the findings).

3.2 *Pragmatic Student Support Structures*

Many of the participants valued the student support structures available on campus to provide mental and emotional, physical, academic, financial and administrative support. The on-campus availability of psychological services provided by qualified psychologists were especially mentioned by some participants: 'Knowing that there are people willing to help me, should I need or ask for it, e.g. psychologists' (Student, F, BEd Foundation Phase). A mentorship programme that allocates new students to more experienced students for assistance with personal and campus matters was also shown to contribute to well-being. In the university residences, a similar guardian programme was followed. Some participants mentioned workshops (such as about time management, exam preparation and well-being) and informative pamphlets as promoting their well-being. Overall, the university residences were mentioned frequently as a source of support: 'Being part of residence also helps me to make new friends and they encourage both academics and sport. This really helps me to balance my student life and it makes me happy to be able to do everything I'm interested in' (Student, F, BEd Foundation Phase).

Access to free medical care also contributed to well-being, again mentioned especially by students from rural areas. Regarding academic support, the university mentorship programme, an official university-wide programme to keep students on track to complete their degrees in the minimum allowed time, easily available tutors, and the role of lecturers emerged as further situational support factors. The role of the lecturers in providing academic support was expected, but the data analysis showed the extent of their support to also incorporate general care for the total well-being of participants. One student (Student, M, BEd) stated that 'lecturers who truly care about their students academically and on a deeper human level' was important. The data analysis revealed that support by lecturers was by no means an isolated occurrence, but quite prevalent across the Faculty of Education in various departments. Several participants mentioned the importance of a competent and knowledgeable faculty support advisor to assist with academic and other study-related matters: 'FSA assist with academic, personal, career goals' (Student, F, BEd).

Financial support through a financing scheme or bursaries, general support by staff and administrative support were also some of the support structures mentioned by several participants. Again, the role of the residences in providing support in respect of all the previously mentioned areas was also noted by the participants.

3.3 The Quality of the Academic Experience and the Vital Role of Lecturers

The importance of lecturers surfaced as an important theme. The content of the lectures and the way the lecturers presented the content were mentioned as situational factors that greatly supported the well-being of the pre-service teacher. One study participant (Student, F, BEd Foundation Phase) reflected the opinion of several fellow participants by appreciating 'the attitudes and enthusiasm of the lecturers'. It seems that the well-being of undergraduate education students was boosted by the mere professionalism of the lecturers in presenting their lectures and the dedication they show towards their own teaching.

The value of technological support to augment the lecture content and presentation via online platforms of the university was recognised: 'the availability of the modern technology like the use of online communication between lectures and their students' (Student, M, BEd). Students appreciated the blended learning model used at the institution. The participants were aware of the university's high ranking in Africa and felt that their well-being was improved by the knowledge that the tertiary institution (and thus the degree for which they were enrolled) had high standing. This situational support factor – which is one that may take years to cultivate – may not always be easy to identify. Another subtheme related to the academic degree programme was the nature of some timetables, which allowed students time between lectures to be with friends.

3.4 Feelings of Safety

A fourth theme that emerged as promoting the well-being of participants was the feeling of safety on campus. Participants felt that physical safety was important to live, learn and exercise freely. Student cards as access control were specifically mentioned as providing a feeling of safety, together with the campus security officers who were visible and helpful. The importance of emotional safety to experience well-being also emerged from the students' responses. Some participants mentioned that they could study without being bullied, they felt free to express themselves (Student, F, BEd Foundation Phase), they felt accepted, and that diversity was respected. Safety was cited numerous times by multiple participants. Some participants merely mentioned 'safety', while others elaborated on the specificities of feeling safe on campus: 'safety contributes to my well-being, knowing I am safe, at no risk of being a victim of crime is very important to my well-being' (Student, F, BEd Participant).

3.5 *Opportunities for Socialisation*

Several participants mentioned that the opportunities for social connection outside the formal academic programme were critical to their well-being. The campus setting, as mentioned before, facilitated social connection, and the residences also featured prominently in social connection: 'social well-being – you get to know people with different characters and attitudes' (Student, F, BEd). However, participants also specifically mentioned activities and societies available to residential as well as non-residential students (e.g., singing competitions, dancing, informal sports matches) to promote their well-being: 'Participating on activities like social groups and sport, participating in sporting activities such as soccer and volley ball' (Student, M, BEd Natural Sciences). For the participants in the current study, the diversity of social connection opportunities that were offered was integral to their well-being.

4 Discussion

The findings from this study suggest a variety of situational support factors that contributed to the well-being of pre-service teachers. The campus environment and facilities, the pragmatic student support structures, the quality of the academic experience and the vital role of lecturers in the learning experience of students, together with feelings of safety and opportunities for socialisation outside of the formal academic programme – all contribute to student well-being. In and of themselves, these findings may not necessarily be new. What was 'new', was how closely the participants in this study related these seemingly 'non-human agency' factors to their own well-being. Students mentioned basic needs such as food, water, and feeling safe as integral to their well-being. They also mentioned access to facilities, the use of technology, and the quality of their lectures. Whilst these findings may perhaps be context-specific due to the high vulnerability of some of the students in the study, the findings pronounced a dimension to student well-being that may be fairly muted in student well-being literature at the moment.

In the same way that buildings 'do not just reflect our values; they later become causes in their own right' (Orr, 2006, p. 2), campus environments may not only reflect the values of a university but potentially become a cause of student well-being in their own right. This symbiosis has already been established with regard to campus environments and student *learning*. According to Strange et al. (2015, p. 2), colleges and universities

> ... establish conditions to attract, satisfy, and retain students for purposes of challenging them to develop qualities of the educated person, including a capacity for complex critical reasoning, communication, and leadership; a sense of identity and purpose; an appreciation for differences; and a commitment to lifelong learning.

Nonetheless, the symbiosis between the environment (situational support) and student *well-being* has received only limited attention in psychological and educational studies. In the context of sustainability, DeLind and Link (2004, p. 124) indeed argue that we cannot understand ourselves as human beings, or our behaviours, in disembodied, generic ways.

> People must come to know and care for (show affection and responsibility for) the places they inhabit. Yet place is a concept of many dimensions – a shape shifter of sorts. It can be tangible, sensual. It can exist under our feet; it can literally ground us, anchor us, give us roots. But place can also be social and spiritual. It can be as intangible as history, as creative as culture, as mystical as creation myths. Instead of something absolute, place can be a matter of shifting identities, shared understandings, and relationships not only among ourselves but among all living creatures. (DeLind & Link, 2004, p. 124)

The findings from this study extend the reciprocity between students and the 'places' they inhabit during their years of study. In the same way that people take care of their environment, aspects within the environment also seemed to support the well-being of the students in this study.

What are then the implications of these findings? They are truly multi-layered. Even though the study was conducted in only one African context, some of the findings may potentially resonate with pre-service teachers in other developing contexts too. The education students in this study mentioned 'water in the taps' or being able to study on a 'full stomach' as factors that supported their well-being. In some contexts, these considerations may well be the factors that support the well-being of in-service teachers (Abdelgafar, 2019) by having their basic needs met.

The participants in my study also mentioned the close proximity of student support services and the resources that were available to them in the library. All of these aspects were ingrained in the environment and provided situational support for their well-being.

Yet, whenever optimal student support for future teachers is conceptualised, it is usually limited to having psychological support services strengthened. Although psychological support services are critical for undergraduate students, it seems that the context within which students live and learn may be of equal importance. The situational factors for supporting the well-being of undergraduate education students/pre-service teachers are frequently neglected and the findings from this study suggest that a deeper understanding of these factors is required to contribute to their well-being. In addition, the study suggests that improved situational support may contribute to the well-being of many future teachers, since investment in the environment is hugely beneficial to them.

Within the Sustainable Development agenda, the notion of well-being has gained much momentum since the launch of Agenda 2030 in 2015. Correspondingly, the importance of quality education within the global context has also garnered the increased attention of policy-makers, teacher education institutions and civil society organisations. It is within the nexus of sustainable development goals 3 and 4 (good health and well-being; quality education) that the current study positioned itself.

The global goal of quality education (SDG 4) states that it aims to 'ensure inclusive and equitable quality education and promote lifelong learning opportunities for all' (United Nations, 2015). Within the ten targets of SDG 4, Target 4.c pertinently expresses the intention to substantially increase the supply of qualified teachers by 2030 (United Nations, 2015). The supply and demand for qualified teachers are particularly critical in sub-Saharan Africa, and globally teachers

> ... are the key to achieving all of the SDG 4 targets. It requires urgent attention, with a more immediate deadline, because the equity gap in education is exacerbated by the shortage and uneven distribution of professionally trained teachers, especially in disadvantaged areas. As teachers are a fundamental condition for guaranteeing quality education, teachers and educators should be empowered, adequately recruited and remunerated, motivated, professionally qualified, and supported within well-resourced, efficient and effectively governed systems. (UNESCO, n.d.)

It can therefore be argued that investment in the situational factors that support the well-being of future teachers has the potential to support quality education. When teachers are doing well, teaching and learning benefit.

The advantages of investment in the well-being of future teachers also extend beyond the obvious benefit of quality education (SDG 4) (UNESCO, n.d., online). SDG 4 is directly connected to several targets encapsulated within other sustainable development goals. For instance, Target 3.7 of the sustainable development goal on health and well-being (SDG 3) – which seeks to ensure universal access to sexual and reproductive healthcare services, health information and education, increased family planning, and ultimately the integration of reproductive health services at the national level – rests heavily on quality education. Similarly, at the systemic level, Target 5.6 of the sustainable development goal on gender equality (SDG 5) seeks to improve the number of countries with laws and regulations that guarantee access to sexual and reproductive health care services, and concurrent health information and education programmes for women aged 15 to 49 years. In this regard, teachers play a pivotal role, especially in the African context, where teachers might be the key (and only) access point to health information for young women.

The sustainable development goal on decent work and sustainable growth (SDG 8) states in its Target 8.6 that the proportion of youth not in employment, education or training should be substantially reduced by 2030. Again, education is key. In the same way, SDG 12 on responsible consumption and production wishes to ensure that awareness of sustainable lifestyles in harmony with the natural environment be heightened and that people everywhere be equipped with the necessary information to make choices that improve sustainability (SDG 12, Target 12.8). Furthermore, Target 13.3 in the sustainable development goal on climate change mitigation (SDG 13) mentions education specifically when it states the intention to 'improve education, awareness raising and human and institutional capacity on climate change mitigation, adaptation, impact reduction, and early warning' (UNESCO, n.d.).

It seems then that the well-being of future teachers is intricately connected to a multitude of sustainability targets within Agenda 2030, thereby providing an urgent rationale for gaining a deeper understanding of the complexities of teacher well-being. In fact, the findings from this study suggest that situational support factors are key to pre-service teachers' well-being.

5 Conclusion

The study in hand blurs the lines of existing conceptualisations of the *agency for well-being* and argues that the assumption of environments as 'static' should be expanded. Predominantly, studies on (pre-service and in-service) teacher well-being tend to amplify human and social resources as support for teacher well-being. The current study contributes to the knowledge base regarding the connection between the physical environment, its inherent situational support factors, and pre-service teacher well-being. Its findings suggest that a deeper understanding of and investment in situational support factors may contribute to the well-being of pre-service teachers.

In terms of the quality of teacher education, this study suggests that situational support should be integrated into long-term strategic planning processes for teacher education programmes. Developing the quality of teacher education, and the teaching within teacher education programmes, may entail more than mere quality curricula, optimal use of technology, supportive assessment practices and excellent lecturers. It may also entail that the quality of the learning environment, the aesthetics of the physical environments within which learning takes place, and intentional decisions to prioritise pre-service teacher well-being, is emphasised.

References

Abdelgafar, A. I. (2019). The quality of life of teachers in Sudan. In I. Eloff (Ed.), *Quality of life in African societies* (pp. 359–372). Springer.

Barlett, P. F., & Chase, G. W. (2004). *Sustainability on campus: Stories and strategies for change*. The MIT Press.

Cefai, C., & Cooper, P. (2017). *Mental health promotion in schools: Cross-cultural narratives and perspectives*. Springer.

DeLind, L. B., & Link, T. (2004). Place as the nexus of a sustainable future: A course for all of us. In P. F. Barlett & G. W. Chase (2004). *Sustainability on campus: Stories and strategies for change* (pp. 121–138). The MIT Press.

Department of Basic Education. (2020). *2019 School realities report*. EMIS Statistical Publications, Department of Basic Education.

De Stercke, J., Goyette, N., & Robertson, J. E. (2015). Happiness in the classroom: Strategies for teacher retention and development. *Prospects: Quarterly Review of Comparative Education, 45*(4), 421–427.

Ebersöhn, L. (2020). Collective resilience to global challenge: A collective wellbeing agenda to transform towards sustained equitable education. *Praxis Educativa, 15*, 1–14.

Eloff, I., & Graham, M. (2020). Measuring mental health and wellbeing of South African undergraduate students. *Global Mental Health, 7*, E34. doi:10.1017/gmh.2020.26

Jian, H. (2021). Teacher wellbeing. *English Language Teaching Journal, 75*(1), 116–118.

Orr, D. W. (2006). *Design on the edge: The making of a high-performance building.* The MIT Press.

Painter, J. E., Wansink, B., & Hieggelke, J. B. (2002). How visibility and convenience influence candy consumption. *Appetite, 38*(3), 237–238.

Santos, L. (2018). *The science of well-being – what psychological science says about the good life: Situation Support* [Coursera lecture notes]. Yale University. Retrieved March 18, 2021, from https://www.coursera.org/lecture/the-science-of-well-being/part-1-situation-support-59tJc?redirectTo=%2Flearn%2Fthe-science-of-well-being%3Faction%3Denroll

See, B. H., Morris, R., Gorard, S., Kokotsaki, D., & Abdi, S. (2020). Teacher recruitment and retention. A critical review of international evidence of most promising interventions. *Education Sciences, 10*(10), 1–45.

Seligman, M. E. P. (2011). *Flourish: A visionary new understanding of happiness and wellbeing.* Free Press.

Strange, C. C., Banning, J. H., & Strange, C. C. (2015). *Designing for learning: Creating campus environments for student success.* John Wiley & Sons.

Turner, K. & Thielking, M. (2019). Teacher wellbeing: Its effects on teaching practice and student learning. *Issues in Educational Research, 29*(3), 938–960.

UNESCO. (n.d.). SDG-Education 2030 Steering Committee Secretariat. *Sustainable Development Goal 4 (SDG 4).* UNESCO.

United Nations. (2015). *The 17 goals. Department of economic and social affairs sustainable development.* United Nations. https://sdgs.un.org/goals/goal4

Van der Vyver, C. P., Kok, M. T., & Conley, L. N. (2020). The relationship between teachers' professional wellbeing and principals' leadership behaviour to improve teacher retention. *Perspectives in Education, 8*(2), 86–102.

Wansink, B., Bhana, H., Qureshi, M., & Cadenhead, J. W. (2016). Using choice architecture to create healthy food interventions in food pantries. *Journal of Nutrition Education and Behavior: Supplement, 48*(7), S36. https://doi.org/10.1016/j.jneb.2016.04.096

Wansink, B., Bhana, H., Cadenhead, J. W., & Qureshi, M. (2016). Behavioral nutrition interventions in food pantries: Lessons and strategies. *Journal of Nutrition Education and Behavior: Supplement, 48*(7), S35. https://doi.org/10.1016/j.jneb.2016.04.095

Wissing, M. P., Potgieter, J. C., Guse, T, Khumalo, I. P., & Nel, L. (2020). *Towards flourishing embracing well-being in diverse contexts.* Van Schaik.

CHAPTER 9

Educating for Sustainability and Global Citizenship in Uncertain Times

A Case Study with In-service Teachers in Portugal

Mónica Lourenço and Ana Isabel Andrade

Abstract

This chapter describes a case study conducted in 2021 with a group of twenty in-service teachers in Portugal who participated in an online professional development course titled 'Education for sustainability: diversity, dialogue and inclusion'. The research aims to understand the impact of the course on teachers' professional learning, focusing on changes related to their conceptualisations of education for sustainability and global citizenship (ESGC), their pedagogical repertoires, their understandings of the purposes of education and of the teacher's role in a globalised and uncertain world, and their motivations and commitment to teach according to ESGC principles. The teachers' individual written reflections were gathered at the end of the course and explored using content analysis. Findings suggest that the teachers developed clearer conceptualisations of ESGC, updated their pedagogical knowledge, and learned how to approach these topics in an interdisciplinary manner. They also gained confidence and motivation to teach ESGC in a more intentional and meaningful manner. The implications of this study for quality teaching and teacher education in uncertain times are discussed.

Keywords

education for sustainability – global citizenship education – in-service teacher education – quality in teacher education – professional learning – professional knowledge – case study

1   **Introduction**

Educating global citizens for a more sustainable world is one of the bedrocks of quality education inscribed in the 2030 Agenda. However, for many of the world's teachers these concepts are puzzling or unknown (Hopkins, 2020). Considering the fundamental role teachers play in advancing progress towards meeting target 4.7 of the Sustainable Development Goals, it is important to promote on-going teacher education to ensure teachers develop the necessary confidence, knowledge and skills to teach about and for sustainability and global citizenship.

This chapter describes a case study conducted in 2021 with a group of twenty in-service teachers in Portugal who participated in an online professional development course entitled 'Education for sustainability: diversity, dialogue and inclusion'. The course was developed within the Erasmus+ project TEDS – Teacher education for sustainability, which was coordinated by the University of Aveiro in Portugal (project code: 2019-1-PT01-KA201-060830).

The study aims to understand the impact of the course on teachers' professional learning, focusing on changes related to their conceptualisations of education for sustainability and global citizenship (ESGC), their pedagogical repertoires, their understandings of the purposes of education and of teacher's role in a globalised and uncertain world, and their motivations and commitment to teach according to ESGC principles. Individual reflections written by the teachers were gathered at the end of the course and explored using content analysis (Schreier, 2012). Findings were interpreted considering a concept of professional development rooted in teachers' commitment to the transformative role of education.

The chapter begins with an overview of key literature and recent research on teacher education for sustainability and global citizenship, teacher professional learning, teacher professional knowledge and teacher quality. Then, it describes the study, namely the context, participants and methodological design. This is followed by a presentation of the results according to each category of analysis. The chapter ends with a discussion and a conclusion where the main findings and limitations of the study are examined and implications for quality teacher education are addressed.

2 Teacher Education for Sustainability and Global Citizenship

The first decades of the 21st century have been marked by a series of interconnected social, political, environmental and economic crises that have affected communities and individuals worldwide: terrorism, climate change, poverty and unemployment, mass migration, gender and racial discrimination, and, more recently, a global pandemic are but some examples of the 'bigger-than-life' challenges facing society. In light of these challenges, humanity is called upon to make decisions and choose a path regarding the legacy we wish to leave for future generations. On one side, lies the defence of human rights and freedoms, and concerted efforts to address multiple inequalities, as well as the present and growing threats of global climate change; on the other side, lie increased attacks on the marginalised and more vulnerable populations of the world, the rise of xenophobic populism and hate speech, and acceleration in the degradation of Planet Earth.

In this context, sustainability and global citizenship appear as a 'real utopia', or to quote Paulo Freire (2018), 'um inédito viável', i.e., a possible dream to help us rethink our relationships with each other and nature, and to guide us on the path towards transformative change. The Sustainable Development Goals (SDGs), a collection of 17 interdependent goals designed to be a blueprint to achieve a better and more sustainable future, are perhaps the best expression of this possible dream. Despite their contradictions and fallacies (McCloskey, 2019), the SDGs represent an unparalleled effort and a commitment towards social justice for all and the planet, perhaps only matched with the Human Rights Declaration of the 20th century. Within the SDGs, Target 4.7 remains the most critical and ambitious goals, focusing specifically on the transformative potential of education in building peaceful and sustainable societies, 'among others, through *education for sustainable development* and sustainable lifestyles, human rights, gender equality, promotion of a culture of peace and non-violence, *global citizenship* and appreciation of cultural diversity and of culture's contribution to sustainable development' (United Nations, 2015).

It is not surprising, then, that global citizenship education (GCE) and education for sustainability (EduS), or for sustainable development (ESD), have emerged as educational possibilities to help individuals understand and reflect upon the world, as well as respond to its challenges, tensions and paradoxes. Despite being grounded on separate policy and research foundations, EduS and GCE are interrelated concepts. UNESCO (2020), for instance, sees GCE as a framework for implementation to achieve the goals set out in the 2030 Agenda. Oxfam (2015), on their part, regard sustainable development as one of the themes to be included in GCE-based curricula. However, many tend to consider both projects in conjunction, regarding them as 'the culmination of democratic global cosmopolitanism and cosmopolitan democracy in the twenty-first century' (Torres, 2020, p. XX), embodying a 'state of mindfulness and caring for the planet, all human beings and all other living entities with whom we share the globe' (Hopkins, 2020, p. XXV). We concur with these views, considering education for sustainability and global citizenship (henceforth, ESGC) a useful framework to develop the knowledge, skills, values and attitudes required by citizens to lead productive lives, make informed decisions and assume active roles in facing and resolving current and future global challenges. In a nutshell, ESGC helps individuals construct an internal learning system that will shape their future choices and actions. This is an important aspect of quality education and distinguishes the pursuit of ESGC from either simple training or mere indoctrination.

The alignment of GCE with sustainable development and lifelong quality education for all, as proposed in the Global Education First Initiative (United Nations, 2012), has come to the fore as a global priority for countries around the world. Governments and institutions have highlighted this priority in different ways: some introduced EduS and GCE as separate disciplines or new goals in their study programmes, while others looked for what they were already doing in their education system.

Yet, even if formal inclusion of GCE and/or EduS into curricula has taken place (see, for instance, Batista & Andrade, 2021; Sá et al., 2019; Santamaría-Cárdaba & Lourenço, 2021; Tarozzi & Inguaggiato, 2016), for many teachers around the world at all levels of schooling these concepts are still unknown or perplexing. This is often attributed to conceptual vagueness associated with these terms, to national education systems' propensity to teach national or regional themes, to competing priorities, to lack of administrative or curricular support, and, fundamentally, to a tenuous presence of these themes in teacher education programmes (Lourenço, 2018; Rapoport, 2010). Indeed, although governments and policy-makers are encouraging teacher development programmes to include themes such as cultural understanding, global awareness and sustainability, appropriate teacher education measures specifically addressing EduS and/or GCE are still lacking (Bourn et al., 2017; UNESCO, 2020). Consequently, ESGC is still not embedded in teachers' (and teacher educators') practice in a systematic manner, but it rather remains a sporadic occurrence and an effort often only taken by willing and motivated teachers (Franch, 2020; Gaudelli, 2016; Lourenço, 2021; Yemini et al., 2019).

Considering the above, it is crucial to promote teachers' professional learning through both pre-service and on-going teacher education programmes to ensure teachers develop the necessary confidence, knowledge and skills to introduce students to GCE and EduS effectively.

3 Teachers' Professional Learning and Teacher Quality

It is widely accepted that teachers are amongst the most significant agents in children/student learning and, consequently, in contributing to the quality of education systems. As such, it is important to understand teachers' professional learning as a way to promote their professional knowledge. This will support teachers in developing the increasingly complex competencies their students need to learn as citizens in the 21st century (Jones & O'Brine, 2011; Madalińska-Michalak et al., 2018). As Darling-Hammond et al. (2017, p. 1) write:

> Sophisticated forms of teaching are needed to develop student competencies such as deep mastery of challenging content, critical thinking, complex problem-solving, effective communication and collaboration, and self-direction. In turn, effective professional development (PD) is needed to help teachers learn and refine the pedagogies required to teach these skills.

Teacher professional knowledge is assumed to be central to student learning. Empirical studies have shown the importance of teachers' professional knowledge for quality education and student achievement. Therefore, it is important to create opportunities for professional development throughout teachers' careers. These opportunities should support the construction of diversified and multidisciplinary professional knowledge, centred on the teachers themselves and on the challenges raised by education at a time of globalisation, change and uncertainty, in which the planet's sustainability and citizen participation are fundamental concerns. Teacher education programmes should be designed with the following purposes and characteristics in mind:
– contribute to the improvement of professional learning, creating opportunities for teachers to integrate or expand content and develop pedagogical approaches;
– provide an education that is simultaneously theoretical and practical, which foregrounds educational practice in 'real' teaching/learning situations;
– foster a teaching practice that allows students to learn in order to become active, critical and engaged citizens;
– engage teachers' through reflective, critical and transformative thinking, in order to stimulate educational innovation and professional development.

Professional teaching development is a complex process and difficult to define, as recent studies have shown (Appova & Arbaugh, 2018; Avalos, 2011; Hubers et al., 2020; Taylor, 2017). In this study, professional development is understood as professional learning, anchored in educational practices, in the problems of teaching and learning, but also in the theories and knowledge of educators who can inform these practices through reflection, as evidenced by Schön

(1983, 1987). Thus, we can state as Vélaz de Medrano and Vaillant (2009, p. 12) identify that

> Professional development takes place when it is tied to the daily practice of teachers and to the problems of teaching and learning. Only through this connection it is possible to promote reflections, restructuring and conceptualizations that open up new perspectives and allow planning pedagogical strategies aimed at improving students' learning and understanding.

Understanding this process of 'learning the teaching profession' cannot be detached from identifying the knowledge teachers need (for example, pedagogical knowledge; content knowledge; curriculum and context knowledge; knowledge about learners; knowledge about education and its mission; and self-knowledge, see Shulman, 1986), as well as identifying the factors that make teacher move. In this respect, the role of reflection as a process of teacher professional learning is highlighted, as well as the role of motivation to learn.

The issue of reflection has been often addressed in research on teacher education, being unanimously recognised as fundamental to teacher learning. For many it is the key piece in the construction of professional knowledge, since it allows for a true understanding of the teaching work (Alarcão, 1996). As Beauchamp writes, 'Reflection has become an accepted component of teacher education programs' (2015, p. 123).

Zeichner sees reflection as an important process in teacher education, with consequences for the lives of teachers and students, for the improvement of school life and, consequently, for social life. He states that teacher education programmes need to prepare teachers to be able to reflect on the origins, purposes and consequences of their actions, as well as on the material, social, cultural, and economic constraints that affect the students, the class, the school, and the social context in which they work (Zeichner, 2008; see also Hickson, 2011). In a word, reflection allows teachers to mobilise their learning, analysing (individually or collectively) their pedagogical and didactic repertoire and educational intentions, and making changes in their ways of thinking about and acting in education (Taylor, 2017).

Yet, for reflection to happen in a way that promotes professional learning it is important that teachers are motivated to do so, investing in inter-actions that support them to be 'better' teachers, and responding to the needs that move them towards what they perceive as 'good' teaching. As Appova and Arbaugh state, 'teachers are motivated to engage in PD via job-embedded learning opportunities that are a part of teachers' daily work – without compromising their teaching and their students' learning' (2018, p. 17).

4 The Case Study

4.1 *The TEDS Project*
This study was developed within the Erasmus+ project TEDS, a three-year collaborative project coordinated by the University of Aveiro (Portugal), which started in 2019. The project involves a network of researchers, teacher educators and teachers from other four European universities – the University of Helsinki (Finland), the University of Malta (Malta), the University of Nantes (France) and Vytautas Magnus University (Lithuania) – and counts on the collaboration of teacher education centres and schools in all of these countries.[1]

TEDS main goal is to contribute to teacher education for sustainability in Europe considering the following dimensions: equity and social solidarity; diversity, dialogue and inclusion; natural resources, environment and technology; economy and financial literacy. This goal is to be achieved by promoting professional knowledge about education for sustainability (EduS) both in theory and in practice in in-service teacher education contexts.

The projects' goals are realised through three sequential but interrelated phases: (1) construction of an EduS framework, emerging from a literature review, and characterisation of teachers' and teacher educators' social representations; (2) design, implementation and evaluation of teacher education courses, including action research projects for EduS in schools; (3) construction of a teacher education framework for EduS and dissemination of the project's results at institutional, local, regional, national and European levels.

The study presented in this chapter focuses precisely on the work developed by the University of Aveiro team during the second phase of the project, when a teacher education course was carried out with a group of in-service teachers in Portugal.

4.2 *The Teacher Education Programme*
'Education for sustainability: diversity, dialogue and inclusion' is a 50-hour course accredited by the Scientific and Pedagogical Council for Continuous Training in Portugal. It was developed between March and June 2021, fully online, via the Zoom platform. The course included both synchronous and asynchronous sessions. The synchronous component for all participants consisted of eight 3–4-hour sessions, totalling 25 hours, conducted by groups

of teacher educators, in a total of 25 hours. Asynchronous sessions included autonomous work developed by the trainees in small groups, often with the support of two teacher educators/mentors, also covering a total of 25 hours.

The objectives of this course were the following:
- to create opportunities to develop didactic and pedagogical knowledge about EduS;
- to collaboratively explore the value of diversity (biological, linguistic, cultural, social, …), promoting its integration in the curriculum in order to educate for sustainability;
- to capacitate educators to develop their students' ability to find collective solutions for global and local ('glocal') problems with a focus on issues of inclusion and dialogue between different cultures and languages.

The teacher education programme (TedP) was designed, implemented and evaluated by 11 teacher educators working in the field of education but from different disciplinary backgrounds, and it was attended by 20 teachers from different levels of schooling (from pre-primary to upper secondary education).

The course 'Education for sustainability: diversity, dialogue and inclusion' involved six steps: (i) presentation and discussion of the TedP and identification of representations about EduS; (ii) contact with different concepts, namely EduS and GCE, intercomprehension and inclusion; (iii) analysis of educational contexts (international, national and local) and projects related to ESGC; (iv) collaborative design of educational projects on ESGC and their implementation in schools; (v) presentation by the teachers of the projects developed in schools and their results; (vi) self-evaluation of the impact of the TedP on teachers' professional learning.

The teaching methodology centreed on presenting of different and complementary perspectives on ESGC, and in action research projects conceived, developed and evaluated by the trainees, with the support of two mentors, followed by their presentation and discussion with the whole group.

Teachers were evaluated for the products achieved during the TedP, as follows: field work (10%); narrative power point presenting the project developed in schools (10%); project conception and development in groups (30%); group report about the project development (30%); and individual written reflections (20%). Only these reflections are analysed for this study.

It is important to mention that, within the scope of the TedP, eight educational intervention projects were carried out in schools, approaching different themes related to the ESGC and covering all levels of schooling, in a total of more than 15 classes.

4.3 Participants

Participants in this study were 20 in-service teachers who took the course 'Education for sustainability: diversity, dialogue and inclusion'. All teachers were female, over 40 years of age. They were also well integrated in the schools in which they developed their projects. All teachers had a Bachelor's degree, and two of them also had a Master's degree. Most of the teachers had never attended ESGC teacher education programmes before, and predominantly associated the concept of EduS with the idea of respect for natural resources and the planet.

All participants provided their written informed consent to participate in this study and for the publication of data included in this article. Ethical review and approval was not required for the study in accordance with the local legislation and institutional requirements.

4.4 Methodology

The study reported in this chapter aims to understand the impact of the course 'Education for sustainability: diversity, dialogue and inclusion' on the participant teachers' professional learning. In particular, the study sought to identify changes in:
– teachers' conceptualisations of EduS and GCE;
– teachers' pedagogical repertoires;
– teachers' understandings of the purposes of education in a globalised and uncertain world;
– teachers' understandings of their role as educators for a more sustainable world;
– teachers' motivations and commitment to teach according to ESGC principles.

To address these objectives, a qualitative case study was developed (Yin, 2009) to provide the teacher educators in this TedP with a more systematic and integrated view of the course, i.e., the case under analysis. For that matter, teachers' discourses were taken as a reference point in order to identify clues or traces that could reavel changes triggered by the course in their professional knowledge. In line with these aims, the individual reflections (IR) written by the 20 teachers at the end of the course (in June 2021) were collected. Reflective writing has been regarded as an essential part of any teacher's professional growth, as it enables teachers to tap into knowledge gained through experiences, to develop critical analysis, to make connections between disparate sets of information, and to take new perspectives on issues (Scanlon et al., 2002). For this study, the IR written by the teachers were considered content-rich texts and appropriate to have access to the professional learning developed during the course.

The IR were analysed using content analysis (Schreier, 2012). This methodological procedure allows researchers to systematically and objectively analyse textual data and to infer about the analysed content, aiming to respond to the proposed research objectives. In this study, we built upon predefined categories of analysis, drawing on literature related to teacher professional learning and teacher professional knowledge (see, for instance, Lourenço et al., 2017; Martins, 2006; Shulman, 1986). Four categories of analysis were defined – *professional content knowledge* related to EduS and GCE; *pedagogical knowledge; knowledge of educational ends, purposes and values;* and *self-knowledge*. Table 9.1 offers a description of each category.

The two researchers/authors of this chapter were involved in the process of data analysis, and multiple instances for peer debriefing were carried out in order to validate data coding.

TABLE 9.1   Categorisation matrix

Categories	Description
Content knowledge	Knowledge of EduS in its various dimensions and of the key competencies for sustainability: systems thinking competence, anticipatory (futures thinking) competence, normative (values thinking) competence, strategic competence, and interpersonal competence (see Wiek, Withycombe, & Redman, 2011). Knowledge of GCE principles and methodologies.
Pedagogical knowledge	Knowledge of classroom organisation and management, including (interdisciplinary) learning strategies and assessment methods for creating effective teaching and learning environments for all students.
Knowledge of educational ends, purposes and values	Knowledge of the guiding principles of education, the goals and theories of education and their philosophical and historical grounds.
Self-knowledge	Teachers' self-perception of their role, individual practices and theories, which allows them to (re)define future strategies and demonstrate motivation to continue learning, so as to be able to transform individuals, contexts and communities to make the world a better place.

5 Findings

Research findings are presented below according to each category of analysis. Statements are illustrated by quotations from teachers' IR, which were translated from Portuguese into English to reach a broader readership. Teachers' names were anonymised to maintain the confidentiality of the participants.

5.1 *Content Knowledge*

Overall, all teachers considered the course to have contributed to both their personal and professional learning, classifying it as 'motivating', 'enriching' and 'inspiring'. Concerning the content of the course, this was deemed to be 'relevant', 'timely' and 'exciting'. Some teachers confessed that, prior to the course, they had little knowledge of ESGC, although they had relevant roles in school as coordinators of environmental projects (such as Eco Schools, the largest worldwide sustainable schools programme) or responsibilities associated with the new curriculum component of Citizenship and Development. As summarised by one of the teachers,

> The contents covered in the sessions were exciting and very relevant. They were a good complement to the little prior knowledge I had about these themes. I developed knowledge in the field of biodiversity to promote better student learning (…). Since I perform the duties of Coordinator of the Eco Schools Programme in my school, environmental themes already had a special place in my heart. However, with this course I realised how rudimentary my knowledge was. (JD, IR, p. 1)

In particular, the course allowed teachers to become acquainted to or to develop knowledge about the concepts of EduS and GCE, discovering links between the two:

> I learned that education for sustainability is an integral part of education for citizenship, assuming by its transversality a privileged position in the promotion of attitudes and values, as well as in the development of skills essential to meet the challenges of today's society. (JC, IR, p. 1)

The teachers understood the complexity of these approaches and were able to reflect about the multiple dimensions of EduS. In this respect, they felt they changed their initial conceptions. As highlighted by one of the teachers: 'Initially, I associated sustainability almost exclusively with the environmental dimension, but after the first session of this workshop I changed my perspective' (LP, IR, p. 1).

Teachers came to understand that sustainability touches not only the environmental dimension but the 'various dimensions of Life' (PB, IR, p. 1). This enabled them to discover links between sustainability and other topics such as linguistic and cultural diversity, global citizenship, circular economy, or even gender equality. The following quotes highlight this issue:

> Early on I understood how vast and comprehensive the word sustainability is. When I thought about sustainability, I focused only on the basics that are connected with protecting the environment and the planet (such as waste separation, recycling, reusing…). I learned that the concept was much broader. I was surprised and I was able to work on a theme that is very dear to me: gender equality. (LP, IR, p. 1)

> Education for sustainability is about much more than environment/nature, it is based on integrated education for adopting and changing attitudes and behaviours towards the environment, human rights and social justice. (JT, IR, p. 2)

In general, teachers recognised that they had changed their perspectives about the concepts of EduS and GCE and about the need to articulate the two, thus discovering a sort of a new subject.

5.2 *Pedagogical Knowledge*

The course also allowed teachers to develop pedagogical content knowledge and to update their teaching practice, as well as to expand their pedagogical repertoires (Causa, 2012). This was mentioned by some teachers as one of the main reasons for taking this course:

> Decree-Law 55/2018, which grants schools more autonomy and flexibility in curriculum management to promote essential learning competencies, together with the introduction of the Citizenship and Development component, requests more interdisciplinary work being carried out by the teachers and the commitment to project work. Therefore, the need for pedagogical updating in these areas was indisputable. I felt that this course was relevant, as topics related to sustainability are very broad; they can be used in project work and include different subject areas. During my practicum, I learned how to develop projects, but this was a long time

ago. I had never done training in this area before, which is really necessary. (CC, IR, p. 1)

> Within this framework I felt that it was urgent to improve and renew myself in terms of methodologies and teaching strategies. As a teacher I need to have new tools that I can put into practice in my professional activity. It is, therefore, important to recycle, learn and reflect about new pedagogical practices. (JT, IR, p. 1)

Apart from updating their practice with new strategies and approaches, namely 'developing skills to carry out project-based work' (SL, IR, p. 2), teachers also discovered new tools and resources in the course, mentioning that they would like to use them in the near future. One of the teachers points out, for instance, the use of Padlet:

> We became acquainted with several resources, some of which I have not yet had the opportunity to thoroughly explore. One example is Padlet, which I was not aware of. This is a good communication tool to use with the school community and with parents to showcase the activities and work developed by the students. It is user-friendly, practical, and very intuitive. It's a tool to keep on using. (CC, IR, p. 2)

More importantly, all teachers mentioned that, as a result of the course and of the action research projects they developed themselves, and that were also shared by the different groups, they learned how to integrate EduS and the key competencies for sustainability in the curriculum: 'Throughout the sessions I became aware of the key competencies for sustainability, realizing how we can operationalize each one of them in our teaching practice' (LS, IR, p. 1).

All in all, the course provided teachers with a catalogue of resources and best practices to approach these themes effectively with their groups of students, as illustrated by the quote:

> Due to the work shared in the course, I will be able in the future to work on various topics with children, based on the videos and power point presentations made available by the trainers and the trainees. (LP, IR, p. 1)

Hence, we can say that the teachers felt they learned about new teaching and learning strategies and were able to integrate them into their pedagogical and didactic repertoire. This professional learning was created by the opportunity of talking with different people, including colleagues from other schools. The discussion in small groups and as a whole group of new 'ways of doing' in schools, based on exchange of experiences, was a clear opportunity for professional learning highlighted by all.

5.3 Knowledge of Educational Ends, Purposes and Values

The course also played an important role in helping teachers reflect about the major purposes of education and, consequently, to (re)consider the demands of teaching activities in a globalised world:

> Being a teacher is also helping pupils to think, to build their own thinking system, and encourage action when something is not right. In an issue as important as the sustainability of our planet, it is necessary to act immediately. With little things we can do a lot. (CC, IR, p. 3)

Several trainees expressed the need for education to be rooted in values that lead to sustainability and global citizenship and for teachers to promote in their students 'the accountability for their actions and awareness/engagement in society' (SM, IR, p. 2). As expressed by one of the teachers, education for sustainability is about adopting and changing attitudes and behaviours towards the environment, catering for human rights and social justice (JT, IR, p. 2).

In order to promote these values, schools also need to change: 'A school «closed to the world» needs to be replaced by a school capable of developing in students a sense of responsibility and local and global citizenship' (SM, IR p. 2).

As a result, teachers considered the course to be relevant not only for teachers, but also for the whole school community. This is evident in the following statement:

> This is a very current and transversal issue that I think is very important for all teachers and students. This is why I think this course should be extended to all interested parties. The topics discussed and the knowledge developed are fundamental for all educational peers (teachers of all subject areas, non-teaching staff, parents, guardians and the entire community). (LP, IR, pp. 1–2)

5.4 Self-Knowledge

As previously discussed, throughout the course, teachers had multiple opportunities for discussion and reflection beyond the texts they wrote at the end of the course. During the sessions and in the regular meetings they had with the mentors, teachers had the opportunity to discuss key literature in the field, debate the pros and cons of particular pedagogical resources and strategies, and, as previously highlighted, to reconsider the purposes of education in current (and uncertain) times. This was expressed by some teachers in their IR:

> The course was designed from a perspective of practical application of knowledge, promoting debate and the exchange of experiences and knowledge (...) There was a lot of sharing of experiences, discussions and very pertinent reflections. (SM, IR, p. 1)

> This course, organised as a "Workshop", offered a more practical and attractive component, forcing me to question, reflect and reformulate the way I approached certain themes. (PB, IR, p. 1)

Hence, the course provided teachers with meaningful times and spaces to reflect about their personal and professional selves. As emphasised by one of the teachers:

> School leaves little time to have contact with the outside world, with reality (and these two years were even worse), to promote knowledge and a taste for nature, to teach the importance of preserving the environment and our cultural heritage, to educate active and engaged citizens and to develop skills through active, experiential and collaborative learning situations directed towards solving problems both locally and globally [...] teachers should have training like this to broaden our horizons, to encourage us to do more and better, to remind us of how important our role is and our contribution to a more sustainable world. (SM, IR, pp. 2, 3)

In their final reflections teachers considered that the course allowed them to gain confidence about their own abilities to integrate ESGC in their teaching practice, especially as they were able to conduct action research projects with their own students and to see other projects developed by their peers. As teachers highlight,

> I believe that the lessons learned were immense, I really feel more capable. The work shared by the other teachers and the resources suggested by the trainers gave me a lot of ideas to develop future projects that can secure a more sustainable world and a more sustainable education, taking into account the goals of sustainable development and the key competencies for sustainability. (CC, IR, p. 3)

Teachers, therefore, expressed their willingness to continue integrating these topics in their teaching, particularly in light of their students' sometimes differing responses to the projects they implemented. While some teachers stress the enthusiasm of the students with the themes they chose for their project, others mention their unawareness of and passivity about relevant topics as important catalysts to continue the work carried out so far. As one of the teachers points out:

> I found a passivity and lack of sensitivity towards the subject [of gender equality] on the part of the children that surprised me and reinforced the importance of implementing this project and continuing it in the upcoming years. (LP, IR, p. 1)

In short, and in line with the literature on professional learning (Appova & Arbaugh, 2018; Taylor, 2017), the teachers show motivation and volition in their reflections about the opportunities created by the teacher education programme feeling that they have changed and that they are better teachers able to respond to the transformative purpose of Education.

6   Discussion

This study sought to understand the impact of an online teacher education course, titled 'Education for sustainability: diversity, dialogue and inclusion', on the professional learning of a group of 20 in-service teachers in Portugal. In particular, it explored how these teachers changed from a professional pointed of view when approaching and introducing ESGC in their teaching practice. With these objectives in mind, the individual reflections written by the teachers at the end of the course were gathered and explored using content analysis, considering four key categories: professional content knowledge (related to EduS and GCE); pedagogical knowledge; knowledge of educational ends, purposes and values; and self-knowledge.

Regarding content knowledge, teachers developed a clearer and wider understanding of EduS and GCE, discovering multiple dimensions and intersections. Initially, most teachers associated EduS with the environmental dimension, however, after the course they were able to notice other dimensions (such as the social and economic) that are fundamental in achieving sustainable development. This enabled them to select their projects themes that they were already interested in, or which were already part of the curriculum (such as citizenship, diversity, inclusion, or gender equality), and to place these themes within this broader framework of ESGC. This conceptualisation provided meaning and a sense of direction to their work.

These results are aligned with prior research, which has also reported an evolution in teachers' understandings of EduS and GCE as a result of professional development courses, particularly when these are supported by a combination of theoretical and practical activities, such as readings of key literature, concept maps, or construction and implementation of resources and lesson plans (see, for instance, Lourenço, 2021; Lourenço et al., 2018; Myers & Rivero, 2019; Sá, 2008). According to the literature, when these activities are appropriately framed and supported with enough room for discussion and reflection, teachers are able to overcome the complexity they often identify in these concepts and to discover links with the curriculum, which allows them to commit more fully to these transformative forms of education.

Another important feature highlighted by the teachers in their IR is related to the development of their pedagogical repertoires. In particular, teachers made extensive references to the contribution of the TedP for the discovery of new strategies, approaches, tools and resources to not only introduce ESGC in their classrooms and thus respond to curriculum reforms, but also to update their overall teaching skills. This was considered by teachers to be a result of the projects developed both by themselves and by the other trainees, but also a consequence of the online sessions, which used tools and software teachers were previously unfamiliar with. Most importantly, teachers felt that the TedP allowed them to understand that it is possible to integrate ESGC in the classroom and to learn how to do this in a meaningful way.

The format and characteristics of the TedP – a workshop, which used an action research methodology – also provided opportunities for teachers to reflect about the ends, purposes and values of education in an uncertain world, and to (re)consider their own role as educators. According to the teachers, education should be rooted in values that lead to global citizenship and sustainability, such as valorisation of (linguistic and cultural) diversity, preservation of natural resources, defence of human rights and freedoms, social justice, and social responsibility. Therefore, they feel that they have an important role to play in their students' lives, especially in helping them develop the necessary knowledge, skills and dispositions to be able to secure a more peaceful, sustainable and inclusive world than the one they have inherited.

Still, they seem to be aware that this task should not rest solely on their shoulders and should be undertaken together with the non-teaching staff, the students, their families and the whole community. Despite their increased motivation to teach for about ESGC and to continue the projects developed during the TedP, the teachers understand that there is a need for ESGC to be dealt with in a systematic and interdisciplinary manner, as well as to be infused in the ethos and mission of their schools to achieve the desired goals (Henck, 2018; Mogren et al., 2019).

Overall, the results of this study suggest that the TedP was useful in helping the 20 in-service teachers develop clearer conceptualisations of ESGC, learn how to approach these topics in an interdisciplinary manner, and to gain confidence and motivation to teach ESGC in a more meaningful and intentional manner. The TedP provided opportunities for teachers to reflect critically, to become more aware of their capabilities and challenges, to work in collaboration, to justify their teaching practice, to be more resilient and open to innovation and change, and to increase their commitment and motivation, which are all aspects central to teacher quality (Heck & Ambrosetti, 2018; Madalińska Michalak et al., 2018). Data also shows that teachers are looking for more quality in their professional knowledge and practices, which in itself is a characteristic of quality teachers.

However, this study is not without limitations. The first shortcoming is related to the participants and to their profiles. Those enrolled in the course represent a sample of in-service teachers who were motivated to select the course theme and may have had initial 'buy-in' to the perspectives, curriculum, and pedagogies enacted.

Secondly, as a qualitative case study conducted by two researchers who were also teacher educators in the course, subjectivity and positionality are omnipresent and might have influenced data analysis. Adding to researcher bias, participant bias is also a possibility. Considering that the IR were part of the teachers' assessment in the professional development course, there was a risk that they wrote their texts in a way they believed corresponded to what the teacher educators were looking for.

Finally, it should not be forgotten that, although teachers revealed a better understanding of ESGC and showed signs of personal and professional development, that does not necessarily mean that they have effectively integrated ESGC in their teaching identities, or that the optimism and motivation that the TedP apparently inspired will last long. Longstanding peer and leadership support, as well as continuing professional development on these topics, will be fundamental to ensure that their confidence does not fade.

In light of the above, it might be worthwhile to conduct a follow-up study of these teachers supported by classroom observation. This would contribute to understanding the long run effects of the TedP, illuminate areas for improvement, and permit a more rigorous analysis of its effects on teacher quality and quality teaching. Indeed, quality can only be identified in longitudinal studies that follow up teachers in their own contexts and actions for a longer period.

7 Conclusion

The 2030 Agenda for Sustainable Development and the leadership provided by the UN and UNESCO made the themes that are at the heart of this chapter gain increased prominence amongst policy-makers since the beginning of the 21st century. Still, policy initiatives on ESGC do not seem to have been followed up by increased resources and appropriate measures to build capacity, expertise and confidence within the teaching profession. ESGC is a complex and controversial field, which is often seen as being marginal or counter to dominant pedagogical approaches within teacher education. This prevents EduS and GCE themes from being included in teacher education programmes (both pre-service and in-service) and to gain the desired relevance in the often-packed syllabi.

Yet, the project of educating environmentally informed, global citizens has a particular urgency given the global imperative. Therefore, it is crucial to ensure pupils are prepared to deal with the challenges of an uncertain world. The literature suggests that teacher education is a key starting point, which should be recognised (Bourn et al., 2017). This means infusing ESGC throughout teacher preparation courses, shifting these themes from the peripheries of teacher education (where they are often seen as optional extras); supporting in-service teachers (but also school leaders and non-teaching staff) in understanding and enacting ESGC; and promoting school partnerships and ESGC communities of practice (linking teachers, universities and civil society organisations) to provide teachers with times and spaces to (re)construct professional knowledge and develop their confidence and skills to be agents of change.

Integrating ESGC in teacher education programmes is a necessity, but it also represents an opportunity to support quality teaching and quality teacher education, especially in times of uncertainties. The complexities and demands of a constantly changing society open up possibilities to rethink teacher education, namely by designing teacher education programmes that prepare teachers as committed agents of change. Researchers suggest that 're-orientating education to address sustainability is a deep process that involves changes in programmes, practices and policy, as well as awareness, knowledge, skills and values and acceptance of the sustainability paradigm' (McKeown, 2014, p. 129). Furthermore, as highlighted in this chapter, ESGC seems to amplify questions about the purpose and contribution of teachers in society, especially the extent to which they have a role beyond simply imparting knowledge and skills, including promoting themes such as social justice, greater equity in the world and a sense of environmental responsibility.

Hence, more initiatives and research linking ESGC and teacher education are fundamental to prepare globally-aware educators and to redirect the current trajectory of our planet.

Acknowledgements

This work was co-funded by the Erasmus+ Programme of the European Union under the project TEDS – Teacher education for sustainability. Schools educating for sustainability: Proposals for and from in-service teacher education (project code: 2019-1-PT01-KA201-060830), coordinated by the University of Aveiro (Portugal). This work was also financially supported by National Funds through FCT – Fundação para a Ciência e a Tecnologia, I.P., in the scope of the framework contract foreseen in the numbers 4, 5, and 6 of the article 23, of the Decree-Law 57/2016, of August 29, changed by Law 57/2017, of July 19.

Note

1   http://teds.web.ua.pt

References

Alarcão, I. (1996). Reflexão crítica sobre o pensamento de Donald Schön e os programas de formação de professores [Critical reflection about Donald Schön and teacher education programmes]. *Revista da Faculdade de Educação da Universidade de São Paulo*, 22(2), 11–42.

Appova, A., & Arbaugh, F. (2018). Teachers' motivation to learn: Implications for supporting professional growth. *Professional Development in Education*, 44(1), 5–21.

Avalos, B. (2011). Teacher professional development in teaching and teacher education over ten years. *Teaching and Teacher Education*, 27(1), 10–20.

Batista, B. F., & Andrade, A. I. (2021). Educating for biocultural diversity and sustainable development in first years of schooling: An analysis of documents from the Portuguese educational system. *Frontiers in Education*, 6(652196). https://doi.org/10.3389/feduc.2021.652196

Beauchamp, C. (2015). Reflection in teacher education: Issues emerging from a review of current literature. *Reflective Practice: International and Multidisciplinary Perspectives*, 16(1), 123–141.

Bourn, D., Hunt, F., & Bamber, P. (2017). *A review of education for sustainable development and global citizenship education in teacher education*. Paper commissioned for the 2017/8 Global Education Monitoring Report, Accountability in education: Meeting our commitments. UNESCO.

Causa, M. (2012). Le répertoire didactique. Une notion complexe. In M. Causa (Ed.), *Formation initiale et profils d'enseignants de langues. Enjeux et questionnements* (pp. 15–72). De Boeck.

Darling-Hammond, L., Hyler, M. E., & Gardner, M. (2017). *Effective teacher professional development*. Learning Policy Institute.

Franch, S. (2020). Reconceptualising citizenship education towards the global, the political and the critical: Challenges and perspectives in a province in Northern Italy. In P. Bamber (Ed.), *Teacher education for sustainable development and global citizenship: Critical perspectives on values, curriculum and assessment* (pp. 144–155). Routledge.

Freire, P. (2018). *Pedagogia do oprimido [Pedagogy of the oppressed]* (3rd ed.). Afrontamento.

Gaudelli, W. (2016). *Global citizenship education: Everyday transcendence*. Routledge.

Heck, D., & Ambrosetti, A. (Eds.). (2018). *Teacher education in and for uncertain times*. Springer.

Henck, A. (2018). Looking beyond the classroom: Integrating global citizenship education throughout your whole school. *Childhood Education, 94*(4), 75–77.

Hickson, H. (2011). Critical reflection: Reflecting on learning to be reflective. *Reflective Practice, 12*(6), 829–839.

Hopkins, C. A. (2020). Foreword. In P. Bamber (Ed.), *Teacher education for sustainable development and global citizenship: Critical perspectives on values, curriculum and assessment* (pp. XXIII–XXV). Routledge.

Hubers, M. D., Endedijk, M. D., & Van Veen, K. (2020). Effective characteristics of professional development programs for science and technology education. *Professional Development in Education*. https://doi.org/10.1080/19415257.2020.1752289

Jones, K., & O'Brien, J. (2011). Professional development in teacher education: European perspectives. *Professional Development in Education, 37*(5), 645–650.

Lourenço, M. (2018). Internationalizing teacher education curricula: Opportunities for academic staff development. *On the Horizon, 26*, 157–169.

Lourenço, M. (2021). From caterpillars to butterflies: Exploring pre-service teachers' transformations while navigating global citizenship education. *Frontiers in Education, 6*, 651250. https://doi.org/10.3389/feduc.2021.651250

Lourenço, M., Andrade, A. I., & Martins, F. (2017). Formar para a diversidade linguística e cultural na educação infantil: possibilidades de construção de conhecimento profissional [Educating for linguistic and cultural diversity in pre-primary education:

possibilities for the construction of professional knowledge]. *Revista Internacional de Formação de Professores, 2*(2), 76–99.

Lourenço, M., Andrade, A. I., & Sá, S. (2018). Teachers' voices on language awareness in pre-primary and primary school settings: Implications for teacher education. *Language, Culture and Curriculum, 31*(2), 113–127.

Madalińska-Michalak, J., O'Doherty, T., & Flores, M. A. (2018). Teachers and teacher education in uncertain times. *European Journal of Teacher Education, 41*(5), 567–571.

Marcelo, C. (2009). Desenvolvimento profissional docente: passado e futuro [Teacher professional development: past and future]. *Sísifo – Revista de Ciências da Educação, 8*, 7–22.

Martins, A. P. (2006). O poder da colaboração na (re)construção do conhecimento profissional docente: um estudo em contexto [The power of collaboration in the (re)construction of professional teaching knowledge: A study in context] [Unpublished MA thesis]. Universidade de Aveiro.

McCloskey, S. (2019). The sustainable development goals, neoliberalism, and NGOs: It's time to pursue a transformative path to social justice. *Policy and Practice: A Development Education Review, 29*, 152–159.

McKeown, R. (2014). The leading edge of teacher education and ESD. *Journal of Education for Sustainable Development, 8*(2), 127–131.

Mogren, A., Gericke, N., & Scherp, H. (2019). Whole school approaches to education for sustainable development: A model that links to school improvement. *Environmental Education Research, 25*(4), 508–531.

Myers, J. P., & Rivero, K. (2019). Preparing globally competent preservice teachers: The development of content knowledge, disciplinary skills, and instructional design. *Teaching and Teacher Education, 77*, 214–225.

Oxfam. (2015). *Education for global citizenship: A guide for schools*. Oxfam.

Rapoport, A. (2010). We cannot teach what we don't know: Indiana teachers talk about global citizenship education. *Education, Citizenship and Social Justice, 5*, 179–190.

Sá, P. (2008). *Educação para o desenvolvimento sustentável no 1º CEB: contributos da formação de professores* [*Education for sustainable development in primary school: contributions from teacher education*] [PhD thesis]. University of Aveiro. http://hdl.handle.net/10773/1457

Sá, P., João, P., & Rodrigues, A. (2019). Sustainable development in primary education – A perspective from official Portuguese guiding documents. In A. Costa, L. Reis, & A. Moreira (Eds.), *WCQR 2019: Computer supported qualitative research, advances in intelligent systems and computing* (pp. 262–273). Springer.

Santamaría-Cárdaba, N., & Lourenço, M. (2021). Global citizenship education in primary school: A comparative analysis of education policy documents in Portugal and Spain. *Iberoamerican Journal of Development Studies, 10*(2), 130–158. https://doi.org/10.26754/ojs_ried/ijds.585

Scanlon, J. M., Care, W. D., & Udod, S. (2002). Unravelling the unknowns of reflection in classroom teaching. *Journal of Advances in Nursing, 38*, 136–143.

Schön, D. A. (1983). *The reflective practitioner*. Temple Smith.

Schön, D. A. (1987). *Educating the reflective practitioner: Toward a new design for teaching and learning in the professions*. Jossey-Bass.

Schreier, M. (2012). *Qualitative content analysis*. Sage.

Schulman, L. S. (1986). Those who understand: Knowledge growth in teaching. *Educational Researcher, 15*(2), 4–14.

Tarozzi, M., & Inguaggiato, C. (Eds.). (2016). *Global citizenship education in Europe. A Comparative study on education policies across 10 EU countries*. Research deliverable issued within the European project 'Global Schools'. Provincia Autonoma di Trento.

Taylor, P. (2017). Learning about professional growth through listening to teachers. *Professional Development in Education, 43*(1), 87–105,

Torres, C. A. (2021). Series Editor Foreword. In P. Bamber (Ed.), *Teacher education for sustainable development and global citizenship: Critical perspectives on values, curriculum and assessment* (pp. XX–XII). Routledge.

UNESCO. (2020). *Education for sustainable development: A roadmap*. UNESCO.

United Nations. (2012). *Global education first initiative*. United Nations.

United Nations. (2015). *Transforming our world: The 2030 Agenda for sustainable development*. United Nations.

Vélaz de Medrano, C., & Vaillant, D. (Eds.). (2009). *Aprendizaje y desarrollo profesional docente*. Santillana, OEI.

Wiek, A., Withycombe, L., & Redman, C. L. (2011). Key competencies in sustainability: A reference framework for academic program development. *Sustainability Science, 6*(2), 203–218.

Yemini, M., Tibbitts, F., & Goren, H. (2019). Trends and caveats: Review of literature on global citizenship education in teacher training. *Teaching and Teacher Education, 77*, 77–89.

Yin, R. K. (2009). *Case study research: Design and methods* (4th ed.). Sage.

Zeichner, K. (2008). A critical analysis of reflection as a goal for teacher education. *Educação & Sociedade, 29*(103), 535–554.

CHAPTER 10

Teacher Education in Conflict-Affected Societies

The Case of Mosul University after the Demise of the Islamic State

Vasileios Symeonidis, Felix Senger, Heike Wendt, Amal Fatah Zedan, Saraa Salim Dawood and Fawzi Habeeb Jabrail

Abstract

In crisis situations, during armed conflicts or after natural disasters, education systems often fail to provide access to the quality of education that is arguably crucial for conflict stabilisation, peacemaking, and development, particularly in countries recovering from war. Challenges to educational provision in (post-)crisis situations and the demands of curriculum change are well discussed and thoroughly documented in the literature. However, the critical role of teachers is often discussed in general terms but not well understood. Furthermore, little is known about the challenges with initial teacher education in post-crisis contexts, or about the quality of teaching in such contexts.

This study aims to identify the challenges with providing quality teaching and teacher education in crisis situations by studying the case of Mosul University in Iraq. Focusing on developments after the demise of the Islamic State, the study looks at expert interviews as a means of exploring the perspectives of teacher educators at different faculties of Mosul University. It also analyses the teacher education curriculum and its development and implementation. Our findings provide an insight into teacher education structures in Iraq and the broader challenges presented by crisis contexts. A core challenge appears to be the centralised curriculum, which focuses on subject specific knowledge rather than other types of knowledge that are of key importance for prospective teachers in areas affected by conflict. Finally, the article provides suggestions for improving the teacher education curriculum at Mosul University and for addressing the challenges presented by crisis contexts.

Keywords

teacher education – post-conflict societies – curriculum – University of Mosul – Iraq

1   Introduction

In crisis situations, education systems often fail to provide access to education and/or the requisite quality of education. This means that young people are deprived of their fundamental right to education, which should enable them to acquire knowledge and skills, become socialised, and develop their identity. Educational institutions cannot provide the protection, qualification, socialisation, and subjectification that are arguably crucial for stabilisation, peacebuilding and development, particularly in countries recovering from war (Smith, 2010). Challenges relating to educational provision in (post-)crisis situations and the need for curriculum change are well discussed and documented in the literature (Barakat et al., 2013; Barrios-Tao et al., 2017; Smith, 2010). However, even though the availability of qualified teachers is one of the crucial factors for enabling access to, and the provision of, quality education for all, the critical role of teachers is often discussed in general terms but not well understood. Furthermore, little is known about challenges to initial teacher education in post-crisis contexts, or about the quality of teaching in such contexts.

This chapter aims to identify the challenges with providing quality teaching and teacher education in crisis situations, by studying the case of Mosul University in Iraq. Teacher education in Iraq has faced major upheavals and transitional phases, having been instrumentalised to ensure teachers' conformity with the ideologies of the different forces that have occupied the country in recent years. Focusing on developments after the demise of the Islamic State in Iraq and Syria (ISIS), the chapter describes the context and structure of teacher education, the development and implementation of teacher education curricula, and the experiences of teacher educators at Mosul University, one of Iraq's oldest and most renowned higher education institutions and one that was severely impacted by violent conflict during the city's occupation. Before looking at the case study, the following section reviews the challenges facing teachers in post-conflict settings, their perceived role, and the role of teacher education in such contexts.

2   The Realities Faced by Teachers in Post-conflict Settings, and Their Perceived Mission

In post-conflict societies, teacher education is caught between the reality of the context that teachers are facing and the dominant narrative that wants teachers to act as agents of change. In the following sections, we describe the challenges faced by the teaching profession in contexts of crisis and illustrate the normative view of teachers as agents of sustainable peace, social cohesion and development, as promoted by certain stakeholders and agencies.

2.1 Workforce-Related Challenges

Ensuring educational provision and access to education requires competent people to be able to, and to want to, work as teachers. Hence we cannot talk about the role of teacher education in post-conflict societies without talking about context, and specifically issues including teacher status, pay and working conditions. Three major challenges can be identified: teacher qualification; teacher recruitment, selection, and employment; and teacher retention (UNESCO-IIEP, 2010). These factors, along with teachers' reduced autonomy and decision-making ability due to standardised curricula and accountability mechanisms, are indications of a deprofessionalisation process within the teaching profession (Locatelli, 2018; MacBeath, 2012; Symeonidis & Stromquist, 2020) that is likely to have a long-term destabilising effect on the education system.

Teacher retention is a challenge in schools in (post-)conflict situations (Novelli & Sayed, 2016; Sayed et al., 2018; UNESCO-IIEP, 2010). Previous studies have shown that in locations affected by conflict the social status of teachers can decline, attrition rates can increase and working conditions can be increasingly eroded (Novelli & Sayed, 2016). Safety, low or irregular payment, displacement, stress, behavioural problems and increasingly diversified student needs, combined with inadequate resources and working conditions and a lack of support or acknowledgement may induce teachers to look for alternative employment. Low or irregular payment arises in some cases from the lack of effective teacher salary systems rather than from a lack of financial resources (Dolan et al., 2012), whereas safety issues are mostly the result of attacks by state and non-state-actors such as rebel groups, militias, or criminal gangs for political, military, ideological, ethno-religious, sectarian or criminal purposes (Global Coalition to Protect Education from Attack [GCPEA], 2014). Teachers themselves are also likely to be subject to the same challenges as the general population, or parts of it, during conflict or crisis. As human beings, teachers may be negatively affected by war, displacement and crisis, both physically and mentally. Their professional role as government representatives may put them at increased risk, as reported in cases where teachers and educational personnel have been threatened, abducted, or attacked by insurgent groups (GCPEA, 2014). Furthermore, their professional role of providing children with support can lead to additional pressure if teachers are unable to cope or act professionally in certain circumstances (Sayed et al., 2018).

Research clearly shows that crisis, war, and disaster can affect children's and young adults' well-being and socio-emotional and academic development

(Cervantes-Duarte & Fernández-Cano, 2016; Frounfelker et al., 2019). Teachers are often the first to respond to students' socio-emotional needs in such situations and are regularly involved in delivering interventions in these contexts, often without adequate support or training. Adebayo (2019) argues, in relation to post-conflict Liberia, for example, that the multiplicity of roles that teachers are required to perform, such as second parents, guardians, and counsellors, leads to an intensified workload. Teachers may feel unable, or be unable, to provide adequate support for emotional needs and behavioural problems; and working with traumatised individuals may affect teachers' own mental health and can lead to secondary traumatic stress (Müller & Goldenberger, 2020).

In consequence, recruiting, selecting and employing teachers may become more difficult (UNESCO-IIEP, 2010). Studies have shown that in crisis situations, prospective teachers may join the profession reluctantly (Novelli & Sayed, 2016). However, obtaining government employment through a teaching position may provide a relatively secure income, social prestige and the prospect of a decent retirement. Combined with the expansion of public employment that is generally observable in post-conflict settings and especially in resource-rich countries, this may still lead to an increase in the teacher workforce. It is important to bear in mind, however, that stable remuneration can also attract untrained and unqualified individuals who may want to become teachers by claiming that they have the necessary qualifications and who may draw a teacher's salary but not actually work, leading to the phenomenon of 'ghost' teachers and the need for rigorous selection processes (UNESCO-IIEP, 2010, p. 5). The hiring of unqualified personnel, without any certification, is also a common practice when it comes to teacher shortages and has a negative impact on teacher status (Symeonidis & Stromquist, 2020; Stromquist, 2018). In contexts where teachers have a low professional status, the feminisation of the teaching profession is more likely to occur (Kelleher, 2011) and so is the expansion of private education through low-fee private schools which impact negatively on teachers' working conditions (Locatelli, 2018).

Finally, getting teachers qualified and developing their knowledge, skills and attitudes through teacher education and capacity building programmes can be a significant challenge in post-conflict situations. It is, however, a prerequisite for the success of any overall education sector policy plan that takes account of conflict (Novelli & Sayed, 2016; Sayed et al., 2018; Smith, 2010). The greatest barrier to quality professional development in fragile contexts is the difficult working conditions in which teachers work, and which impact on their professional identity, efficacy and professionalism (Burns, 2015). Quite often, there is also a lack of personnel qualified to help teachers master material, since long-term conflicts can result in a brain-drain into higher education programmes (Muthanna & Sang, 2018). If there are opportunities for professional development, their impact may be limited by problems related to coordination between providers or between bodies that evaluate teachers (Burns, 2015). In contexts where conflict is still present, it may simply be dangerous for teachers to participate in professional development activities, since the providers of such activities may be seen as closely aligned with an unpopular government (Burns, 2015). Another barrier relates to poorly designed professional development, which can be episodic rather than sustained and intensive, reflecting budget constraints, the lack of qualified trainers, volatility, and logistical challenges (Burns, 2015). It can also reflect misconceptions on the part of policy-makers or donors about the role of teachers and how they learn. Non-state providers play a significant role in capacity building programmes, because of their perceived ability to address states' failure to deliver services effectively and efficiently (Teamey, 2007), but the quality of such programmes for teachers is often criticised and perceived as irrelevant (Burns, 2015; Burns & Lawrie, 2015).

2.2 *Training Teachers to Be Agents of Change*

From a political perspective, education is often discussed as long-term investment in conflict stabilisation, peacemaking and development. The (re-)establishment of functioning educational institutions may (re-)enforce the legitimacy of government (Thyne, 2006), help people to return to, or to resettle, areas in order to attend school or go to work, or force them to do so (BIICL, 2016), and may protect young people against being recruited into armed combat (Barakat & Urdal, 2009; Urdal, 2004, 2006). In situations affected by conflict, education can on the one hand contribute to conflict transformation and support attempts at peacebuilding; on the other, it can act as a driver of conflict by fueling grievances, stereotypes, xenophobia and other antagonisms, or by promoting inequality and political dominance and the marginalisation of certain societal groups (Davies, 2010; Stewart, 2011). Accessible and available educational institutions, schools' ethos and culture, curricula, educational materials and pedagogy are all key mechanisms in this context. Teachers are key agents of political socialisation, providing unambiguous knowledge and socialising students with regard to the government and the state, attitudes towards others and parties involved in conflict, the value of education and knowledge sources, and who should be regarded as a citizen.

In post-conflict settings, teachers are often required to serve as agents of sustainable peace, social cohesion and development, and their training needs to focus on supporting life skills, citizenship and peace education, moral and ethical education, child protection, human rights, skills for sustainable livelihoods, challenging gender inequalities, and learner-centreedness (Novelli & Sayed, 2016). These are topics that can promote conflict sensitivity and are cited as important indicators of the values that the education system communicates to new generations of young people (Smith, 2010). However, teacher education curricula tend to approach these topics superficially, focusing instead on the development of subject knowledge and skills for curriculum delivery (Sayed et al., 2018). This tension is exacerbated when teacher education is mostly lecture-based and delivered by external experts, cascade programmes or unqualified teacher educators (Adebayo, 2019; Ghosn-Chelala, 2020). Colonial roots also continue to influence teacher education curricula in some developing regions (Namubiru, 2014). These issues are indicative of a culture of avoidance rather than diversity and critical thinking, and of a need to transform the curriculum (Ghosn-Chelala, 2020; Namubiru, 2014). Such transformation implies moving away from approaches based on knowledge transmission and that prioritise nationalistic principles towards empowering teachers to integrate progressive teaching and dialogue with students on conflict-related issues.

The agency of teachers as peacebuilders can be seen as static, fixed and essentialised or as multidimensional, situated and dynamic (Sayed et al., 2018). This agency is not exercised in isolation from teachers' surroundings, and there are cases where teachers may act as agents of change (e.g. promoting respect, justice and inclusion among students) or as agents of conflict (e.g. perpetuating inequity and conflict among ethnic, religious or socio-economically disadvantaged groups) (Sayed et al., 2018). The lines between these two conflicting roles are sometimes blurred and they may play out simultaneously in certain contexts. After describing the predominant narrative of teachers as change agents, the section below highlights some of the implications of this narrative for teacher education in post-conflict settings.

3   The Role of Teacher Education

A number of countries are concerned about shortfalls in the quality of their teacher workforce. Irrespective of whether they are experiencing crisis situations or not, many countries struggle to ensure they have enough teachers with the knowledge and skills to meet schools' needs, and to provide teacher education and continuing professional development opportunities to substantially improve the quality of teaching. Achieving change within systems that have developed over many years of history is difficult for many reasons. Policy with regard to teacher education is fundamentally political and increasingly influenced by a globalisation that is based on the ideas of neoliberalism

(Cochran-Smith & Fries, 2011). As such, teacher education involves the negotiation of conflicting values and assumptions about the purposes of schooling, the responsibilities of teachers, and the role of education in improving a nation's ability to compete in the global economy (Cochran-Smith, 2013). In many circumstances, political elites are likely to want to use education for their own purposes and view teachers and the quality of teaching as 'a key issue in the economic development of a country, in safeguarding a socially coherent society and in conserving the cultural heritage of a country' (Snoek & Zogla, 2009, p. 25).

Teacher education in its various forms, from initial training to continuing professional development, is thus crucial if society is to be transformed through education. And while the critical role of teachers in post-conflict recovery is generally accepted in the literature, little is known about the challenges faced by teacher education or about teacher quality in such contexts. At all levels of the education system, governance is a crucial issue (Wendt, 2012). Existing arrangements for teacher representation and participation in consultation, decision-making and governance may be potential sources of conflict, or they may be opportunities for inclusion and the resolution of grievances. Arrangements to ensure transparency and accountability also reflect the system's capacity to accept and address inequalities that might otherwise become sources of conflict. Although decentralising education systems may have the potential to increase participation and ownership, it may leave education open to manipulation as part of local politics. This highlights the need for systems and structures to insulate the education sector from political bias, potential corruption and interference in operational decisions. Policies on teacher education reflect the prevailing ideologies amongst those in power, and in contexts of crisis and conflict, this control is exercised more thoroughly. In such contexts, conflicting notions of the desired outcomes and the purpose and delivery of teacher education are often intensified due to resource constraints and weak governance systems. Therefore, we propose to start by mapping the desired outcomes of teacher education in post-conflict settings as documented in the literature, before moving on to describe what takes place in practice.

Initial teacher education and continuing professional development are essentially connected to the idea of preparing teachers to be agents for social cohesion and peacebuilding (Novelli & Sayed, 2016; Sayed et al., 2018). Seen from that perspective, the role of teachers is redefined: they switch from being deliverers of curricula and educational reforms to being agents of sustainable peace, social cohesion and development, whose capacity to influence their conflict-driven surroundings is of paramount importance (Adebayo, 2019; Novelli & Sayed, 2016). This implies that teachers develop the theoretical knowledge and pedagogical expertise to become autonomous professionals and reflexive practitioners, aspiring to democratic values and fostering critical thinking. According to Sayed et al. (2018), research on the teacher education systems of Rwanda and South Africa indicates that professional development activities need to be underpinned by explicitly articulated theories of social cohesion and enable the creation of supportive professional networks for teachers, both within and between educational organisations. They also recommend the development of bilingual pedagogies for multilingual contexts, adequate resourcing for initial teacher education, and the strengthening of partnerships between schools and teacher education institutions.

In post-conflict societies, teacher education is viewed as supporting peace education efforts. However, the focus of this interaction is often on helping teachers to develop the right competencies to promote peace, resolve conflict and prevent violence in classrooms; teacher education programmes in societies affected by conflict and post-conflict societies rarely cover the perpetuation of different forms of conflict and violence that result from nation-state structures (McGlynn et al., 2009). Adopting a 'critical peace education' perspective that considers the consequences of structural inequalities and nation-state structures, Bekerman and Zembylas (2014) argue that teachers in post-conflict societies should become 'critical design experts'. This means that teachers should develop expertise in the contexts in which they operate and the ways in which interactions are engineered in those contexts, so as to be able to critique the everyday practices of nation-state structures and develop appropriate interventions to disrupt such structures. At the same time, they should look for adaptive strategies to survive within the system while trying to improve it. To this end, 'teacher education programmes need to be redesigned to encourage prospective teachers to become explorers who uncover the ways society is organised and have the knowledge and skills to envision an alternative "design" of this society' (Bekerman & Zembylas, 2014, p. 58). This redefined notion of the relationship between teacher education and peace education implies a need for critical assessment of the normative premises upon which knowledge claims are made, and consideration of the power relations involved in ontological and epistemological assumptions about identity, culture and education.

Moreover, teacher education can open up space in which teachers can engage with painful personal legacies of the past, enabling them to integrate issues of moral and ethical decision-making into their teaching (Weldon, 2010). This was the case with the South African teacher development program, Facing the Past, for example, which helped teachers examine how conflict affected them as individuals and as teachers, so that they could in turn facilitate difficult conversations about the past with their students, with a view to building a democratic future (Weldon, 2010). This value-driven and ethically defensible approach to teacher education can promote social justice and equity, enabling teachers 'to not only change hearts and minds but also the difficult societal structures and inequalities that underpin conflicts' (Sayed et al., 2018, p. 6).

4 Methods

The literature review in the two preceding sections looks at the discourse around the requirements and conditions that school teachers might be facing in post-conflict settings and the necessity for teacher education to ensure that prospective teachers are adequately prepared. Most of the literature reviewed above refers to the importance of the context in which teacher education and schooling is delivered as well as the need to provide prospective teachers with specific knowledge – especially with regard to helping their students understand the importance of social cohesion, peace and equity.

In this chapter, we explore the extent to which the observations in the literature also hold true for the Mosul region and for initial teacher education at Mosul University. We look at governance, education finances, context, teacher status, and the structure and curriculum of initial teacher education as well as opportunities to engage with painful personal legacies of the past. We have taken Mosul University as a case study because it is one of the oldest and largest universities in Iraq and has always been – and remains – on the frontline of conflicts; this has a big impact on the quality of academic teaching, equality of academic opportunity and academic life as a whole. In order to examine teacher education in one of the world's most prominent crisis contexts, we took a variety of approaches to data collection.

Policy documents were sourced via official authorities and translated into English. Salary information used to consider teacher status was collected through official government documents provided by university administrators at the University of Mosul. Contextual information drew on field notes, the professional knowledge of the authors working as teacher educators at Mosul university and transcripts of two online focus group meetings with 25 educators in March 2021. In order to examine the overall structure of teacher education, three in-depth semi-structured interviews were conducted with renowned teacher education experts at Mosul University. The Iraqi interviewees were professors at Mosul University from different faculties, including Mathematics and English. They all played central roles in overseeing the structures of their own department and were well informed about the structures of departments involved in teacher education. Interviews were carried out primarily in English and lasted an average of 112 minutes. Due to travel restrictions in the context of the COVID-19 pandemic, these interviews were undertaken by means of video phone calls and recorded with permission; whenever participants were uncomfortable with this, recording was stopped and their points noted down by hand.

In order to enable analysis of curriculum content, the curricula of different subjects and departments were collected and translated into English. For our analysis we selected curricula for pre-school education (n = 1), special education (n = 1) humanities for primary education (n = 4), science for primary education (n = 3), humanities for secondary education (n = 4), and science for secondary education (n = 2). We took courses as analytical units and coded them using a deductive approach, building on the model of professional teacher knowledge proposed by Baumert and Kunter (2013) and distinguishing between subject knowledge, pedagogical content knowledge, pedagogical/psychological knowledge, and counselling knowledge. Subject knowledge refers to a 'deep understanding' of the relevant school subject, while pedagogical content knowledge refers to knowledge of how to explain the relevant subject, and how to encourage students to think and perform tasks relating to the subject (2013, p. 29). We coded courses on teaching methodology and approaches to this knowledge domain. According to Baumert and Kunter (2013, p. 36), counselling knowledge refers to a 'socially distributed and largely non-subject specific form of knowledge that has to be bundled and interpreted in a given counselling situation'. Organisational knowledge refers to all aspects of school governance, management, school quality and legal and other institutional factors (Baumert & Kunter, 2013, p. 36). Inductively, we added three categories: citizenship education, computer science and languages. These subjects do not fit within any of the knowledge domains but are still frequently part of teacher education at Mosul University and could be best represented in these three categories. All coding were reviewed and checked on the basis of detailed descriptions of course content. Primary data was supplemented by archival reports and documents to ensure that data was triangulated from different sources.

5 The Context and Structure of Teacher Education in Iraq

5.1 *Governance*

When reflecting on education in Iraq, it is important to consider that one is actually dealing with two education systems – one established in the Iraqi Central State and one in the Kurdish Autonomous Region. The two systems 'rarely, other than through the Constitution and the national budget, converge into a centralized, consolidated national education system' (UNESCO, 2011, p. 16). Mirroring the situation on the ground, different governmental departments

TABLE 10.1 Annual budget of the ministries responsible for education and higher education since 2016 (figures in trillion IQD)

Year	Budget of MOE	Budget of MHESR
2016	7.8	2.2
2017	1.5	2.2
2018	2.8	2.3
2019	2.2	2.4

deal with education in both parts of the country: The Ministries of Higher Education and Scientific Research (MHESR/MHESR-K) oversee tertiary level education and the Ministries of Education (MOE/MOE-K) are in charge of school education.

The Iraqi education system is highly centralised and all aspects of administrative processes, from quality monitoring to decisions on educational content and teaching methods, are highly regulated (Alnuaimi, 2018). Initial teacher education is comprised of a four-year university-level course.

5.2 *Education Finances*

Due to ongoing crisis situations in the past two decades as well as cuts in oil revenues, the education system has been subjected to substantial financial pressures, which also affect the quality of TE. The MOE in particular has experienced swinging cuts in its annual budget allocation, from more than 7 billion IQD in 2015 to less than 2 billion IQD in 2019, which now represents less than 2% of Iraq's total national budget (Ministry of Finance, 2020).

Over the same period, the budget of the MHESR also remained low, coming in at between 2 and 4 billion IQD and hence accounting for between 2 and 4% of the total budget (Ministry of Finance, 2020, see Table 10.1). It has been argued that the budget shortfalls and fluctuations have inhibited long-term strategic planning at the ministries concerned (El-Ghali et al., 2010).

6 Major Challenges to Education Following the Demise of ISIS in the Nineveh Region

Challenges to education in Mosul following the demise of ISIS are:
– Education infrastructure in the region has been largely destroyed due to abuses during occupation and the liberation war. Many schools on the

right side of Mosul and in other areas in the region that were (almost) completely damaged are not yet reopened. Therefore, many families have not yet returned 'home' and cannot ensure access to schooling for their children. 4 years after liberation, there are still not enough schools: platooning (operating on the basis of shifts) is common with reduced learning hours for everyone; classes are overcrowded, with classes of 60–70 students not uncommon. Teacher absenteeism is another challenge, mainly resulting from the fact that many teachers are not living in the neighborhood of schools but safer communities and even Kurdistan region.

- The whole Nineveh region suffers from a general shortage of teachers with death, migration, retirement as well as refusal of teachers to work in unsafe places being the main reasons. Other reasons include low payment and status, as well as teachers feeling incapable of working under the existing conditions. Shortages are especially apparent in special education, mathematics and English language.
- Many students and teachers died or lost family members during the times of terror; with crimes of mass murder, ethnic cleaning, enslavement, abduction and mass rape against the Yazidi, Christian and Shia minorities, the situation has been officially recognised as a genocide. Members of all non-Arab and non-Sunni Muslim communities were systematically targeted with many being directly affected by experiences of torture, death threats or other forms of violence and being forced to flee their homes, losing all their belongings. Under occupation, civilians within the city were subjected to a regime of terror (e.g. looting, mass executions, abduction, imprisonment, death threats, bans and curfews, lack of medication and basic facilities, bombings and shootings, religious indoctrination) with few escaping trauma. Today, many suffer from post-traumatic stress, and many are not ready to attend school. In schools, teachers struggle to provide support and guidance and deal with behavioural problems.
- As an occupying force, ISIS took over the functioning parts of Mosul's education system (Arvisais & Guidère, 2020). ISIS issued legal opinions (fatwas) declaring government education provided by the Iraqi and Syrian regimes in schools and universities to be infidel and implemented its own curricula (Olidort, 2016). Courses on art and music, civics, sculpting, social studies and history, sports, philosophy, sociology, psychology, Islam, and Christianity were removed from the curriculum; concepts such as patriotism, nationalism, democracy, elections, core economic theories, evolution and polytheism were banned from the curriculum and strict gender separation was enforced. Students were not only taught fundamental religious values and given military training, they were also educated to become overseers of

morals at home. Students and teachers who took part in the government's education system or who refused to participate in the new system installed by ISIS risked severe punishments, ranging from public flogging to partial or total expropriation of property to the death penalty (Arvisais & Guidère, 2020). However, the degree of control and hence participation varied. Based on UNICEF data, Arvisais and Guidère (2020) estimated that over 45,000 children and young adults living in the Nineveh region were enrolled in a school under ISIS occupation, at least for a time. Others who fled occupied regions participated in emergency education or joined regular schools in Iraq or outside the country. As a consequence, almost all students have suffered interrupted education, some being out of school for 5 years.

– When schools reopened in 2017 the Ministry of Education decided that students would continue to be allocated to classes by age. As a consequence, achievement levels for almost every class are distributed over a span of 5 school years.
– When schools reopened after the liberation, the Ministry of Education decided that with the reopening of schools students would still be allocated to classes according to their age. As a consequence, almost every class achievement level ranges over a span of 5 school years.
– The whole region does not have any governmental schools catering for students with special needs. Few private sector education centres offer some care and education programmes of varying quality. All of them not free of charge.
– Schools in the Nineveh region were additionally affected by the recent pandemic situation, as not all regions have guaranteed basic infrastructure and many families have no suitable digital devices or internet to participate in online-based instruction. Furthermore, teachers lack didactical and organisational knowledge to provide education especially for younger students. It is estimated that about 50% of primary schools simply fail to have contact with students since the outbreak of the pandemic.

6.1 *Teacher Status*

Compared to other government positions, the salary accorded to the teaching profession is fairly low. Table 10.2 shows the annual salary for public servants in Iraq, providing an overview of the earnings of government officials at various levels. The salary scheme distinguishes between ten functional classes with class 10 being the lowest and assigned to unqualified personnel and class 1 being the highest, reserved for high ranking government officials. Educational level is a core criterion for assignment to functional classes, with a Bachelor's degree corresponding to class 7, a Master's degree to class 5 and a Doctoral

TABLE 10.2 Annual salary for public servants in Iraq (Teaching sector, amounts in USD)

Functional class	Old salary	New salary/years of services											Annual bonus	Number of years promoted
		1	2	3	4	5	6	7	8	9	10	11		
1	790	790	806	823	840	856	873	890	906	923	940	956	16	—
2	631	631	645	660	674	688	702	716	730	745	756	773	14	5
3	517	517	527	537	547	557	567	577	587	597	607	617	10	5
4	424	441	450	458	466	475	483	491	500	508	516	525	5	5
5	357	408	414	420	425	431	437	443	499	455	460	466	5	5
6	301	383	388	393	398	403	408	413	418	423	428	433	5	4
7	246	350	355	360	365	370	375	380	385	390	395	400	4	4
8	200	308	312	316	320	324	328	333	337	341	345	350	4	4
9	154	275	279	283	287	291	295	300	304	308	312	316	4	4
10	116	250	253	256	360	263	266	269	273	276	280	283	2.5	4

degree to class 3. Promotion to the next functional class is granted every 4 to 5 years. Whereas these classes are generally set for all government employees, additional allowances are granted by different ministries and there are hence differences across sectors. A school teacher with a Masters' degree, for example, receives much lower pay than a police officer who only has a secondary school leaving certificate (Salary explorer, 2021). In addition, factors such as marital status, children or the need to commute are associated with additional allowances. Such sector-based financing results in considerable differences between wages, even within the education sector: an individual with the same formal degree, work experience and personal status as a school teacher can earn an annual salary that is up to three times higher (Salary explorer, 2021). In consequence the status of teachers in Iraq is low and it is not uncommon for school teachers to work another job in order to meet their financial needs (Taha, 2020).

However, at the same time, government positions increasingly require university degrees, which – considering that Iraq is now facing youth unemployment of more than 25% – offer the only way to ensure a reliable source of income (Statista, 2020; Taha, 2020). Another factor in the high demand for academic training, and the take up of teaching positions, is the centralised system for allocating study places: In Iraq, study places in general, and places at students' university of choice in particular, are allocated almost exclusively on the basis of the score achieved in the final high school examination (DAAD, 2018). Such procedures have been criticised elsewhere for promoting concentration of the most competent students in particular subject areas such as medicine or law (Buckner, 2013). Given the comparably low score required to enter teacher education, this system leads to a high demand for the only government position obtainable by students who have performed less well in the final high school examination (Taha, 2020).

6.2 *Initial Teacher Education*

As with all university education in areas affected by conflict, there is an impact on the physical, human and social dimensions of teacher education (Barakat & Milton, 2015). The crises, especially in the immediate aftermath of the Iraq War and throughout the occupation of parts of the Iraqi territory by the ISIS militia, also had an immediate effect on the capacity of universities to provide quality teacher education. The higher education sector was already in a weak condition before the third Gulf War due to UN sanctions and the systematic neglect of the late Hussein era (Buckland, 2005; Lawler, 2003). After the war however, 84% of Iraqi university infrastructure was destroyed, looted or damaged (Reddy, 2005). Much later, too, substantial shortages in technical devices, laboratory equipment and teaching materials were reported (Mahmud, 2013).

Moreover, an estimated 30% of all professors left the country between 2003 and 2007 (Krieger, 2007; Milton & Barakat, 2016) and more than 500 university professors were killed between 2003 and 2015 (Barakat & Milton, 2015), depriving universities of the expertise required to maintain quality teacher education. In effect, only 28% of university teaching staff held doctoral degrees, whereas 39% held a Master's and 33% a Bachelor's degree (Reddy, 2005).

When it comes to social challenges, teacher education is required to cope with high numbers of traumatised students, with estimates ranging between 20 and 70% depending on location and measurement method (Abdullah et al., 2010; Almousawi, 2017; Al-Hadethe et al., 2014; Al-Shawi et al., 2011). Furthermore, the Iraqi Teacher Education system has to deal with a vast number of displaced students, and varying individual requirements as regards administrative and organisational support and recognition of educational certificates (Anselme & Hands, 2012; Bajwa et al., 2017). With ISIS occupying vast areas of Iraq, the situation was exacerbated for universities in affected cities such as Tikrit, Ramadi and Mosul (Walker, 2014). Universities were forced to operate in exile and/or were replaced by a university system imposed by the occupiers (Glum, 2014; Siira & Hill, 2016). A variety of colleges and departments including education were eliminated, and training for other relevant fields such as social sciences was substantially shortened (Arvisais & Guidère, 2020). In these difficult circumstances, the quality of teacher education fell and the demand for places on teacher education courses rose. Due to interruption in their studies because of the aforementioned circumstances, a high number of students are now resuming their studies in Iraq in general resulting into overcrowded classes. However, even though student numbers are increasing, professors across all departments experience the learning motivation as rather low.

6.3 *Structure*

The curriculum provides a framework structure for teacher education in Iraq. Reflecting this, most universities have different colleges catering for teacher education. At the University of Mosul, which serves as the case study here, five different colleges offer teacher education. The College of Basic Education, prepares teachers for work in kindergarten, preschool and primary school; the Colleges for Science Education, Humanities Education and Physical Education prepare their students to teach at middle or high school level.

Admission requirements differ for the different colleges, with the College of Basic Education having a lower entry requirement than the colleges catering for secondary education, and the colleges for humanities and sciences requiring candidates to have specialised during high school. A fifth college delivering teacher education is the College of Education for Girls. This college prepares female teachers for teaching positions, also at middle school/high school level, and has been established in order to enable women who would be prevented from studying in a co-educational setting because of their family traditions (Taha, 2020). Instructors at this college, however, can be either male or female.

6.4 *Curriculum*

Teacher education in Iraq is organised at university level and generally lasts four years. Curricula are centralised and there is little variation between institutions.

Due to the highly centralised structure of the Iraqi education system mentioned above, it is highly likely that courses at other Iraqi universities are similarly structured. To understand and illustrate the emphasis given to different content in the teacher education curricula, we distinguish between subject knowledge, pedagogical/psychological knowledge, organisational knowledge, counselling knowledge, citizenship education, languages and computer science. Table 10.3 shows the key results as regards the percentage distribution of courses across each of the respective categories.

As can be seen from this analysis, most courses tend to put heavy emphasis on the delivery of subject knowledge, which constitutes more than half of the initial education of teachers of humanities and sciences at both primary and secondary level (for humanities at secondary level the figure is over 70%). Pedagogical knowledge also plays an important role here, even though it is predominantly presented as general pedagogical/psychological knowledge rather than as subject-specific pedagogical knowledge. The situation is different for pre-school and special education teachers. Here, the proportion of courses dealing with subject knowledge is much lower and a large proportion of the courses taught refer to pedagogical/psychological knowledge (for special education, the majority of this content relates to information about impediments to learning and special educational needs). For all subjects there is only a limited emphasis on organisational and counselling knowledge and citizenship education, representing between 1 and 8% of the total number of courses taught in initial teacher education at Mosul University.

Overall, there is a lack of practical focus in teacher education, with limited opportunities offered for undertaking practice teaching. Student teachers undertake a practicum phase towards the end of their studies, having to identify the school themselves and to receive permission from the relevant school authorities before starting their practicum. During this phase, two supervisors working at the university, one subject specialist and one education specialist, visit the school two or three times and provide their feedback so that student teachers can improve their practice, before the supervisors assess their

TABLE 10.3 Percentage of knowledge domains addressed in teacher education at Mosul University

Courses	Preschool	Special Ed.	Humanities (Primary level)	Sciences (Primary level)	Humanities (Secondary level)	Sciences (Secondary level)
Content knowledge[a]	10%	2%	56%	54%	71%	52%
Pedagogical content knowledge[b]	14%	8%	6%	6%	6%	0%
Pedagogical/psychological knowledge[c]	37%	60%	12%	15%	10%	22%
Organizational knowledge[d]	8%	3%	4%	3%	1%	5%
Counselling knowledge[e]	3%	3%	2%	3%	1%	3%
Citizenship education[f]	3%	3%	4%	3%	3%	5%
Languages[g]	17%	16%	12%	11%	6%	8%
Computer skills[h]	7%	5%	5%	6%	3%	5%

Anchor examples:
a Victorian novel 1830–1900, partial differential equations.
b Teaching methods.
c Growth psychology.
d Educational management and supervision, curricula and textbooks.
e Guidance and psychological health, educational counselling.
f Human rights, philosophy (e.g. for science or mathematics teachers).
g Arabic, English (when Arabic and English is not subject taught).
h Computer skills.

performance in the last meeting. According to our interviewees, no student has ever failed this assessment.

7 Initiatives at Mosul University Offering Space for Teachers to Engage with Painful Personal Legacies of the Past

Between 2015 and 2017 the University ran in exile, offering undergraduate education programmes for about 14,000 exiled students. Teacher education programmes were offered in various places in the Kurdistan region. This also provided stability and gave students and academics the opportunity to discuss their experiences and provide each other with social and emotional support in times of crisis. Many lecturers report that responding to such needs, especially between 2015 and 2017, took up some of their teaching time. Since 2016 Mosul University, in partnership with the Technical University of Dortmund in Germany (Wendt, 2020) has offered university-wide student conferences, which are one-week long academic events for up to 400 students to support the rehabilitation of the university as a place of science and academic dialogue. These extra-curricular events are carefully designed to create safe opportunities for dialogue on issues that are crucial to reconstruction and reconciliation in the university. More than 1200 students and 120 academics have taken part in these activities, with about a quarter of them being students and academics from teacher education colleges. Overall, the activity is perceived as positive by lecturers and students (see Wendt, 2020). Evaluations conducted by academics from the education departments show that these interventions have had a positive impact on students' well-being, motivation to learn and achievement compared with those who did not participate (Sharif & Qadir, 2020; Zedan, 2020).

8 Conclusions

The case of teacher education in Iraq post-ISIS, and initial teacher education at Mosul University in particular, in many ways seems to validate theoretical assumptions and empirical findings regarding the nature of teaching and teacher education in areas affected by conflict. In Iraq, teacher education curricula are highly centralised and – at least in the case of Mosul University – focus on subject knowledge rather than emphasising other types of knowledge that might be of key importance for prospective teachers in areas affected by conflict, especially knowledge relating to counselling, citizenship education and organisation. In contexts where teachers are required to deal with large numbers of students with specific conflict-related issues such as displacement, trauma or prolonged interruptions to schooling, they are also tasked with contributing to the education of young citizens in accordance with post-transformation principles – which in the case of Iraq concern the newly-established democratic order and the commitment to human rights. Another preventative factor in this context could be that pedagogical knowledge is mostly delivered in a highly generalised form and not so much as pedagogical content knowledge, which could also serve as a framework for introducing student-centreed learning and other approaches that could in turn help to transfer democratic models into Iraqi classrooms. Practical phases for teaching are also limited given the current challenges and curriculum limitations, so that it becomes necessary to improve the offerings for practical teaching in the curriculum, as well as to introduce an induction period with mentors for novice teachers.

In our analysis of the content presented in initial teacher education at Mosul University, we rely primarily on the curricula that are currently in place. This methodology has allowed us to examine the basic structures of teacher education delivery; in-depth analysis of the content of teacher education is beyond the scope of this study. However, our findings regarding the curricula of teacher education, as discussed here, also indicate that the teacher education system in Iraq would require radical reform before it could meet the high standards required for quality teacher education. This aligns with other findings, which indicate, that the ways in which material is delivered in Iraqi higher education in general, and hence also in teacher education, are 'old fashioned' (Al-Janabi & Anderson, 2011), or even supportive of ethno-religious discrimination (Al-Kubaisi, 2012; Shanks, 2016). In the case of teacher education, it has been pointed out that in the immediate aftermath of the third Gulf War, little more was done than replacing the 'social philosophy' courses of the Saddam era with courses in 'human rights' which are oriented towards US-American or European concepts of citizenship education (Agresto, 2007, p. XVI). Our interviews confirmed that this remains the case today (Taha, 2020). The fact that the specific course is taught by law specialist and political scientists, rather than teacher educators, implies the need to review its purpose in terms of how to better integrate human rights and citizenship education in the realities of the classroom and thus empower students.

Interplay with other factors, such as the huge financial pressures on the entire education system and hence also on teacher education, and the rigid admissions policy for all fields of study, leaving teacher education courses with comparably low achieving students, means that education in the Mosul area is deprived of one of its most valuable resources – well trained and highly motivated teachers who could act as catalysts for the transformation and reconciliation of post-conflict society. To counter this situation, basic resources, such as physical infrastructures, textbooks and schooling materials, are urgently needed, while the international community should provide its support with targeted interventions that reflect the needs of Iraqi teachers. For example, academics from privileged educational contexts could show solidarity by offering basic knowledge and resources, acting as critical friends and carefully listening to the challenges faced by teacher educators and teachers at the local level.

To improve the quality of teacher education and enhance quality teaching in conflict-affected societies, our findings highlight among the most important factors the provision of basic material resources, the supply of well-qualified teacher educators with pedagogical expertise, the adaptation of teacher education curricula to local needs, and sharpening the focus of the curricula on pedagogical content knowledge. And while many of these factors might sound as common sense when it comes to the quality of teacher education in general, this is not the case for conflict-affected societies where the lack of resources and political will exacerbates existing tensions. Thus, quality teaching and teacher education in post-conflict societies should move higher in the agenda of policy-makers who need to allocate adequate funds and allow for more autonomy in the design and delivery of teacher education programmes.

References

Abdullah, E. K., Ibrahim, R. H., & Sedan, M. S. (2010). Post-traumatic stress among university students. *Jordan Medical Journal, 44*(4), 427–431.

Adebayo, S. B. (2019). Emerging perspectives of teacher agency in a post-conflict setting: The case of Liberia. *Teaching and Teacher Education, 86*, 1–10.

Agresto, J. (2007). *Mugged by reality: The liberation of Iraq and the failure of good intentions*. Encounter Books.

Al-Hadethe, A., Hunt, N., Thomas, S., & Al-Qaysi, A. (2014). Prevalence of traumatic events and PTSD symptoms among secondary school students in Baghdad. *European Journal of Psychotraumatology, 5*(1), 23928, 1–5.

Al-Janabi, S. T. F., & Anderson, D. (2011). Reforming the higher education system in Iraq: Internationalization via decentralization. *I-Manager's Journal of Educational Technology, 8*(3), 1–14.

Al-Kubaisi, Y. (2012). A Journey of learning: The curriculum In Iraqi schools and higher education. In H. Brunskell-Evans & M. Moore (Eds.), *Reimagining research for* reclaiming the academy in Iraq: Identities and participation in post-conflict enquiry (pp. 53–63). Sense Publishers.

Almousawi, A. (2017). War-related trauma and post-traumatic stress disorder prevalence among undergraduate students in Iraq in 2010. *Iraqi Journal of Public Health, 1*(2), 35–41.

Alnuaimi, A. S. (2018). Iraq. In A. S. Weber & S. Hamlaoui (Eds.), *E-learning in the Middle East and North Africa (MENA) region* (Vol. 17, pp. 123–138). Springer International Publishing.

Al-Shawi, A., Al-Hemiary, N., Al-Diwan, J., & Tahir, D. (2011). Post-traumatic stress disorder among university students in Baghdad: A preliminary report. *Iraqi Journal of Communal Medicine, 24*(4), 287–290.

Anselme, M. L., & Hands, C. (2012). Access to secondary and tertiary education for all refugees: Steps and challenges to overcome. *Refuge, 27*(2), 89–96.

Arvisais, O., & Guidère, M. (2020). Education in conflict: How Islamic state established its curriculum. *Journal of Curriculum Studies, 52*(4), 498–515.

Bajwa, J. K., Couto, S., Kidd, S., Markoulakis, R., Abai, M., & McKenzie, K. (2017). Refugees, higher education, and informational barriers. *Refuge, 33*(2), 56–65.

Barakat, B., & Urdal, H. (2009). *Breaking the waves? Does education mediate the relationship between youth bulges and political violence?* Policy Research Working Paper. The World Bank.

Barakat, S., Connolly, D., Hardman, F., & Sundaram, V. (2013). The role of basic education in post-conflict recovery. *Comparative Education, 49*(2), 124–142.

Barakat, S., & Milton, S. (2015). *Houses of wisdom matter: The responsibility to protect and rebuild higher education in the Arab World*. https://www.brookings.edu/research/houses-of-wisdom-matter-the-responsibility-to-protect-and-rebuild-higher-education-in-the-arab-world/

Barrios-Tao, H., Siciliani-Barraza, J. M., & Bonilla-Barrios, B. (2017). Education programs in post-conflict environments: A review from Liberia, Sierra Leone, and South Africa. *Revista Electrónica Educare, 21*(1), 1–22.

Baumert, J., & Kunter, M. (2013). The COACTIV Model of teachers' professional competence. In M. Kunter, J. Baumert, W. Blum, U. Klusmann, S. Krauss, & M. Neubrand (Eds.), *Cognitive activation in the mathematics classroom and professional competence of teachers* (Vol. 29, pp. 25–48). Springer US.

Bekerman, Z., & Zembylas, M. (2014). Some reflections on the links between teacher education and peace education: Interrogating the ontology of normative epistemological premises. *Teaching and Teacher Education, 41*, 52–59.

BIICL. (2016). *Protecting education in the Middle East and North Africa Region: Report*. https://www.biicl.org/documents/37_1263_protecting_education_in_the_mena_region_-_full_report_-_june_2016__web_version_v2.pdf

Buckland, P. (2005). *Reshaping the future: Education and postconflict reconstruction.* Worldbank.

Buckner, E. (2013). *How university admissions distorts some Arab societies.* Al Fanar. https://www.al-fanarmedia.org/2013/05/how-university-admissions-distorts-some-arab-societies/

Burns, M. (2015). *4 Barriers to teachers' professional development in fragile contexts.* https://www.globalpartnership.org/blog/4-barriers-teachers-professional-development-fragile-contexts

Burns, M., & Lawrie, J. (Eds.). (2015). *Where it's needed most: Quality professional development for all teachers.* Inter-Agency Network for Education in Emergencies.

Cervantes-Duarte, L., & Fernández-Cano, A. (2016). Impact of armed conflicts on education and educational agents: A multivocal review. *Revista Electrónica Educare, 20*(3), 238–261.

Cochran-Smith, M. (2013). Introduction: The politics of policy in teacher education: International perspectives. *The Educational Forum, 77*(1), 3–4.

Cochran-Smith, M., & Fries, K. (2011). Teacher quality, teacher education and diversity: Policy and politics. In A. Ball & C. Tyson (Eds.), *Studying diversity in teacher education* (pp. 339–361). American Educational Research Association.

DAAD. (2018). *Irak: Kurze Einführung in das Hochschulsystem und die DAAD-Aktivitäten|2018*. DAAD. https://www2.daad.de/medien/der-daad/analysen-studien/laendersachstand/irak_daad_sachstand.pdf

Davies, L. (2010). The different faces of education in conflict. *Development, 53,* 491–497.

Dolan, J., Golden, A., Ndaruhutse, S., & Winthrop, R. (2012). *Building effective teacher salary systems in fragile and conflict-affected states.* https://www.brookings.edu/research/building-effective-teacher-salary-systems-in-fragile-and-conflict-affected-states/

El-Ghali, H., Chen, Q., & Yeager, J. (2010). Strategic planning in higher education in the Middle East: The case of Non-Gulf-Countries. In D. Obst & D. Kirk (Eds.), *Global education research reports: Vol. 4. Innovation through education: Building the knowledge economy in the Middle East* (pp. 43–59). Institute of International Education.

Frounfelker, R. L., Islam, N., Falcone, J., Farrar, J., Ra, C., Antonaccio, C. M., Enelamah, N., & Betancourt, T. S. (2019). Living through war: Mental health of children and youth in conflict-affected areas. *International Review of the Red Cross, 101*(911), 481–506.

GCPEA. (2014). *Protecting education personnel from targeted attack in conflict-affected countries.* https://reliefweb.int/report/world/protecting-education-personnel-targeted-attack-conflict-affected-countries-enfr

Ghosn-Chelala, M. (2020). Global citizenship education in conflict-affected settings: Implications of teachers' views and contextual challenges for the Lebanese case. *Teaching and Teacher Education, 93,* 1–11.

Glum, J. (2014). ISIS takeover in Iraq: Mosul University students, faculty uncertain about the future of higher education. *International Business Times.*

https://www.ibtimes.com/isis-takeover-iraq-mosul-university-students-faculty-uncertain-about-future-higher-1731468

Kelleher, F. (2011). *Women and the teaching profession: Exploring the feminisation debate*. Commonwealth Secretariat and UNESCO.

Krieger, Z. (2007). Iraq's universities near collapse. *Chronicle of Higher Education, 53*(37), 35–39.

Lawler, A. (2003). After the war. Iraq's shattered universities. *Science, 300*(5625), 1490–1491.

Locatelli, R. (2018). *The implications of education privatization on teachers in lower-income countries*. Report submitted to the 13th session of the joint ILO–UNESCO Committee of Experts on the Application of the Recommendations concerning Teaching Personnel (CEART). https://www.ilo.org/sector/activities/sectoral-meetings/WCMS_675242/lang--en/index.htm

MacBeath, J. (2012). *The future of the teaching profession*. Education International.

Mahmud, S. F. (2013). The higher education in Iraq challenges and recommendations. *Journal of Advanced Social Research, 3*(9), 255–264.

McGlynn, C., Zembylas, M., Bekerman, Z., & Gallagher, T. (Eds.). (2009). *Peace education in conflict and post-conflict societies: Comparative perspectives*. Palgrave, Macmillan.

MHESR. (2013). *Humanities curricula*. www.mohesr.gov.iq/uploads/pdf/Book%202013.pdf

Milton, S., & Barakat, S. (2016). Higher education as the catalyst of recovery in conflict-affected societies. *Globalisation, Societies and Education, 14*(3), 403–421.

Ministry of Finance. (2020). *Where does the money go?* http://www.mof.gov.iq/obs/en/Pages/WDMGChart.aspx

Müller, L. M., & Goldenberg, G. (2020). *Education in times of crisis: The potential implications of school closures for teachers and students*. https://chartered.college/education-in-times-of-crisis-the-potential-implications-of-school-closures-for-teachers-and-students/

Muthanna, A., & Sang, G. (2018). Brain drain in higher education: Critical voices on teacher education in Yemen. *London Review of Education, 16*, 296–307.

Namubiru, P. S. (2014). Ideological trends in initial teacher education curricula: The case of East African universities. *Tuning Journal for Higher Education, 2*(1), 129–159.

Novelli, M., & Sayed, Y. (2016). Teachers as agents of sustainable peace, social cohesion and development: Theory, practice & evidence. *Education as Change, 20*(3), 15–37.

Olidort, J. (2016). *Inside the caliphates classroom: Textbooks, guidance literature, and indoctrination methods of the Islamic State*. The Washington Institute for Near East Policy.

Reddy, J. (2005). *Iraq: 5/6ths of Iraq's higher learning institutions burnt, looted, wrecked; 48 profs slain; UNU calls for world help to repair system*. https://reliefweb.int/report/iraq/iraq-56ths-iraqs-higher-learning-institutions-burnt-looted-wrecked-48-profs-slain-unu

Salary explorer. (2021). *Scale of salaries and wages of police officers in Iraq.* http://www.salaryexplorer.com/ar/salary-survey.php?loc=103&loctype=1&job=504&jobtype=3#disabled

Sayed, Y., Badroodien, A., Omar, Y., Ndabaga, E., Novelli, M., Durrani, N., Barrett, A., Balie, Lorna, B., Salmon, T., Bizimana, B., Ntahomvukiye, C., & Utomi, J. (2018). *The role of teachers in peacebuilding and social cohesion in Rwanda and South Africa.* ESRC/DFID Research Report, University of Sussex. https://www.gov.uk/research-for-development-outputs/the-role-of-teachers-in-peacebuilding-and-social-cohesion-in-rwanda-and-south-africa-synthesis-report

Shanks, K. (2016). *Education and ethno-politics: Defending identity in Iraq.* Routledge, Taylor & Francis Group.

Sharif, I., & Qadir, B. (2020). *Self-efficacy expectations for Mosul University students. Internal evaluation.* College of Basic Education, Mosul University.

Siira, K., & Hill, T. (2016). *The University of Mosul could show the way in post-war reconstruction.* Al Fanar. https://www.al-fanarmedia.org/2016/11/university-mosul-show-way-post-war-reconstruction/

Smith, A. (2010). *The influence of education on conflict and peace building.* Background paper prepared for the Education for All global monitoring report 2011 The hidden crisis: Armed conflict and education. UNESCO.

Snoek, M., & Zogla, I. (2009). Teacher education in Europe: Main characteristics and developments. In A. Swennen & M. van der Klink (Eds.), *Becoming a teacher educator: Theory and practice for teacher educators* (pp. 11–27). Springer.

Statista. (2020). *Youth unemployment in Iraq.* https://www.statista.com/statistics/812116/youth-unemployment-rate-in-iraq/

Stewart, F. (2011). *Horizontal inequalities as a cause of conflict: A review of CRISE findings.* World Development Report.

Stromquist, N. P. (2018). *The global status of teachers and the teaching profession.* Education International.

Symeonidis, V., & Stromquist, N. P. (2020). Teacher status and the role of teacher unions in the context of new professionalism. *Studia Paedagogica, 25*(2), 23–45.

Taha, A. (2020, November 9). *Teacher education in Iraq.* Unpublished interview transcript drafted by H. Wendt, V. Symeonidis, & F. Senger.

Teamey, K. (2007). *Whose public action? Analyzing inter-sectoral collaboration for service delivery: A literature review on relationships between government and non-state providers of services.* Economic and Social Research Council, University of Birmingham.

Thyne, C. L. (2006). ABC's, 123's, and the golden rule: The pacifying effect of education on civil war, 1980–1999. *International Studies Quarterly, 50*(4), 733–754.

UNESCO. (2011). *UNESCO country programming document for the Republic of Iraq.* https://unesdoc.unesco.org/ark:/48223/pf0000213680

UNESCO-IIEP. (2010). Identification, selection and recruitment of teachers and education workers. In UNESCO-IIEP (Ed.), *Guidebook for planning education in emergencies and reconstruction* (pp. 1–24). https://inee.org/resources/identification-selection-and-recruitment-teachers-and-education-workers

Urdal, H. (2004). *The devil in the demographics: The effect of youth bulges on domestic armed conflict, 1950–2000*. World Bank. https://documents.worldbank.org/en/publication/documents-reports/documentdetail/794881468762939913/the-devil-in-the-demographics-the-effect-of-youth-bulges-on-domestic-armed-conflict-1950-2000

Urdal, H. (2006). A Clash of generations? Youth Bulges and political violence. *International Studies Quarterly, 50*(3), 607–629.

Walker, K. (2014). Islamic State plunges research in Iraq into darkness. *Nature Middle East*. https://www.natureasia.com/en/nmiddleeast/article/10.1038/nmiddleeast.2014.238

Weldon, G. (2010). Post-conflict teacher development: Facing the past in South Africa. *Journal of Moral Education, 39*(3), 353–364.

Wendt, H. (2012). *Die Vergleichende Einzelfallstudie. Ein Beitrag zum methodologischen Diskurs am Beispiel der Transformation des Schulsystems in Südafrika*. Waxmann.

Wendt, H. (2020). Hochschullehre in Krisenregionen. Nach dem IS: Die Universität Mosul beim schwierigen Neuanfang. *Weiterbildung: Zeitschrift Für Grundlagen, Praxis Und Trends, 3*, 38–41.

Zedan, A. (2020). *The achievement motivation among the participating and not participating students in the workshop of Mosul University. Internal evaluation*. Mosul University, College of Basic Education.

PART 3

Strengthening Quality Teaching and Teacher Education: Looking to the Future

CHAPTER 11

Teacher Education for the 31st Century?

Preparing Teachers for Unknown Futures

A. Lin Goodwin

Abstract

Current education reform efforts are focused on teachers – their preparation, retooling and upgrading, professional development, and assessment. Indeed, there is ample empirical data indicating that teachers are essential to student achievement and that quality teachers produce quality outcomes. Yet, how should teacher preparation and ongoing development change to meet the needs of an unknown and constantly evolving future? It certainly is commonplace across the world, to talk about *preparing teachers for 21st century skills and competencies*. But what knowledges or competencies are fundamental and enduring enough to serve society long beyond the 21st century? In what ways might these competencies, in turn, influence and shape curriculum and teaching so as to best prepare young people for their tomorrow? This chapter begins with a brief look at globalisation and some of the contemporary issues that are global stressors. It then describes prevailing modes of teaching and perceptions of learning that contradict practices now called for in response to a rapidly changing global landscape. Five domains of knowledge for teaching are offered to help us think anew about teacher competencies and understandings, with a focus on teacher preparation curriculum, as well as some insights for continuing professional development and for teacher educator learning – what should teachers at all levels know and be able to do if they are to capably drive curriculum change for deep learning and meaningful student engagement? I argue that these five knowledge domains can enable us to reimagine teaching and learning, and reform the teaching profession in ways that can support, nurture and sustain the creative, thinking, agentic professionals we need, not just for the 21st century but for the 31st.

Keywords

teacher – teacher education – modes of teaching and perceptions of learning – five knowledge domains and fundamental competencies – education reforms – reimagine teaching and learning – globalisation – unknown future

1 Introduction

Many current reform efforts in education are focused on teachers – their preparation, re-tooling and upgrading, professional development, and assessment. Indeed, there is wide acceptance (backed by empirical data) that teachers are essential to student achievement and that quality teachers produce quality outcomes (Chetty et al., 2014; European Commission, 2018; Hattie, 2003; OECD, 2018a). Yet, how should teacher preparation and schools of education change to meet the needs of an unknown and constantly evolving future? And how should we think differently about teachers' ongoing growth, learning and continued professional development? It certainly is commonplace across the world, to talk about *ensuring quality teachers for the 21st century* or *teaching 21st century skills and competencies*. But what might be knowledges or competencies that are fundamental and enduring, such that they can serve society long beyond the 21st century? In what ways might these competencies, in turn, influence and shape curriculum – what we teach, and how – so as to best prepare young people for their tomorrow? These questions are especially salient as the world emerges from a devastating and extended global pandemic that has shaken the very definition of 'normal' or 'typical' in all aspects of society, particularly education, promoting a collective rethinking of how teaching should look and how schooling needs to be different as we face forward into tomorrow.

This discussion begins with a brief look at globalisation and some of the contemporary issues that are stressing our global community. This serves as a backdrop for modes of teaching and perceptions of learning that remain stubbornly in place, versus what has been called for in response to a rapidly changing global landscape. Five domains of knowledge for teaching are offered to help us think anew about teacher competencies and understandings, with a focus on teacher preparation curriculum, as well as some insights for continuing professional development and for teacher educator learning – what should teachers at all levels know and be able to do if they are to capably drive curriculum change for deep learning and meaningful student engagement? I argue that these five knowledge domains can enable us to reimagine teaching and learning, and reform the teaching profession in ways that can support, nurture and sustain the creative, thinking, agentic professionals we need, not just for the 21st century but for the 31st (see Goodwin, 2020a).

2 Globalisation and Global Stressors

Any contemporary conversation about globalisation must acknowledge the massive impact of COVID-19 which was declared a global pandemic by the

World Health Organization on March 11, 2020. A simple comparison of the state of the world pre-versus post-COVID illuminates the exacerbating effect of the pandemic on key quality of life-markers.

2.1 Before/after March 2020

An opinion piece by *New York Times* columnist Nicholas Kristof reflecting on the 2019 year, highlighted the progress humankind had made in the world in terms of reducing poverty, raising literacy levels, providing access to clean water and to electricity, lowering infant mortality rates, and more. Indeed, 'extreme poverty', as one example, had 'plunged to less than 10% of the world's population' compared to 40 years ago (Kristof, 2019, para. 8). Yet, in October 2020, the World Bank (2020) documented a rise in 'global extreme poverty… for the first time in over twenty years', foreseeing that COVID-19 will 'add as many as 150 million extreme poor by 2021' (para. 1). In 2017, 'nearly 20 million refugees… [were]… forcibly displaced from their own countries. An additional 40 million people… were internally displaced due to conflict and violence'; among these were 27 million children (UNICEF, 2018, para. 1). By 2020 '34 million refugees and asylum seekers… have been forcibly displaced from their own countries – half of them children' (UNICEF, 2021, para. 2), a significant rise over 2017 figures. According to the World Meteorological Organization (WMO), '2019 conclude[d] a decade of exceptional global heat, retreating ice and record sea levels driven by greenhouse gases from human activities' (2019, para. 1), plus scores of extreme weather events around the world. But the negative trends continued in 2020 which 'was one of the three warmest years on record' as '[c]oncentrations of the major greenhouse gases, CO_2, CH_4, and N_2O, continued to increase despite the temporary reduction in emissions' due to COVID lockdowns (WMO, 2021, p. 5)

Thus, even while human existence improves, there is still much volatility in a world that is experiencing exponential change in terms of climate, economies, human mobility, technology and the explosion of knowledge, recently further re-defined or accelerated by the pandemic. Young people today are facing many new challenges and global stressors, and need to be equipped to manage, lead, and direct positive change. The World Economic Forum is calling for 'new models, new standards and a new momentum for action to transform the future of education' that prepare young people for 'new job types that do not yet exist' and 'foster human-centric skills – cooperation, empathy, social awareness and global citizenship' (WMO, 2021, pp. 4–6). Similarly, the OECD Learning Framework 2030 project (OECD, 2018b), has brought together a wide and varied group of stakeholders from around the world to articulate the competencies that will enable young people to be 'future ready' and 'apply their knowledge in unknown and evolving circumstances' (p. 5). These skills include the 'cognitive and meta-cognitive... social and emotional... practical and physical' (OECD, 2018b, p. 5). These 'future ready' skills are echoed by the Council of the European Union (2018) which has recommended such key competencies for lifelong learning as problem solving, critical thinking, ability to cooperate, creativity, computational thinking, self-regulation.

3 Teaching for Now versus Teaching for the Future

Given an uncertain and ambiguous future, static knowledge or content can no longer be seen as adequate; international discourse around teaching and learning for the unknown ahead of us calls for flexible thinking, the ability to imagine creative solutions in concert with others, the willingness to take risks and experiment, and fearlessness in the face of likely failure, at least initially. Yet, even as policy-makers, government agencies and corporate leaders are emphasising so-called soft skills (which are really not soft at all but actually very challenging to teach or achieve) and transversal skills such as critical reasoning and collaboration, schools, curriculum and teaching practices continue to emphasise subjects taught as isolated, disciplinary siloes, and discrete content knowledge packaged as immutable 'truths', privileging the 'simple linear, mechanistic, or deterministic' (Pearce et al., 2012, p. 419). As WEF observes, 'developed and developing economies alike still rely heavily on passive forms of learning focused on direct instruction and memorization' (2021, p. 5).

The reification of neoliberal principles that prize competition, free market economies, and profit margins, has fueled global competitiveness, which has, in turn, driven high stakes accountability movements and the quantification of learning (Taubman, 2009). We are preoccupied with measuring results, sorting and categorising students, and rankings on league tables; education is now 'a vehicle that assists the growing market economy' (McLaren & Farahmandpur, 2001, p. 139). Classrooms the world over are recognizable for the commonly practiced one-way transmission of knowledge from teacher to pupil. Paulo Freire (1984) termed this the 'banking approach' of teaching, where students are treated as empty vessels who passively receive knowledge deposited by teachers. We are well into the 21st century and yet are still aspiring to 21st century competencies such as creativity, teamwork, problem-solving and intellectual agility for our students. There is a great deal of discussion around the world about learner diversity, but instruction continues to be generic, designed for the average student who does not actually exist, aiming more for conformity than openness and personal growth. It seems that 'education systems have grown increasingly disconnected from the realities and needs of global economies and societies' (WEF, 2021, p. 5). By depersonalising education, 'schools kill creativity' (Robinson, 2015); the one-size-fits-all curriculum assumes sameness in a world student body that is full of variation. It is not surprising then, that in the TALIS survey (OECD, 2019b), teachers across 48 countries expressed their lack of preparedness for diversity amongst learners, whether cultural, intellectual, physical, socioeconomic, national origin, home language, immigrant status, and so on. Moreover, '[d]uring the pandemic, remote learning became a lifeline for education', even while TALIS data indicated that ICT training was teachers' second most identified professional development need even prior to COVID-19 (Schleicher, 2020, p. 16), adding another layer to the complex knowledge and skills today's teacher requires.

The world is changing quickly, and teachers must change as quickly; learning can only be different if teaching is different. It is still often assumed that students are learning if they can recite or regurgitate information teachers give them and that all students learn and can be taught in the same way. This approach wastes talent because it fails to capitalise on the inherent diversity in classrooms, or nurture the different capacities, interests and needs students embody. So, how can teacher preparation and continuing professional development be different so that teaching is different?

This article suggests five knowledge domains for teaching, or big ideas that can support teacher learning and teaching that is integrated, inquiry-based, and holistic. In my own extensive work in teacher education and development, they have enabled me to see and stretch beyond teaching as an imitative process; rather, I have been guided to view (and enact) good teaching as the consequence of multiple decisions and reflective praxis which grow out of the dialogue, competing agendas, and varied contexts surrounding teaching. Rather than focus on discrete behaviours and competencies only, these domains have widened my gaze, along with my colleagues, to attend to the kinds of teachers we need to prepare and support in order to achieve the quality education we say we want for all children. These knowledge domains for teaching are:

1. personal knowledge/autobiography and philosophy of teaching;
2. contextual knowledge/understanding children, schools and society;
3. pedagogical knowledge/content, theories, teaching methods, and curriculum-making;
4. sociological knowledge/diversity, cultural relevance, and social justice; and
5. social knowledge/cooperative, democratic group process, and conflict resolution.

4 Knowledge Domains for Teaching

4.1 *Personal Knowledge*

Teaching is unique among all professional activities in that it is subject to the daily scrutiny of millions of lay people, i.e., 'students' who are not of or in the profession, yet are still afforded an intimate view of what teaching is (who teachers are) and how it plays out in the classroom from year to year. Dan Lortie (1975) termed this close-up view of teaching/teachers 'the apprenticeship of observation', one that every person entering the teaching profession has undergone. Today that apprenticeship may last as long as 16 years as a baccalaureate is frequently (and increasingly) a standard requirement for teacher qualification, meaning new teachers begin their careers with well-formed impressions about teachers' role and work based on years of observation and study in elementary, secondary, and even university classrooms. Consequently, every student who enters a teacher preparation program cannot but be filled with all kinds of expectations, beliefs, preconceived notions, assumptions and implicit theories about teaching, learners, teachers, and schools (Goodwin, 2002; Fives & Gill, 2015; Pajares, 1992). These preconceptions are very powerful, with prospective teachers' personal knowledge becoming the foundation upon which teaching practice is built, rather than professional knowledge and experiences offered by a preservice program (Goodwin, 2002; Feiman-Nemser, 2001; Richardson, 1996).

Teacher preparation can therefore be seen as a transition between the person one has been in the past and the professional one aspires to be in the future. Teacher education programmes should be a space for the intersection of student teachers' autobiographies and the formal course of study. This will enable each student teacher to draw upon personal knowledge and prior experience alongside the teacher preparation curriculum and teaching practice, so as to reconstruct these in such a way as to derive meaning that is simultaneously relevant personally and professionally. In the absence of meaningful – and deliberate – reconstruction, transformation or behaviour change are unlikely as new information, skills, and attitudes presented by the teacher preparation program fail to be integrated into student teachers' thoughts and actions. This leaves teachers candidates to rely on past meaningful experience, histories and personal knowledge that are deeply entrenched, able to powerfully, yet implicitly, shape their pedagogical decisions and curriculum choices as teachers (Fives, Lacatena, & Gerard, 2015; Goodwin, 2002; Richardson, 1996).

'Education is high on the agenda of governments around the globe' (Robinson, 2015, p. 6), as nations move to upgrade teachers and reform teaching so as to improve their standings on international assessments, especially PISA, 'the global yardstick for measuring success in education' (Schleicher, 2017, p. 123, cited in Ledger et al., 2019). Many high performing jurisdictions have been actively re-conceptualising 'learning' and therefore re-defining teacher quality. For example, in Singapore, educators' practice is being reshaped by an ongoing national commitment to 'Teach less, learn more', resulting, for example, in a 30% reduction in the curriculum to create more 'white space' for creativity and deep learning, and a move towards child-centreed instruction. Instruction in Finnish schools is 'phenomenon-based', taking an inquiry approach to learning that engages students in asking big questions and solving authentic problems. Regardless of the country or context, every innovation depends on teachers for successful implementation.

Such exciting changes notwithstanding, internationally, most teachers still share in common experiences (their own) with schooling that emphasised rote learning and memorisation, factual knowledge over understanding and learner passivity versus active engagement. These shared memories and images of school must be consciously examined and challenged, otherwise they can block meaningful learning (Rios, Montecinos, & van Olphen, 2007), leaving teachers, both new and less so, to teach as they were taught, to replicate their own experiences as students. Initiating this deliberate interrogation of lived experiences and tacit understandings requires teacher education to focus on 'cognitions, beliefs, and the making of meaning' (Richardson, 1998, p. 145) and engage student teachers in critically assessing their prior knowledge and practical theories in order to '[restructure] their cognitive maps with reformed and/or new understandings' (p. 147). Otherwise,

> The failure to see how one's accumulated life experiences bridge to one's continuing growth is to miss the opportunity to make them relevant to the future. Therefore, attention must be given to personal knowledge, building on what the student teacher already knows, on who the student teacher is, and on the preconceptions student teachers bring with them as they begin their preparation. (Goodwin, 2010, p. 23)

4.2 *Contextual Knowledge*

No individual program, regardless of how comprehensive, can prepare teacher candidates for all possible classroom contingencies. As teacher educators, we certainly aim to expose our student teachers to a wide variety of scenarios, settings, curricula, and issues, so as to equip them to deal with the complexity that characterises all classrooms, and to help them develop the agility and flexibility they will need to manage the uncertainties inherent in teaching. But as complex and dynamic places, classrooms, and the children who inhabit them, defy categorisation, so how should teacher preparation help develop in fledgling teachers' readiness for the myriad situations that *will* arise in the classroom. Since we cannot possibly identify a priori all that our student teachers will need to know in order to be successful with the diversity of human beings with whom they will work and in the diversity of settings in which they will do this work, what kinds of transversal skills should we be emphasising – ways of thinking about teaching and learners that can be applied to make sense of perplexing problems, no matter where or how they emerge?

Contextual knowledge begins with the students at the centre – who they are as people, not small or young versions of adults, but unique and agentic individuals in their own right. And just like their teachers, they come to the learning enterprise with their own personal knowledge, beliefs, truths, (mis)conceptions and experiences – they bring all of who they are into the classroom. But students do not exist in a vacuum, they are members of numerous communities – families, neighborhoods, cultural groups – interlocking micro-societies, each with its own norms, values, traditions, and beliefs. These micro-societies are all nested within multiple macro-contexts that are political, historical, social, cultural, institutional, economic, and so on, and are in turn embedded within governmental (both local and national) structures, regulations and policies. Thus, contextual knowledge is not merely the immediate and proximate, but includes keeping in view broader influences that may be political, structural, historical, or cultural and which have an impact on teachers' planning and the kinds of decisions they make.

For example, in the United States given changes in immigration laws and policies, coupled with rising nationalistic fervor and increased xenophobia, immigrants and their children face grave difficulties within an ever more challenging environment. By law, regardless of immigrant status, all children have the right to be educated. Thus, school districts across the country are serving large numbers of students who are entitled to schooling and who will require a range of supports. These do not stop at academic supports or curriculum content reflective of their experiences, but may include language, health, legal, employment, housing, and other daily living supports because immigrant students are part of a social eco-system and so can only be well cared for if the eco-system in which they are embedded also receives care and support. This means that a teacher (and the school) must attend to multiple contexts that are intertwined, taking into account students' needs, capacities and issues, ways to work with students' communities, and policies, laws and societal norms that exert daily impact on students' lives and security, all of which will affect their ability to learn and be successful.

It is important also to remember that contextual knowledge also operates on a global scale, bringing into sharp relief the many changes all societies have undergone, as well as the many complexities that now characterise the daily lives of young people. Quality teachers need to be cognizant of these myriad realities. For example, millions of young digital natives comfortably navigate a digital environment, creating virtual, yet lived, worlds of which few adults are familiar or even aware. Today's youth also frequently traverse transnational spaces and move easily across time zones (Rong & Preissle, 2009). The ease and frequency of transnational travel has heightened cultural borrowing and redefined traditional notions of home, family, friendship, and relationships (Goodwin, 2020b). Moreover, capitalism and the rapid expansion of world economies has fueled desires, expectations, and interactional modes that were unknown only a few decades ago (Banks, 2008; Farmer, 2005). Clearly, an understanding of context involves more than a sense of position or place, and today's teacher must integrate this understanding into all that occurs in classrooms. Contextual knowledge propels teachers beyond subject or instructional strategy to examine learners' needs as nested within multiple socio-cultural-economic-political locations, to ask questions, gather information, and invent practice according to ever shifting circumstances.

4.3 Pedagogical Knowledge

Dictionary definitions of pedagogy range from the concrete: teaching methods, to the more philosophical: the art or science of teaching. A cornerstone of teacher education programmes is 'methods', defined as strategies or teaching tools, equipping teachers to *do* teaching – structure lessons, deliver content, design learning activities, assess learning. Sometimes termed 'tool kits', or even 'bag of tricks', they are often what new teachers clamor for because they are seen as practical, very concrete and can be applied right away in the classroom. They also 'feel' like teaching, because they represent typical teacher actions, or what all teachers are supposed to do – instruct. Armed with 'tricks of the trade' is comforting to beginning teachers because it provides them a sense of security, they are *ready* to teach and *ready* for teaching.

Unfortunately, this sense of security is often short-lived because there are few 'tricks of the trade' that will work in every situation, for every student – or even for the same group of students at another time – or for every subject. Undoubtedly it is important for student teachers to learn a variety of methods and develop a repertoire of "things to do" in the classroom. However, a repertoire of teaching strategies involves more than mastering a series of techniques or steps. Rather, teacher actions should represent ways of thinking about learners and learning, as disciplinary knowledge, theories of human and brain development, the sciences of learning, and methods and models of teaching are all brought to bear. More valuable than a collection of 'how tos' is the ability to study a situation, notice what students need, and invent contingently responsive practices (Darling-Hammond & Bransford, 2005). This ability comes from habits of mind more than from the technical implementation of discrete methods. Habits of mind or habits of practice are developed as student teachers are challenged to thoughtfully integrate disciplinary expertise and pedagogical content knowledge with prior experience and current student teaching practice. Content, theories, and methods of teaching become the building blocks for curriculum development.

Teacher preparation programmes are more likely to focus on curriculum implementation skills than on curriculum design and creation. Teaching is often viewed primarily as an instructional or implementation problem, one which can be considered quite apart from what is taught (Bolin & Panaritis, 1992). Hence, the predominant model with which teachers are familiar is delivery of a curriculum, i.e., content developed and sequenced by external experts. A full discussion of what 'curriculum' actually means is beyond the scope of this chapter. Curriculum is a complex field for a reason and so is much more than the prevailing conception of curriculum as synonymous with lessons, the scope and sequence of content, the syllabus, standards or goals and objectives. Suffice it to say that in general, definitions and understandings of curriculum are persistently narrow and technical, even amongst teachers and teacher educators. It is not surprising then that teaching is similarly seen in specific and technical terms and teachers are taught to do teaching accordingly.

A much more powerful role for the teacher is as curriculum maker – one who designs a curriculum that grows out of the needs and interests of students (Goodwin, 1997; Schoonmaker, 2002). This does not require that teachers continually create curriculum from the blank page, or that commercial or mandated resources should be disregarded. What it does mean is that teachers as curriculum makers embrace 'several capacities of mind... of heart... of the physical body and the spiritual soul' – ways of seeing the world, respecting and being with others, and maintaining balance between one's inner self and the outer world (McIntosh, 2005, p. 23). Expertise in curriculum development enables even the novice teacher to critically evaluate and adapt assigned materials, to make adjustments such that one-size-fits-all curricula can actually be relevant to students' diversities. Adaptation is a key step on a curriculum development continuum along which teachers move from modification of what is, to the envisioning of what might or needs to be, to the enactment of that vision through the creation of curriculum that emerges from and is meaningful to students' unique contextual, cultural, academic, and personal needs. Finally, pedagogical knowledge must transcend the formal curriculum – that which is sanctioned by the state – to include deep understanding of the informal, cultural, or personal curriculum that children embody. For example, the curriculum of home, the curriculum of community/ies, the curriculum of lived experiences. Pedagogy alone is insufficient; curriculum makers embrace pedagogies.

4.4   *Sociological Knowledge*

Our world is marvelously diverse and requires teachers who respect, comprehend, and meet that diversity. Yet diversity is often seen as a problem versus an asset, mostly associated with issues and conflicts, while the goal of equity not only seems to be receding further and further into the distance, but oftentimes does not seem to be a priority at all as we witness in daily newsfeeds and social media threads the human struggle to live in harmony, not conflict.

We are also living in an era of unprecedented global mobility; there has been an '83 per cent increase of the international migrant population globally from 153 million in 1990 to 281 million in 2020' (UNICEF, 2021, para. 3). This mobility is physical as air travel has become more affordable and accessible, moving millions of people across the world each day. But it is also virtual as technological advances put people in constant and close communication through social media platforms, smart phones, and a host of AI applications, especially evident during the pandemic. All these factors have 'intensified global interconnectivity' (Pauwel, 2019, p. 257) and brought people, geographies and multiple discourses into close relief.

The massive sociological changes we are witnessing on a global scale, are having an impact on our schools and on what it means to teach well. No school or teacher, no teacher education program, is immune to these rapid transformations as society grows in complexity. Global competitiveness in tandem with neoliberal policies that favor capitalism and focus on profits, have turned education into a commodity for sale. This has exacerbated the rationing of quality schools and teachers as well as rich and meaningful curriculum, further widening the achievement gap between those in the dominant majority, and those in the marginalised minority. Historically, the narrative has been consistent: the best of education has always been reserved for the privileged, while schools have served to replicate social stratifications and inequities, grooming students for future life roles as predetermined by their class and race.

Without question, this knowledge domain is the most challenging because issues of race, class, gender, sexuality and nationality are sensitive, loaded with meaning and emotion, and are integrally connected to deep-seated beliefs and values (Banaji & Greenwald, 2013). We have always lived in a diverse world; but now that diversity has been brought into high definition by forces of globalisation and digital technologies; what happens 'there' to 'them' now affects what happens 'here' to 'us'. Globalisation also heightens our interdependence, especially as so-called developed countries in the Global North, experience rapidly aging populations and economic slowdowns, compared to so-called developing countries in the Global South which are younger and demonstrate accelerating economies. This means that none of us can afford to ignore the too many children (female, brown and black, poor, immigrant, language minority) who do not have access to or have been denied the quality and caring education they need to help them grow into informed, thinking, moral, and empowered citizens who are equipped to care for the earth.

New teachers will need to confront their fears, prejudices, and misconceptions if they are to teach children of all races and ethnicities, children who have disabilities, children who are immigrants, migrants, refugees, second language learners, gay and lesbian, poor, academically talented and struggling, homeless, children who are different from them as well as those who mirror them, and so on. Many of these children have been/are ostracised and ignored; many have been/are considered worthless, uneducable, damaged. Teacher preparation will need to become uncomfortable, a space for interrupting low expectations, deficit thinking, racism, classism, xenophobia, and all other kinds of isms, if our intention is to develop teachers who can uphold the rights of children and are equipped to interrupt schooling practices that are discriminatory and harmful. Diversity in and among teachers is not simply a noun or a state of being; diversity is a mindset, a concept, a way of thinking, perceiving, living, and teaching. It is a quality, characteristic, disposition, and perspective that all teachers, each person, must seek.

4.5   *Social Knowledge*
The rapidity of change in contemporary society does not show any signs of slowing down, but instead seems to be accelerating with many troubling signs of a negative and intolerant turn in the past five years alone, given the worrying rise of nationalism and, xenophobic tendencies, ongoing wars and conflicts, trade wars and deficits, gun violence and terrorist attacks, cyber bullying, and fake news. This pessimistic state of our world is being further driven downward by poor leadership – it has become commonplace for politicians and government heads of too many countries to lie or deceive with impunity, serve their own interests and the interests of the wealthiest, simultaneously deny climate change and pillage natural resources, violate human rights agreements, exclude and commit egregious acts against the most vulnerable, and openly display their racism, misogyny and cruelty.

Given this new reality, coupled with climate change (which is resulting in climate anxiety among young people), an ever-widening income gap, fears of job automation and poor job prospects, and concerns about the utility, and accessibility, of higher education, it is understandable why people are angry. Their anger and disillusionment have been expressed in protests in numerous countries including France, Ecuador, Hong Kong SAR, Iraq, Chile, Catalonia, so much that 2019 was dubbed by the United Nations: 'a year of protest' (Garguilo, 2019). In the midst of this, advances in technology have had a profound impact on these social movements as protestors, many of whom are young adults and teenagers, connect with, communicate and learn from each other across space and national boundaries through social media. Trans-globally, they are voicing their strong dissatisfaction with government polices – actions and inactions – that affect their daily lives and livelihoods, and will have a profound impact on their futures

In this rapidly shrinking and increasingly complex universe, social knowledge must be more than acquiring skills that enable one to cooperate with others and get along. The very nature of how we as a global community will move forward together – or not – is at stake. We are at a crucial juncture in human existence when we literally have the power to destroy ourselves and the world. Learning how to solve our differences using peaceful means designed to include rather than exclude, and support democratic participation, are essential for our mutual survival. And it is teachers who can, and should, play a key role in helping young people work towards these goals and to embrace humanity – both theirs and the humanity they share with others. Social knowledge for teachers begins with skillfulness at managing and facilitating interactions with individuals and groups, regardless of background, culture and beliefs, recognising that different dynamics are at work with each, but that finding common ground and consensus are possible and necessary. Additionally, teachers must have expertise in democratic group processes, so they are able to create classroom settings where cooperation, fairness, mutuality, and equality are the norms. There is much evidence in the world that we do not, as a world community, live by these norms. Children can experience such democratic environments and learn to live by and advocate for these basic principles of justice only if teachers are capable of modeling and creating them.

These visions of democratic classrooms and processes have no associated political agenda. Admittedly, all teaching is political – whether implicitly or explicitly – but the concepts underlying this discussion of democratic classrooms are non-partisan and universal: equity, inclusion, diversity, cooperation, full participation, peace. These ideas are equally important on a world stage, and there is much work to be done if we are to prosper, develop and thrive as a world family. After all, 'we are depending on all our children to take hold of society and remake it with wisdom, compassion, love, and hope, to re-imagine a good life that includes rather than excludes, and to act in the interests of the common good' (Goodwin, 2010, p. 27).

4.6 Knowledge Domains for Teacher Education across the Professional Continuum

The conversation thus far has focused on foundational teacher education, the initial preparation of new professionals. But the five knowledge domains are relevant across the professional continuum and have meaning for the development and learning – and therefore will shape the teaching – of early career teachers, seasoned professionals and teacher educators who are charged with teaching teachers.

In terms of *Personal Knowledge*, teachers at all levels bring into their work a variety of beliefs and implicit theories about that it means to teach, to teach well, and to teach well in a variety of subjects as well as contexts (Fives & Gill, 2015). Teacher educators are also not immune and similarly enter their profession with many preconceived notions about how quality teaching looks and how it can be achieved, given the many years they too have spent as apprentice-observers (Goodwin & Kosnik, 2013; Murray & Male 2005). Thus, the careful assessment and interrogation of one's personal knowledge and beliefs about teaching must be a continuous self-initiated process that is sustained by experienced educators over their career trajectory. These habits of mind, if first introduced during preservice teaching, can (indeed must) be further cultivated and supported by continuous professional development and through learning communities. Otherwise, experienced practitioners can just as easily hold fast to, or revert to, implicit biases (Banaji & Greenwald, 2013) and inaccurate assumptions that research has shown to be especially harmful to children who are perceived as different and therefore marginalised as deficient (Carter & Darling-Hammond, 2016; Goodwin, 2020c; Lynch, 2014). Similarly, research has shown that teacher educators, in the absence of formal preparation for their role, reach into their own histories and replicate past experiences in their work with teachers, informing present day teacher education curriculum by relying on likely obsolete practices (Goodwin et al., 2014) and thus perpetuating the status quo.

Contextual Knowledge is a critical aspect of teacher educator knowledge without which preservice teacher education curriculum will continue to be narrow and focused on discrete skills, subject matter knowledge, and too often, the past. Teacher educators are often criticised for their irrelevance in countless surveys where early career teachers have repeatedly indicted their teacher preparation programmes for not preparing them for the 'real world' of classrooms. It is contextual knowledge that brings the 'real world' into view and ensures that academic or theoretical knowing can translate to meaningful practice that addresses the many intertwining complexities that affect learning and student understanding. Contextual knowledge is at the heart of meaningful and future-oriented instruction as teachers leave their initial preparation and enter into the classroom as teachers of record. Preparing young people for an uncertain future is a ubiquitous goal, especially given the shock the COVID-19 gave the world that found itself far from ready for sudden devastation. In the absence of accurate prediction about what lies ahead, future-oriented teaching requires teachers whose continuing professional development focuses on analysis, application and adaptation to a constantly changing context – using knowledge flexibly and creatively versus simply acquiring knowledge. Professional development for teachers cannot continue as it has: discrete skills focused, short term, context-free (Darling-Hammond et al., 2009; OECD, 2019b), but must be sustained, contextually-grounded, and collaborative (Darling-Hammond, Hyler, & Gardner, 2017).

Preservice students are often exposed in their preparation to different pedagogical models, but then find themselves unable to implement these models in the schools they join where there is a powerful pull towards keeping practice constant (Goodwin, Roegman & Reagan, 2016). The stand-and-deliver model of instruction remains cemented in schools (WEF, 2021) as high stakes testing has resulted in 'the narrowing of curriculum' (Crocco & Costigan, 2007) to focus on what is measured. 21st century competencies include creativity, collaboration, and critical thinking; but these cannot find their footing in curriculum that is prescriptive and locked too tightly around subject matter knowledge that teachers must first deliver, for students' absorption and performance. Research has shown that teachers are most satisfied with their work and feel most motivated and efficacious when they are involved in decisions that affect their teaching, but not many teachers around the world indicated this level of decision-making around pedagogy and curriculum (OECD, 2019b). *Pedagogical Knowledge* is critical if educators aspire to teach for the future and break out of the curriculum = content mindset and embrace curriculum = experience. This mindset change can facilitate thinking differently about and doing differently with what is known versus simply knowing what is known. *Pedagogical Knowledge* enables seasoned teachers to utilise multiple pedagogies to transform instruction – multiple pedagogies are not simply variations of strategies, but different conceptual lenses for viewing and redefining knowledge and connecting it to students and their lives. This knowledge domain has the power to ignite teachers because it calls upon them to make critical decisions about teaching, to deeply engage with what is worth knowing and therefore teaching, and centres them on *who* they are teaching versus *what* they are teaching.

It has almost become cliché to talk about the increasing diversity of classrooms and how teachers need to be ready to meet the needs of students who embody many differences and identities. And yet, students the world over do not experience the same quality of education, even within the same classroom, but are marginalised and penalised for their race, class, national origin, immigrant status and more (Carter & Darling-Hammond, 2016; European Commission, 2013; OECD, 2019a, 2019b). The global pandemic has laid bare the vast inequities in U.S. public education' (Strauss, 2020), and worsened existing inequities, such as in education, everywhere in the world (United Nations Development Program, 2020). There continue to be calls for focused professional development for teachers, both in-service and preservice, in order to be better equipped to educate all children well. These calls are not new, and history reveals that often our rhetoric is more robust than our actions as students of diversity have less access to quality schooling and teachers (Goodwin, 2020c; OECD, 2019a; UNESCO, 2019; US Commission on Civil Rights, 2018), and 'schools are fraught with dehumanizing and racialised beliefs about students of Color' (Kohli, 2019, p. 39). Research also reveals that those instructing teachers demonstrate limited understanding of cultural diversity and its critical impact on learning and teaching, given little awareness of their own biases and limited knowledge (Goodwin & Darity, 2019; Goodwin et al., 2014). *Sociological Knowledge* is essential for teachers at all levels, in all schools, hailing from all countries, teaching all subjects – in essence every teacher inclusively. What was stated earlier bears repeating: diversity in teachers and of teachers is not simply a noun or a state of being; diversity is a mindset, a concept, a way of thinking, perceiving, living, and teaching. It is a quality, characteristic, disposition, and perspective that all teachers, each person, must seek. Our very own futures depend on every student from every walk of life being well-educated and well-cared for, so they can care well for us and our world.

Caring for the world depends on citizens of the world working together to ensure the common good in peaceful, unselfish, caring and purposeful ways. The adults of the world have not demonstrated to the next generation that we are able to work together, resolve conflict and genuinely support forward progress for everyone. We have not shown how to share, to care, to protect the weak, save the planet, be truthful. If ever there was a need for all teachers to reaffirm the need for *Social Knowledge*, that need is surely now.

4.7 *Epilogue*

I stated previously that these knowledge domains for teaching enabled me and my colleagues to look beyond discrete skills and specific teacher moves, and to envision the kinds of teachers we believe are needed if we are to achieve the goal that is oft repeated but seldom achieved – a quality teacher for each child, able to teach in ways that support deep and engaged learning. In keeping with the five domains, teacher preparation and continuing professional development should focus on nurturing classroom practitioners who are:

1. *Critically conscious, self-examiners*: supporting teachers to critically examine the preconceived biases/beliefs/ideas/stereotypes they bring into teaching (from their own lived experiences as students and adults), to ensure these implicit theories about teaching and learning and the worth of some human beings over others are exposed and cannot negatively influence instructional decisions and block change;
2. *Enquirers and observers*: educating and continually supporting teachers to be observers, enquirers, and problem solvers so they are able to thoughtfully respond to the unforeseen, and make informed judgments about the wide variety of complex learning and teaching issues they will encounter daily in their classrooms;
3. *Curriculum makers*: developing teachers' skills as curriculum makers/designers, not just deliverers/implementers, so they have greater ownership over the curriculum and are better equipped to be active partners in educational reform;
4. *Equity advocates*: developing and fortifying teachers who can interrupt the harmful practices, curriculum, structures and systems that have long denied (and still deny) children from marginalised and minoritised groups full access to the benefits of school and society;
5. *Community builders*: building teachers' capacity to create inclusive communities in their classrooms, in their schools and within the teaching profession where students and teacher communities learn across differences to cooperate, collaborate and work through problems together.

Ultimately, our welfare depends on the success of every child; there are no throw away children, no children to waste. We can only save ourselves if we care for and love 'other people's children' (Delpit, 1995) as if they truly mattered as much as our own; we can only save ourselves if we care for and love one another, as if we all truly matter.

References

Banaji, M. R., & Greenwald, A. G. (2013). *Blindspot: Hidden biases of good people.* Random House.

Banks, J. (2008). Diversity, group identity, and citizenship education in a global age. *Educational Researcher, 37,* 129–139.

Bolin, F., & Panaritis, P. (1992). Searching for a common purpose: A perspective on the history of supervision. In C. Glickman (Ed.), *Supervision in transition: 1992 yearbook of the Association for Supervision and Curriculum Development* (pp. 30–43). Association for Supervision and Curriculum Development.

Carter, P., & Darling-Hammond, L. (2016). Teaching diverse learners. In D. Gitomer & C. A. Bell (Eds.), *Handbook of research on teaching* (5th ed., pp. 593–638). American Education Research Association.

Chetty, R., Friedman, J. N., & Rockoff, J. E. (2014). Measuring the impact of teachers II: Teacher value-added and student outcomes in adulthood. *American Economic Review, 104*(9), 2633–2679.

Council of the European Union. (2018). *Council recommendation of 22 May 2018 on key competencies for lifelong learning.* https://eur-lex.europa.eu/legal-content/EN/TXT/?uri=uriserv:OJ.C_.2018.189.01.0001.01.ENG

Crocco, M. S., & Costigan, A. T. (2007). The narrowing of curriculum and pedagogy in the age of accountability urban educators speak out. *Urban Education, 42*(6), 512–535.

Darling-Hammond, L., & Bransford, J. (Eds.). (2005). *Preparing teachers for a changing world: What teachers should learn and be able to do.* Jossey-Bass.

Darling-Hammond, L., Hyler, M. E., & Gardner, M. (2017). *Effective teacher professional development.* Learning Policy Institute.

Darling-Hammond, L., Wei, R. C., Andree, A., Richardson, N., & Orphanos, S. (2009). *Professional learning in the learning profession.* National Staff Development Council.

Delpit, L. (1995). *Other people's children: Cultural conflict in the classroom.* New Press.

European Commission. (2013, July). *Supporting teacher competence development for better learning outcomes.* https://ec.europa.eu/assets/eac/education/policy/school/doc/teachercomp_en.pdf

European Commission. (2018). *Boosting teacher quality: Pathways to effective policies.* Publications Office of the European Union.

Farmer, P. (2005). *Pathologies of power. Health, human rights, and the new war on the poor.* University of California Press.

Feiman-Nemser, S. (2001). From preparation to practice: Designing a continuum to strengthen and sustain teaching. *Teachers College Record, 103*, 1013–1055.

Fives, H., & Gill, M. G. (Eds.). (2015). *International handbook of research on teacher beliefs.* Routledge.

Fives, H., Lacatena, N., & Gerard, L. (2015). Teachers' beliefs about teaching (and learning). In H. Fives & M.G. Gill (Eds.), *International handbook of research on teacher beliefs* (pp. 249–265). Routledge.

Freire, P. (1984). *Pedagogy of the oppressed.* Continuum.

Garguilo, F. (2019). *2019: A year of protest.* https://reliefweb.int/report/world/2019-year-protest

Goodwin, A. L. (Ed.). (1997). *Assessment for equity and inclusion: Embracing all our children*. Routledge.

Goodwin, A. L. (2002). The case of one child: Making the shift from personal knowledge to professionally informed practice. *Teaching Education, 13*, 137–154.

Goodwin, A. L. (2010). Globalization and the preparation of quality teachers: Rethinking knowledge domains for teaching. *Teaching Education, 21*(1), 19–32.

Goodwin, A. L. (2020a). Changing teaching to change learning: Teacher preparation for the 31st century. In *Conference proceedings, Regional Center for Educational Planning-UNESCO, 5th international conference: Drivers of the future of education* (pp. 18–29). UAE.

Goodwin, A. L. (2020b). Globalization, global mindsets and teacher education. *Action in Teacher Education, 42*(1), 6–18.

Goodwin, A. L. (2020c). Learning to teach diverse learners: teachers and teacher preparation in the U.S. In *Oxford research encyclopedia of education*. Oxford University Press. https://doi.org/10.1093/acrefore/9780190264093.013.913

Goodwin, A. L., & Darity, K. (2019). Social justice teacher educators: What kind of knowing is needed? *Journal of Education for Teaching, 45*(1), 63–81. doi:10.1080/02607476.2019.1550606

Goodwin, A. L., Roegman, R., & Reagan, E. (2016). Is experience the best teacher? Extensive clinical practice and mentor teachers' perspectives on effective teaching. *Urban Education, 51*(10), 1198–1225. doi:10.1177/0042085915618720

Goodwin, A. L., Smith, L., Souto-Manning, M., Cheruvu, R., Tan, M. Y., Reed, R., & Taveras, L. (2014). What should teacher educators know and be able to do? Perspectives from practicing teacher educators. *Journal of Teacher Education, 65*(4), 284–302.

Hattie, J. A. C. (2003). *Teachers make a difference: What is the research evidence?* Retrieved November 7, 2020, from http://research.acer.edu.au/research_conference_2003/4/

Kohli, R. (2019). Lessons for teacher education: The role of critical professional development in teacher of color retention. *Journal of Teacher Education, 70*(1), 39–50.

Kristof, N. (2019, December 28). This has been the best year ever. *New York Times*. https://www.nytimes.com/2019/12/28/opinion/sunday/2019-best-year-poverty.html

Ledger, S., Thier, M., Bailey, L., & Pitts, C. (2019). OECD's approach to measuring global competency: Powerful voices shaping education. *Teachers College Record, 121*(8), 1–40.

Lortie, D. (1975). *Schoolteacher*. University of Chicago Press.

Lynch, M. (2014, December). *Deciphering the sociopolitical context of school reform*. https://www.theedadvocate.org/deciphering-the-sociopolitical-context-of-school-reform/

McIntosh, P. (2005). Gender perspectives on educating for global citizenship. In N. Noddings (Ed.), *Educating citizens for global awareness* (pp. 22–39). Teachers College Press.

McLaren, P., & Farahmandpur, R. (2001). Teaching against globalization and the new imperialism: Toward a revolutionary pedagogy. *Journal of Teacher Education, 52*(2), 136–150.

OECD. (2018a). *Effective teacher policies: Insights from PISA*. OECD Publishing. Retrieved September, 2020, from https://read.oecd-ilibrary.org/education/effective-teacher-policies_9789264301603-en#page2

OECD. (2018b). *The future of education and skills, education 2030*. https://www.oecd.org/education/2030/E2030%20Position%20Paper%20(05.04.2018).pdf

OECD. (2019a). *PISA 2018 results: Vol. II. Where all students can succeed*. OECD Publishing. https://dx.doi.org/10.1787/b5fd1b8f-en

OECD. (2019b). *TALIS 2018 results (Volume I): Teachers and school leaders as lifelong learners*. TALIS, OECD Publishing. https://doi.org/10.1787/1d0bc92a-en

Pajares, M. F. (1992). Teachers' beliefs and educational research: Cleaning up a messy construct. *Review of Educational Research, 62*(3), 307–332.

Pauwels, L. (2019). Exposing globalization: Visual approaches to researching global interconnectivity in the urban everyday. *International Sociology, 34*(3), 256–280.

Pearce, C., Kidd, D., Patterson, R., & Hanley, U. (2012). The politics of becoming… making time… *Qualitative Inquiry, 18*(5), 418–426.

ReliefWeb. (2019, December 20). *2019: A year of protest*. https://reliefweb.int/report/world/2019-year-protest

Richardson, V. (1996). The role of attitudes and beliefs in learning to teach. In J. Sikula (Ed.), *Handbook of research on teacher education* (2nd ed., pp. 102–119). Macmillan.

Richardson, V. (1998). Teacher education and the construction of meaning. In G. Griffin (Ed.), *The education of teachers: The ninety-eighth yearbook of the National Society for the study of education, Part I* (pp. 145–166). University of Chicago Press.

Rios, F., Montecinos, C., & van Olphen, M. (2007). Lessons learned from a collaborative self-study in international teacher education: Visiones, preguntas, y desafios. *Teacher Education Quarterly, 43*, 57–74.

Robinson, K. (2015). *Creative Schools, the grassroots movement that transforming education*. Penguin Books.

Rong, X. L., & Preissle, J. (2009). *Educating immigrant students in the 21st century*. Corwin.

Schleicher, A. (2020). *The impact of COVID-19 on education: Insights from education at a glance 2020*. OECD Publishing. https://www.oecd.org/education/the-impact-of-covid-19-on-education-insights-education-at-a-glance-2020.pdf

Schoonmaker, F. (2002). *Growing up teaching*. Teachers College Press.

Strauss, V. (2020, April 14). How COVID-19 has laid bare the vast inequities in U.S. public education. *Washington Post*. https://www.washingtonpost.com/education/2020/04/14/how-covid-19-has-laid-bare-vast-inequities-us-public-education/

Taubman, P. M. (2009). *Teaching by numbers: Deconstructing the discourse of standards and accountability in education.* Routledge.

UNESCO. (2019). *Migration, displacement and education: Building bridges, not walls.* https://unesdoc.unesco.org/ark:/48223/pf0000265866

UNICEF. (2018). *Child migration.* https://data.unicef.org/topic/childmigration-and-displacement/migration/

UNICEF. (2021, April). *Child migration.* https://data.unicef.org/topic/child-migration-and-displacement/migration/

U.S. Commission on Civil Rights. (2018). *Public education funding inequity.* Author.

WEF. (2015). *New vision for education: Unlocking the potential of technology.* http://www3.weforum.org/docs/WEFUSA_NewVisionforEducation_Report2015.pdf

WEF. (2020). *Schools of the future: Defining new models of education for the fourth industrial revolution.* Author. http://www3.weforum.org/docs/WEF_Schools_of_the_Future_Report_2019.pdf

WMO. (2019, December 3). *2019 concludes a decade of exceptional global heat and high-impact weather.* https://public.wmo.int/en/media/press-release/2019-concludes-decade-of-exceptional-global-heat-and-high-impact-weather

WMO. (2021). *State of the global climate 2020.* Author. https://library.wmo.int/doc_num.php?explnum_id=10618

World Bank. (2020). *COVID-19 to add as many as 150 million extreme poor by 2021.* https://www.worldbank.org/en/news/press-release/2020/10/07/covid-19-to-add-as-many-as-150-million-extreme-poor-by-2021

CHAPTER 12

Developing Teachers

A Necessary Condition for Quality Retention

Qing Gu

Abstract

This chapter builds upon but extends current understanding of the conditions for sustaining teachers' learning and development over the course of their professional lives. From a social-ecological perspective and grounded in a synthesis of empirical research over the last two decades, the chapter explores variations in the needs of teachers' professional learning and development over the course of their professional lives, and the ways in which the increasingly complex and diverse landscape of teaching supports or hinders their capacity to teach to their best in different schools and in different phases of their professional lives.

A central argument of the chapter is that a continuing dialectic between the teacher and their practices is more likely to occur in schools where there is a supportive and trusting environment for individuals' professional learning and development. Rather than focussing on the physical retention of teachers, there is a compelling argument for those responsible for raising standards in schools to take measures to ensure, as far as possible, the personal, professional, organisational and policy conditions of teachers' work and lives are conducive to nurturing their learning and fostering their professional fulfilment, so that schools will retain teachers who are willing and able to teach to their best – what we call 'quality retention'.

Keywords

teacher development – professional learning and development – teacher retention – quality retention

1   Introduction

Building and sustaining the quality of teachers is not only an agenda for the future (Day, 2017), but equally importantly, for the well-being, learning and achievement of the children who attend schools today. The COVID-19 pandemic has highlighted and exacerbated many of the profound pre-existing inequalities in education provision worldwide, including the hundreds of millions of children who were not in school before the pandemic, and those not learning while in school (Save the Children, 2021). The reported learning loss is found to be especially acute in schools with higher levels of disadvantage (Crenna-Jennings, Perera, & Sibieta, 2021); and because of deprivations of schooling and learning, an entire generation of children in the poorest countries and in most marginalised regions have been consigned to poorer life chances (Save the Children, 2020; World Bank, 2020).

Improving education quality holds the hope of ending learning poverty for the most disadvantaged and marginalised children and young people around the world. For these children especially, school represents an *oasis of safety and hope* where they can learn, play, grow and achieve. Although schools alone cannot address many of the centuries' old issues of educational and social inequalities that still challenge many children's fundamental right to quality education in modern times, they are spaces where many committed and caring teachers are dedicated to inspiring the learning and achievement of young minds.

The question of how to retain the hearts, minds and effectiveness of teachers who work in intellectually, emotionally and physically challenging places called 'school' (Goodlad, 2004) has been contemplated for many years in many countries. In essence, this is a *quality* retention question. In confronting this question, we encounter more fundamental issues of what constitutes teacher quality, why quality retention matters (as opposed to teachers' *physical* retention), and what schools and systems can do to enable them to learn to live new lives in which they are able to sustain their capacity to teach to their best over time.

2 Why *Quality* Retention Matters

The important role of a high-quality teaching profession in raising standards and transforming educational outcomes cannot be better emphasised in research papers nationally and internationally. Research on teacher effectiveness consistently reports that teachers' classroom practices have the largest effects on student learning and achievement (Hallinger, 2005; Leithwood et al., 2006; Rivkin, Hanushek, & Kain, 2005; Rockoff, 2004). The positive effects of high-quality teaching are especially significant for pupils from socio-economically disadvantaged backgrounds. Evidence suggests that when taught by very effective teachers, pupils can gain an extra year's worth of learning (Hanushek, 1992, 2011). Internationally, comparative research evidence from the Organisation for Economic Co-operation and Development (OECD) affirms that 'teacher quality' is the single most important school variable influencing student achievement (OECD, 2005). Indeed, its Teaching and Learning International Surveys (TALIS) have repeatedly concluded that making teaching a more attractive and more effective profession must be the priority in all school systems if they are to secure and enhance effective learning (OECD, 2009, 2011, 2018a).

It remains the case, however, for diverse and complex socio-economic and political reasons, that for many countries retaining and developing committed and effective teachers is a real challenge. In many low- and medium-income countries, for example, where school enrolment is on the rise, an acute shortage of primary teachers represents one of the greatest hurdles to providing education for all school-age children (UNESCO, 2011, 2014, 2015). A lack of resources and financial incentive packages to attract qualified personnel into teaching has meant that quantity, rather than quality, continues to be a primary concern in their efforts to provide basic education. This has meant that, unfortunately, children in countries needing teachers the most, tend to be taught by the least qualified personnel (UNESCO, 2006, 2015, 2020).

In contrast, in the world of high-income countries, such as the USA, the UK and many European countries, shortage of teacher supply tends to be a particularly pressing problem for core subject areas such as maths, modern foreign languages and science (European Commission, 2012, 2014; European Parliament, 2019) and for schools serving socioeconomically deprived communities (Allen & McInerney, 2019; Boyd et al., 2008; Guarino et al., 2006; Ingersoll, 2001). There are also troubling indicators which suggest that leadership turnover is especially higher and teacher quality is especially lower in schools serving high-need communities (Boyd et al., 2008; Goldhaber & Hansen, 2009; Loeb et al., 2005; Sibieta, 2020) where most children, who are already disadvantaged in accessing or benefiting from rich capital and social capital in their early years, are then denied access to the quality education to which they are entitled when entering the formal school system.

3 'Retention First, Recruitment Second'

Concerns about teacher supply and quality are not new. Significant falls in the proportion of graduates applying for teacher training programmes across many European countries have culminated in an urgent call to increase efforts to transform the conditions of teaching and through this, attract more suitably qualified people to the profession (Auguste et al., 2010; OECD, 2011; European Commission, 2012; European Parliament, 2019). At the same time, the ageing population of the existing teaching workforce (Aaronson, 2008; Chevalier & Dolton, 2004; European Commission, 2012, 2014; Grissmer & Kirby, 1997; Guttman, 2001; OECD, 2005) poses pressing challenges to the nature of its composition in the future. Only 7% of all primary and secondary teachers in the EU are under 30 years old, whilst around more than 1 in 3 (36%) are 50 or older (European Parliament, 2019). In England, for example, close to half of the full-time teachers (46%) are aged over 40, with 19% of these aged over 50 (Department for Education, 2020). This situation is the most pronounced in Italy where more than half of all teachers are older than 50 (European Commission, 2012, 2013; European Parliament, 2019).

Moreover, high rates of attrition of teachers in their first five years of teaching (Burghes et al., 2009; Darling-Hammond, 1997; Department for Education, 2020; Ingersoll, 2003; Kados & Johnson, 2007; Shen & Palmer, 2009; OECD, 2005, 2011) remain a persistent teacher retention problem. Although some studies show that on average, early career leavers tend to be less effective than stayers as measured by the test score gains of the students in their classrooms (Boyd et al., 2011; Goldhaber et al., 2011; Henry et al., 2011), others suggest that teachers with stronger qualifications and more competitive university backgrounds are more likely to exit early (Boyd et al., 2008; Guarino et al., 2006; Feng & Sass, 2011; Lankford et al., 2002).

The reasons behind teachers' decision to leave are complex. A common critique has, at least in part, attributed teacher attrition to a whole-sale redefinition of teacher professionalism driven by 'a culture of accountability, performance, and measurability' (Luke, 2011, p. 370; see also Rots & Aelterman, 2008; Smith & Kovacs, 2011). Luke (2011, p. 368) laments that 'the normative, the ethical, the cultural – matters of value – have quietly slipped from policy discussion (Ladwig, 2010), overridden by a focus on the measurable, the countable, and what can be said to be cost efficient and quality assured'. Within such a performativity culture, teacher professionalism has become more closely aligned with national educational policy which tends to define educational success in relatively narrow, instrumental terms (Furlong, 2008). Alongside this, the power of government regulatory bodies for the setting and adjudication of standards has been increased significantly over time. This has been complemented by more detailed and bureaucratic monitoring of what teachers do in their classrooms and how they do it – irrespective of whether what they are required to do is educationally and/or culturally meaningful (Luke, 2011). Thus, whether or not teachers agree with the centrally prescribed policy agendas and strategies, they are expected to conform to them in their day-to-day practice (Furlong, 2008).

It is perhaps, then, no surprise that this highly prescriptive culture of neoliberal accountability and performativity has been criticised by scholars as having contributed to a wide-spread lack of deep trust in teachers' professional standing, judgment and capability. For some years now, a substantial number of studies on teacher retention have been overly concerned with a narrow problem-focussed agenda. Although this body of research has improved our understanding of the factors which may cause some teachers to struggle and/or exit, it offers rather limited explanation as to why so many other teachers who are working with similar challenges embedded in outcomes driven educational systems are willing, able and committed to continue to teach to their best. What tends to be absent from many of the investigations of teacher stress, attrition and job satisfaction of individual teachers is the integral role that teachers' professional, role and organisational identities, well-being and sense of vocation play in enabling them to meet the daily challenges of teaching and learning (Day & Gu, 2014); and the part played by school leaders in mediating the sometimes negative effects of educational policies and through this, shaping and influencing many, if not all, teachers' sense of job fulfilment, commitment and effectiveness (Gu, Sammons, & Chen, 2018).

The positive impact of strong leadership on student learning through building supportive school culture and creating favourable working conditions for teachers is well documented in the teacher development, school improvement and school effectiveness literature (Day et al., 2011; Gu et al., 2008; Hallinger, 2005; Johnson, 2004; Leithwood et al., 2004, 2006; Sammons et al., 2011). Grissom's (2011) study found that higher teacher turnover rates in disadvantaged schools result in part from the ineffectiveness of the principal. His analysis of national school and teacher surveys showed that teacher satisfaction is likely to be lower, and that the probability for teachers to leave schools is significantly greater when the leadership of the principal is weak and ineffective.

Recent research on scaling up innovations for better teaching and learning outcomes in England also points to the significance of leadership in enabling sustained teacher professional learning, development and change (Gu et al., 2019, 2020, 2021). The research shows that leadership support for professional learning and development is a prerequisite for change in school culture which shapes the intellectual, social and organisational environments that are necessary for change in teacher practice and improvement in pupil engagement in learning. Put simply, 'A "good" research-informed innovation can rarely travel into the day-to-day realities of classrooms on its own merits without school leaders that can help teachers engage with it and apply and adapt it to their own classroom contexts' (Gu et al., 2021, p. 19). In line with these research findings is the observation of the strong and positive associations between school leaders' administrative support and low teacher retention rates (Boyd et al., 2011; Ladd, 2009). A strong sense of staff collegiality has been found to be crucial in building intellectual, emotional and social capital in schools so that teachers, and especially those working in schools serving socioeconomically deprived communities, are able to maintain their integrity and commitment in times of change (Gu & Day, 2007; Allensworth et al., 2009; Day et al., 2011; Holme & Rangel, 2012).

In his reflection of his leadership journey in education, Sir John Dunford (2016) argued that schools and the education system at large should place 'retention first' and 'recruitment second' in their endeavour to secure an effective workforce to meet the learning entitlements of every student in every school in every country of the world. It would indeed be more fruitful and educationally more meaningful if greater attention were paid to the factors which enable teachers who decide to stay to maintain committed to their own learning and the learning and achievement of their pupils. This is, in essence, a quality retention issue because, as Johnson and her colleagues (2005, p. 2) have argued, the physical retention of teachers, 'in and of itself, is not a worthy goal':

> Students are not served well when a district retains teachers without regard to quality. Little can be achieved (and much might be lost) when a district succeeds in reducing teacher turnover if some of those teachers are incompetent, mediocre, disengaged, or burnt out. Instead, student learning is the goal, and schools must seek to retain teachers who demonstrate that they are skilled and effective in the classroom, are committed to student learning, and are ready and able to contribute to the improvement of their school.

However, we all know that to teach at one's best over time is not easy. In reflecting on her professional work with teachers over the course of her career, Nieto's (2011, p. 133) expressed the greatest respect for such teachers: 'My belief in teachers is stronger than ever because I have seen the best of them do unbelievable work in sometimes harsh circumstances'. These are the teachers who give witness to the essential meaning of 'everyday resilience' that Day and Gu (2014) have elaborated in their work on the work, lives and effectiveness of teachers.

Over the years, scholars have used different conceptual and methodological lenses to explore issues around improving the quality of provision of teaching and learning in schools. We have chosen *resilience* in our recent work because it provides a useful conceptual lens for teachers, school leaders and policy-makers to understand how and why many teachers have managed to weather the often unpredictable 'storm' of school and classroom life (Patterson & Kelleher, 2005) and sustain their commitment and motivation in the profession. It also enables us as researchers to probe deep into teachers' inner and external professional worlds to explore why many are able to remain committed and passionate about making a real difference and continue to do so – irrespective of the unpredictable nature of every school and the many physical, emotional and intellectual challenges that are associated with this. More importantly, we know from research that pupils of highly committed and resilient teachers are more likely to perform better academically (Day et al., 2007).

In the remainder of the chapter, I associate teacher quality with the purpose, value and beliefs in teachers' inner worlds which enable them to endure the persistence of hope and endeavour to do their best to reach and engage every student in learning, regardless of the challenges which this may bring. I will do so in the knowledge that teacher quality is not fixed as individuals' capacity to express the conviction of their vocational commitment is almost certain to fluctuate over the course of a career. The extent to which individual teachers are able to exercise their capacity to be committed and resilient will depend not only upon their individual histories and their personal resources, but also upon the influence of the school environment, their colleagues and the quality of their school leadership.

4 Teacher Quality Revisited: Purpose, Value and Beliefs at the Core

There is strong and consistent research evidence that teachers' classroom practices have the largest effects on student learning achievement (Barber & Mourshed, 2007; Hallinger, 2005; Leithwood, 2019; Leithwood et al., 2006; Mourshed, Chijioke, & Barber, 2010; Rivkin, Hanushek, & Kain 2005; Rockoff 2004). At the systems level, the two McKinsey's reports (Barber & Mourshed, 2007; Mourshed, Chijioke, & Barber, 2010) show that getting the right people into the teaching profession and developing them to become effective teachers have played a central role in enabling the world's most improved school systems to come out on top, and more importantly, keep getting better. Put simply, teacher quality is the most critical school-level and system-level predictor of student success.

Depending on the theoretical and methodological interests and preferences of educational researchers, the definitions and measures of teacher quality vary considerably. At times, the meaning of *teacher* quality is used interchangeably with that of *teaching* quality. For example, in some studies where the research focus was on investigating increases in the quality of teach*ing*, value-added scores and learning gains were used to measure and categorise the quality of teachers rather than what they do in the classroom (e.g., Bowen & Mills, 2017; Chetty, Friedman, & Rockoff, 2014).

It is necessary to make a distinction between teach*er* quality and teach*ing* quality because, as Kennedy (2010, p. 591) argues, 'the qualities teachers bring with them to their work are not always enough to ensure better teaching practices'. A profound difference is that the former is essentially concerned about the person in the professional teacher, whilst the latter is about the practice of the professional. Put differently, teacher quality concerns *who the teacher is, what being a teacher means to the person,* and *what the values, capacity and, capabilities they have* that influence, positively or negatively, student learning and achievement. In contrast, teaching quality is primarily concerned with *what the teacher does in the classroom* (i.e., processes and activities of instruction) and *how well they do it* (i.e., impact of instruction on student learning). Thus, quality teach*ing* as against quality teach*ers* will be influenced, as Kennedy (2010) reminds us, not only by the 'enduring personal qualities that they bring with them' but will also be 'a function of schedules, materials, students, institutional incursions into the classroom, and the persistent clutter of reforms that teachers must accommodate' (2010, p. 597).

Teacher quality has remained central to policy debate about teacher supply and demand in many countries. This is because, at least in part, teacher quality attends to the ethical and vocational values, passion and resilience, as well as cognitive, social and psychological resources and dispositions of the person *in* the teacher – all of which influence, powerfully and profoundly, teachers' capacity to teach well over the course of their professional lives. Their commitment, enthusiasm and resilience – qualities that are harder to measure – are fundamental to how teachers feel about their work, how they think about themselves as professionals, and importantly, how they are (or are not) able to fulfil their professional values and core purposes by making a real difference to children's learning and achievement.

In this chapter, I focus on two inner resources of teacher quality: *altruistic values* and *efficacious beliefs*. The reasons are twofold. First, these inner resources are expressions of the personal values and strengths of the *person* in the professional teacher that define the ethical character and professional quality of the teacher. Second, and related to the first, they enthuse and enable teachers to improve their capabilities to fulfil the personal and social meaning of teaching, and therefore explain *why* some can 'maintain equilibrium and a sense of commitment and agency in the everyday worlds in which teachers teach' (Gu & Day, 2013, p. 26) whilst others cannot.

4.1 Purpose and Values: Soulfulness of Quality

In his seminal work on teaching as a calling and vocation, Hansen (1995, 2021) argues persuasively that the idea of vocation underscores the fact that it is not the teaching *role* itself but 'the person within the role and who shapes it who teaches students' (1995, p. 17). In describing teaching a calling and vocation, Hansen invites us to probe deeply into understanding the soulfulness and passion in teaching as well as the social origins of the *practice* of teaching which embodies teachers' aesthetic (e.g., having a feeling and a sense for work done well), moral, and intellectual endeavours and inspirations to enact their inner urge to make a difference to the learning and achievement of their students. The language of vocation takes us *inward* to recognise that when the person is called to '*be* a teacher rather than just to *do* or *perform* a job that others might easily accomplish in their place (Sherman, 2013, 2020)' (Hansen, 2021, p. 23), we see the identity of the person in the teacher and get closer to understand why for many teachers, teaching is much larger than a job.

> The sense of vocation finds its expression at the crossroads of public service and personal fulfilment. It takes shape through involvement in work that has social meaning and value. ... Vocation is also expressed over time. ... a person cannot will a sense of service into existence nor wake up one day and decide to be of service. Those dispositions grow and take shape over time, through interaction with people and through the attempt to perform the work well. (Hansen, 2021, pp. 3–4)

What follows is that the person's altruistic values and principles shape the ways in which they derive the social, intellectual and moral meanings from their role as a teacher. Recognising how these inner meanings motivate teachers to improve their ability to teach well is integral to understanding why the teaching profession is regarded by many committed and dedicated teachers as a 'lifestyle' (Day & Gu, 2014).

Altruism as a philosophical concept has long been used in education to describe an ethical principle and moral purpose that drive many teachers to build caring relationships with their students (Nias, 1989; Noddings 1992), and remain committed and passionate about giving their best to the students whom they serve (Ayers, 2010; Day, 2004; Gu & Li, 2013; Hansen, 1995; Nieto, 2003, 2015). Altruistic principles and values are internal to the calling that has drawn many teachers into the practice of teaching. However, to view teaching as an 'altruistic vocation' (Schwarz & Alberts, 1998, p. 155) is not, as sceptics might argue, an unsustainable 'ethical ideal' which requires teachers to sacrifice a high degree of selflessness (e.g. Higgins, 2011). Nor does it deny that teachers' material needs (such as pay and income) are important. Our research on teachers' subjective well-being in China shows that teachers' altruistic values have no direct associations with their income satisfaction, but positive and direct associations with their satisfaction with work (Song, Gu, & Zhang, 2020). When teachers' salaries have met the 'basic threshold' of income, those with stronger altruistic values and higher efficacious beliefs tend to report smaller effects of income on their work satisfaction.

Over the last decade evidence from our own research in England and China and international surveys of teachers (OECD, 2014, 2018b) repeatedly shows that the majority of teachers in the profession are still hopeful, committed and passionate about making a difference to the learning and lives of the children – for whom they care and feel responsible. Bullough and Pinnegar (2009) argue that it is in moments when teachers were meeting their ethical obligations to children that they felt elevated and were reminded of why they were first 'called to teach' (2009, p. 246).

Therefore, in our analysis of teachers' work and lives, we consider altruism as the essence of teachers' ethical values, principles and obligations, which according to Hansen (1995), enable them to see work as a 'service to others' and gain 'personal satisfaction in the rendering of that service' (1995, p. 3). This view 'turns the focus of perception in such a way that the challenges and the complexity in teaching become sources of interest in the work, rather than barriers or frustrating obstacles to overcome' (Hansen, 1995, p. 144). Such a view of teaching leads to a positive and productive emphasis on learning, growth and development – which regards teachers' need for intellectual challenge and capacity building as an indispensable part of their moral responsibility. It reveals profoundly that the good life of teaching entails both an *intellectual* act and a *moral* enterprise (Day & Gu, 2010, 2014; Goodlad, Soder, & Sironik, 1990; Hansen, 2021; Huberman, 1993; Palmer, 2007). It is this inner meaningfulness – intellectually, emotionally and spiritually – that influences, deeply and powerfully, teachers' own sense of identity and well-being.

> Becoming a wonderful teacher, or a great or awesome teacher, is a lifetime affair. This is because good teaching is forever pursuing better teaching; it is always dynamic and in motion, always growing, learning, developing, searching for a better way. Teaching is never finished, never still, never easily summed up. 'Wonderful Teacher' might be inscribed on someone's lifetime achievement award, printed on a retirement party banner, or etched on a tombstone, but it is never right for a working teacher. (Ayers, 2010, p. 16)

From the perspective of social change and evolution, Welzel and Inglehart's (2010) seminal work on values and well-being reminds us of the importance of considering the social-markers and cultural sources of values when investigating teachers' internal worlds. This is because 'humans internalise most of their values fully unconsciously in an unquestioned process of socialisation' – through which they are 'familiarised with what is socially accepted in their society' (Welzel & Inglehart, 2010, p. 47). For example, in the Chinese culture and society where the self is viewed as 'a connected, fluid, flexible, and committed being who is bound to others' (Lu, 2010, p. 335), and where the prevalent Confucian moral discourse has long stressed the importance of supressing selfish desires to serve the collective, the origins of Chinese teachers' sense of purpose and meaningfulness as well as intellectual and social connections in their worlds of work reside not only in their personal motives and goals, but more profoundly, the fulfilment of their moral obligations as a professional for the society. In this sense, Chinese teachers' satisfaction with the quality of their professional lives encapsulates the attainment of purpose and goals that meet both their own intrinsic professional needs and those of the larger professional community and society – to which they belong. The identification of culture-specific values in shaping Chinese teachers' perceptions of the meaning and goals of their work highlights the need for a deep understanding of *what matters to whom* and *in what contexts* in future research on teachers and teaching.

4.2 *Efficacious Beliefs: Psychological Functioning That Enhances Quality*

Bandura's (1986) social cognitive theory defines perceived self-efficacy as individuals' beliefs about their capabilities to exercise control over events that affect their lives, to produce expected performance, and to influence others. People with strong beliefs in their capabilities make things happen by setting themselves challenging goals, thinking strategically in the face of difficulties, and remaining resilient, motivated and task-focussed (Bandura, 1997). Bandura (1997) thus rejects the view that that efficacy beliefs are mere inert predictors of performance accomplishment. Rather, he argues that they are 'a vital personal resource' (Bandura, 2000, p. 120) which function as a key contributor to effective functioning and human flourishing.

> When faced with obstacles, setbacks, and failures, those who doubt their capabilities slacken their efforts, give up, or settle for mediocre solutions. Those who have a strong belief in their capabilities redouble their effort to master the challenges. (Bandura, 2000, p. 120)

Bandura's argument, together with findings from the latest research on teachers' self-efficacy (e.g., Klassen et al. 2011; Renshaw, Long & Cook, 2015;

Zee & Koomen, 2016), offers conceptual and empirical ground for the argument that teachers' efficacy beliefs are their self-referent judgments of their own capacity and capability to perform at certain levels (Kelley & Finnigan, 2003; Zee & Koomen, 2016). Over the last thirty years research has consistently reported that self-efficacious teachers tend to suffer less emotional exhaustion and burnout symptoms, and experience more confidence in mastering challenging tasks and higher levels of responsibility for teaching, commitment, personal accomplishment, and job satisfaction (e.g. Klassen & Chiu, 2010; Pillay, Goddard, & Wilss, 2005; Skaalvik & Skaalvik, 2010; Schwerdtfeger, Konermann, & Schonhofen, 2008; Song, Gu, & Zhang, 2020; Zee & Koomen, 2016). These findings lend support for the view that the strengths of teachers' judgements of their performance capability enhance, or constrain, the strengths of their aspiration, commitment, and effort to fulfil different task demands in given circumstances and through these, influence, positively or negatively, their emotional outlook and satisfaction with the quality of their work and life.

Values and efficacious beliefs are both key aspects of psychological functioning (OECD, 2013). Our recent research on teachers' well-being (Song, Gu, & Zhang, 2020) offers additional evidence emphasising the importance of psychological functioning in explaining human flourishing (see also, Diener et al., 2010; OECD, 2013). Although strong altruistic values can fulfil teachers' satisfaction of 'becoming the kind of teacher and person they desire to be' (Bullough & Pinnegar, 2009, p. 246), the enactment and fulfilment of these values is mediated by their efficacious beliefs. On the one hand, purpose and meaning, as 'powerful regulators of human behaviour' (Welzel & Inglehart, 2010, p. 47), empowers (or limits) individuals' efficacious beliefs in their capacity to perform proficiently in context. On the other hand, teachers need to feel efficacious in what they do in order for there to be a positive effect on work satisfaction from their strong values. Put another way, only when teachers' care and love for students are enacted in ways which enable them to master the challenges and thus continue to teach to their best can they experience higher levels of satisfaction with the quality of their work as a teacher.

5 Developing Teacher Quality: Why Schools Matter

5.1 *A Social Ecological Approach to Researching Teacher Quality*

Over the years, we have worked with teachers also who, despite their hard work, commitment, moral purpose and dedication to the education of their students, struggle to improve outcomes. Those teachers who excel and whose students excel with them do not just do so on their own. Whilst it is clearly the responsibility of each teacher to teach to their best, it is the responsibility of each individual school, school district and national government to ensure that they are able to do so through high-quality leadership and the provision of physical and other resources. Strong and consistent evidence from educational research suggests that the social and intellectual organisation of the school, and by extension, schools' connections with local communities, society, and the policy structure – when characterised with supportive and trusting relationships between different stakeholders – fosters teachers' collective capacity, commitment, resilience and effectiveness (Bryk & Schneider, 2002; Day & Gu, 2010, 2014; Sammons et al., 2007; Tschannen-Moran & Barr, 2004).

Such evidence invites us to use a social-ecological approach to analyse how the environments in which teachers work and live influence, and are influenced by, their capacity to teach well over the course of their professional lives. The relevance of the social-ecological approach to researching teachers' quality are at least threefold.

First, an *environment-centred approach* to human development reinforces the importance of emphasising the impact of multilevel contexts on the growth of teachers over the course of their professional lives, especially in terms of their capacity to maintain a sense of commitment and agency in the everyday worlds in which they teach. The theoretical underpinning of the social ecology of teachers' work, lives and professional development emerged from Bronfenbrenner's (1979) ground-breaking work on human development which is, in essence, concerned with the interconnectedness and interactions between multilevel systems and the ways they shape the course of human development throughout the life span. Bronfenbrenner defined human development as 'the person's evolving conception of the ecological environment, and is relation to it, as well as the person's growing capacity to discover, sustain, or later its properties' (1979, p. 9).

The same argument applies to teacher development. The quality of the reciprocating systems in education influences the quality of the intellectual, social and organisational conditions in which teachers work – which in turn impact, positively or negatively, on their professional identities and their capacity to be committed, efficacious and effective (Beltman, 2015; Day & Hong, 2016; Gu, 2014; Gu & Day, 2007, 2013; Johnson et al., 2016). Amongst these, the environments of schools are found to be particularly significant in shaping why and how many teachers are able to continue to commit their time, energy and passion to a profession which can make them 'feel a sense of invisibility and powerlessness' (Nieto, 2015, p. 252; see also Gu & Johansson, 2013; Johnson, 2004; OECD, 2016; UNESCO, 2015). I will unpack why schools and school leadership especially, matter to teacher development and teacher quality in more detail later.

Second and related to the first, the social ecological model of person x environment interaction (Ungar, Ghazinour, & Richter, 2013) enables us to place teachers in their complex worlds of work and analyse the ways in which their capacity to teach to their best *influences* and *is influenced* by their professional worlds. Unlike children whose individual resources (e.g. optimism and efficacy) are believed to be 'only as good as the capacity of his or her social and physical ecologies that facilitate their expression and application to developmental tasks' (Ungar, 2011, p. 6), teachers are 'moral and political agents' (Soder, 2004, p. 11) whose moral values form the hub of a school's culture which energise teachers' collaboration, learning and development. For teachers, if their role expectations were primarily defined by prescribed standards, methods and techniques, then these expectations would have missed a simple but fundamental truth about 'a good teacher':

> Good teachers possess a capacity for connectedness. They are able to weave a complex web of connections among themselves, their subjects and their students so that students can learn to weave a world for themselves. ... The connections made by good teachers are held not in their methods but in their hearts – meaning heart in its ancient sense, as the place where intellect and emotion and spirit and will converge in the human self. (Palmer, 2007, p. 11)

The voice of the *heart* flows from the identity and integrity of the inward teacher (Palmer, 2007) and speaks out why many teachers in many countries regard teaching as 'a way to live in the world' (Nieto, 2015, p. 1). As I have elaborated earlier in this chapter, understanding the role of moral values and vocation in influencing what many teachers do and why they do it in their schools and classrooms is key to understand the dynamic and complex nature of the interaction between the teacher and their context of work. Deal and Peterson (2009) argue that 'like a butterfly, a school must be nurtured by its inner energy in order to thrive' (2009, p. 180). This reinforces the observation that teachers' actions, commitment and beliefs also influence, individually and collectively, the social and organisational culture and contexts in which they work and live. Buchanan (2015) found in her research on teacher identity and agency that the discourse of education policy and structures do not completely redefine teachers' self-concepts: teachers are more complex and multifaceted than that, because individual teachers bring with them 'a unique mix of personal and professional experiences and commitments' (Buchanan, 2015, p. 700):

> Teachers therefore confront the policies and professional discourses they encounter not as tabulae rasae, but rather actively use their own preexisting identities to interpret, learn from, evaluate, and appropriate the new

conditions of their work in schools and classrooms. In this process, their identities are reformed and remade – and professional agency is carved out.

Last but not least, the social ecological understanding of teachers' work and lives emphasises a *process-oriented, developmental-contextual* approach to viewing and supporting teacher development. Teacher quality, or put differently, teachers' capacity to develop and sustain their qualities to teach well is nurtured, learned and acquired in their context of work. Over time such capacity unfolds progressively in a developing individual (Schön, 2012) as they learn to navigate and negotiate their way to the intellectual, social/relational and technical resources in their immediate external environment that enable them to continue to learn, to grow, and to enact their values and capacity to teach well. For many teachers who have managed to sustain their commitment and motivation in the profession, the ability to weather the often unpredictable 'storm' of school and classroom life (Patterson & Kelleher, 2005) is not an option, but a necessity. Sustained pursuit of continuing professional learning and development is what makes good teachers and great teaching. This is a career-long moral commitment and 'a sustainable investment for professional capital' (Hargreaves & Fullan, 2012, p. 186).

5.2 *Why Schools Matter in Developing and Sustaining Teacher Quality*

The conceptual strengths of the social ecological approach to researching teachers' work and lives highlight the significance of schools as 'finders and keepers' (Johnson, 2004) of committed, resilient and quality teachers. Despite the reform and societal pressures on teachers, research consistently shows that three interrelated conditions – teachers' vocational selves, social and professional relationships with colleagues, and leadership support and recognition – are found to be integral in enabling them to sustain their educational purposes and successfully manage the 'unavoidable uncertainty' (Shulman, 1987, p. 1) inherent in the everyday life of a teacher (Gu & Day, 2013). Amongst the three, school leadership comes first and acts as a necessary organisational condition that enables teachers to fulfil their professional commitments in collaboration and partnership with their colleagues.

Recent research evidence on teacher retention shows that teacher leavers are not necessarily 'escaping' from pupils' poor behaviour. Rather, they are escaping from poor leadership and dysfunctional school cultures. Toxic cultures devalue our need of others, impede our ability to turn to them for support, and challenge our capacity to form supportive and collegial relationships to learn and develop (Jordon, 2006, 2012). At a result, with a heavy heart, we continue to observe in our research that some teachers seeing teaching behind closed doors as a reality of the profession. Many of these teachers, more often than not, have struggled to understand why their sheer hard work has failed to bring about the levels of progress and achievement that they would like to see in their students (Matthews et al., 2014).

Our decades of research on school leadership and school improvement shows that principal leadership is instrumental in bringing about improved learning outcomes in schools. They contribute to student learning largely *indirectly* through leadership activities and influence, particularly through building school capacity and (re)designing structural, socio-cultural, and relational processes that are conducive to promoting professional learning communities and raising the quality of teaching and learning (Bryk et al., 2010; Day et al., 2011; Gu & Johansson, 2013; Hallinger & Heck, 2010a, 2010b; Leithwood, Harris, & Strauss, 2010; Leithwood, Sun, & Pollock, 2017; Sun & Leithwood, 2012, 2015). The quality and professional capability of leadership also defines the extent to which individual schools are to be engaged with externally initiated improvement effort and the ways in which the new learning is to be aligned with, as well as advance, the existing culture and capacity for change and sustained improvement.

In this process, school leaders, and school principals especially, are the *architects* of social relations and learning cultures in their schools. Their ability to drive professional development and improvement in their own schools (leader self-efficacy) and to develop sustained collaboration with other leaders and schools (leader collective efficacy) shapes the *base* capacity to be engaged with improvement initiatives within local school systems and 'the *new* capacities that must be developed to sustain and extend these initial efforts over time' (Bryk et al., 2010, p. 220, original emphasis; also Leithwood & Louis, 2012). It is perhaps then no surprise that in high-performing schools a key defining aspect of principal leadership is an unrelenting focus on fostering consistent values, expectations, and standards, and through these, empowering and transforming staff capacities and organisational conditions to embrace change and improvement.

6 Concluding Remarks

A central task for all concerned with enhancing quality and standards in schools is, therefore, not only to have a better understanding of what influences teachers' quality over the course of a career, but also the means by which the teacher quality necessary for these to be sustained may be nurtured in the contexts in which they work. Promoting and cultivating healthy individual and collective learning and achievement cultures in schools is essential to how they feel about themselves as professionals.

Establishing consistency and coherence in school structures, cultures, and improvement processes holds the key to engaging the heads, hearts and hands of the school community to achieve sustained and sustainable performance over time. Such consistency and coherence were reflected in understandings – between those who led and those who were led – of how and why their schools were able to become successful and, as importantly, to stay successful. They helped to shape the day-to-day practice of school life and enabled schools in our research to remain focused on the core business of schools – quality provision of teaching and learning – irrespective of external pressures of change (Gu, Sammons, & Chen, 2018).

References

Aaronson, D. (2008, September). The impact of baby boomer retirements on teacher labor markets. *Chicago Fed Letter*, *254*. http://www.chicagofed.org/publications/fedletter/cflseptember2008_254.pdf

Allen, B., & McInerney, L. (2019). *The Recruitment gap: Attracting teachers to schools serving disadvantaged communities*. Sutton Trust.

Allensworth, E., Ponisciak, S., & Mazzeo, C. (2009). *The schools teachers leave: Teacher mobility in Chicago public schools*. Consortium on Chicago School Research.

Auguste, B., Kihn, P., & Miller, M. (2010). *Closing the talent gap: Attracting and retaining top-third graduates to careers in teaching*. McKinsey & Company.

Ayers, W. (2010). *To teach: The journey of a teacher* (3rd ed.). Teachers College Press.

Bandura, A. (1986). *Social foundation of thought and action: A social cognitive theory*. Prentice Hall.

Bandura, A. (1997). *Self-efficacy: The exercise of control*. W. H. Freeman.

Bandura, A. (2000). Cultivate self-efficacy for personal and organizational effectiveness. In E. A. Locke (Ed.), *Handbook of principles of organization behavior* (pp. 120–136). Blackwell.

Barber, M., & Mourshed, M. (2007). *How the world's best performing school systems come out on top*. McKinsey and Company.

Beltman, S. (2015). Teacher professional resilience: Thriving not just surviving. In N. Weatherby-Fell (Ed.), *Learning to teach in the secondary school* (pp. 20–38). Cambridge University Press.

Bodenheimer, G., & Shuster, S. (2020). Emotional labour, teaching and burnout: Investigating complex relationships. *Educational Research*, *62*(1), 63–76.

Bowen, D., & Mills, J. (2017). Changing the education workforce? The relationships among teacher quality, motivation and performance pay. *Teachers College Record, 119*, 1–32.

Boyd, D., Grossman, P., Lankford, H., Loeb, S., & Wycoff, J. H. (2008). *Who leaves? Teacher attrition and student achievement.* NBER Working Paper No. W14022.

Boyd, D., Lankford, H., Loeb, S., Ronfeldt, M., & Wyckoff, J. (2011). The role of teacher quality in retention and hiring: Using applications-to-transfer to uncover preferences of teachers and schools. *Journal of Policy Analysis and Management, 30*(1), 88–110.

Bronfenbrenner, U. (1979). *The ecology of human development: Experiments by nature and design.* Harvard University Press.

Bryk, A. S., & Schneider, B. L. (2002). *Trust in schools: A core resource for improvement.* Russell Sage Foundation.

Bryk, A., Sebring, P., Allensworth, E., Luppescu, S., & Easton, J. (2010). *Organising schools for improvement: Lessons from Chicago.* University of Chicago Press.

Buchanan, R. (2015). Teacher identity and agency in an era of accountability. *Teachers and Teaching: Theory and Practice, 21*(6), 700–719.

Bullough, R., & Pinnegar, S. (2009). The happiness of teaching (as eudaimonia): Disciplinary knowledge and the threat of performativity. *Teachers and Teaching: Theory and Practice, 15*(2), 241–256.

Burghes, D., Howson, J., Marenbon, J., O'Leary, J., & Woodhead, C. (2009). *Teachers matter: Recruitment, employment and retention at home and abroad.* Politeia.

Chetty, R., Friedman, J. N., & Rockoff, J. E. (2014). Measuring the impacts of teachers II: Teacher value-added and student outcomes in adulthood. *American Economic Review, 104*(9), 2633–2679.

Chevalier, A., & Dolton, P. (2004). Teacher shortage: Another impending crisis? *CentrePiece*, Winter, 15–21.

Cooper, J. M., & Alvarado, A. (2006). *Preparation, recruitment and retention of teachers.* IIEP education policy series No. 5. UNESCO.

Crenna-Jennings, W., Perera, N., & Sibieta, L. (2021). *Education recovery and resilience in England.* Education Policy Institute.

Darling-Hammond, L. (1997). *Doing what matters most: Investing in quality teaching.* National Commission on Teaching & America's Future.

Day, C. (2004). *A passion for teaching.* RoutledgeFalmer.

Day, C. (2017). *Teachers' worlds and their work.* Routledge.

Day, C., & Gu, Q. (2010). *The new lives of teachers.* Routledge.

Day, C., & Gu, Q. (2014). *Resilient teachers, resilient schools: Building and sustaining quality in testing times.* Routledge.

Day, C., & Hong, J. (2016). Influences on the capacities for emotional resilience of teachers in schools serving disadvantaged urban communities: Challenges of living on the edge. *Teaching and Teacher Education, 59*, 115–125.

Day, C., Sammons, P., Leithwood, K., Hopkins, D., Gu, Q., & Brown, E., with Ahtaridou, E. (2011). *School leadership and student outcomes: Building and sustaining success.* Open University Press.

Day, C., Sammons, P., Stobart, G., Kington, A., & Gu, Q. (2007). *Teachers matter: Connecting lives, work and effectiveness.* Open University Press.

Deal, T. E., & Peterson, K. D. (2009). *Shaping school culture* (2nd ed.). Jossey-Bass.

Department for Education. (2020). *School workforce in England.* https://explore-education-statistics.service.gov.uk/find-statistics/school-workforce-in-england

Diener, E., Wirtz, D., Tov, W., Kim-Prieto, C., Choi, D., Oishi, S., & Biswas-Diener, R. (2010). New well-being measures: Short scales to assess flourishing and positive and negative feelings. *Social Indicators Research, 97*(2), 143–156.

Dunford, J. (2016). *The school leadership journey.* John Catt Educational Ltd.

European Commission. (2012). *Key data on education in Europe 2012.* Education, Audiovisual and Culture Executive Agency.

European Commission. (2014). *Study on policy measures to improve the attractiveness of the teaching profession in Europe.* European Commission.

European Parliament. (2019). *Teaching careers in the EU.* https://www.europarl.europa.eu/RegData/etudes/BRIE/2019/642220/EPRS_BRI(2019)642220_EN.pdf

Feng, L., & Sass, T. (2011). *Teacher quality and teacher mobility.* National Center for Analysis of Longitudinal Data in Education Research Working Paper 57.

Furlong, J. (2008). Making teaching a 21st century profession: Tony Blair's big prize. *Oxford Review of Education, 34*(6), 727–739.

Goldhaber, D., Gross, B., & Player, D. (2011). Teacher career paths teacher quality and persistence in the classroom: Are public schools keeping their best? *Journal of Policy Analysis and Management, 30*(1), 57–87.

Goldhaber, D., & Hansen, M. (2009). National board certification and teachers' career paths: Does NBPTS certification influence how long teachers remain in the profession and where they teach? *Education Finance and Policy, 4*(3), 229–262.

Goodlad, J. I. (2004). *A place called school.* McGraw-Hill.

Goodlad, J. I., Soder, R., & Sirotnik, K. A. (1990). *Places where teachers are taught.* Jossey-Bass.

Grissmer, D., & Kirby, S. N. (1997). Teacher turnover and teacher quality. *Teachers College Record, 99*(1), 57–61.

Grissom, J. A. (2011). Can good principals keep teachers in disadvantaged schools? Linking principal effectiveness to teacher satisfaction and turnover in hard-to-staff environments. *Teachers College Record, 113*(11), 2552–2585.

Gu, Q. (2014). The role of resilience in teachers' career long commitment and effectiveness. *Teachers and Teaching: Theory and Practice, 20*(5), 502–529.

Gu, Q., & Day, C. (2007). Teachers resilience: A necessary condition for effectiveness. *Teaching and Teacher Education, 23,* 1302–1316.

Gu, Q., & Day, C. (2013). Challenges to teacher resilience: Conditions count. *British Educational Research Journal, 39*(1), 22–44.

Gu, Q., Hodgen, J., Adkins, M., & Armstrong, P. (2019). *Incentivising schools to take up evidence-based practice to improve teaching and learning: Evidence from the evaluation of the Suffolk Challenge Fund: Final project report.* Education Endowment Foundation. https://educationendowmentfoundation.org.uk/public/files/Campaigns/Suffolk_Challenge_Fund.pdf

Gu, Q., & Johansson, O. (2013). Sustaining school performance: School contexts matter. *International Journal of Leadership in Education, 16*(3), 301–326.

Gu, Q., & Li, Q. (2013). Sustaining resilience in times of change: Stories from Chinese teachers. *Asia Pacific Journal of Teacher Education, 41*(3), 288–303.

Gu, Q., Rea, S., Seymour, K., Smethem, L., Bryant, B., Armstrong, P., Ahn, M., Hodgen, J., & Knight, R. (2020). *The research schools network: Supporting schools to develop evidence-informed practice.* Evaluation report. Education Endowment Foundation. https://educationendowmentfoundation.org.uk/public/files/RS_Evaluation.pdf

Gu, Q., Sammons, P., & Chen, J. (2018). How principals of successful schools enact education policy: Perceptions and accounts from senior and middle leaders. *Leadership and Policy in Schools, 17*(3), 373–390.

Gu, Q., Sammons, P., & Mehta, P. (2008). Leadership characteristics and practices in schools with different effectiveness and improvement profiles. *School Leadership & Management, 28*(1), 43–63.

Gu, Q., Seymour, K., Rea, S., S, Knight, R., Ahn, M., Sammons, P., Kameshwara, K., & Hodgen, J. (2021). *The research schools programme in opportunity areas: Investigating the impact of research schools in promoting better outcomes in schools.* Evaluation report. Education Endowment Foundation.

Guarino, C. M., Santibanez, L., & Daley, G. A. (2006). Teacher recruitment and retention: A review of the recent empirical literature. *Review of Educational Research, 76*(2), 173–208.

Guttman, C. (2001, October). A hard sell for teaching. *The Courier UNESCO.*

Hallinger, P. (2005). Instructional leadership and the school principal: A passing fancy that refuses to fade away. *Leadership and Policy in Schools, 4*(3), 1–20.

Hallinger, P., & Heck, R. (2010a). Collaborative leadership and school improvement: Understanding the impact on school capacity and student learning. *School Leadership and Management, 30*(2), 95–110. doi:10.1080/13632431003663214

Hallinger, P., & Heck, R. H. (2010b). Leadership for learning: Does collaborative leadership make a difference? *Educational Management, Administration and Leadership, 38*(6), 654–678.

Hanushek, E. A. (1992). The trade-off between child quantity and quality. *Journal of Political Economy, 100*(1), 84–117.

Hanushek, E. A. (2011). The economic value of higher teacher quality. *Economics of Education Review, 30*(3), 466–479.

Hansen, D. (1995). *The call to teach.* Teachers College Press.

Hansen, D. (2021). *Reimaging the call to teach.* Teachers College Press.

Hargreaves, A., & Fullan, M. (2012). *Professional capital: Transforming teaching in every school.* Teachers College Press.

Henry, G. T., Bastian, K. C., & Fortner, C. K. (2011). Stayers and leavers: Early career teacher effectiveness and attrition. *Educational Researcher, 40*(6), 271–280.

Higgins, C. (2011). *The good life of teaching: An ethics of professional practice.* Wiley-Blackwell.

Holme, J., & Rangel, V. (2012). Putting school reform in its place: Social geography, organizational social capital, and school performance. *American Educational Research Journal, 49*(2), 257–283.

Huberman, M. (1993). *The lives of teachers.* Continuum.

Ingersoll, R. M. (2001). Teacher turnover and teacher shortages: An organizational analysis. *American Educational Research Journal, 38*(3), 499–534.

Ingersoll, R. M. (2003). *Is there really a teacher shortage?* Consortium for Policy Research in Education, University of Pennsylvania.

Johnson, S. M. (2004). *Finders and keepers.* Jossey-Bass.

Johnson, S. M., Berg, J. H., & Donaldson, M. L. (2005). *A review of the literature on teacher retention.* Harvard Graduate School of Education.

Johnson, B., Down, B., Cornu, R., Peters, J., Sullivan, A., Pearce, J., & Hunter, J. (2016). *Promoting early career teacher resilience.* Routledge.

Jordan, J. (2012). Relational resilience in girls. In S. Goldstein & R. B. Brooks (Eds.), *Handbook of resilience in children* (pp. 73–86). Springer.

Kardos, S. M., & Johnson, S. M. (2007). On their own and presumed expert: New teachers' experience with their colleagues. *Teachers College Record, 109*(9), 2083–2106.

Kelley, C. J., & Finnigan, K. (2003). The effects of organisational context on teacher expectancy. *Educational Administration Quarterly, 39*(5), 603–634.

Kennedy, M. M. (2010). Attribution error and the quest for teacher quality. *Educational Researcher, 39*(8), 591–598.

Klassen, R. M., & Chiu, M. M. (2010). Effects on teachers' self-efficacy and job satisfaction: Teacher gender, years of experience, and job stress. *Journal of Educational Psychology, 102*(3), 741–756.

Klassen, R. M., Tze, V. M., Betts, S. M., & Gordon, K. A. (2011). Teacher efficacy research 1998–2009: Signs of progress or unfulfilled promised? *Educational Psychological Review, 23,* 21–43.

Ladd, H. (2009). *Teachers' perceptions of their working conditions: How predictive of policy-relevant outcomes.* National Center for Analysis of Longitudinal Data in Education Research Working Paper No. 33. CALDER.

Ladwig, J. G. (2010). Beyond academic outcomes. *Review of Research in Education, 34,* 113–141.

Lankford, M., Loeb, S., & Wyckoff, J. (2002). Teacher sorting and the plight of urban schools: A descriptive analysis. *Educational Evaluation and Policy Analysis, 13*(3), 256–268.

Lee, J. K., & Yin, H. B. (2011). Teachers' emotions in a mandated curriculum reform: A Chinese perspective. In C. Day & J. K. Lee (Eds.), *New understandings of teacher's work. Professional learning and development in schools and higher education* (pp. 85–104). Springer.

Leithwood, K. (2019). *Leadership development on a large scale: Lessons for future success.* Corwin.

Leithwood, K., Day, C., Sammons, P., Harris, A., & Hopkins, D. (2006). *Seven strong claims about successful school leadership.* National College for School Leadership.

Leithwood, K., Harris, A., & Strauss, T. (2010). *Leading school turnaround: How successful leaders transform low-performing schools.* Jossey-Bass.

Leithwood, K., & Louise, K. S. (2012). *Linking leadership to student learning.* Jossey-Bass.

Leithwood, K., Seashore Louis, K., Anderson, S., & Wahlstrom, K. (2004). *How leadership influences student learning.* Center for Applied Research and Educational Improvement.

Leithwood, K., Sun, J., & Pollock, K. (Eds.). (2017). *How school leaders contribute to student success: The four paths framework.* Springer.

Loeb, S., Darling-Hammond, L., & Luczak, J. (2005). How teaching conditions predict teacher turnover in California schools. *Peabody Journal of Education, 80*(3), 44–70.

Lu, L. (2010). Chinese wellbeing. In M. H. Bond (Ed.), *The Oxford handbook of Chinese psychology* (pp. 327–342). Oxford University Press.

Luke, A. (2011). Generalizing across borders: Policy and the limits of educational science. *Educational Researcher, 40*(8), 367–377.

Matthews, P., Rea, S., Hill, R., & Gu, Q. (2014). *Freedom to lead: A study of outstanding primary school leadership in England.* National College for School Leadership.

Mourshed, M., Chijioke, C., & Barber, M. (2010). *How the world's most improved school systems keep getting better.* McKinsey and Company.

Nias, J. (1989). *Primary teachers talking.* Routledge.

Nieto, S. (2003). *What keeps teachers going?* Teachers College Press.

Nieto, S. (2011). Critical hope, in spite of it all. In R. F. Elmore (Ed.), *I used to think ... and now I think* (pp. 127–133). Harvard Education Press.

Nieto, S. (2015). *Why we teach now?* Teachers College Press.

Noddings, N. (1992). *The challenge to care in schools*. Teachers College Press.

OECD. (2005). *Teachers matter*. OECD.

OECD. (2009). *Creating effective teaching and learning environments: First results from TALIS*. OECD.

OECD. (2011). *Building a high-quality teaching profession: Lessons from around the world*. OECD.

OECD. (2013). *OECD guidelines on measuring subjective well-being*. OECD Publishing.

OECD. (2014). *TALIS 2013 results: An international perspective on teaching and learning*. OECD.

OECD. (2016). *Education at a glance: OECD indicators*. OECD Publishing.

OECD. (2018a) *Where all students can succeed* (Vol. II). OECD.

OECD. (2018b). *TALIS 2018 results: Teachers and school leaders as lifelong learners* (Vol. 1). OECD.

Palmer, P. (2007). *The courage to teach* (10th ed.). Jossey-Bass.

Patterson, J., & Kelleher, P. (2005). *Resilient school leaders: Strategies for turning adversity into achievement*. Association for Supervision and Curriculum Development.

Pillay, H., Goddard, R., & Wilss, L. (2005). Well-being, burnout and competence. Implications for teachers. *Australian Journal of Teacher Education, 30*, 22–33.

Renshaw, T. L., Long, A. C. J., & Cook, C. R. (2015). Assessing adolescents' positive psychological functioning at school: Development and validation of the student subjective wellbeing questionnaire. *School Psychology Quarterly, 30*(4), 534–552.

Rivkin, S. G., Hanushek, E. A., & Kain, J. F. (2005). Teachers, schools and academic achievement. *Econometrica, 73*(2), 417–458.

Rockoff, J. E. (2004). The impact of individual teachers on student achievement: Evidence from panel data. *American Economic Review Papers and Proceedings, 94*(2), 247–252.

Rots, I., & Aelterman, A. (2008). Two profiles of teacher education graduates: A discriminant analysis of teaching commitment. *European Educational Research Journal, 7*, 523–534.

Sammons, P., Day, C., Kington, A., Gu, Q., Stobart, G., & Smees, R. (2007). Exploring variations in teachers' work, lives and their effects on pupils: Key findings and implications from a longitudinal mixed-method study. *British Educational Research Journal, 33*(5), 681–701.

Sammons, P., Gu, Q., Day, C., & Ko, J. (2011). Exploring the impact of school leadership on pupil outcomes. *International Journal of Educational Management, 25*(1), 83–101.

Save the Children. (2020). *Save our education*. Save the Children.

Save the Children. (2021). *Build forward better*. Save the Children.

Schön, I. (2012). Temporal and contextual dimensions to individual positive development: A developmental-contextual systems model of resilience. In M. Ungar (Ed.), *The social ecology of resilience: A handbook of theory and practice* (pp. 143–156). Springer.

Schwarz, G., & Alberts, J. (1998). *Teacher lore and professional development for school reform*. Bergin & Garvey.

Schwerdtfeger, A., Konermann, L., & Schönhofen, K. (2008). Self-efficacy as a health-protective resource in teachers? A biopsychological approach. *Health Psychology Official Journal of the Division of Health: Psychology American Psychological Association, 27*, 358.

Shen, J., & Palmer, L. B. (2009). Inadequate preparation does impact teacher attrition. In J. Shen (Ed.), *School leaders: Professional and demographic characteristics* (pp. 125–140). Peter Lang.

Sherman, S. (2013). *Teacher preparation as an inspirational practice: Building capacities for responsiveness*. Routledge.

Sherman, S. (2020). Evolving enactments of personal fulfilment and service in teaching. In D. M. De Marzio (Ed.), *David Hansen and the call the teach: Renewing the work that teachers do* (pp. 13–26). Teachers College Press.

Shulman, L. S. (1987). Knowledge and teaching. *Harvard Educational Review, 57*, 1–22.

Sibieta, L. (2020). *Teacher shortages in England: Analysis and pay pptions*. Education Policy Institute.

Skaalvik, E., & Skaalvik, S. (2010). Teacher self-efficacy and teacher burnout: A study of relations. *Teaching and Teacher Education, 26*, 1059–1069.

Skaalvik, E., & Skaalvik, S. (2011). Teacher job satisfaction and motivation to leave the teaching profession. *Teaching and Teacher Education, 27*(6), 1029–1038.

Smith, J. M., & Kovacs, P. E. (2011). The impact of standards-based reform on teachers: The case of 'No Child Left Behind'. *Teachers and Teaching: Theory and Practice, 7*(2), 201–225.

Soder, R. (2004). When I get my own classroom. In J. Goodlad & T. McMannon (Eds.), *The teaching career* (pp. 1–18). Teachers College Press.

Song, H., Gu, Q., & Zhang, Z. H. (2020). An exploratory study of teachers' subjective wellbeing: Understanding the links between teachers' income satisfaction, altruism, self-efficacy and work satisfaction. *Teachers and Teaching: Theory and Practice*. https://doi.org/10.1080/13540602.2020.1719059

Sun, J., & Leithwood, K. (2012). Transformational school leadership: Effects on student achievement. *Leadership and Policy in Schools, 11*(4), 418–451.

Sun, J., & Leithwood, K. (2015). Leadership effects on student learning mediated by teacher emotions. *Societies, 5*, 566–582.

Tschannen-Morgan, M., & Barr, M. (2004). Fostering student learning: The relationship of collective teacher efficacy and student achievement. *Leadership and Policy in Schools, 3*(3), 189–209.

UNESCO. (2006) *Teachers and educational quality: Monitoring global needs for 2015.* UNESCO.
UNESCO. (2011). *The global demand for primary teachers – 2011 Update.* UNESCO.
UNESCO. (2014). *Wanted: Trained teachers to ensure every child's right to primary education.* UNESCO.
UNESCO. (2015). *Education for all 2000–2015: Achievements and challenges.* UNESCO.
UNESCO. (2020). *Global education monitoring report: Inclusion and education: All means all.* UNESCO.
Ungar, M. (2011). The social ecology of resilience: Addressing contextual and cultural ambiguity of a nascent construct. *American Journal of Orthopsychiatry, 81*(1), 1–7.
Ungar, M., Ghazinour, M., & Richter, J. (2013). Annual research review: What is resilience within the social ecology of human development? *Journal of Child Psychology and Psychiatry, 54*(4), 348–66.
Welzel, C., & Inglehart, R. (2010). Agency, values, and well-being: A human development model. *Social Indicators Research, 97*(1), 43–63.
World Bank. (2020). *Ending learning poverty: What will it take?* World Bank.
Zee, M., & Koomen, H. M. Y. (2016). Teacher self-efficacy and its effects on classroom processes, student academic adjustment, and teacher wellbeing: A synthesis of 40 years of research. *Review of Educational Research, 86*(4), 981–1015.

CHAPTER 13

The Teacher, Teacher Careers and Teacher Education

Conditions for a Career Long Dedication and Passion

Marco Snoek

Abstract

Career opportunities play an important role in keeping teachers passionate and motivated in their profession. As such opportunities contribute to growth, challenge, variation and recognition, they can both attract high quality candidates to the profession and keep talented teacher in the profession for a longer time. However, the traditional view on the teacher profession can be considered as static with little career opportunities. This raises the questions: how teacher careers can be understood, and what the implications for such a more dynamic understanding are for education systems, school heads, teachers and for teacher education.

Taking into account this questions, six international reports on teacher careers that aim to support national systems to strengthen career opportunities for teachers are explored in this chapter. These reports from the European Commission's Working Groups on Schools, the Commissions data network Eurydice, OECD and UNESCO, all emphasise the importance of strengthening career opportunities for teachers, but vary in their focus, as most report focus on formal career structures that are embedded in national legislation, while the EC's Working Group Schools report from 2020 takes a somewhat wider perspective, taking the perspective of teacher more as a starting point in identifying career options.

From the reports the implications for teachers, school heads and teacher education can be derived, including the need for a wider and more dynamic view on the profession, leading to a wider professional identity, the need for the development of career competencies for teachers and the need for initial teacher education institutes to actively support teachers not only during their initial development, but throughout the different stages of their career.

Keywords

teacher – teacher career – teacher education – career ladders – professional development – teacher continuum – teacher policy

1 The Importance of Teacher Careers

Teachers' motivation for teaching is an important factor in the motivation and learning outcomes of pupils and students (Roth et al., 2007). This raises the question how teachers can stay motivated during their teaching career. Research shows that allowing teachers more agency to work towards different promotion opportunities can offer a strong incentive to remain in the profession (Cabus et al., 2020; Calvert, 2016; Cordingley et al., 2019; Tournier et al., 2019).

Although many countries have some kind of career structure for the teacher profession in place, many of these teacher career structures are based on a single salary scale, where teachers earn promotions based solely on academic qualifications or years of experience, irrespective of the quality of teaching (Chimier & Tournier, 2018; Crehan, 2016; European Commission/EACEA/Eurydice, 2018; UNESCO, 2019). Crehan (2016) and Tournier et al. (2019) show that such models that emphasise salary scales, can reduce teacher motivation as it mainly focuses on extrinsic and controlled motivation while neglecting intrinsic and autonomous motivation. This is supported by Herzberg's dual factor theory of motivation (Herzberg, 1968) that emphasises that factors like salaries and working conditions mainly have impact on the dissatisfaction with regard to the profession, while beyond a certain point it is not financial incentives but job-related factors like recognition, responsibility, and growth which contribute to a positive motivation (Crehan, 2016).

The existing career opportunities often are of a vertical and hierarchical nature as they are connected to more coordinating and managerial roles (European Commission/EACEA/Eurydice, 2018). This creates the risk that tasks and qualities that are related to leadership and management are seen as of higher value than tasks and qualities that are related to supporting classroom learning. As a result, teachers who want to develop themselves and have a 'career' are forced to leave the primary process of classroom teaching (Evers, 2007; Gerrichhauzen, 2007).

Career opportunities do not only play a role in teachers' retention, but also in attracting high quality candidates into the profession. A profession is not only attractive because of its prestige, status and the esteem based on high standards that are maintained by its members (Hargreaves, 2009), but also because of the opportunities it offers for development and growth. This is confirmed in studies that specifically focus on career opportunities within the teacher profession (Coldwell, 2017; Van der Aa & Van den Berg, 2018; Vermeulen & Van der Aa, 2011; Vrielink & Hogeling, 2011). In a recent Dutch study on the reasons why secondary school students choose or reject a teacher career, more than half mentioned the lack of opportunities for career growth (Bahlmann et al., 2018).

As a consequence, to keep teachers motivated within the profession, it is not only important to create a working environment where teachers have the opportunity and professional autonomy to design their daily work (job crafting) (Hulsbos et al., 2012; Onderwijsraad, 2016), but also an environment that offers opportunities for designing the development of their role over time (career crafting) (Akkermans & Tims, 2017). The notion of career crafting indicates that career development of employees is not only a task for the organisation where a professional is employed, but that the main responsibility lies with the employee himself (Van der Heijden & De Vos, 2015). Being successful in crafting your own career as a teacher requires specific competencies to reflect on your career (including both reflection on what underlying values are important in your work and on the qualities that you possess), to explore different career options and how they relate to your values and qualities, to act on this and to actually take career steps, and the ability to use networks to support your career steps (Kuijpers et al., 2006). Such personal related factors are also emphasised within the area of vocational psychology – where constructs like individual developmental phases, personal interests, personal values, ambition, meaning, recognition and agency are indicated as important elements that impact successful career development within professions (McIlveen, 2009; Runhaar et al., 2009; Swanson, 2013; Van der Sluis, 2011).

However, next to personal qualities of teachers in shaping and crafting their career, organisational support is still needed (Forrier et al., 2018). Career support and career tools can support teachers in making career decisions (European Commission/EACEA/Eurydice, 2018), while explicating different possibilities, steps and roles within the teacher profession can help teachers in navigating their career. Different actors in and around schools can pay a role in this: education employers, local authorities, career advisors, school leaders and colleagues. Creating a coherent career support structure that can help teachers to remain passionate in their work over the years, is part of the area of personnel and human resource policies where strategic organisational aims like processes, external demands, tasks and renumeration need to be combined with elements from vocational psychology like ambition, recognition and agency.

The way in which these strategic organisational aims can be connected to individual psychological factors is influenced by the wider national context and the way in which the teacher profession is perceived. When the teacher profession is mainly understood as a static and narrow profession (Snoek et al., 2019), both teachers and schools will encounter difficulties in navigating and supporting a career paths that is inspiring and enriching and helps to keep high quality teachers for a longer period in the profession.

Different actors can play a key role in supporting teachers and schools to strengthen career development of teachers. First actor are national governments. As in most countries career structures within the teacher profession are defined at a national level, strengthening career opportunities for teachers requires action with regard to national teacher policies focusing on career structures, teacher support and support of schools. Career structures offering more options and choice can improve teacher motivation, but such structures are complicated to implement and typically lead to upheaval in established systems (Chiriboga Montalvo & Pinto Haro, 2019; Sayed & de Kock, 2019; Tournier et al., 2019).

A second key actor are teacher education institutes. Through initial teacher education they can contribute to the development of career competencies and the agency of teachers. But they can also support teachers' career development through in-service teacher education, where they can support teachers in developing qualities and competencies that are needed for new roles or for expert roles.

This all raises the question how international and European policies can support nations to strengthen the conditions for career development of teachers and what the possible implication of such policies can be for teacher education institutions.

In this paper we will explore this question by analysing recently published international policy advices that aim to support national governments in strengthening career opportunities for teachers. In this analysis we will use three leading questions:
– How are careers for teachers understood?
– What implications are identified for teachers, schools and national policies?
– What are the implications for initial and post-initial teacher education?

For this analysis, we identified policy advices or reports on teacher careers that have been published recently by the three major transnational policy bodies or thinktanks that aim to support national governments to strengthen the quality of their education system: the European Commission, OECD and UNESCO. With the three leading questions in mind, these documents were carefully read to identify elements that could contribute to answering these questions.

2 European Policy Guidance for Teacher Careers

Although education is considered as one of the key factors in strengthening the European Union in terms of economic growth and social cohesion, the European Commission has no legislative authority with respect to education. Therefore, the realisation of ambitions regarding the quality of education within the

European Union, is in the hands of the individual member states. However, the European Council and the European Commission still have a number of policy tools to support the development of national education policies through the so called 'open method of co-ordination' (Büchs, 2007; Radaelli, 2003). One of the key elements of this method is the use of peer learning, within working groups where policy representatives from different member states and European stakeholder organisations exchange policy examples and dilemmas. This process is supported by thematic and comparative analyses of national policies. Both the comparative data and the exchange of national policy examples aim to inspire national governments to improve their policies. Through the exchange between member states, a closer understanding of policy issues is reached which is summarised in policy recommendations that aim to guide and support national policy development.

From 2005 several working groups have addressed issues regarding schools and teachers and published numerous policy guides. Two of these address the topic of teacher careers: Shaping career-long perspectives on teaching: A guide on policies to improve Initial Teacher Education (ET2020 Working Group on Schools Policy, 2015) and Supporting teacher and school leader careers: A Policy Guide (ET2020 Working Group Schools, 2020). To provide the working group and member states with comparative data on teacher careers in different member states, the European Union's information network Eurydice has provided a comparative report on teacher careers in Europe (European Commission/EACEA/Eurydice, 2018), followed by a wider report on teacher careers, development and well-being (European Commission/EACEA/Eurydice, 2021).

2.1 ET2020 *Working Group on Schools Policy: Shaping Career Long Perspectives on Teaching*

The 2015 policy guide emphasises the teacher profession as a continuum of teacher preparation, teacher induction and teacher continual professional development (ET2020 Working Group on Schools Policy, 2015). The guide provides five parallel perspectives on this continuum: a pedagogical perspective connected to the concerns of teachers themselves, which will vary in different phases of the professional continuum, an instrumental perspective related of the support system that aims to support teachers in different phases of their career, a professional perspective related to the competencies that teachers need and competence frameworks that may act as reference frames to guide next steps in development, a cultural perspective related to learning cultures in schools that can support or hinder teacher learning and the way in which teaching and learning by teachers are integrated, and a career perspective, related to growth and development in tasks and responsibilities. Key message is that these five perspectives are interconnected and that coherence between these five perspectives is strengthened when there is a shared vision on the (continuum of the) teacher profession, on (support for) teacher learning and on teacher development in terms of competencies and roles.

> It is essential to create career and support structures that recognize, reward and stimulate the different phases of the continuum. Therefore, it is important that all stakeholders – ITE providers, schools, education authorities, policymakers, as well as teacher unions and associations – work as partners at each phase and across these phases, aligning the different perspectives of the continuum. (ET2020 Working Group on Schools Policy, 2015, p. 17)

Based on this overarching perspective on the teaching profession, the guide provides policy examples from different countries that aim to support the continuum of the profession. The majority of these examples focus on the instrumental perspective: the support of the professional development of teachers, with a special focus on the support of newly qualified teachers. Some examples focus on conditions for career development, in terms of the mechanisms for teacher appraisal and assessment as a requirement for further career steps.

> In Hungary, a new teacher career scheme has recently been introduced, under which teachers' competencies are assessed before they enter a new career stage. A network of advisors and counsellors has been established in order to support teacher development and advancement under this scheme. (ET2020 Working Group on Schools Policy, 2015, p. 11)

Based on discussions within the working group, the guide recommends policy makers to pay attention to a number of topics: the connection between different phases of the continuum, and the embedding of continuous professional development in the system and in school structures and cultures. At the same time, the guide recognises the importance of ownership of teachers towards their CPD through professional reflection, through engagement in innovation and through the recognition of formal, non-formal and informal learning activities. According to the guide, sustainable partnerships between schools and providers of initial teacher education and post-initial teacher education can support this.

The guide emphasises a developmental perspective on the profession:

> ... when teaching is seen as a profession (where teaching is considered as an adaptive process based on professional autonomy, responsibility

and norms and also personal judgement) (see Biesta, 2014) or as an art (where teaching is considered as a continuous creative process of design and reflection), a teaching career is more likely to be an attractive and stimulating option. Teachers will be challenged to be innovative and entrepreneurial, to be critical and reflective, and to take responsibility for professional growth and improvement of teaching and learning. (ET2020 Working Group on Schools Policy, 2015, p. 28)

This professional growth and improvement should be reflected in career opportunities for teachers:

> To support teacher development and flexibility in teachers' careers, decision makers should recognize the range of roles and entry points to the profession and create inclusive policies that value and certify different skills and experiences and give opportunities for career steps, both within and outside the classroom. Initiatives could focus on specific teaching roles (e.g. counsellor, ICT specialist, school-based teacher educator, teacher leader) through certificated Continuing Professional Development courses, or could focus on opening up the teaching profession by creating opportunities midcareer for entrance into or departure out of the teaching profession. (ET2020 Working Group on Schools Policy, 2015, p. 32)

The guide recognises that professional development and growth in competencies of teachers need to be recognised and rewarded within schools. This recognition and reward can be given through changes in roles and responsibilities. This implies that professional development is closely connected to school development and that these two processes need to be aligned as a way of strengthening each other. If this alignment is missing, it can be a source of frustration for teachers who have developed new qualities that they are unable to apply in their schools or are not recognised for having these qualities.

The Working Groups warns to avoid a single-minded focus on the traditional career step from teacher to school leader. It suggests that challenging tasks and roles need to be created to keep excellent teachers in the classroom. As possible interesting career paths and roles the guide mentions: school-based teacher educators, teacher researchers, teacher leaders, authors of lesson materials and learning media, or teacher-entrepreneurs. Additionally, it is emphasised that career models should avoid focusing only on the education sector as closed and unidirectional perspectives on the profession are best avoided.

Summarising the guide recommends that

To support teacher development and flexibility in teachers' careers, decision makers should recognise the range of roles and entry points to the profession and create inclusive policies that value and certify different skills and experiences and give opportunities for career steps both within and outside the classroom. (ET2020 Working Group on Schools Policy, 2015, p. 35)

2.2   *Eurydice: Teacher Careers in Europe*

In response to the policy guide, the European Commission emphasised the need to make teaching careers more attractive and to changing the paradigm of the profession from static to dynamic (European Commission, 2017, p. 8). In this, strengthening the career possibilities of teachers is considered as one of the key issues:

Pay, contractual status and clear career prospects are important for the attractiveness of the profession. (…) Clearly defined competence levels and career structures enhance teachers' appreciation of career prospects.

To support member states governments in strengthening career opportunities, the Commission's information network on education Eurydice studied the way in which existing teacher careers are structured and supported in the different European member states.

The report Teacher Careers in Europe: access, progression and support (European Commission/EACEA/Eurydice, 2018, p. 70) focuses on the description of national career systems and career mechanisms that are in place. In this description, a distinction is made between flat or single-level career structures and multilevel career structures:

In multi-level career structures, the levels are usually defined by a set of competencies and/or responsibilities. Within a multi-level career structure, different career levels are structured in terms of ascending complexity and greater responsibility. A salary scale may be linked to the career structure, but is not its determining feature. Career structures with only one level are referred to as 'flat career structures' in this report. A salary scale may be in use but it usually relates to years spent in service and, possibly, performance. A flat career structure may allow for a teacher to widen their experience or take on additional tasks or responsibilities.

In the report, career development – which is understood both in terms of progression through the various levels of the career structure and progression in terms of experience gained through undertaking additional responsibilities – is considered as an important factor in helping teachers remain motivated throughout their career. The report both explores how teachers can move through different levels of the career structure (in those countries where such career levels exist) and how teachers can develop their career by taking on additional roles and responsibilities next to teaching. The exploration is limited to career steps that are directly related to teaching responsibilities, so promotion to administrative headship is not included.

In education systems with multi-level career structures, the different levels vary, from development towards more coordinating roles like head teacher, to different levels of expertise or to roles in addition to teaching (e.g. as mentor for colleagues, as advisor on curriculum development or school development or as teacher researcher). Promotion within multi-level career systems is mostly connected to a raise in salary and may be based on positive evaluation or appraisal, length of professional experience, demonstration of specific competencies or specific professional development. Depending on the national structure and its level of (de)centrality, the decisions on promotion are taken at different levels, varying from the top national authority, the local authority, to the school management.

In the Eurydice report (European Commission/EACEA/Eurydice, 2018), a clear definition of the concept of careers remains a challenge. The distinction between flat career structures and multi-level career structures is not always clear. Salary steps based on ancienity, qualification level or performance assessment are not considered as part of multi-level career structures with different levels with ascending complexity and greater responsibility. However, in systems with a flat career structure, the reports indicates the possibility to combine teaching roles with additional roles and responsibilities like a mentor of co-ordinator, but within the system this is not recognised as a different 'career level' although financial incentives might be involved. This raises the question whether there is a fundamental difference between career opportunities for teachers between flat career systems or multi-level career systems. The difference seems mainly based on how career steps are formally recognised and formalised within the system.

The report recognises that teacher careers cannot be taken for granted, as teachers might need support in managing and planning their progression within the teaching profession. This career guidance might include the provision of information, coaching or counselling with a view to advancing a teacher's career (p. 76). The report identifies 'career guidance' as a possible way to provide this support to teachers. However, in only three countries (France, Hungary and Austria), this career guidance is recognised as part of the career system and career counsellors are available for teachers that wish to make career steps.

2.3 Eurydice: Teachers in Europe: Careers, Development and Well-being

Within the recent report Teachers in Europe: Careers, development and well-being (European Commission/EACEA/Eurydice, 2021), Eurydice elaborates its policy inventory on teacher careers. The new report looks more closely to the requirements that are used for decisions on career progressions steps. Three criteria are identified within the countries that are studied by the report. Most countries use years of service as a criterium for promotion. When this is the only criterium, career steps are open for every teacher after a given number of years of service as a teacher. The second criterium is CPD implying that for a specific career step certain CPD courses are conditional. Finally, teacher appraisal or assessment can play a role in decisions regarding career progression. This teacher appraisal can be a task for the school head, a local or national authority or regulatory body. In some countries all three criteria play a role.

The career steps themselves can be defined in different ways: as increase of salaries (in most countries), an increase of prestige and status, or an change of roles. Prestige and status can be related to the recognition of teacher expertise by positions as expert teacher, or master teacher. A change or roles creates the opportunity for diversifying the work of teachers. Such roles might relate to managerial roles, pedagogical roles (e.g. related to student guidance or counselling), or roles related to teacher support (as mentor or teacher trainer) or school support (e.g. coordinating curriculum development, ICT coordination or CPD activities). When career progression implies taking up new roles, this might be connected with time compensation, leading to less teaching hours.

The report concludes that strengthening education systems in terms of career opportunities for teachers, required an orchestrated effort within national systems, looking at opportunities, compensation, recognition, support and a shared understanding of the dynamics of the profession.

> For both models, there is scope for reflection and reform by articulating career paths that allow teachers to evolve in different roles, depending on school and systemic needs, as well as teachers' wishes, talents and life plans. Elaborating such paths also entails clarifying issues around compensation and reward mechanisms, considering formal recognition and tailoring the criteria used for career progression. Teaching should cease to be seen as an isolated profession with limited or no career evolution and become a part of the larger family of school education professions instead. (European Commission/EACEA/Eurydice, 2021, p. 60)

2.4 ET2020 *Working Group Schools: Supporting Teacher and School Leaders Careers: A Policy Guide*

The Eurydice reports are limited in their scope as they address three types of career paths: a path towards more managerial roles, a path towards other roles next to teaching and a path towards being an expert teacher. Within the ET2020 Working Group Schools, a wider perspectives on possible career paths for teachers was developed (ET2020 Working Group Schools, 2020). Based on exchange between policy representatives from different countries and on expert sessions, three other possible career paths were identified: a path that involved changing workplaces towards different school contexts (between schools or sectors), a path that involved roles within different levels within the system (e.g. take roles at school level, local level or national level next to teaching at classroom level), or a path that involved moving in or out the education sector (in terms of hybrid or circular careers). These career paths are not so much part of formal career systems and might not be related to the needs of schools or the education system, but can provide career steps that connect with the ambitions and needs of teacher and help them to stay passionate over the years.

> Even if not all paths are supported by formal policy measures, many of the potentially inspiring opportunities described above might still be possible for a teacher to experience during their own career. Having a range of paths available can create an attractive suite of career opportunities for

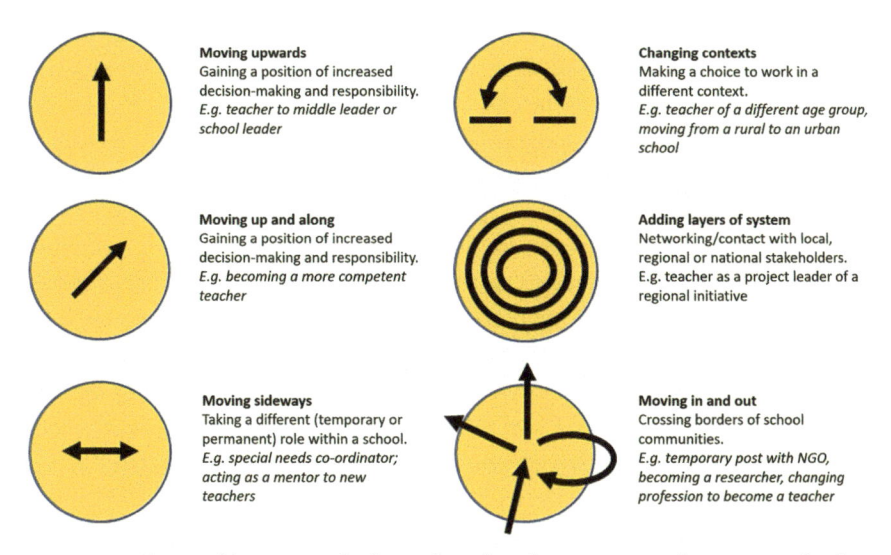

Moving upwards
Gaining a position of increased decision-making and responsibility.
E.g. teacher to middle leader or school leader

Changing contexts
Making a choice to work in a different context.
E.g. teacher of a different age group, moving from a rural to an urban school

Moving up and along
Gaining a position of increased decision-making and responsibility.
E.g. becoming a more competent teacher

Adding layers of system
Networking/contact with local, regional or national stakeholders.
E.g. teacher as a project leader of a regional initiative

Moving sideways
Taking a different (temporary or permanent) role within a school.
E.g. special needs co-ordinator; acting as a mentor to new teachers

Moving in and out
Crossing borders of school communities.
E.g. temporary post with NGO, becoming a researcher, changing profession to become a teacher

FIGURE 13.1   Six possible career paths for teachers (based on ET2020 Working Group Schools, 2020, p. 23)

teachers and contributes to a richer education system, benefiting from the external influences that teachers encounter and experience. (p. 22)

These six career paths are not independent from each other. They can be combined or may vary over time when teachers move from one career path to another.

The guide motivates the attention for teacher careers from the perspective of teacher retention:

> Not only do European school education systems need to continually recruit enough suitable teachers and school leaders, they also need to keep and nurture them for as long as best suits those individuals and systems. (ET2020 Working Group Schools, 2020, p. 8)

Key challenge for education systems is how to create a profession that is attractive and fulfilling, not only at the start of the profession, but throughout the professional life of teachers.

> Therefore the question is not only how to attract dedicated and passionate teachers to the profession, but also – and maybe even more importantly – how to ensure they stay dedicated and passionate over time. For this, growth, development, variation and recognition are essential. (ET2020 Working Group Schools, 2020, p. 14)

Therefore the guide aims to stimulate policy makers to recognise and support diverse career paths that genuinely nurture individual motivation and abilities, whilst providing a range of opportunities where they have the opportunity to apply these motivation and abilities and can grow and progress (see Appelbaum et al., 2000). Teacher careers are not so much understood as formal steps on a given career ladders, but a journey of personal choice:

> [...] careers of teachers and school leaders are built on the choices they make, every bit as much as on the priorities of the system. This principle leads logically to policies that increase and diversify opportunities, and ensure that they are visible and accessible. The idea of choice also leads inevitably to acceptance that the career path of a teacher is not inevitably a hierarchical progression through to school leadership, but can take many twists and turns. (ET2020 Working Group Schools, 2020, p. 5)

This perspective of individual choice, calls for 'increased attention to the agency of teachers as individuals in determining their own career pathways' (ET2020

Working Group Schools, 2020, p. 14). This recognition of individual choice in career paths strengthens the idea that 'not all teachers have the same profile. The variation of roles and expertise within a school can contribute to a stronger community of professionals that, in cooperation, is able to solve the variety of challenges that a school encounters' (ET2020 Working Group Schools, 2020, p. 23).

At the same time this choice and agency of teachers asks for teachers to be able to guide their own career choices and career steps. This could be considered as a 'career competence':

> the capacity of teachers and school leaders to adopt an imaginative approach to their career, taking themselves in bold and interesting directions that will still benefit the school. (ET2020 Working Group Schools, 2020, p. 6)

In this, the guide makes a distinction between professional development and career development:

> Generally, professional development involves enhancing teachers' capacity to meet changing job requirements as subject content develops or curricula changes are introduced. [...] it is firstly a mechanism for school improvement, and tends to fit a plan established by the school and the wider education system. A teacher's career, on the other hand, is individual and unique. It may even include periods away from teaching and the education system altogether. It will be determined in part by personal ambition and realizable goals. (ET2020 Working Group Schools, 2020, p. 14)

However, the choices and agency of teachers is partly defined by the professional identity of teachers: the perception of one's self as a professional actor based on an individual life journey. This professional identity is shaped through the professional life of a teacher and influenced by teacher education and the mental models regarding the teacher profession that are dominated in the system.

> Education systems should take into account and carefully consider what kind of professional identity is being constructed and by whom – by the system (central authorities and/ or other institutions), by the teachers as a collective, or by individuals for themselves. (ET2020 Working Group Schools, 2020, p. 18)

Secondly the guide aims to identify how policy makers can coherently approach the support of career opportunities for teachers. For this, it is suggested to make use of a framework that can establish a shared vision and language regarding the teacher profession and teacher career opportunities. Such a framework can consist of several elements: an overview and mapping of existing paths, roles and other opportunities for progression and variation in work, competencies that might be needed and required for these paths and roles, opportunities for developing or acquiring these competencies through CPD activities, support structures and resources for teachers or for those that support them; recognition or reward mechanisms (e.g. in terms of salaries and working conditions or contractual status) that are related to career steps, and element of quality assurance regarding teacher careers.

At the level of schools, it requires an approach that aligns teacher development coherently with school development through:

> the development of local human resource strategies in schools, including supporting the capacity of the leadership to guide such development and decision making with effective dialogue, as well as foster a collaborative – rather than purely competitive or isolated – community of professionals. (ET2020 Working Group Schools, 2020, p. 28)

As this alignment is still a challenge in most systems, the European Commission has launched a follow-up initiative to identify inspiring examples of the development of more dynamic career frameworks:

> The Council, therefore, invites EU Member States to develop national career frameworks for teachers (46). Following on the conclusions, the European Commission in its communication on the European education area aims at developing 'European guidance for the development of national career frameworks during 2021–2022, thus supporting the career progression of school education professionals. (European Commission, 2020, p. 19)

3 International Policy Guidance for Teacher Careers

The issue of teacher careers is not restricted to the European continent, but creates challenges for education systems all over the world. As a consequence, international policy think tanks like OECD and UNESCO have published studies and reports on the question how to strengthen career opportunities for teachers. In addition to the European reports discussed in the previous section, in this chapter we will analyse two of such international reports to see whether perspectives that extend beyond the European context can provide new ideas with regard to the research questions.

3.1 OECD: *Working and Learning Together: Rethinking HR Policies in Schools*

In 2019, OECD published its report on human resource policies in schools, focusing on 'actions that shape who school staff are and what they do, through decisions on careers, staff distribution, and professional learning' (OECD, 2019, p. 3). Aim of the document is 'to help countries learn from one another by exchanging best practices, and to gather and disseminate evidence on effective school resource policies' (OECD, 2019, p. 3). The report is based on the experience from 21 countries that were actively involved in the preparation of the document. The report recognises that teachers are a vital resource within the school education systems as they have a positive impact on student learning, and that human resource policies can strengthen, recognise and preserve this impact. Creating career opportunities can 'attract talented individuals to a career in school education and sustain their motivation over time' (OECD, 2019, p. 15) and thus keep talented and motivated teachers in the classroom. Career structures can be 'a means to recognise good performance, match individuals to responsibilities that fit their skills and interests, and increase long-term motivation and retention' (OECD, 2019, p. 20).

> The traditional teaching career has often been described as 'flat' and providing few opportunities for advancement or diversification. It is therefore possible for many teachers to have the same set of responsibilities from the first to the last day of their career. In such contexts, the only way for motivated teachers to grow in their careers may be to leave the classroom and take up roles in school leadership or the education administration. This can be to the detriment of student learning since it risks depriving them of their most effective teachers.

Articulated career structures can also contribute to the recognition of teachers, compensating the often existing lack of external recognition and formal feedback and avoiding that teachers mostly need to rely on self-motivation through their working life.

The report recognises both vertical or hierarchical career opportunities, 'structured around a succession of formal positions or roles with distinct task profiles and progressively increasing responsibility within the classroom', often connected to increased salaries, and horizontal or lateral career opportunities 'with opportunities to focus on and assume responsibilities in a specific area of expertise inside or outside the classroom, often involving specialisation in a particular aspect of the teaching profession' (OECD, 2019, p. 20).

Within the hierarchical multistage structures, the number of stages can vary – often with the first stage(s) reserved for novice teachers. Higher stages often include increased responsibilities and higher expectations, sometimes associated with a wider impact beyond the classroom, within or beyond schools. The report promotes a transparent process for career advancement that is voluntary and meritocratic. A country analysis shows that criteria and processes can vary and be based on qualification, competencies, experience, performance or professional development, be decided in a process of evaluation or certification (involving school heads or examination board at school level, local authority level or national level in terms of a national teaching agency or teacher council) and lead to open ended or fixed term appointments (e.g. connected to mandatory renewal or re-certification). Differentiated teacher standards can support promotion decisions as they describe what is expected from teachers at different career levels and create guidelines for professional development courses.

Horizontal career structures create the opportunity to recognise the capacity of teachers for leadership in a specific area by creating specialist roles where they can apply their expertise. Such lateral career moves often are connected to reduced teaching hours rather than additional pay. Horizontal career structures can have specific benefits:

> First, allowing teachers to focus on the area of their work that they are most productive in can improve the allocation of tasks and result in a more efficient use of teachers' time, knowledge and skills. Second, it provides teachers with increased autonomy to shape their career based on their interests, which constitutes an important source of long-term motivation. Finally, besides changes to the staffing mix in schools, the creation of new roles may be an effective response to new needs or policies that call for schools to build professional capacity and expertise in a specific area. (OECD, 2019, p. 125)

By introducing specialist roles, opportunities for further career development are created without having to move to administrative or formal leadership roles. Horizontal career steps might also involve roles beyond the individual school by taking on responsibilities at system level, often on a temporary base, e.g. as a consultant, or coach.

Although the report promotes the development of career structures – preferable with a combination of vertical and horizontal structures – it also gives a warning as it

> can create uncertainty among teachers and be perceived as threatening the profession's egalitarian norms. [...] A lack of clarity around what new

roles would entail and how to move into them, concerns that the reform would create divisions among teachers, or its perceived association with other changes to teachers' working conditions can contribute to the failure of career structure reforms. (OECD, 2019, p. 21)

As a consequence the report advices to pilot changes in career structures on a small scale and to give teachers and school leaders a prominent voice in the design of career pathways and their associated professional standards as this is

> critical to guarantee their relevance and alignment with the day-to-day experience and needs of schools. It can also be an effective means to strengthen teachers' voice and sense of self-agency, their involvement in the profession's self-regulation and to generate a sense of ownership that is critical for a new career structure to be accepted, implemented and contribute to the profession's attractiveness. Teachers' participation in the process recognises their professionalism, the importance of their skills and experience and the extent of their responsibilities. (OECD, 2019, p. 178)

The report also indicates specific challenges while developing career systems. Such challenges are related to the link between career steps and salaries, which will impact both motivation and financial sustainability, and to assessments procedures for promotion as the bar could be set too low, leading to reduced credibility and high costs, or too high, leading to frustration and reduced motivation. Another challenge is how to facilitate teachers in time to take on other roles. Although the tasks that teachers perform outside of the classroom are increasingly recognised as an integral part of their professional roles, the report indicates that this recognition is often not reflected in how working time of teachers reflects the diversity of tasks:

> in many OECD school systems, service codes and other statutes that regulate how teachers spend their time are based on a narrow conception of the profession. They primarily regulate teaching hours, (i.e. the time teachers are expected to spend on classroom instruction) while only vaguely defining non-teaching time. (OECD, 2019, p. 162)

3.2 UNESCO: Teacher Career Reforms

As many governments are looking for ways to diversify teacher career structures and to widen career advancement opportunities in order to attract and retain high performing teachers, UNESCO's International Institute of Education Planning launched a project to support policy makers in identifying options and implications for reforming their teacher career structures (Tournier et al., 2019). Aim of the project was to identify options for organising and managing teacher careers within the public school sector, the perceived effects of teacher careers on teacher motivation, attraction and retention, and the implications for managing processes of career reforms. The project included a review of the literature, a mapping exercise including ten countries and in-depth studies of three countries.

The study makes a distinction between first and second generation career models. First generation models are based on a single salary schedule model with automatic salary increases and promotions based on seniority and experience, including the possibility for promotion towards administrative or leadership positions replacing teaching duties. Second generation models fit with a shift towards accountability, evaluation and merit-pay as they are based on performance-based incentives. Within the second generation career models, the report identifies three different approaches: one-time bonus pay based on positive appraisal, appraisal based salary progression, and career ladders which focus on promotion to new roles and responsibilities with additional salary, based on appraisal.

The IIEP study specifically focused on career models that included a career ladder diversifying the professional course of teachers and widening advancement options. Such career ladders can both refer to vertical opportunities (with promotion to administrative or leadership functions in which teachers stop teaching) or to horizontal opportunities (in which teaching in the classroom remains key to the work of teachers). The study identifies career ladders as a promising and attractive model as

> career schemes are expected to motivate teachers 'from the inside'. Looking at proxy indicators of teacher autonomous motivation, this research finds that, overall, teachers very positively welcome having more opportunities for career progression while still being able to stay in the classroom. (OECD, 2019, p. 14)

In several of the countries that were studied, career schemes include pathways, in which different directions (horizontal) and levels (vertical) are combined, mostly making a distinction between the teaching direction and the management direction.

One of the elements the study looked at was the aspect of teacher collaboration:

> Our research shows that collaboration is not automatically fostered by emerging career schemes, but must be clearly formalized through the

career structure, for instance by giving experienced teachers the authority and extra time to support their peers. (OECD, 2019, p. 14)

Teacher collaboration was also influenced by the type of criteria that are used to decide on teacher promotion.

> Utilizing a norm-referenced system (only top performers are promoted) is more likely to lead to decreased collaboration between teachers and a limited sense of self-determination, whereas criterion-referenced systems (all applicants who meet the criteria are promoted) may encourage responsibility and autonomy without damaging interpersonal relationships. (OECD, 2019, p. 16)

The study shows that well-designed and -implemented career system reforms can have a positive impact. Although the career schemes had limited impact on the attractiveness of the profession, the study found a positive influence on teacher retention. 'Having more horizontal promotion opportunities contributes to teachers' willingness to stay in the profession. It also helps keep the best teachers in the classroom' (OECD, 2019, p. 14). Career opportunities also impact the perceived agency of teachers, not only with respect to their professional mobility, but also with respect to decision-making in schools, as teachers who progressed to higher levels felt that they gained a voice in discussions around curriculum and pedagogical issues and felt empowered to affect change in schools. When teacher career schemes are accepted within the school systems and certain career steps aim at supporting colleagues, career schemes heave the potential to strengthen collaborative cultures in schools. However, when promotion opportunities are limited, it can lead to stronger competition between teachers.

The study also indicates important conditions to reach this impact: adequate salaries and working conditions, clear, coherent and progressive differentiation in roles and responsibilities, a transparent and meritocratic process for career advancement decisions, support and training opportunities to prepare for new roles, and the importance of building trust and a shared vision among all parties.

Finally the report warns that teacher career reform processes need to be planned and executed carefully, taking into account careful planning in terms of teacher numbers, consideration of resource constraints in terms of salary implications, calculation of the costs and organisational burdens of performance evaluation systems, and the need for human resources for implementation at various levels (e.g. regarding the ability of school heads to conduct teacher evaluations). Finally, the report emphasises the importance of teacher buy-in and participation in the reform process.

4 A Common Understanding of Teacher Careers?

The above analysis provides an answer to the first question: How are careers for teachers understood? The policy documents all stress the importance of career opportunities as a key condition for teacher's long term motivation. This is not only beneficial to teachers themselves, but also to pupils as (horizontal) career opportunities can stimulate experienced, excellent and ambitious teachers to stay in the classroom. Also on macro level, teacher's career opportunities can contribute to the attractivity of the profession and attract high quality candidates to the profession.

The documents all emphasise that to have opportunities for growth in the profession, to be challenged, to have variation in tasks, roles and responsibilities over time, and to be recognised in qualities, ambitions and contributions are all important underlying elements during the working life of teachers. The career opportunities need to recognise different ambitions and interests of teachers and avoid a narrow understanding of careers as a hierarchical growth in status, salary and (leadership) position, leading to positions out of the classroom. As a large group of teachers find their passion and motivation in their direct interaction with pupils and students, stressing managerial roles as key career path might reduce passion and recognition of teachers as it can create the impression that their daily work with pupils is of less value.

Although all five documents emphasise that teachers careers are more than seniority or performance related salary increments, they differ in the way in which teacher careers are defined. Both the Eurydice studies OECD report and the UNESCO report focus on formal opportunities within a country's education system. In the design of the studies, there is a strong focus on formal career ladders that are integrated in the national legislative structure. Both the focus on single and multi-level systems (Eurydice) or on second generation career systems with career ladders (UNESCO), might create the illusion that the formally recognised career steps are the only steps available.

However, the recent report of the EC's Working Group Schools takes a wider perspective on teacher careers by taking the teachers' perspective as the starting point instead of the system. Through this perspective a wider understanding of teacher careers is created. The six career opportunities that are identified in the report are not all related to formal career steps that are available within the system, but also include career steps that are diverge from the formal steps in career ladders, but include opportunities that that are not formalised, but that still exist and that some teachers take to shape their careers by following their dreams and passions. It recognises that a career is more than taking formally recognised career steps with a career system.

This wider perspective shows that a focus on formal system level career opportunities might create a too narrow view on careers. Multi-level career systems with career ladders can make specific opportunities visible and recognised and thus support career development, but at the same time they limit career perspectives to the steps that are formally defined. At the same time, defining a system as a single-level career system might give the impression that there are no formal career steps possible, while there still are lots of opportunities, even though they might be hidden for many teachers. When the decisions on tasks, roles and responsibilities are taken at school level, the number of career possibilities in single-level systems might be even broader and more varied than in formalised multi-level career systems. This implies that not only the requirements and mechanisms for career progression as defined by legislation at the national level should be taken into account. Next to these national legislative regulations, local mechanisms for career progression might exist under the authority of school heads, school boards or local authorities, creating a wider variety of career opportunities. From this perspective, the Netherlands might create an interesting policy example as the strongly decentralised system leaves all authority on career decisions to local school boards. Within that context not nationally defined career steps exist (which explains why it was excluded from the Eurydice analyses), while it at the same times creates a wide variety of informal opportunities for career development of teachers.

5   Implications for Teachers, Schools and National Policies

This also leads to an answer to the second question: What implications are identified for teachers, schools and national policies?

The first implication relates to the need for a shared and broad understanding of the teacher profession. This broad understanding is based on diversification within the profession, as teachers might have different roles, profiles and responsibilities, based on their expertise and ambitions. They can act as classroom teachers at different levels of expertise, as expert in a certain domain supporting colleagues or processes of curriculum innovation or school improvement, with different responsibilities. This diversification is close related to the understanding that all these roles and levels of expertise are needed in a concerted team effort to address the complicated challenges of schools to deal with the needs of pupils in a diverse, competitive and complex society and to the notion of distributed leadership in schools (Snoek, Hulsbos, & Andersen, 2019). Through such a shared and broad understanding of the profession, opportunities for career development can become more explicitly visible for both teachers working in schools and candidates who consider a career in the teacher profession. This visibility is important as the traditional perspective of a static profession where teachers have little career possibilities is still a dominant view within society. As the OECD study indicates, this is not only a question of identifying possible roles for teachers, but also of facilitating teachers to these roles. When financial systems are mainly dominated by the amount of teaching hours, it is complicated to recognise and compensate time for teachers to take on additional roles. This implies that the budgetary system should reflect the broad understanding of the teacher profession.

The second implication is the importance to recognise that career systems are no aim in themselves, but a means to keep the teacher's profession attractive over the years by providing opportunities for growth, challenge, variation and recognition. Formal career structures can support this by creating formal pathways within the system, but it is important to recognise that these structures do not represent all opportunities that exist. To support (potential) teachers in their career choices, it is important to make a wide variety of career choices visible, both formal career paths and non-formal career paths, e.g. through inspiring narratives of teachers that walked these paths.

The third implication is that supporting career paths of teachers asks for balancing two perspectives: the needs of the system and the individual needs of teachers. In many cases these two perspectives might be aligned and combined easily, in other cases they might be seen as conflicting, e.g. when the ambitions of an individual teachers might divert from the priorities in the school. This can be the case when teachers aspire to combine their classroom teaching with other roles outside the classroom. Especially when there is a teacher shortage and every teacher is needed in the classroom, school heads might be reluctant to grant that ambition. However, on the long run, the impact might be that teachers lose their passion and decide to leave schools altogether, creating an even bigger problem.

Finally, strengthening career opportunities calls for action by different stakeholders at different levels. National policy makers need to create a policy context that is supportive to teacher careers, e.g. through the measures that have been mentioned above in terms of national career systems, but also by making both formal and informal career opportunities visible for teachers and schools. At local level, career steps ask for actions from education employers (like school boards or local authorities), school heads that have direct conversations with teachers (e.g. in terms of teacher appraisal or development ambitions and plans), and teachers themselves that need to decide to take career steps or not. Especially the 2020 EC's Working Group Schools guide gives valuable suggestions on what is needed to support local actors, varying from providing background theory on teacher careers, supportive tools for school heads to initiate career support dialogues, to identify opportunities inside and outside schools and ways to recognise and support teachers in their development, and supportive tools for teachers to manage their careers.

6 Implications for Teacher Education

When the teacher profession is considered as a continuum, linking initial teacher education, induction and continuous professional development of teachers during their career, the question is how teacher education institutes can support this continuum. In other words, what are the implications of strengthening teacher career opportunities for initial and post-initial teacher education? As both the Eurydice, OECD and UNESCO reports focus on the formal career structures, they do not pay attention both: to initial teacher education and the role it has to play in strengthening teacher careers. Only the 2020 report of the EC's Working Group Schools addresses the role of initial and post-initial teacher education in a number of implicit and explicit ways.

As teacher identity is a key underlying factor that shape the actions and choices of teachers, it is important to consider how teacher identities are shaped and how they support a dynamic understanding of the teacher profession and the agency of teachers to shape their work and careers. As initial teacher education plays a key role in shaping teachers professional identities, teacher education institutes should consider how their curriculum reflects the future profession as a dynamic profession characterised by lifelong learning during the different stages of the teacher career.

However, shaping one's career requires a number of career competencies:
– Reflection on capacities: What is my strength?
– Reflection on motives: What drives me?
– Work exploration: What and where are opportunities and possibilities?
– Career directedness: What steps can I take?
– Networking: Who can help me?

These five qualities do not only apply to young people in schools, but also to teachers. However, in most countries these qualities do not get much attention during initial teacher education. Support systems and frameworks that aim to strengthen career possibilities of teachers need to support the development of these qualities (ET2020 Working Group Schools, 2020).

This raises the question to what extent these career competencies can be addressed more explicit within national competence frameworks for teachers and within initial teacher education curricula. Part of this can be to help student teachers to explore the career possibilities for teachers both when recruiting students to the teachers education programme, during the teacher education programme and at the end. Such exploration might help student teachers to avoid a static image of the profession, develop a wider and dynamic perspective on their future profession and to explore the ambitions and directions that are fit for them.

Finally, acknowledging that the teacher profession needs to be considered as a continuum with a variety of career opportunities, also implies that the professional development of teachers is not restricted to the phase on initial teacher education, but is a life-long process. New challenges in school will require new and deeper knowledge and skills, new roles will ask for new competencies and qualities that need to be developed over time. This raises the question how support structures like initial teacher education and induction programmes are extended to the whole of the teacher career. Where can teachers prepare for roles like being a (teacher) leader, a mentor to colleagues, a classroom expert, a curriculum developer, a teacher-researcher, or a subject advisor, once they have decided to opt for such a career direction? All these directions ask for a deepening of the initial qualities that they developed during initial teacher education. However, in many countries, roles of teacher education institutes are restricted to the phase of initial teacher education, while other support institutes for continuous teacher development have a key role after initial teacher education. This strict separation between the different phases of the teacher continuum are often reflected in the financial systems as the main funding system of universities is focused on the number of students in initial teacher education. To enable coherence across the system and stages, institutes for initial teacher education need to extend their support for teachers beyond the phase of initial teacher education, supporting their students not only in the initial phase but also during the next phases of their professional career. As these phases often also imply a career dialogue between teachers and their employers or school heads, such career support asks form a close collaboration between teacher education institutes and schools in such a way that career opportunities within the system, support programmes to develop the qualities for these career choices and the ambitions of teachers strengthen each other. This actually asks for erasing the old dichotomy between initial teacher education and in-service education and to replace that by a perspective of continuous development within a dynamic profession.

References

Akkermans, J., & Tims, M. (2017). Crafting your career: How career competencies relate to career success via job crafting. *Applied Psychology, 66*, 168–195.

Appelbaum, E., Bailey, T., Berg, P., & Kalleberg, A. L. (2000). *Manufacturing advantage: Why high performance work systems pay off.* Cornell University.

Bahlmann, M., Eustatia, B., & Pillen-Warmerdam, D. (2018). *Optimale inrichting van lerarenopleidingen. Resultaten van een vignette- en motievenonderzoek onder havisten, vwo'ers en mbo-4 studenten* [Optimal design of teacher education. Results of a survey among students in upper secondary education]. Qompas.

Büchs, M. (2007). *New governance in European social policy: The open method of coordination.* Palgrave Macmillan.

Cabus, S., Haelermans, C., & Flink, I. (2020). *Evaluating a certificate programme on educational mentorship and coaching leading to induction activities for new teachers in Rwandan primary schools.* HIVA-KU.

Calvert, L. (2016). *Moving from compliance to agency: What teachers need to make professional learning work.* Learning Forward and NCTAF.

Chimier, C., & Tournier, B. (2018, November 21). Three initiatives to foster teacher motivation [Blog]. Learning Portal, IIEP-UNESCO. https://learningportal.iiep.unesco.org/en/blog/three-initiatives-to-foster-teacher-motivation

Chiriboga Montalvo, C., & Pinto Haro, J. (2019). *Reforma de la carrera docente en Ecuador: Estudio de caso* [Reform of teacher careers in Ecuador. A case study]. IIEP-UNESCO.

Coldwell, M. (2017). Exploring the influence of professional development on teacher careers: A path model approach. *Teaching and Teacher Education, 61*, 189–198.

Cordingley, P., Crisp, B., Johns, P., Perry, T., Campbell, C., Bell, M., & Bradbury, M. (2019). *Constructing teachers' professional identities.* Education International.

Crehan, L. (2016). *Exploring the impact of career models on teacher motivation.* IIEP-UNESCO.

ET2020 Working Group on Schools Policy. (2015). *Shaping career-long perspectives on teaching: A guide on policies to improve initial teacher education.* Publications Office of the European Union.

ET2020 Working Group Schools. (2020). *Supporting teacher and school leader careers: A policy guide.* Publications Office of the European Union.

European Commission. (2017). *Communication from the Commission to the European Parliament, the council, the European Economic and Social Committee and the Committee of the regions. School development and excellent teaching for a great start in life.* SWD(2017) 165 final. COM(2017) 248 final. Retrieved April 11, 2021, from http://eur-lex.europa.eu/legal-content/EN/TXT/PDF/?uri=CELEX:52017DC0248&qid=1513677437956&from=FR

European Commission/EACEA/Eurydice. (2018). *Teaching careers in Europe: Access, progression and support*. Eurydice Report. Publications Office of the European Union.

European Commission/EACEA/Eurydice. (2021). *Teachers in Europe: Careers, development and well-being*. Eurydice report. Publications Office of the European Union.

Evers, G. H. M. (2007). *Advies omtrent bevordering implementatie functie- en beloningsdifferentiatie in PO, VO en BVE* [Advisory reports regarding the implementation of job and salary differentiation in primary, secondary and vocational education]. Organisatie voor Strategisch Arbeidsmarktonderzoek.

Forrier, A., De Cuyper, N., & Akkermans, J. (2018). The winner takes it all, the loser has to fall: Provoking the agency perspective in employability research. *Human Resource Management Journal, 28*(4), 511–523.

Gerrichhauzen, J. T. G. (2007). *De lerende en onderzoekende docent* [The learning and inquiring teacher] [Inaugural lecture]. Open Universiteit, Ruud de Moor Centrum.

Herzberg, F. (1968). *Work and the nature of man*. Staples Press.

Hulsbos, F., Andersen, I., Kessels, J., & Wassink, H. (2012). *Professionele ruimte en gespreid leiderschap*. Open Universiteit.

Kuijpers, M., Schyns, B., & Scheerens, J. (2006). Career competencies for career success. *Career Development Quarterly, 55*(2), 169–179.

McIlveen, P. (2009). Career development, management, and planning from the vocational psychology perspective. In A. Collin & W. Patton (Eds.), *Vocational psychology and organizational perspectives on career: Towards a multidisciplinary dialogue* (pp. 63–89). Sense.

OECD. (2019). *Working and learning together: Rethinking human resource policies for schools*. OECD Reviews of School Resources. OECD Publishing.

Onderwijsraad. (2016). *Een ander perspectief op professionele ruimte in het onderwijs* [Another perspective on professional freedom in education]. Onderwijsraad.

Radaelli, M. (2003). *The open method of coordination: A new governance architecture for the European Union?* Swedish Institute for European Policy Studies.

Roth, G., Assor, A., Kanat-Maymon, Y., & Kaplan, H. (2007). Autonomous motivation for teaching: How self-determined teaching may lead to self-determined learning. *Journal of Educational Psychology, 99*, 761–744.

Runhaar, P., Sanders, K., & van Rijn, M. (2009). *Human Resource Management (HRM) voor professionele ontwikkeling in het onderwijs: Een literatuuronderzoek naar de wijze waarop HRM de professionele ontwikkeling van leraren kan stimuleren* [Human Resource Management for professional development in education: A literature review on the way in which HRM can stimulate professional development of teachers]. KPC Groep.

Sayed, Y., & De Kock, T. (2019). *Teacher career pathways in South Africa: Insights from the Western Cape*. IIEP-UNESCO.

Snoek, M., Dengerink, J., & De Wit, B. (2019). Reframing the teacher profession as a dynamic and multifaceted profession: A wider perspective on teacher quality and teacher competence frameworks. *European Journal of Education, 54*, 413–425.

Snoek, M., Hulsbos, F., & Andersen, I. (2019). *Teacher leadership: Hoe kan het leiderschap van leraren in scholen versterkt worden?* Hogeschool van Amsterdam.

Swanson, J. L. (2013). Traditional and emerging career development theory and the psychology of working. In D. L. Blustein (Ed.), *The Oxford handbook of the psychology of working* (pp. 49–69). Oxford University Press.

Tournier, B., Chimier, C., Childress, D., & Raudonyte, I. (2019). *Teacher career reforms: Learning from experience.* IIEP-UNESCO.

UNESCO. (2019). *Teacher policy development guide.* UNESCO.

Van der Aa, R., & van den Berg, D. (2018). *De arbeidsmarkt in het MBO. Update op basis van gegevens tot en met 2016* [The labour market in middle vocational education. Update based on data until 2016]. Intern document CAOP.

Van der Heijden, B. I. J. M., & De Vos, A. (2015). Sustainable careers: Introductory chapter. In A. de Vos & B. I. J. M. van der Heijden (Eds.), *Handbook of research on sustainable careers* (pp. 1–19). Edward Elgar Publishing.

Van der Sluis, L. (2011). Talentontwikkeling op de arbeidsmarkt [Talent development in the labour market]. In J. Kessels & R. Poell (Eds.), *Handboek human resource development* (pp. 134–144). Bohn Stafleu van Loghum.

Vermeulen, L., & Van der Aa, R. (2008). *Wat leraren bindt aan het onderwijs? Onderzoek naar de rol van begeleiding en professionalisering bij het behoud van leraren in het onderwijs* [What binds teachers in education? Study on the role of support and professional development in teachers' retention in education]. Ministerie van OCW.

Vrielink, S., & Hogeling, L. (2008). *Tevreden blijven werken in het onderwijs* [Continue working with satisfaction in education]. Sectorbestuur Onderwijsarbeidsmarkt.

CHAPTER 14

Mobilising Policy to Reframe Teaching and Teacher Education in Europe

The European Commission's Emerging Role within the Teacher Quality Agenda

Conor Galvin, Panagiotis Kampylis, Deirbhile Nic Craith, Joanna Madalinska-Michalak and Noel Purdy

Abstract

Recent initiatives by the European Commission (EC) have returned the issue of teacher quality to the forefront of policy work across Europe. These have also taken the Commission's policy activity in a direction and to a scale previously unseen. We believe that a sense of urgency driving the establishment of the European Education Area (EEA) is facilitating a new, increasingly assertive and practice-centred policy method on the part of the Commission, and that this involves mobilising policy in ways that are already starting to significantly reframe teaching and teacher education in Europe.

A defining characteristic of this new method is an increased willingness and rising confidence on the part of the EC to lead on interventionist policy-work that engages the spectrum of policy activity from the European to the national and even includes policy experimentation at the level of individual schools and school systems. We propose that policy action in this modality represents a largely unmarked but significant change in how EC policy work is led and undertaken.

This development offers both possibilities and potential problems. Consequently, the central focus of our chapter rests on unpacking the changing policy practices of the Commission in pursuit of its teacher quality agenda over recent years. We detail and critique the move to new policy method and consider its implications for teachers and teacher education, and specifically what it will likely mean for teacher education policy work in Europe of the near future. To close, we consider how positive and proactive engagement with the new policy work realities by the teacher education research community in Europe can help strengthen and deepen the pluralism and diversity of teachers and their education in ways that both the Commission and teacher education professionals can readily value and share. This however is not something that can be taken for granted – meaningful access to spaces of influence and the relevant policy fora to do so will need to be argued for and occupied.

Keywords

policy method – European Commission – teacher quality – teacher education

1   Introduction

In recent years across the European Union, there has been an increased focus on policy reforms to improve teacher and teaching quality. This is accompanied by greater emphasis on improving the quality of teacher education, including initial and in-service teacher education. Recent initiatives by the European Commission have returned the issue of teacher quality to the forefront of policy work and activity across Europe and have taken the Commission's activity in this area in a direction and to a scale previously unseen. Teacher quality is a central theme in the Council conclusions on European teachers and trainers for the future (EC, 2020) where teacher quality is linked consistently with the provision of relevant, inclusive and equitable quality education and training, and related concerns for instruction in attitudes, values and behaviours, enabling [citizens] to thrive professionally and personally and be active and responsible participants in society (Council of the European Union, 2020).

Most importantly however, policy action for teacher quality is an anchor feature in the emerging lines, actions and programmes supporting the Council Resolution on a strategic framework for European cooperation in education and training towards the European Education Area and beyond (2021–2030) – the EC flagship proposals for establishing the European Education Area by 2025. It also features prominently in two major EC initiatives launched in 2020, the Digital Education Action Plan (DEAP) with arrangements for teacher development clearly evident within the plan, and the European Green Deal particularly in relation to the role envisaged for teachers in advancing conceptualisations of 'just transition' and 'equity'. This represents European policy attention at a level of granularity not previously seen. The EU is not alone in this. Since 2018, the OECD has been engaged in the Teachers' Professional Learning (TPL) initiative which seeks to reframe the policy environments that support the professional growth of teachers down to the level of the language used to describe such activity and the ownership of the process. Additionally, in 2020 the OECD also initiated school-level policy experimentation around the development of the Platform for Innovative Learning Assessments, PILA (OECD, 2020). This is described as a new initiative to promote innovative assessments of/as/for learning in the classroom that harness the potential of digital technologies to improve learning and assessment. Underpinning this initiative is the intention to produce a free hub for educators looking for engaging and research-based tools to support their students' growth as autonomous, lifelong learners (OECD, 2020, p. 3).

In this chapter we propose that policy action in this modality represents a largely unmarked but significant change in how policy work on teacher quality is led and undertaken; globally and regionally a new policy method is emerging. A defining characteristic of this method is an increased willingness and rising confidence on the part of trans-national policy orchestrators such as the European Commission and OECD to lead on interventionist policy-work that engages the spectrum of policy activity from supranational to national and even to policy experiments at the level of individual schools and school systems. In the EU context, arguments for the urgency in establishing the European Education Area, EEA, are seen to warrant an increasingly assertive and practice-centred policy focus by the Commission on quality teachers and teaching in relation to quality teacher education. We suggest that this unprecedented mobilisation of policy offers both possibilities and potential problems. The central focus of this chapter rests on the changing policy practices of the European Commission in pursuit of its teacher quality agenda over recent years. The chapter details and critiques this move and considers its implications for teacher education, and specifically what it will likely mean for teacher education policy work in Europe of the near future. A better understanding of this agenda will allow the teacher education community to proactively position itself to engage with the new policy work realities.

The chapter is in three main sections. It opens with a short but necessary outline of the previous practices against which the new policy method needs to be set. In section two, the role of evidence and influence in contemporary EU policy work is considered. In section three, the changing technical and political purposes in EU policy work are discussed.

The significance of these are then discussed in light of previous of work by the European Commission on mobilising policy to strengthen teaching and teacher education in Europe. In conclusion, we consider how positive and proactive engagement by the teacher education community in Europe can – and should – help strengthen and deepen the pluralism and diversity of teachers and their education that both Commission and teacher education professionals can readily value and share.

2 Understanding Contemporary Teacher Education Policy in Europe

In this section we consider both the traditional and emerging policy methodologies engaged by the European Commission in framing and strengthening teaching and teacher education. We look first at education policy work in a traditional reading and set this against the politics of working beyond the conventionally recognised competence of the EU. We then consider the increasingly complex context of teacher and teacher education policy in Europe under the emerging EEA agenda and the role of evidence and influence in EC teacher policy action. We then examine the scale of change currently taking place in terms of the technical and political purposes of EU policy work for teacher education under the EEA agenda. This includes a detailed discussion of the key policy work concepts of competence, subsidiarity and proportionality, and the rising importance of ideating around science for policy and the turn to policy experimentation as the EC policy-making apparatus moves inexorably beyond traditional OMC-based methods alone.

2.1   European Teacher Education Policy Work in a Traditional Reading

Teacher education policy and practice across Europe is the result of both local and global actions over the last few decades and increasingly represents the development of shared European education interests and concerns. Acknowledging its complexity, teacher education can be described as 'an activity system whose aims and outcomes are culturally shaped by its contexts, rules, roles and actors' (Caena, 2017, p. 179). Teacher education can be characterised by ongoing contradictions and change, constantly interacting with other activity systems, and not only responding to external pressures, as Caena suggests (2017, p. 179) but influencing them as well. In this view, any analysis of teacher education policy work needs to take stock of situated, context-driven features and needs and should be perceived especially in connection with higher education in Europe (Madalińska-Michalak, 2018, p. 17). It should also be considered as a policy field that is deeply contested and often politicised (Menter, 2016).

In this context, it is worth mentioning two significant developments concerning teacher education in Europe in the last two decade or so – the Bologna Process which led to the formal creation of the European Higher Education Area (EHEA) in 2010 and the selection of Education Sciences/Teacher Education as the first area of attention under the hugely ambitious EU TUNING project (TUNING, 2009) with, as Caena (2014, p. 4) notes, its EHEA-consistent guidelines for teacher education programmes and competence-based outcomes. These are important because they unequivocally site teacher education within higher education in Europe but equally within the EU's increasingly econometric focus, and also set a very specific reading of individual competency at the heart of the teacher quality process.

The focus of these initiatives represents one of the first indications of what Lawn and Grek (2012) describe as the gradual increase in the velocity and scope of education policy, practice and instruments across Europe – however, both were decidedly 'traditional' in the slow, consensus-building policy design that they used. This slower-paced policy methodology is discussed later in this chapter; for now, it is enough to note that it was the process of choice of the EC policy makers of the time and that it was embraced by the various academics and field-experts called on to engage with both Bologna and TUNING.

In policy work terms these policy developments are also important in other ways. They provide early examples of the Commission carving out new European policy spaces with all the hallmarks that we have come to associate with this type of policy action; policy content developed by experts, mobilised by networks of actors, projects and associations, constructed by comparative data, and 'de-politicized' by the use of standards and data (Lawn & Grek, 2012). Each also represents an attempt to radically redefine teacher education across the EU and embodies a policy-making ethic that now seems very much of its time.

Of the two, the Bologna Process has had the more public history and the more visible successes. Following the signature of the Bologna Declaration in 1999 and the Lisbon Strategy in 2000 and despite the initial hesitancy of some European HE systems, a first decade of preparation for the EHEA through Bologna saw remarkable changes in higher education systems in Europe, in their national degree systems, quality assurance and internationalisation. These changes set higher education systems across Europe on a shared path. However, many of the changes were contested and even resisted in parts of Europe which slowed significantly the scale and pace of change – a point that proponents needed to accept given that the EU has no legal competence (jurisdiction) in relation to the educational activities of its member states (Galvin et al., 2020). In any event, this decade of preparation was followed by a time that focused on steadily implementing processes to progress and support Bologna principles and arrangements that continues to the present. The changing EC policy infrastructures and practices that accompanied this were, we suggest, critical to this effort. Consequently, the Bologna Process Implementation Report (European Commission/EACEA/Eurydice, 2020) shows notable progress made over the two decades in creating the European Higher Education Area and in how European higher education systems advanced with concerted national reforms. The European Higher Education Area has become a new place of work and research through interconnected institutions, networks and commercial enterprises, and continues to be constructed through the flow of policy ideas, knowledge and practices from place to place, sector to sector, organisation to organisation, and across borders. And although only one of many areas of concern under the Bologna Process, this, we suggest has had the effect of keeping teacher education on the policy agenda – partly because of its HE connections, and partly because of the increasing power of global narratives connecting teacher quality – and hence teacher education – to enhanced economic outcomes. As Lawn and Grek (2012, p. 154) noted, this sparked a unifying search, shared by the European Union and its member states, for economic competitiveness and a knowledge economy, worked to expand the role and scope of contemporary European education policies which would include teacher and teacher education policy work.

2.1.1 The Politics of EU Policy Work

Interestingly, where teacher education is concerned the TUNING project has been considerably less successful – failing singularly to attract from the sector the critical mass of interest and support needed to radically recast teacher education in Europe in the proposed education sciences modality, although, arguably, the Commission policy makers and the stewarding institutions learnt much from this early effort to put teacher education 'at the heart of the European project' (TUNING, 2009, p. 19) – lessons that have been built into other subject and area frameworks developed subsequently through the TUNING process. Remarkably, the TUNING discourse around competency framing, clinical placement within Initial Teacher Education (ITE), the professional 'lifelong' learning continuum and so on continues to present in Commission initiatives and policy activity relating to teacher education. In a sense, TUNING continues to have a marked but secret rather than public hold in EC policy.

One reading of why one succeeded where the other faded would suggest that the key difference in policy action terms between the initiatives was that the Bologna Process was anchored more publicly and visibly in the politics of the EU. Sitting firmly within the increasingly important EU drive towards a knowledge economy, the Bologna Process was consequently promoted with considerably more energy that TUNING. What is really fascinating in policy terms is how the political status of the Bologna Process was elevated and systematically woven into the European Research Area discourse through foregrounding in various high-profile EU pronouncements such as the *Paris Communiqué* (2018) and especially through the deployment of novel policy instruments to progress its activities – particularly its inclusion in the *Education & Training Monitor* cycle.

Another reading of how the EC approach to policy work has shifted noticeably over the past two decades centres on the advantages associated with what Rauh (2019) has described as the political aspects of policy work and what Lawn and Grek (2012) term *explanatory elements* that may escape notice if purely national or institutional perspectives are taken when considering the nature and purposes of European education policy work. In particular, they note the formidable and formative nature of the shift from 'traditional' policy work *into a space dominated by comparison and data* and the turn to policy science within the European Commission that has largely enabled this. That is the aspect of new method policy work by the Commission to which we now turn.

2.2 Evidence and Influence in Contemporary EU Policy Work

2.2.1 An Ever More Complex Policy Context

Any account of recent developments in European policy for education must acknowledge the increasing structural complexity of European Commission policy work and, correspondingly, the increasing range of its constituencies, arrangements, and concerns – including the technical architecture used to coordinate and align the policy objectives of member states in the interests of the wider European project. Fundamentally, the EU has no legal *competence* (jurisdiction) concerning the educational activities of its member states; education remains an acknowledged area of subsidiarity and as such is recognised as essentially a question for the member state itself (Wallace et al., 2020; Galvin et al., 2020). And yet in recent years, the Commission has intervened assertively in this area with increasing frequency.

As noted above, each EU member state is responsible for its education and training systems including its teacher education programmes. This has been a defining context for policy work. However, education has always been an area of interest for the Union. The first meeting of Education Ministers in the 1970s saw the beginning of increased European cooperation in education, and a political will to cooperate. Early cooperation initiatives in education among EU member states focused on higher and vocational education and training, migrant education, foreign language teaching and the European dimension of schooling (European Commission, 2006a, 2006b, 2006c). These centred on transnational action involving training initiatives, transition to working life and pilot studies (Antunes, 2006), but the importance of education and training to the economic development of Europe was not lost on the EU's leaders even then (European Commission, 2006c; Pépin, 2007). Current policy cooperation among member states and the EU institutions is based on strategic frameworks for European cooperation in education and training, such as ET2020, and the recent Council Resolution on a *Strategic Framework for European cooperation in education and training towards the European Education Area and beyond* (2021–2030). These resolutions and actions are profoundly important for two reasons; they shape the policy message flowing to the national/member state level, and they open access to EU funding relating to the strategic direction aimed at increasing European integration. In this way, teacher education has come to form a central plank in the EU's education and training agenda and the context for policy work has shifted markedly from the singularly memberstate arrangements of the past.

In summary: European cooperation increasingly involves a focus on education policy in the context of Europe to the point where, arguably, the European Commission has become a major policy player in education (Lawn & Lingard, 2002; Moos, 2006; Antunes, 2006; Pépin, 2007) particularly since the launch of the Lisbon Strategy in 2000 (Pépin, 2007). Antunes (2006, p. 43) described this growth in cooperation as a maturing of the 'Europeification' process which was slowly gestating in the decades before the Lisbon Strategy. We see this influence most clearly in the emergence of policy-led initiatives such as *eTwinning* – which has reached almost 1m teachers in 225k schools across Europe in 2021[1] and *SELFIEforSCHOOLS* – which has had 1.7 million users from 82 countries in the three years since it was launched (SELFIE, 2021).

2.2.2 The Idea of Education as a European Policy Space

According to Lawn and Normand (2015, p. 2) 'the EU actively constructs European spaces that it is capable of governing and works to create new policy networks and spaces within which it can deploy European solutions to European problems'. It is unsurprising so to see Lawn and Lingard (2002), Ball and Youdell (2008) and Grek et al. (2009) refer to the idea of a European policy space, as one occupied by various players from member states and the EU, and involving interaction between small groups of linked professionals, EC managers and experts, which is being shaped by various Commission bodies, networks and cultural and economic projects. The creation of such a space allows for the speeding up of flows of ideas and people, and is considered a useful method for considering changes in educational policy production in an era of globalisation (Lawn & Lingard, 2002). It is in the European Education space that commission and country experts meet and engage in policy discussion, thereby facilitating policy convergence across member states. Dale describes the European Education space as an opportunity structure framed *formally* by the Treaty [of Lisbon], *substantively* by the Lisbon Agenda, and *historically* by the pre-2000 European education initiatives (2009, p. 32). Since the Maastricht Treaty (1992), the EU has had a role in contributing to the development of quality education by encouraging cooperation between member states and, if necessary, by supporting and supplementing their action.

Reforms in education, including teacher education, do not occur in a vacuum and cannot be seen in isolation from the economic and social context of the times. In our globalised environment, policy for teacher education is influenced by multiple groups, agencies and organisations such as the EU which cut across the boundaries of individual nation-states (Olssen, Codd, & O'Neill, 2004). A feature of the European education policy context is that the Commission has been highly successful in seeding and promoting its policy agenda through an increasingly policy-active the EC Directorate-General for Education, Youth, Sport, and Culture (DG-EAC) and the EC Joint Research Centre (JRC) network and has done so largely through the coordination of multiple interests and partners from within the EU. Indeed, the policy-making architecture of the EU is established by joint action of member states and EU institutions (Sabel & Zeitlin, 2008), by a partnership between state actors and non-state actors in a new form of policy-making based on cooperation rather than legislation (Pépin, 2007) and/or by acting as a network hub where member states 'combine the sovereignty they possess to implement coordinated changes' (Antunes, 2006, p. 48). Deliberation, discussion and argument at *comitological* committees, comprising representatives of member states and experts, enables decisions to be made, though this multi-level process can blur the distinction between centralised and decentralised decision-making, changing the norm of representative democracy to a form of networked deliberative decision-making, often among technical elites (Sabel & Zeitlin, 2008). Essentially, *comitological* committee work is an aspect of OMC which can be understood as involving 'soft law' measures which are binding on the member states in varying degrees but which never take the form of directives, regulations or decisions. The basis for the work of this committee is a way in which

Policy communities, policy networks, policy coalitions and key individuals play a central role in such EC policy processes (Ball, 2012) and networks become conduits of policy spread (Grek et al., 2009). According to Ball and Youdell (2008, p. 99) social relations are established between politicians, civil servants, businesses, and voluntary organisations, which inform and influence policy thinking about education. Kriesi, Adam and Johnson (2006) argue that within such networks or social relations the supranational actors – for example EC expert Working Groups – become the most important policy-specific actors. Such EU Working Groups are key commission constructs where EC policy makers and area experts meet, discuss and network around policy solutions to common issues in education.

2.2.3   EU/EC Teacher Education Action
The EU's earlier work regarding teacher education sought to address the lack of coordination between elements of teacher education, and the lack of coherence and continuity, especially between teachers' initial professional education and their subsequent induction, in-service training and professional development, in some member states, by outlining a common framework for

policies to improve the quality of teacher education, providing member states with several broad orientations for developing policies and practices (European Commission, 2005). The European framework document also stressed the need for partnerships between teacher education institutions and schools so that research informs the development of 'best practices' and highlights the importance of developing teacher-education policy.

The European Commission prepared a set of Common European Principles for teachers' competencies and qualifications in 2004–2005 to improve the competencies and qualifications of teachers and trainers to enhance the quality and efficiency of education across the Union (European Commission, 2005, p. 2). The Common Principles espoused a view of the teaching profession as well-qualified, mobile, engaged in professional development and lifelong learning, working with knowledge, technology and information and in partnerships with other stakeholders, acquiring new knowledge, innovating and using evidence to inform their work. The Common European Principles were adapted in a later Communication on the quality of teachers as part of the Education and Training 2010 policy of the European Commission. Teacher Education or professional development for teachers and trainers features in many communications from the European Commission, which, following consultation with the public and with stakeholder organisations, become Council Recommendations.

2.2.4   How EC Policy Work Functions

A complex policy architecture has developed over time to support and facilitate the work of education policy-making within the EC. This is underpinned by an ecosystem of policy actors, agents and brokers who participate in various ways – some public, some less so – to influence and shape the EU policy landscape and exercise influence within it. This has been described as a European 'policy elite in education' (Lawn & Lingard, 2002, p. 302) coming from 'public-private partnerships, knowledge-based organisations, agencies, associations and markets… [that] meet in associations or through projects or networks' (Lawn, 2013, p. 20). Within this nexus, experts registered to the Commission often play a significant and not uncontroversial role (Field, 2013; Ripoll Servent & Busby, 2013).

The EC DG-EAC is the executive branch of the European Union responsible for policy on education. It holds the brief for oversight of all education policy matters, including those relating to teacher education: it also commissions and funds most education-related work and oversees it. Within DG-EAC there is no specific administration Unit or subunit that leads on this; partly because the teams are small and highly agile. Indeed, several Units – the basic EC division of administration – have been involved alone or collaboratively in teacher education aspects of the recent ERASMUS+ Programme Call. For instance Units B1 and A1 together coordinated work on the new *Jean Monnet Teacher Action* but are not involved in the *ERASMUS+ Teacher Academies* aspect of the programme which is fronted up by Unit B2, Unit C1 has been central to the work with JRC. The Education, Audiovisual and Culture Executive Agency (EACEA) is the executive agency of the European Union most directly involved in managing and realising the Teacher Education parts of the Union's programmes in education. It works closely with the policymakers in DG-EAC and has supported various ERASMUS+ initiatives and projects with a teacher education dimension. For instance, following project calls EACEA administered successful *Knowledge Alliance* projects on teacher education under KA2, as well as overseeing the phenomenally successful ERASMUS+ *eTwinning* Programme – which has a growing teacher education element under the heading of eTwinning Future Teachers. It also executes policy experimentation on teacher education related issues under KA3. In all of this, both DG-EAC and EACEA are supported by the EC Joint Research Centre (JRC) the Commission's science and knowledge service. The stated mission of the JRC is to provide independent scientific advice and support to EU policy. In recent years, JRC-Seville's Directorate B; *Growth & Innovation* has been particularly active concerning policy initiatives that affect teacher education such as *DigCompEDU, SELFIEforSCHOOLS*, and now *SELFIEforTEACHERS*. This relationship is discussed in more detail elsewhere in the chapter.

What is important to note is that both the architecture to support such ambitious policy work and the human resources to power it, are assembled and mobilised by the European Commission in ways and at a scale not previously seen concerning teachers and teacher education. We propose that much of this new method can be traced back to a particular moment when the EU decided to take a more active stance on training and education. We would place this in the intensive modification of the Union's policy institutions and practices following from the technical and political fall-out from the Lisbon Agenda. The original warrant for this we would situate in the earlier Maastricht Treaty (1992) which offered the first formal indications of EU interest in education as a policy space.

2.3 Changing Technical and Political Purposes in EU Policy Work for Teacher Education

2.3.1 Competence, Subsidiarity, and Proportionality

Where a policy domain falls within its remit, the Commission has traditionally deployed a systematic set of policy practices that produce collective EU decisions on action (Wallace et al., 2020). Rhinard (2019, p. 616) described this as 'typified by the extensive analysis of a particular problem, long phases of consultation with key stakeholders, the deliberate cultivation of support for proposals, episodic decision-making moments and a focus on long-term implementation'. The consultation and consensus aspects of this are commonly referred to as the EU Open Method of Coordination (OMC). Rhinard (2019, p. 617) goes on to note:

> Virtually all EU policy domains feature tools and procedures for scanning the horizon for potential disturbances, early-warning systems for possible threats and risks, special protocols for alerting political actors when a threat emerges and decision making via abbreviated procedures. Officials prioritize policy speed and a concern to protect both individuals and infrastructure as an important raison d'être of what they do.

Where a policy domain does not rest with the EU, the Commission follows principles of *subsidiarity* and *proportionality* in how it addresses such areas. It is worth mentioning that subsidiarity is a legal and technical term that signifies member-states retain full policy control in an area. Subsidiarity has its origins in Article 5(3) of the Treaty on European Union (TEU) and Protocol (No 2) of the Lisbon Treaty which deals with the application of the principles governing subsidiarity and proportionality in the work of the European Commission. Proportionality refers to the degree to which the Commission will nevertheless support member states through union-level action in relation to an area of subsidiarity, where this is deemed necessary to the broader European project.

As noted earlier, Education and teacher education would fall within this bracket and remain an acknowledged area of *subsidiarity*. However, not having a direct policy remit or *competence* does not mean policy inaction at the EC level; on the contrary, it has led to some of the most interesting and creative policy work undertaken by the Commission in recent years (Galvin et al. 2020, p. 94). Elements of this are explored below, as is the impact of what Rhinard (2019, p. 616) terms the increasing 'crisisification' of the EC policy-making machinery which is of particular interest and relevance here.

2.3.2 The Changing EC Policy-Making Apparatus; Moving beyond the Open Method of Coordination

The most widely known mechanism through which the EC pursues its policy interests in treaty limited/non-*competence* areas is the non-binding, Open Method of Coordination (OMC) mentioned above. The OMC operates through a form of 'soft governance' – deploying guidelines, indicators, benchmarks, and sharing 'best practice' among and between policy makers from member-states.

The focus becomes education systems rather than education policies in member states. Effectively, OMC uses a form of collegial brokerage to drive trends towards greater policy convergence to so generate policy *engrenage* and peer-pressure among national/regional-level policy actors, so helping ensure the implementation of EC agenda policy (Grek et al., 2009). The OMC is also a mechanism for monitoring and supplementing existing EU legislative instruments and authority (Sabel & Zeitlin, 2008), and where education is concerned, it is the central means of defining relationships between the EU and member states (Dale, 2009b).

Through the framework of the OMC and its related *ET 2020* activities, national plans and progress reports are subjected to mutual surveillance and peer review by member-state representatives and opportunities are provided for strengthening mutual learning and deepening the exchange of practice. Essentially, OMC involves 'soft law' measures that are binding on member-states in varying degrees but never take the form of directives, regulations or decisions. As a form of policy convergence, the OMC played a major role in shaping the European Education Space by identifying common problems that are best addressed at the European level (Dale, 2009b, pp. 128–129), leading to the 'Europeification' of policies in fields such as teacher education (Antunes, 2006).

The OMC emerged as a key governance and policy instrument as part of the Lisbon Strategy (2000) and has proved particularly useful in policy fields such as education, where the potentialities for cooperation were more limited by EU treaties (Pépin, 2007). Its architects envisaged the OMC as a 'third way' for EU governance as it was seen as being capable of reconciling the pursuit of common European objectives with respect for national diversity while encouraging mutual emulation and experimental learning through comparison of different approaches to shared problems (Sabel & Zeitlin, 2008), thus enabling the construction of European unity while retaining national diversity. The result has been a steady growth in policy-work and increasing reach for EC policy tools and instruments. In this way, the OMC operates alongside traditional legal frameworks creating a complex system of 'multilevel governance'. In such a system 'informal normative pressures and agenda-setting from the European Commission promises to be as powerful as legal prescription' (Alexiadou, 2007, p. 102). As a governance instrument within the EU repertoire, OMC also provides a framework for cooperation between the member states, whose national policies can be directed towards specific common objectives, thus achieving greater convergence towards the main EU goals (Pépin, 2007).

However, OMC has not been without its criticisms. Initial hopes that OMC would decrease the EU's democratic deficit by creating more participatory policy processes around inclusion and other aspects of social policy have not been wholly realised (Friedrich, 2006; Barcevicius et al., 2014). More significantly in terms of our interest here, the European Parliament in particular has been concerned about the democratic legitimacy of the OMC and warned against the OMC becoming a 'non-transparent and subversive parallel procedure in the EU' (European Parliament, 2014). Nevertheless, OMC remains an important method in relation to policy-action within EC activities around education and training. The challenge for policy makers within the Commission has therefore been to find ways to address what they perceive as the main shortcoming of the method – its inherently unpredictable, sometimes lugubrious and always time-intensive underpinning collegial and consensus-building architecture (Barcevicius et al., 2014; Rhinard, 2019).

Among the responses that have gained traction in relation to education and teacher education policy two stand out: the exponential rise in recent years of involvement by the EC Joint Research Centre across the range of education policy work undertaken by the Commission; and the steady rise of 'in-house', early stage, *policy experimentation* work by DG Education, Youth, Sport and Culture (DG-EAC) with in many cases the assistance and advice of JRC. Both have impacted markedly on the agenda for quality in teaching and teacher education, as discussed below.

2.3.3 The EC Joint Research Centre: Science for Policy and the Turn to Policy Experimentation

The rising role of the Joint Research Centre (JRC) in shaping EU Education, Training and Lifelong Learning policies has been remarkable to observe. The JRC is the Commission's science and knowledge service and carries out research to provide 'independent scientific advice and support' to EU policy. In education, training, and lifelong learning, JRC has progressively taken a more active role not only by providing evidence to Commission policy-makers but also by developing policy protocols and procedures to professionalise policy work and embed a *science for policy* ethic in all its work (see Šucha & Dewar, 2020). Topp et al. (2018) describe this as the JRC's Knowledge Management for Policy (KMP) Professionalisation Programme which has been developed since 2015 to address the problems of providing timely policy advice and to foster 'evidence informed policymaking'. They suggest that the KMP identifies particularly 'the ways in which organisations containing researchers, policy-makers, communicators, and knowledge brokers can adopt pragmatic ways to connect the demand and supply of policy-relevant knowledge' (Topp et al., 2018, p. 2).

However, in parallel with this conceptual capacity building, JRC has also engaged in policy work going far beyond resourcing options and recommendations. On behalf of the Commission, and especially on behalf of DG-EAC, JRC has actively designed, implemented, and evaluated ground-breaking policy for education work in relation to competence frameworks, and has authored related professional development instruments/tools now used widely by teachers in the EU and beyond. The flagship JRC SELFIE for Schools Instrument which is available in over 30 languages was developed to assist schools to self-assess in terms of their usage of digital technology for learning and teaching. This has helped shape and frame the quality agenda in teacher development right down to the level of the school and individual teacher. A brief look at this JRC activity now follows.

Over the past decade, JRC-Seville (the *Human Capital & Employment Unit* of JRC) has played a leading role in developing and implementing European competence frameworks and related self-assessment and self-reflection tools, in collaboration with DG-EAC and DG Employment, Social Affairs and Inclusion (DG-EMPL). This seminal JRC work on competence frameworks started in 2013 and finalised in 2016 with the *European Digital Competence Framework for Citizens* (Vuorikari et al., 2016), which soon became a reference framework at the EU level. JRC then released the *European Framework for Digitally-Competent Educational Organisations* (Kampylis, Punie, & Devine, 2015), where the focus was the digital capacity at the organisation level. The work on digital competence frameworks completed in 2017 with the release of *DigCompEdu: the European Digital Competence Framework for Educators* (Redecker, 2017). As implied by the abbreviations used for the three frameworks, the DigComp suite (DigComp, DigCompEdu, DigCompOrg) are regarded as interconnected and interrelated, capturing the digital competence of citizens (lifelong learners) and educators as well as the digital capacity of educational organisations. They are seen therefore to offer a unique and comprehensive set of conceptual models and a holistic approach for digital competence in education, training, and lifelong settings.

In terms of policy work, the development and release by JRC and DG-EAC of the *SELFIEforSCHOOLS* tool can be seen as a turning point that signals a deliberated move by the Commission away from the development of conceptual models and policy advice to full-spectrum development, testing and implementation of tools that can be used directly by schools, teachers and learners in the EU Member States. Subsequently, JRC has piloted a SELFIE *for Teachers* self-assessment tool in five countries, and released a validated version in

October 2021. Additionally, JRC is at the time of writing supporting the work of the recently launched EU Climate Coalition – both in terms of policy and human resources as well as developing a competence framework for Education for Environmental Sustainability (EES). This suggests a direction of travel rather than simply a once off exploration of a policy method.

In short: over the past decade or so the European Commission has assembled in the JRC a policy machinery and highly-capable supporting personnel that have allowed it to systematically pursue a progressively more active role in policy work – moving beyond monitoring and analysing education and training policies to the point where it can confidently and capably seed, steer and evaluate policy action. The Centre does so by employing a unique, custom-built policy methodology that seeks to combine the science-for-policy fundamentals of its Knowledge Management for Policy (KMP) approach with an education policy activism unprecedented for the Commission in terms of its scale and reach. This has increasingly been an asset in DG-EAC policy activity as the JRC and the directorate work more closely on their shared interests. Much of the detail of this new relation has been shaped through shared policy experimentation work.

2.3.4 Policy Experimentations – Another Way of Promoting EU Education and Training Policies

Of the various EU directorates-general, DG-EAC is the one with the closest and most long-standing connections with education. Down the years, all major actions and programmes associated with education and lifelong learning have been homed in this directorate or its predecessors; for instance Comenius, eLearning, Lifelong Learning, ERASMUS, and now ERASMUS+. These have been the traditional transnational programme routes through which the EU has sought to influence education practices and policy and many – such as the Jean Monnet Actions and eTwinning – have been extremely successful, touching the lives of millions of young Europeans. However, in common with its JRC counterparts, policy-makers within the DG-EAC have been searching in recent years for more efficient and effective ways to influence policy and practice at member-state level. This includes elements of the thinking Rhinard (2019) observed when he described the emerging policy work of the Commission as being increasingly characterised by 'a prioritization of speed in decision-making, new perceptions of which actors matter, and new narratives on the role and purpose of the EU' (Rhinard, 2019, p. 629).

Additionally, the traditional activities of DG-EAC have recently seen a rise in alternative modalities such as the adding of teacher education to the Jean Monnet Actions for the first time and the introduction of an important new line affecting teachers and teacher education in the ERASMUS+ Teacher Academy initiative.

Moreover, DG-EAC has also been making use of *policy experimentation* within the ERASMUS+ framework for some time now. The idea itself is not that new – policy experimentation has been attracting interest among policymakers since 2011, when the joint World Bank/ OECD/Brazil National Development Bank (BNDES) conference on Innovation Policy for Inclusive Growth was held in Rio de Janeiro in October. However, two features of the DG-EAC policy experimentation mark it as different: First, is its explicit aim to support transnational cooperation and mutual learning among public authorities at the highest institutional level (i.e. Ministry or equivalent) with responsibility for developing and implementing education, training, and youth policies. Arguably, such experimentations in real world settings enable policy-makers to perform reality checks through field trials in several countries to assist with informed choices against more objective and realistic outcomes. Second, is the funding scale and number of projects involved. The EU has funded 37 projects under Erasmus+ Key Action 3 – *Support for policy reform* since 2014 at an indicative grant cost of €58.8m. This is an impressive investment in the method with many of the projects involved focussing on aspects of teaching and teacher education. Indeed, one of the two priorities in the most recent (2020) call for European Policy Experimentations in education and training was 'teaching and teachers'. Nine out of eleven projects funded under the call involved interventions related directly to empowering, training, supporting, and upskilling prospective and in-service teachers.

From the above, it is evident that policy experimentation is another tool that the EC now uses for promoting policy work on teacher education and training at the highest level. *Teachers and Trainers* – Framework Priority Area 3 of the recent EU Council recommendation on advancing the European Education Area (EU, 2021) – seems to be deliberately aligned with policy experimentation and so continues the development of the method.

In summary: policy experimentation in a particular modality with a particular purpose is another element of the new policy methodology being embraced by the Commission when it comes to education policy action. The conceptualisation of the European Education Area as an incubator of new policy methodology and approaches that valorises policy solutions to a designated challenge (in this case, high-quality, inclusive, and future-oriented education and training) is not a totally new construct. The EU has developed similar initiatives in affiliated sectors such as the *European Higher Education Area* and the *European Research Area* (cf. Vukasovic, 2017; Meijer & van de Klippe, 2020). In this context, the EEA is central to a Europeanisation of Commission-led policy work which can be best understood as a process of (a) construction (b) diffusion (c) institutionalisation of formal and informal rules, procedures, policy paradigms, styles, 'ways of doing things' and shared beliefs and norms which are first defined and consolidated in the making of EU decisions and then incorporated in the logic of domestic discourse, identities, political structures and public policies (Alexiadou, 2007; Radaelli, 2004). For those seeking to understand and influence EU teacher education policy the shift is both significant and potentially concerning.

3 Discussion

In this chapter we have considered the emergence of a new dynamic in how the EC pursues policy for education, including teacher education, as it progresses the European Education Area agenda. At the core of this sits a move to extend EU authority in the governance of education. We have pointed to the growing strength and reach of the new EC policy methodology as the Commission develops capacity and deploys instruments such as policy experimentation to further its policy ends. We have sought in this way to clarify the EC policy narrative on the nature and intention of its education policy work generally and to alert to its formidable potential.

On the positive side, we have found that the *deliberative supranationalism* (Joerges & Neyer, 2006) which has been a marked feature of strong policy work by the Commission in recent years has endured into the new arrangements and thinking. The DG-EAC Working Groups mandate has been renewed as part of the build towards the EEA. With this the more consultative and deliberative nature of key aspects of its policy work has largely been maintained. The temptation must have existed to move to more reactive forms of policy agenda work but this seems to have been resisted; planning lines and activities may have been extended to accommodate the impacts of the pandemic but they were maintained. For instance, the new Digital Education Action Plan was launched later than expected but it has gone ahead. Similarly, open public consultations (OPC) on EC Working Group agendas for *Pathways to School Success* and *Education for Environmental Sustainability* (EES) started reasonably close to the original datelines. Additionally, EC action has taken place on the launch of novel *Jean Monnet* and the ERASMUS+ Teacher Academies action. All of these have implications for teachers and teacher education.

In all of this an interesting and potentially powerful trend towards more open opportunities for contribution by experts, coalition building, and co-design of policy scoping has characterised EC action. We see this in new departures such as the framing up of the *European Digital Education Hub* and the novel *Jean Monnet* and ERASMUS+ *Teacher Academies* mentioned immediately above. Opportunities to work with the EU JRC on its various projects such as competence frameworks for teachers and education institutions, to contribute to 'Seville Process' workshops where EEA policy lines are developed, and to work with DG-EAC on policy experimentation can be expected to present as the EEA agenda gathers pace. It is essential that the teacher education community responds in a spirit of academic openness and optimism, and participates actively in these. Teacher educators and education researchers are well placed to make a meaningful contribution within the framework of the new policy methodology *if the opportunity is taken to do so*.

However, optimism and willingness to participate are not necessarily enough to ensure this happens. There is a need also for proactively and ethically seeking out opportunities to be involved. The uncharacteristic speed with which the Commission is advancing the EEA agenda has a possible darker side. In a very real sense, the remove of EC policy work from public attention facilitated by the COVID pandemic may have accentuated alternative trends that further erode the subsidiarity of education policy work. The most concerning of these relates to possible unchecked convergence of policy positions resulting from lack of *sufficient* sector expert insight. Commission experts and small numbers of education sector experts from individual member states have continued to work together over the pandemic to progress education policy ideas, so enabling a flow of ideas to continue but possibly causing drift towards group/convergent thinking in some areas of EU education policy work. Indeed, this type of insider influence has long been acknowledged as problematic in the literature. For instance, Ball and Youdell (2008) argued that the considerable association of personnel involved in EU policy work meant the distinctions between advice, support and lobbying for work can be hard to see (p. 8), arguably creating a privatisation of education policy 'through advice, consultation, research, evaluations and forms of influence'. Additionally, Alexiadou and Jones (2001) and Gornitzka and Holst (2015) both suggest that convergence around a small inner circle shifts attention from critical policy analysis in local contexts to building consensus around policy goals and the technical means by which European policy aims can be realised and measured. Field (2013) has also commented critically on this practice.

Consequently, a key question for all of us in teacher education about the EEA relates to who sits at the table when European education policy is made, how they get there, and how they operate 'to exert influence and affect processes and outcomes' (Field, 2013, p.2). This has implications for transparency and for meaningful access to these flows for those outside the circles of experts involved. Where teacher quality and quality teacher education are concerned, it is essential that expert capture is not allowed to continue.

Notwithstanding the best intentions of those driving the integration aspects of the EEA agenda, much of the fabric of teaching and teacher education are embedded inextricably in local contexts, histories and practices in ways that convergent policy at the EU level can never properly accommodate; particularly if the driving ethic of educational policy work is linked primarily to the economic project of the EU. The more confident and assertive policy methodology emerging at the European Commission and the narratives that underpin this will need not only to be watched but also influenced by teacher education interests if a shared and meaningful future is to be achieved. For us in teacher education and teacher education research, it is important to understand and essential that we seek actively to influence the new EC policy narrative and the emerging policy method detailed above as these are likely to have profound implications for teacher education policy work and indeed education policy work more generally in Europe in the future.

4   Conclusion

Traditionally EC policy work for teacher quality, teacher education and teacher development has both facilitated and been shaped by a transnational flows of people, ideas and practices across European borders. Such teacher education policy work challenges the nationalist tradition present in all education systems, albeit more strongly in some than in others (Symeonidis, 2018). For example, the visions of a 'European teacher' (Schratz, 2014; Madalińska-Michalak, 2018) or 'quality teacher' (Snoek, 2021) have characteristics of pluralism and identification with 'unity in diversity' that both Commission and teacher education professionals can readily value and share. These values and flows cannot be assumed automatically to remain central to EC thinking and policy work as the EEA takes shape – particularly if a more limited discourse of the lifelong learning teacher workforce were to prevail and as what Mayer (2021) notes about the current reframing of what counts as research and policy evidence starts to take hold. It is important therefore for the teacher education community to take every opportunity offered to become actively and continually involved in realising the better possibilities of the European Education Area. According to pronouncements such as those from the Gothenburg Summit of European Leaders (2017) the governance and mission of this emerging area will – as specified by the Council of the European Union at Brussels on 19 February 2021 – rest on 'a spirit of co-creation' (Council of the European Union,

2021, p. 7) which will actively seek to foster cooperation between the member states and to engage sector expertise to enrich the quality and inclusiveness of national education and training programmes, including teacher and teacher education quality. It is on us to seize this moment and to ensure that a shared and meaningful future is achieved.

Note

1 See https://www.etwinning.net/en/pub/index.htm

References

Alexiadou, N. (2007). The Europeanisation of education policy: Researching changing governance and 'new' modes of coordination. *Research in Comparative and International Education*, 2(2), 102–116. https://doi.org/10.2304/rcie.2007.2.2.102

Alexiadou, N., & Jones, K. (2001, September 26–29). *Travelling policy/local spaces* [Paper]. Congress Marx International 111 Le Capitale et L'Humanite University of Paris X, Paris.

Antunes, F. (2006). Globalisation and Europeification of education policies: Routes, processes and metamorphoses. *European Educational Research Journal*, 5(1), 38–55.

Ball, S. (2012). *Global education Inc.: New policy networks and the neoliberal imaginary*. Routledge.

Ball, S., & Youdell, D. (2008). *Hidden privatisation in public education. A preliminary report to Education International 5th World Congress*. University of London.

Barcevicius, E., Weishaupt, J. T., & Zeitlin, J. (2014). *Assessing the open method of coordination. Institutional design and national influence of EU social policy coordination*. Palgrave Macmillan.

Caena, F. (2014). *Initial teacher education in Europe: An overview of policy issues*. European Commission. ET2020 Working Group of Schools Policy. https://ec.europa.eu/assets/eac/education/experts-groups/2014-2015/school/initial-teacher-education_en.pdf

Caena, F. (2017). Weaving the fabric: Teaching and teacher education ecosystem. In B. Hudson (Ed.), *Overcoming the fragmentation in teacher education policy and practice* (pp. 179–200). Cambridge University Press.

Council of the European Union. (2009). *Council conclusions of 12 May 2009 on a strategic framework for European cooperation in education and training*. EU 2009/C 119/02.

Council of the European Union. (2020). *Council conclusions on European teachers and trainers for the future*. EU 2020/C 193/04.

Council of the European Union. (2021). *Council resolution on a strategic framework for European cooperation in education and training towards the European Education Area and beyond (2021–2030)*. EU 2021/C 66/01.

Dale, R. (2009a). Introduction. In R. Dale & S. Robertson (Eds.), *Globalisation and Europeanisation in education* (pp. 7–19). Symposium Books.

Dale, R. (2009b). Studying globalisation and Europeanisation in education: Lisbon, the open method of coordination and beyond. In R. Dale & S. Robertson (Eds.), *Globalisation and Europeanisation in education* (pp. 121–140). Symposium Books.

European Commission. (2005). *Common European principles for teacher competences and qualifications*. European Commission, Directorate-General for Education and Culture.

European Commission. (2006a). *Delivering on the modernisation agenda for universities: Education, research and innovation*. COM (2006) 208 final.

European Commission. (2006b). *Progress towards the Lisbon objectives in education and training. Report based on indicators and benchmarks*. SEC (2006) 639.

European Commission. (2006c). *Efficiency and equity in European education and training Systems. Communication from the Commission to the Council and the European Parliament*. COM (2006) 481 final.

European Commission. (2018). *2019 annual work programme for the implementation of "Erasmus+": the Union programme for education, Training, Youth and Sport*. C(2018) 6572 of 11 October 2018. https://europa.eu/youth/d8/sites/default/files/youth-strategy-library/annual-work-programme-c-2018-6572.pdf

European Commission. (2020a). *Digital education action plan 2021–2027: Resetting education and training for the digital age*. COM(2020) 624 final. https://ec.europa.eu/education/education-in-the-eu/digital-education-action-plan_en

European Commission. (2020b). *Supporting school self-evaluation and development through quality assurance policies: Key considerations for policy makers*. Report by ET2020 Working Group Schools.

European Commission. (2020c). *Communication from the Commission to the European parliament, the Council, the European Economic and Social Committee and the Committee of the Regions on achieving the European Education Area by 2025*. 30.9.2020 COM 625 final.

European Commission. (2021). *The European pillar of social rights action plan*. Publications Office of the European Union.

European Commission/EACEA/Eurydice. (2020). *The European Higher Education Area in 2020: Bologna process implementation report*. Publications Office of the European Union.

European Parliament. (2014). *The open method of coordination. At a glance*. https://www.europarl.europa.eu/EPRS/EPRS-AaG-542142-Open-Method-of-Coordination-FINAL.pdf

Field, M. (2013, July). The anatomy of EU policy-making: Appointing the experts. *European Integration online Papers* (EIoP). *European Community Studies Association Austria (ECSA-A)*, *17*. http://eiop.or.at/eiop/pdf/2013-007.pdf

Friedrich, D. (2006). Policy process, governance and democracy in the EU: The case of the open method of coordination on social inclusion in Germany. *Policy & Politics*, *34*(2), 367–383.

Galvin, C., Austin, R., Revyakina, E., & McMorrough, A. (2020). Building cultural awareness and understanding in Europe's schools: Insights from the European Commission's eTwinning programme. In W. J. Hunter & R. Austin (Eds.), *Blended and online learning for global citizenship: New technologies and opportunities for intercultural education* (pp. 92–121). Routledge.

Gornitzka, Å., & Holst, C. (2015). The expert-executive nexus in the EU: An introduction. *Politics and Governance*, *3*(1), 1–12.

Grek, S., Lawn, M., Lingard, B., Ozga, J., Rinne, R., Segerholm, C., & Simola, H. (2009). National policy brokering and the construction of the European Education Space in England, Sweden, Finland and Scotland. *Comparative Education*, *45*(1), 5–21.

Joerges, C., & Neyer, J. (2006). 'Deliberative supranationalism' revisited. Working Paper, EUI LAW, 2006/20. https://cadmus.eui.eu/handle/1814/6251

Kampylis, P., Punie, Y., & Devine, J. (2015). *Promoting effective digital-age learning: A European framework for digitally-competent educational organisations*. EUR 27599 EN. Publications Office of the European Union.

Kriesi, H., Adam, S., & Jochum, M. (2006). Comparative analysis of policy networks in Western Europe. *Journal of European Public Policy*, *13*(3), 341–361.

Lawn, M. (2013). The understories of European education. The contemporary life of experts and professionals. *SISYPHUS Journal of Education*, *1*(1), 18–35.

Lawn, M., & Grek, S. (2012). *Europeanizing education: Governing an emerging policy space*. Symposium Books.

Lawn, M., & Lingard, B. (2002). Constructing a European policy space in educational governance: The role of transnational policy actors. *European Educational Research Journal*, *1*(2), 290–307.

Lawn, M., & Normand, R. (2015). Introduction. In M. Lawn & R. Normand (Eds.), *Shaping of European education: Interdisciplinary approaches* (pp. 1–13). Routledge.

Maastricht Treaty. (1992). Treaty on European Union, signed at Maastricht on 7 February 1992. *Official Journal of European Communities*, C 191, 29.7.1992, 1–112.

Madalińska-Michalak, J. (2018). Profile of European teachers. In A. R. Simoes, M. Lourenco, & N. Costa (Eds.), *Teacher education policy and practice in Europe. Challenges and opportunities for future* (pp. 11–25). Routledge.

Mayer, D. (2021). The connections and disconnections between teacher education policy and research: Reframing evidence. *Oxford Review of Education*, *47*(1), 120–134.

Meijer, I., & van de Klippe, W. (2020). Monitoring responsible research and innovation in the European Research Area. The MoRRI project. In E. Yaghmaei & I. van de Poel (Eds.), *Assessment of responsible innovation: Methods and practices* (pp. 171–195). Routledge.

Menter, I. (2016). Introduction. In G. Beauchamp & L. Clarke (Eds.), *Teacher education in times of change* (pp. 14–31). Policy Press.

Moos, L. (2006). What kinds of democracy in education are facilitated by supra-and transnational agencies? *European Educational Research Journal*, 5(3&4), 160–168.

OECD. (2020). *Market consultation: Platform development contractor(s) for the Platform for Innovative Learning Assessments (PILA)*. OECD/Mimeo.

Olssen, M., Codd, J., & O'Neill, A. M. (2004). *Education policy: Globalization, citizenship and democracy*. Sage Publication Ltd. https://dx.doi.org/10.4135/9781446221501

Paris Communiqué. (2018, May 24–25). *Ministerial conference*. Paris. Retrieved August 16, 2018, from http://www.ehea2018.paris/Data/ElFinder/s2/Communique/EHEAParis2018-Communique-final.pdf

Pépin, L. (2007). The history of EU Cooperation in the field of education and training: How lifelong learning became a strategic objective. *European Journal of Education*, 42(1), 121–132.

Radaelli, C. M. (2004). Europeanisation: Solution or problem? *European Integration Online Papers (EIoP)*, 8(16). http://eiop.or.at/eiop/texte/2004-016a.htm

Rauh, C. (2019). EU politicization and policy initiatives of the European Commission: The case of consumer policy. *Journal of European Public Policy*, 26(3), 344–365.

Redecker, C. (2017). *European framework for the digital competence of educators: DigCompEdu*. JRC Working Papers JRC107466. Publications Office of the European Union.

Rhinard, M. (2019). The crisisification of policy-making in the European Union. *JCMS: Journal of Common Market Studies*, 57(3), 616–633.

Ripoll Servent, A., & Busby, A. (2013). Introduction: Agency and influence inside the EU institutions. *European Integration online Papers (EIoP)* (Special Issue 1), 17, Article 3. http://eiop.or.at/eiop/texte/2013-003a.htm

Sabel, C. F., & Zeitlin, J. (2008). Learning from Difference: The new architecture of experimentalist governance in the European Union. *European Law Journal*, 14, 271–327.

Schratz, M. (2014). The European teacher: Transnational perspectives in teacher education policy and practice. *CEPS Journal*, 4, 11–27.

SELFIE. (2021). *SELFIE forum data*. https://ec.europa.eu/education/schools-go-digital/selfie_news/selfie-forum-2021_en

Simoes, A. R., Lourenco, M., & Costa, N. (Eds.). (2018). *Teacher education policy and practice in Europe. Challenges and opportunities for the future*. Routledge.

Snoek, M. (2021). Educating quality teachers: How teacher quality is understood in the Netherlands and its implications for teacher education. *European Journal of Education*, *44*(3), 309–327.

Šucha, V., & Dewar, M. (2020). Institutional framework for the science-policy interaction. In V. Šucha & M. Sienkiewicz (Eds.), *Science for policy handbook* (pp. 21–32). Elsevier.

Symeonidis, V. (2018). Revisiting the European teacher education area: The transformation of teacher education policies and practices in Europe. *CEPS Journal*, *8*(3), 13–34.

Topp, L., Mair, D., Smillie, L., & Cairney, P. (2018). Knowledge management for policy impact: The case of the European Commission's Joint Research Centre. *Palgrave Communication*, *4*, 87. https://doi.org/10.1057/s41599-018-0143-3

TUNING. (2009). *Tuning educational structures in Europe: Reference points for the design and delivery of degree programmes in education*. Universidad de Deusto.

Vukasovic, M. (2017). Stakeholder organizations in the European Higher education area: Exploring transnational policy dynamic. *Policy and Society*, *36*(1), 109–126.

Vuorikari, R., Punie, Y., Gomez, S. C., & Van Den Brande, G. (2016). *DigComp 2.0: The digital competence framework for citizens. Update phase 1: The conceptual reference model*. Luxembourg Publication Office of the European Union.

Wallace, H., Pollack, M. A., Roederer-Rynning, C., & Young, A. R. (Eds.). (2020). *Policy-making in the European Union*. Oxford University Press.

CHAPTER 15

Educating about and through Research
The Role of Research in Pre-service Teachers' Classroom Practices

Stéphane Colognesi and Virginie März

Abstract

Numerous studies have shown how pre-service teachers struggle with a research-practice or theory-practice gap: they find it difficult to implement insights from educational theory within their real-world classroom practices. As a result, student teachers rapidly return to deeply and often traditional rooted beliefs and attitudes. Teacher education institutes, therefore, are challenged to prepare student teachers for seeing the value of educational theory and research for teachers' classroom practices. In this chapter, we focus on bridging the theory-to-practice gap within initial teacher training, by educating student teachers about research through research. More specifically, we evaluated the implementation of a research-training module in the final year of teacher training. This module was characterised as a collaborative research partnership (between student teachers, in-service teachers, teacher educators, and researchers) and focused on developing and evaluating teaching scenarios. Data collection combined focus groups (N = 23 primary school student teachers) with the analysis of student teachers' teaching portfolios. The study findings illustrate how participation in a collaborative research project contributed to student teachers' research conceptions and reflexivity skills. Moreover, collaborative research partnerships enabled to bridge the world of practitioners and researchers, leading them to work together on questions that both consider as being relevant. Our study contributes to the reflection on how to strengthen the quality of teaching and teacher training, by showing how collaborative research can be seen as a valuable professional learning activity.

Keywords

theory-practice gap – initial teacher education – primary education – research participation – collaborative research – qualitative research

1 Problem Statement

Over the last years, we can see considerable attention to the role (teacher) research can fulfill in teacher professional development and in school improvement (Coburn & Penuel, 2016; Dobber et al., 2012). Nevertheless, teachers often struggle with a so-called research-practice or theory-practice gap: they find it difficult to implement educational theory within real-world classroom practices. Recent literature has shown how student teachers believe that the content of their training program (and more specifically theories stemming from research) are far removed from the realities of the classroom.

According to student teachers, initial teacher education often promotes certain evidenced-based practices that they perceive as being disconnected from daily classroom reality (Perez-Roux, 2016). When student teachers go through their traineeship, they therefore often encounter a tension between daily classroom reality and the ideal picture set during teacher training (Altet et al., 2013). Furthermore, research has shown that during their first steps within the teaching profession, student teachers rapidly return to deeply (and often traditional) rooted beliefs and attitudes (Caena, 2011; Shulman & Shulman, 2004). As such, teacher education institutes are challenged to convince student teachers of the value of educational theory and research: showing the relevance and usefulness of theory and research-based training programmes for their classroom practice.

Successfully bridging the research-to-practice gap is important, since it could foster practitioners to use knowledge stemming from research as well as enable researchers to include the preoccupations of the latter within educational research. In this perspective, Austin's (2016) work has shown that incorporating research into teacher education curricula can bring several benefits, contributing to teacher effectiveness in the long term. For instance, research can help teachers find solutions to particular problems, it can provide them with up-to-date sources of information, and it can help determine priorities when introducing educational changes. Hammerness et al. (2005), moreover, identified that teachers who graduated from teacher education programmes that make extensive use of teacher research, experienced higher feelings of preparedness. The study of Cochran-Smith et al. (2009), found that research during teacher education contributes to student teachers' critical reflection, enables them to construct new curricula, as well as facilitates teachers to modify instruction and pedagogy to meet students' needs. Duroisin et al. (2020) have also shown that training in and through research is a key to the development of (future) teachers' reflexivity. Finally, it can also, more broadly, improve teachers' understanding of their professional and socio-cultural context. This last point seems important in relation to the current context of teachers' work. Being a teacher is not only about being a classroom actor, but also about functioning as a member of a school organisation, understanding the micropolitical climate and school culture determining teachers' work (Coppe et al., 2020; März et al., 2019; März & Kelchtermans, 2020).

In a recent study (Van Nieuwenhoven et al., 2021), student teachers were questioned about the effects they experienced of a program where research was incorporated in a teacher training module. The training module concerned the study of pedagogical currents. The researcher presented his latest work on the subject. He then accompanied the students in the process of developing teaching activities for their internship, based on the presented research insights. He also shared with the students the interview protocol from his research concerning their teaching practices. Several aspects emerged from the analysis of the interviews with teacher educators and students. First, in line with Austin's study (2016), we found that the research instruments, data, and the underlying theoretical frameworks provided students with up-to-date knowledge to plan and analyse their teaching scenarios during internships. Second, the student teachers mentioned that interaction with the researcher gave them a better understanding of what a researcher's tasks are. In addition, having access to recent research insights, in this case: pedagogical currents and practices, convinced some students to continue studying by following a master's program in educational sciences. In addition, we found that research, in the context of French speaking Belgium, is almost absent from teacher training programmes. The involved teacher educators, moreover, did not feel competent in the area of research. This can be explained by the fact that in Belgium a Master's degree is sufficient to become a teacher educator in a teacher education institute. Other studies, in other contexts, have also shown that the lack of theoretical knowledge on the part of internship supervisors is a factor that does not facilitate the support of future teachers in the theory-practice articulation (Hernandez & Ducrey-Monnier, 2020).

In this chapter, we will present the findings of a recent study that focuses on bridging the research-practice gap within initial teacher education. More specifically, the aim of our study was to stimulate student teachers to improve their classroom practices by *educating them about and through research*. More specifically, we opted for a collaborative research design (involving student teachers, in-service teachers, teacher educators, and researchers) within the domain of French oral skill-didactics: we evaluated the implementation of a research-training module, while training student teachers through participation in this study to value and use research. The ambition of the chapter is twofold: first, we will describe the design of the research-training module in order to show how student teachers learn to use research as well as adopt a reflexive role. Second, we will observe the impact of this research-training module on student teachers' research competencies. We will describe how student teachers have lived the role of researcher, and examine what it has brought to them.

Based on our findings, we show that a sixth type of professional learning activity is to be added to the five identified in the literature: collaborative teacher research. Collaborative teacher research cannot only improve the quality of teacher education, but as well enable teachers to cope with the multiple facets of the teaching profession (Coppe et al., 2020).

2 Theoretical Foundations

For the design of the research-training module, we were inspired by three guiding theoretical principles: inquiry-based working, professional learning activities, and role diversity.

First, one way to bridge the gap between theory/research and practice, is to engage student teachers in research through inquiry-based working (Baan et al., 2019). Teachers are increasingly expected to be able to use and conduct research to evaluate and improve their own teaching practices (Zeichner, 2003). These new expectations call for the incorporation of a research orientation in teacher education programmes. Therefore, in several countries (such as the Netherlands, Norway, Finland, and Canada), there has been a tendency to integrate an intensive focus on research in the curriculum (Darling-Hammond, 2017; Flores, 2017; Snoek et al., 2017; Van der Linden et al., 2012). For instance, by letting student teachers carrying out research projects during their studies that involve inquiry into pedagogical issues in their schools, often in collaboration with other school actors. Collaborative research aims to bridge the gap between academics and practitioners (Bourassa et al., 2007; Desgagné & Larouche, 2010). According to Rust and Meyers (2003), collaborative teacher research can be a fruitful strategy for teachers to actively participate in the examination of classrooms and schools (see also Cochran-Smith & Lytle, 2009). In addition, collaborative research pursues two objectives: it aims to develop a knowledge producing activity as well as to contribute to the professional development of all actors involved (Mukamurera, 2014). Moreover, collaborative research makes educational research more accessible to teachers, and thus enables to 'redress some of the unequal power dynamics subjugating teachers in educational research' (Christianakis, 2010, p. 110).

Second, in order to face the rapid changes of the teaching profession, research has identified several types of professional learning activities (Geijsel et al., 2009; Janssen & van Yperen, 2004; Kwakman, 2003). The concept of professional learning is understood in terms of a continuum, and starts with initial teacher education (Portelance et al., 2008). These types of professional learning activities are: keeping updated (gathering new knowledge and information), innovation (produce something new in an existing context), experimenting (testing interventions in the classroom), knowledge sharing (sharing of theoretical and experiential knowledge between professionals), and reflective practices (questioning one's knowledge and practices).

The research-teaching module has been developed based on these five types of professional learning activities. They have been treated as principles for the design of the research-training module. To confront future teachers with these types of professional learning activities, it seems important that they are placed in a perspective of integrative alternation (Chaubet et al., 2018; Merhan et al., 2007; Pentecouteau, 2012). Integrative alternation articulates theory and practice in an interactive relationship. It is in fact a matter of working on experiences from the practice field during the learning activities in the training institute. Conversely, it is also about finding a practical use for the theoretical aspects of the training program (Nitonde & Paquay, 2011; Pentecouteau, 2012). Thus, an integrative alternation makes it possible to create a synergy between theoretical and practical knowledge.

Third, in order for these types of professional learning activities to be operationalised during teacher training, it is important that student teachers take on different roles while being engaged in a research activity. A role can be defined as 'a temporary, situated mode of action enacted by an individual according to a project, a task' (Colognesi, 2017, p. 22). It is indeed possible to change roles during the course of a task depending on the goals assigned to it (Lebel et al., 2017; Vivegnis, 2019). In a training program designed to enable teachers working in the same school to introduce an innovation into their teaching practices, Colognesi and Lucchini (in press) guided student teachers through different roles directly related to the types of professional learning activities: Learner (keeping updated), Engineer (innovation), Teacher (experimenting), Observer (knowledge sharing) and Reflective Analyst (reflective practices). This training program is called LETRA. Results show that going through these successive roles allowed teachers to have access to complex skills, facilitating knowledge transfer and pedagogical innovation. Our research-training module takes up these roles, and adds that of researcher (inspired by the collaborative research design).

3   Design of the Research-Training Module

The research-training module, named DIDAC'TIC (Colognesi & Balleux, 2018), has been implemented in the final (i.e. third) year of initial teacher training for primary school teachers (in one teacher education institute in French speaking Belgium). The objective of this module was to develop and experiment with teaching scenarios within the domain of French oral genre-pedagogy (Dolz & Gagnon, 2008; Dolz & Schneuwly, 1998; Horverak, 2016) using digital tablets. For this module, a partnership was created between different actors: student teachers, in-service teachers (of the internship school), teacher educators, a researcher and students conducting research as part of their master studies (within the faculty of psychology and educational sciences). The research-training module takes place from April through June, at the end of the teaching program of future primary school teachers. The student teachers have no other course activities at that time, and can dedicate themselves fully to the activities of this module (for example, the presentation of their research findings is done through a research report).

Within the framework of the research-training module, six roles are distinguished: the students go successively through the roles of learner, engineer, teacher, observer, while the roles of reflective analyst and researcher are transversal to the others. As for the other actors, they intervene jointly in the research process, as described in the steps below.

In a first step, student teachers are trained in oral skill-didactics based on existing research in this domain (i.e. role of learner). Since future teachers do not teach their pupils as how they are told to do so, but rather teach the way they have been taught themselves, we make the student teachers live through the activities themselves, so that they are able to feel what their pupils will experience. This is followed by a moment of reflection (Hatton & Smith, 1995; Schön, 1994), to make evident the levels of learning and to focus on what research on oral skill-didactics has brought to practice.

In a second step, while taking the role of engineer, student teachers are asked to develop a particular teaching scenario with the use of digital tablets. They have to develop this in a sub-group, supported by an in-service teacher and their teacher educators. It is at this moment that, with the support of the researchers, the student teachers also develop tools for data collection, such as pre- and post-tests.

The third step brings forward the roles of teacher and observer. At this stage, student teachers (in pairs), with the support of an in-service teacher, implement their research-based teaching scenario in a classroom practice of the internship school. This is the experimentation-phase. While one pair of students is running the class, another pair is collecting data in the same class: collecting answers to pre- and post-tests, filming the different steps of the teaching scenario. The reactions of three pupils in each class are also filmed and are transcribed. Metacognitive questions (Colognesi et al., 2020) are posed in interviews to these students to gather information about how they function, the difficulties they encounter, the strategies they use, etc. During this step, teacher educators and researchers are involved in supporting the process of data collection.

While the experimentation takes place over a period of two to three weeks, the various actors collaborate in the logic of a Professional Learning Community (Darling-Hammond & Richardson, 2009). This means that they all go through a process of professional development, by collectively sharing expertise, analysing, and discussing practices. As a result, several 'crossed autoconfrontational moments' take place during school internship in the presence of teacher educators and researchers. This is guided by the principle that each activity or action should be analysed on their effectiveness during the implementation (Rix & Lièvre, 2005), as such that the involved actors are confronted with the results of their actions (Falzon & Mollo, 2004).

Even though the roles of reflective analyst and researcher are transversal to all the steps, they are specifically put forward during the fourth step. At the end of the experimentation-phase, the data set is analysed collectively. The student teachers are responsible for the statistical analysis of the quantitative data. They also carry out an analysis of the collected qualitative data: answers to metacognitive questions, traces left by students, etc. All actors are involved in the interpretation of the results, thereby bringing forward the effects of the implemented teaching scenarios.

At the end of the research-training module, students are asked to produce two documents. First, they individually produce a portfolio reflecting upon their professional development. The instructions for this portfolio are to report on perceived professional development, reviewing five aspects: self as a teacher, self and others, technology integration, methodological and pedagogical advances, and their role as a researcher. There are no constraints on the expected format or number of pages. Second, they write in pairs a research report related to their teaching scenario. They indicate the main statistical results related to the experiment. They also add qualitative data (quotes of metacognitive responses, traces of productions, etc.) to explain the quantitative results. They summarise the main results in relation to the literature.

Concerning the first production, the portfolio, a first analysis (Colognesi et al., 2019) already showed several results. First, to identify the levels of reflexivity attained by student teachers, the portfolios were analysed on the basis of the levels of reflexivity of Derobertmasure (2012). In their teaching portfolio, students reflected upon the teaching scenario that they co-constructed with their teacher educators and in-service teachers during internship. By crosschecking the data from the portfolios and the way in which student teachers managed different levels of reflexivity (Derobertmasure, 2012), we were able to identify three main reflexivity profiles.

The first profile was the most present. It refers to student teachers who focus on the teaching scenario they designed and implemented collaboratively. They described it precisely, with a wealth of contextual details and information. The portfolios of students in this profile are characterised by a strong exploitation of the first level of reflexivity (Derobertmasure, 2012): describe, become aware, question themselves, and identify their difficulties. The student teachers representing the second profile not only described the teaching scenario, but also reflected upon their professional development. They talked in terms of 'before' and 'after' the training and emphasised what they have gained by being involved in the module. The processes of 'diagnosis' and 'evaluation' are very present. Student teachers in this profile master the processes of the second level of reflexivity (Derobertmasure, 2012). The third profile was less present. Student teachers in this profile have a more global, integrated view. They use theoretical references to justify and underpin their reflections. This profile presents a more balanced and varied use of the dimensions of reflexivity.

The current research follows up on our previous study, but focuses on studying how student teachers developed the role of researcher.

4 Methodology

The aim of our study was to describe how student teachers have experienced the role of researcher, as well as to examine what it has brought to them. For this, we studied the implementation of a teacher training module with a focus on research, called DIDAC'TIC in the final year of teacher training for primary school teachers. As a reminder, the role of researcher had never been encountered by the students earlier in their training. Moreover, in the context of teacher training in Belgium, research skills are not currently expected from students. The DIDAC'TIC module is optional for student teachers, which means that the other students in the cohort find themselves in other optional modules (such as special education, extracurricular activities, didactics of mathematics, international project). All students were finalising the last year of teacher training for primary school teachers.

This study was conducted in a typical initial primary teacher education program in French Speaking Belgium. Teacher training for primary teachers (6- to 12-year-olds) is a 3-year program at a Haute Ecole. Students are trained in the mastery of 7 major competencies (Conseil supérieur pédagogique, 2010), related to (1) communication, (2) deontology and ethics, (3) teamwork, (4) critical relationship to knowledge, (5) mastery of the contents to be taught and methodological frameworks, (6) planning, implementation and evaluation of learning situations, and (7) classroom management. The decree defining initial teacher training (Decree initial training, 2000) provides for internships organised in real-life situations. This is to enable students to acquire the know-how that is based on the articulation of theory and practice. In the first year, this internship involves two weeks of collaborative practice. In the second year, student conduct and internship of four weeks and in the third year, of ten weeks. Students graduate with a bachelor's degree, which corresponds to level 6 of the Francophone qualifications framework. There is no expectation that they will be formed in research. Nevertheless, a decree (Decree defining the initial training of teachers, 2019, art. 14, p. 7) has rethought teacher training in French-speaking Belgium. A 'new' priority is visible: training for and through research. This will be possible through collaboration in teacher training between the teacher education institutes (Haute Ecoles) and universities. But the decree is struggling to be implemented and the date of implementation is constantly being postponed for the time being.

For the data collection, we made use of the curriculum materials and products produced by students as part of the teacher training module. More specifically, we analysed the portfolios of three editions of the module, i.e. from 2016 to 2019. In these portfolios, students integrated information in relation to the researcher's role they enacted during the collaborative research. In total, productions of 35 student teachers of one teacher education institute were analysed: 12 students from 2016 (2 men and 10 women), 15 students from 2017 (3 men and 12 women) and 8 students from 2018 (8 women).

For data analysis, a content analysis was applied to the 35 selected portfolios (Miles & Huberman, 1994). During data analysis, different strategies were used to ensure the trustworthiness of the findings (Creswell, 2007). In the first step, we reduced the data: all the fragments in which student teachers mentioned the role of researcher were selected. This selection was conducted by three people: two researchers and one teacher educator. The presence of the teacher educator was invaluable in making sense of certain statements. Second, we did a categorical analysis. We categorised the data based on data from previous research (Austin, 2016; Van Nieuwenhoven et al., 2021), and we also allowed new themes to emerge. Third, we have attempted to highlight quotations in order to be able to illustrate each category identified. These two steps were carried out by the two researchers who discussed together the interpretations to be given to enhance the trustworthiness of the analysis (Strauss & Corbin, 1990).

5 Findings

The findings are presented according to the themes resulting from our analyses. Five themes emerged as follows: a complex role for future teachers; research as an opportunity to focus on one particular domain; research as an opportunity to change one's beliefs and update one's knowledge; research as an opportunity to have tools to better understand pupils and regulate teaching; changing representations about research. They are illustrated by carefully selected quotations.

5.1 A Complex Role for Future Teachers

The findings showed that student teachers, at the early stage of the research-training module, considered research as something complex, abstract and of secondary importance. The student teachers emphasised that a research focus was lacking during teacher training.

> The first session as a researcher was not obvious, as I had never done this before. At first, I didn't really know what I was going to use it for. I didn't see what I could do with all the data I collected and how I was going to use it afterwards. I was more of a 'I have to do this because it is required'. (VY)

Another difficulty for the students was accepting that, during the research-training module, they were not going to be in the classroom all day. They had to adjust and accept that they were going to go to class to do the intervention based on the teaching scenario that they have developed, and then spend the rest of the time dealing with the data.

> At the beginning of the research, I had great difficulty placing myself in the role of researcher. In fact, during all my years of training, I was used to being a trainee in a classroom and taking charge of the pupils' entire school day. In this research-training module, it was normal to join 'only' the elementary school to carry out the oral teaching activities and to collect data and to leave afterwards. (FA)

> We were no longer trainees as usual, but research students: we were asked to film, record, transcribe, question, and also analyze the results. At the beginning, it was not simple, we did not know how to do all of that. (DE)

Difficulties in adopting the role of researcher also included the complexity for student teachers of reading a scientific article. They explained that they were not used to it. They mentioned that they have not learned how to do it. They also indicated that this requires a great degree of concentration.

> When we started working on our research paper and read an article, I realized that some things were more difficult. For example, I couldn't concentrate from the beginning to the end because it was a long article and so I ended up dropping out at some point. This is, on the one hand, linked to the length of the article but also to the vocabulary which is linked to the context and therefore is not always easy to understand. (PA)

This idea gradually changed through the course of the research-training module. At the end of the module, students started to value research and educational theory. Several benefits emerged from the portfolio analysis to justify this change.

5.2   *Research as an Opportunity to Focus on One Particular Domain*

The students reported that the research-training module allowed them to focus on one domain: the development of oral skills. This was the first time since the beginning of their training that they have been able to devote all their time to one aspect of teaching/learning. They explained that it was interesting because they were not in 'survival mode', what they experience when they are in charge of classroom management. They expressed that they were able to really focus on a single teaching issue, as well as to take the time to understand what was going on in the instructional program.

> I was privileged to be able to participate in such a large-scale project. I had never had the opportunity to position myself as a researcher to understand a problem. Here, I had the time to dedicate myself to this. (MA)

> Usually, we have to manage everything. From 8:30 am to 3:30 pm. When we go home, we make corrections and prepare for the next day. It's a rush. I must admit that I didn't have much time during my internships to really observe the students. To analyze their mistakes in the exercises. Here, we had time to sit down. There was time during the day for that. And also to watch the videos of our teaching. I really learned a lot. (TA)

5.3   *Research as an Opportunity to Change One's Beliefs and Update One's Knowledge*

Students described in their portfolios that having read recent research in the field of oral education has allowed them to change their beliefs on the subject.

They explained that it were the theoretical frameworks but also the interventions presented in the articles, which are closer to their reality, that contributed to a change in beliefs.

> During my training, I never learned how to develop students' oral communication skills. And the perceptions I had about this learning process were wrong. Through reading the articles, and the interventions presented in them, I was able to adjust my knowledge and also get ideas for my practice. (TO)

Another idea that emerged is that research makes it possible to update its practices. In short, by reading up-to-date studies, student teachers learned about what practices are effective and can be used to aim for student success.

> We read articles, current studies on teaching. It helped me understand the basics to guide me through my practice. With current and proven ideas. It's important to have this information, to educate yourself, in order to be better prepared. (CH)

In addition, it seemed that a lever for students to apprehend scientific articles has been the fact that the text was closely related to what they were doing in training.

> It was the first time I read a scientific article related to an experience I had. It made it really interesting to read because you could identify yourself through the article. (MA)

> A personal contribution that I would also like to emphasize was developed while reading a research article. It was very similar to what we are doing. What I got from this reading was the fact that for the first time I enjoyed reading a scientific article. Indeed, I let myself be carried away by the text, the arguments/explanations of the results. This is certainly due to the fact that for once, before reading this article, I had experienced something similar myself, so I found myself in this project. (AP)

5.4 Research as an Opportunity to Have Tools to Better Understand Pupils and Regulate Teaching

Portfolio analysis showed that student teachers found that the research has given them the opportunity to observe their pupils better. They explained that the data collection tools gave them access to how students functioned. These included metacognitive questions and videos where pupils are active.

> Questioning the pupils and collecting metacognitive data allowed us to really identify our pupils, and to have access to their functioning, their way of thinking, etc. The analysis of these responses allowed me to have an impact on the way I acted with them, to differentiate. I had never taken the time to do that. (MA)

Other tools also allowed student teachers to understand the pupils' level, with more rigour and evidence than usual. For instance, they referred to the tests taken before and after the interventions to measure pupils' progress.

> And that allowed me to observe the students in another way, more carefully, to have identical criteria of success for each student, to carry out an in-depth observation on a particular subject. It allowed me to realize that it is possible to objectively perceive student evolution. (SI)

Besides, having conducted the analyses allowed the student teachers to see where the students' difficulties were situated. They explained that it showed them with certainty whether the intervention worked. It also provided information on aspects of the subject matter that needed to be reworked. In the end, the research seemed to have given students keys to regulate the learning process of their pupils.

> We analysed the data collected. With the researchers, we learned to read the statistical results. This allowed us to really see what the students have integrated well and where there are still problems. I usually do it intuitively. It was a very positive experience. (CH)

> We did statistics based on the pre- and post-test but also based on the children's intermediate productions. My main fear was that there would not be enough significant evolution. But I realized that the students did evolve. The fact that we have these statistics shows if the children have evolved and if they have mastered the subject better. (AR)

> Doing this allowed us to see the analysis that can be done on a project and to see what we will have to modify in the following teaching activities. (AP)

In addition to these various benefits, it also emerged from the portfolio analysis that students have changed their representations from the initial ideas about research.

5.5 Changing Representations about Research

Students explained that the module allowed them to develop new skills: reading a scientific text, being sensitive to data analysis, etc.

> Everything became clearer as time went on and I moved more into a 'It would be interesting to still have this as data for later'. (VY)

> 'Doing statistical analysis? But how? Can someone help me? I don't know what to do with all these numbers!' All these thoughts accompanied me at the beginning. Fortunately, a trainer/researcher was by our side to enlighten us with regard to these reflections. Thus, these numbers, complex for me at the beginning, became clear and understandable, I knew how to analyze them afterwards. (TH)

They mentioned that they finally enjoyed doing it. Many also said that they would be willing to go through this again if possible.

> Finally, I had a lot of fun doing the research report, with the analysis of the graphs, the collection of data from the oral and written pre- and post-test... The interpretation of the numbers and their justification is an aspect that I really like in the role of researcher. (TA)

> Although I wish I had felt more suited to this task from the start, I know that now I could take on this role again and be better prepared, if I had to do it again. (CE)

And finally, some students reported that the experience made them desire to continue their studies through research. They mentioned a master's degree in educational sciences in particular.

> Finally, the last role I had to take on was that of researcher. This was the element of the project that worried me the most, as it was a role that was still unknown to me. The definition of researcher is a member of a team, involved in scientific research. Being a member of a team still appeals to me a lot, and with Noémie, it was easy and pleasant. During my school years, I had never had to do scientific research before. So I had a lot of

questions bubbling up inside of me. Now, having written my personal development and having handed in my final paper, it means, inevitably, that I have done this scientific research and that I have overcome my fear. I enjoyed taking this position of researcher. I can already read a statistical table, describe it, find a question to answer and then develop it. I am proud of what I have accomplished and how far I have come. And I think I will continue to do so next year. (JE)

Already now, I want to finalize my studies with a master's degree and thanks to the discoveries made during this module, I wonder if I wouldn't go for a master's degree in the field of research on school education rather than in the field of remedial education. (BR)

It also seems that, for some, the research module contributed to an additional awareness of the need for further training. This included, according to students, the updating of knowledge through reading studies in the field of education.

It seems essential to me to continue to train myself, in order to be able to act in this society where everything is in constant evolution. Reflective analyses have taught us to know how to question ourselves, and research, through articles and also the instruments to understand what the pupils are doing, can allow us to face up to improve and adapt ourselves. Except that all this will have been for nothing if we take our diploma as the only proof of our competence in teaching. I need to continue to read and keep up to date with research findings. (AL)

6 Discussion

In the current context of school organisations, and with the increasing accountability pressure, teacher research has received increased attention. Future teachers need to be able to use and conduct research to improve their own practices. In many countries, teacher education programmes have incorporated research activities within their curricula, to prepare student teachers to become extended instead of restricted professionals (Afdal & Spernes, 2018). Nevertheless, studies show that it is not easy to make student teachers' see the value of educational research, nor for in-service teachers use research insights. Often, research is seen as being disconnected from their daily classroom practices.

This chapter focused on bridging the theory-to-practice gap within teacher education programmes, by educating student teachers about research through research. We believed that the implementation of a collaborative research design could be a promising strategy to prepare future teachers. Through participation in a research-training module, student teachers gradually changed their perspectives towards educational theory and research. The results show how they were able to co-construct a teaching scenario and analyse its effects. In addition, the module contributed to student teachers' reflexivity (Altet, 2004; Colognesi et al., 2021; Donnay & Charlier, 2008).

The results of this study show how educating about research through research, while going through a variety of roles, is innovative both in the design of the module as well as in the protocol of the research. Firstly, this research-training module bridges the worlds of practitioners and of researchers, leading these partners in education to work together on questions that both consider as being relevant. Secondly, by involving student teachers into a research project, they learn the importance of collaboration in future research projects.

Our study confirms the results of previous studies, in which conducting collaborative research is described as a promising activity in educating student teachers, but only when it is done in a purposeful, deliberate, and reflective way. More specifically, in the teacher-training module, research was not presented as something being disconnected from the teaching activity, but was seen as a continuous part of the teaching practice (Dobber et al., 2012), in a perspective of alternation (Chaubet et al., 2018; Merhan et al., 2007; Pentecouteau, 2012). Moreover, our study confirms how involving student teachers in collaborative research, contributes to their reflective skills, a more innovative stance, and more informed decisions in practice (Hagevik et al., 2012).

Based on our results, we postulate that a sixth type of professional learning activity is to be added to the five identified in the literature (Geijsel et al., 2009; Janssen & van Yperen, 2004; Kwakman, 2003): take on the role of researcher. And we believe that enacting the role of researcher should be a priority in the training of future teachers, as mentioned in the planned reform (Decree defining the initial training of teachers, 2019).

7   Study Limitations and Future Research

This study had some limitations that may suggest future research opportunities. First, data collection focused on student teachers' perspectives, through a portfolio analysis. These portfolios were intended to report on the students' opinions, reactions and developments during the research-training module.

They were to be read by the trainers. In this sense, we do not know if the students' words are sincere or intended to please the readers, although the content was not evaluated. Exploring this aspect, with oral interviews conducted with a researcher from outside the training module, could allow for cross-checking information.

Moreover, since inquiry-based working aims to improve classroom practice, future research needs to study the impact on pupils' outcomes. Since collaborative research implies a partnership between different actors, future research can also take into account the experiences of the different actors involved. In what way did it change teacher educators' beliefs and practices, as well as how did it contribute to school improvement of the involved schools. This is all the more interesting because, in the French-speaking context, some teacher educators feel that they are not competent in the field of research (Van Nieuwenhoven et al., 2021).

Moreover, it is relevant to explore how student teachers once graduated transferred this to their school practices, and analyse the working conditions (structural and cultural conditions) that are necessary to implement inquiry-based working in school organisations. Here, for instance, teacher education institutes could create partnerships with school organisations to create spaces and time where student teachers, in-service teachers, and teacher educators collaborate together.

8 Conclusions

In conclusion, we would argue that it seems necessary that the role of researcher be assumed by the student teacher. We see at least three important conditions for this to be possible. First, teacher candidates should conduct research related to a particular teaching strategy and focused on improving student learning. As such, the research should be directly related to teachers' practices and be concrete to aim for their understanding and improvement. Second, it seems important to give them time to both understand the role of researcher they are taking up, but also to be able to devote themselves to the various activities related to it. In this sense, 'freeing up' the schedule from all other activities allowed the future teachers to focus on the objectives that the research training module was pursuing. Third, for this work to be possible, it seems necessary to have a close partnership with the internship supervisors. Thus, in a collaborative research perspective, they will also be involved in the research because the problematic at hand will also affect them. This is also a way of reducing the gap between the objects of the training and what is experienced during the internship (Hernandez & Ducrey-Monnier, 2020). Our study has shown how conducting research as a professional learning activity, can be a valuable strategy to improve the quality of teaching and strengthen the quality of teacher education (see also Van Katwijk et al., 2021; Willegems et al., 2018). Through the implementation of collaborative research partnerships (here: between student teachers, in-service teachers, teacher educators, and researchers), the involved actors not only developed their research skills, but also other competencies related to the teaching profession. On the long term, these partnerships, could further improve the quality of teacher education, by creating more close synergies between research and practice, and by closing the space between teacher education institutions and schools (Menter & Flores, 2021).

References

Afdal, H. W., & Spernes, K. (2018). Designing and redesigning research-based teacher education. *Teaching and Teacher Education, 74*, 215–228.

Altet, M. (2004). L'analyse de pratiques en formation initiale des enseignants : développer une pratique réflexive sur et pour l'action [Analysis of practice in initial teacher training: Developing a reflective practice on and for action]. *Éducation Permanente, 160*, 101–111.

Altet, M., Desjardins, J., Etienne, R., Paquay, L., & Perrenoud, P. (2013). *Former des enseignants réflexifs: Obstacles et résistances* [*Training reflective teachers: obstacles and resistance*]. De Boeck.

Austin, R. (Ed.). (2016). *Researching primary education*. Sage Books.

Baan, J., Gaikhorst, L., van 't Noordende, J. E., & Volman, M. L. L. (2019). The involvement in inquiry-based working of teachers of research-intensive versus practically oriented teacher education programmes. *Teaching and Teacher Education, 84*, 74–82.

Bourassa, M., Bélair, L., & Chevalier, J. (2007). Les outils de la recherche participative [The tools of participatory research]. *Éducation et Francophonie, 35*(2), 1–11.

Bucheton, D. (2014). *Refonder l'enseignement de l'écriture* [*Refounding the teaching of writing*]. Retz.

Caena, J. (2011). *Literature review: Quality in teacher's continuing professional development*. European Commission.

Chaubet, P., Leroux, M., Masson, C., Gervais, C., & Malo, A. (2018). *Apprendre et enseigner en contexte d'alternance. Vers la définition d'un noyau conceptuel* [*Learning and teaching in a work-study context. Towards the definition of a conceptual framework*]. Presses de l'Université du Québec.

Christianakis, M. (2010). Collaborative research and teacher education. *Issues in Teacher Education, 19*, 109–125.

Coburn, C. E., & Penuel, W. R. (2016). Research-practice partnerships in education: Outcomes, dynamics, and open questions. *Educational Researcher, 45*, 48–54.

Cochran-Smith, M., Barnatt, J., Friedman, A., & Pine, G. (2009). Inquiry on inquiry: Practitioner research and students' learning. *Action in Teacher Education, 31*(2), 17–32.

Cochran-Smith, M., & Lytle, S. L. (2009). *Inquiry as stance. Practitioner research for the next generation.* Teachers College Press.

Colognesi, S. (2017). Un dispositif de recherche-formation sur l'enseignement/apprentissage de l'oral en milieu scolaire : le cas de DIDAC'TIC [A research-training program on the teaching/learning of oral language in schools: the case of DIDAC'TIC]. *La lettre de l'AIRDF, 62*, 21–26.

Colognesi, S., & Balleux, L. (2018). Former les futurs instituteurs primaires à utiliser les tablettes numériques dans leur classe: Une spécialisation optionnelle en Haute École pédagogique [Training future primary school teachers to use digital tablets in the classroom: An optional specialization at the Haute École pédagogique]. *Frantice.net, 14*(1), 7–23.

Colognesi, S., Deprit, A., Coppe, T., Van Nieuwenhoven, C., März, V., & Hanin, V. (2021). Developing student teachers' reflexivity toward their course planning: Implementation of a training program focused on writing and reflective skills. *Sage Open*. https://doi.org/10.1177/21582440211016897

Colognesi, S., Deschepper, C., Balleux, L., & März, V. (2019). Quel accompagnement des étudiants dans la production d'un texte réflexif, à l'intérieur du travail de fin d'études? Le cas d'un module de formation des futurs enseignants du primaire [What support for students in the production of a reflective text, within the end-of-study work? The case of a training module for future primary school teachers]. *Formation et Pratiques D'enseignement en Question, 25*, 79–101.

Colognesi, S., & Lucchini, S. (in press). LETRA: A teacher training program based on the adoption of different roles. *Mc Gill Journal of Education*.

Colognesi, S., Piret, C., Demorsy, S., & Barbier, E. (2020). Teaching Writing – with or without metacognition? An Exploratory study of 11-to 12-Year-old students writing a book review. *International Electronic Journal of Elementary Education, 12*(5), 459–470.

Conseil Supérieur Pédagogique. (2010). *Référentiel des compétences de l'enseignant* [*Teacher competency framework*]. Fédération Wallonie Bruxelles.

Coppe, T., Raemdonck, I., März, V., Parmentier, M., Brouhier, Q., & Colognesi, S. (2020). L'insertion professionnelle des enseignants au travers des multiples aspects de la socialisation au travail. ISaTE : un instrument de mesure pour les appréhender

[Teachers' induction through the multiple aspects of work socialization. ISaTE: a measurement instrument]. *Mesure et Évaluation en Éducation, 43*(3), 67–102.

Creswell, J. (2007). *Qualitative inquiry and research design: Choosing among five approaches* (2nd ed.). Sage.

Darling-Hammond, L. (2017). Teacher education around the world: What can we learn from international practice? *European Journal of Teacher Education, 40*, 291–309.

Darling-Hammond, L., & Richardson, N. (2009). Research review. Teacher learning: What matters? *How Teachers Learn, 66*(5), 46–53.

Décret 'formation initiale': Décret de la Fédération Wallonie-Bruxelles du 12 décembre 2000 définissant la formation initiale des instituteurs et des régents. 2000. *Moniteur belge*, 19 janvier, p. 25501. https://www.gallilex.cfwb.be

Décret définissant la formation initiale des enseignants : Décret de la Fédération Wallonie – Bruxelles du 7 février 2019 définissant la formation initiale des enseignants. 2019.

Derobertmasure, A. (2012). *La formation initiale des enseignants et le développement de la réflexivité ? Objectivation du concept et analyse des productions orales et écrites des futurs enseignants* [Initial teacher training and the development of reflexivity? Objectivation of the concept and analysis of the oral and written productions of future teachers] [Thèse de doctorat]. Université de Mons. https://tel.archives-ouvertes.fr/tel-00726944

Desgagné, S., & Larouche, H. (2010). Quand la collaboration de recherche sert la légitimation d'un savoir d'expérience [When research collaboration serves the legitimization of experiential knowledge]. *Recherches en Éducation, 1*, 7–18.

Dobber, M., Akkerman, S. F., Verloop, N., & Vermunt, J. D. (2012). Student teachers' collaborative research: Small-scale research projects during teacher education. *Teaching and Teacher Education, 28*(4), 609–617.

Dolz, J., & Gagnon, R. (2008). Le genre du texte, un outil didactique pour développer le langage oral et écrit [The text genre, a didactic tool for developing oral and written language]. *Pratiques, 137/138*, 179–198.

Dolz, J., & Schneuwly, B. (1998). *Pour un enseignement de l'oral : initiation aux genres formels publics* [For a teaching of the oral language: introduction to public formal genres]. ESF.

Donnay, J., & Charlier, E. (2008). *Apprendre par l'analyse de pratiques. Initiation au compagnonnage réflexif* [Learning through the analysis of practices. Initiation to reflective companionship]. Presses Universitaires de Namur.

Duroisin, N., Beauset, R., & Simon, L. (2020). Description d'un dispositif de formation de type 'lesson study' basé sur la collaboration entre étudiants d'Université et de Haute École : former à et par la recherche [Description of a 'lesson study' type of training system based on collaboration between university and college students: Training in and through research]. *Revue Hybride de L'éducation, 4*(4), 114–152.

Falzon, P., & Mollo, V. (2004). Auto- and allo-confrontation as tools for reflective activities. *Applied Ergonomics, 35*, 531–540.

Flores, M. A. (2017). Practice, theory and research in initial teacher education: International perspectives. *European Journal of Teacher Education, 40,* 287–290.

Geijsel, F., Sleegers, P., Stoel, R., & Krüger, M. (2009). The effect of teacher psychological, school organizational and leadership factors on teachers' professional learning in Dutch schools. *The Elementary School Journal, 109*(4), 406–427.

Hagevik, R., Aydeniz, M., & Rowell, C. G. (2012). Using action research in middle level teacher education to evaluate and deepen reflective practice. *Teaching and Teacher Education, 28*(5), 675–684.

Hammerness, K. M., Darling-Hammond, L., Bransford, J., Berliner, D., Cocharan-Smith, M., McDonald, M., & Zeichner K. (2005). How teachers learn and develop. In L. Darling-Hammond & J. Bransford (Eds.), *Preparing teachers for a changing world: What teachers should learn and be able to do* (pp. 358–389). Jossey-Bass.

Hatton, N., & Smith, D. (1995). Reflection in teacher education: Towards definition and implementation. *Teaching and Teacher Education, 11*(1), 33–49.

Hernandez, S., & Ducrey-Monnier, M. (2020) 'Je n'utilise pas la théorie dans ma pratique de tous les jours'. Echanges entre praticiens formateurs et enseignants HEP autour de concepts théoriques issus des didactiques ['I don't use theory in my everyday practice'. Exchanges between practitioner trainers and HEP teachers around theoretical concepts from didactics]. *Formation et Pratiques D'enseignement en Questions, 26,* 17–36.

Horverak, M. O. (2016). An experimental study on the effect of systemic functional linguistics applied through a genre-pedagogy approach to teaching writing. In *Yearbook of the Poznań linguistic meeting 2* (pp. 67–89). De Gruyter.

Janssen, O., & van Yperen, N. W. (2004). Employees' goal orientations, the quality of leader-member exchange, and the outcomes of job performance and job satisfaction. *Academy of Management Journal, 47,* 368–384.

Kwakman, K. (2003). Factors affecting teachers' participation in professional learning activities. *Teaching and Teacher Education, 19,* 149–170.

März, V., Gaikhorst, L., & Van Nieuwenhoven, C. (2019). Entrer dans le métier, c'est plus qu'enseigner. Comment préparer les futurs enseignants à assumer leur rôle organisationnel? [Entering the profession is more than just teaching. How do we prepare future teachers to assume their organizational role?] *Éducation & Formation, 315,* 65–81.

März, V., & Kelchtermans, G. (2020). The networking teacher in action: A qualitative analysis of early career teachers' induction process. *Teaching and Teacher Education, 87,* 102933. doi:10.1080/02619768.2021.1928070

Menter, I., & Flores, M. A. (2021). Connecting research and professionalism in teacher education. *European Journal of Teacher Education, 44,* 115–127.

Merhan, F., Ronveaux, C., & Vanhulle, S. (2007). *Alternance en formation* [Alternation in training]. De Boeck.

Meyers, E., & Rust, F. (2003). *Taking action with teacher research*. Heinemann.

Miles, M., & Huberman, A. (1994). *Qualitative date analysis*. Sage Publications.

Mukamurera, J. (2014). Le développement professionnel et la persévérance en enseignement. Éclairage théorique et état des lieux [Professional development and perseverance in teaching. Theoretical background and state of the art]. In L. Portelance, S. Martineau, & J. Mukamurera (Eds.), *Développement et persévérance professionnels en enseignement. Oui mais comment?* (pp. 9–33). Les presses de l'Université du Québec.

Nitonde, F., & Paquay, L. (2011). Vers quelles pratiques de stage en formation initiale des enseignants du secondaire? Analyse des conceptions des enseignants de l'ENS au Burundi [Towards what practices of internship in initial training of secondary school teachers? Analysis of the conceptions of ENS teachers in Burundi]. *Education & Formation, 295*, 143–164.

Pentecouteau, H. (2012). L'alternance dans une formation professionnelle universitaire. De l'idéal épistémologique aux contradictions pédagogiques [The alternation in a university professional training. From the epistemological ideal to pedagogical contradictions]. *Revue Internationale de Pédagogie de L'enseignement Universitaire, 28*(1), 1–11.

Perez-Roux, T. (2016). Formation des enseignants et mobilisation des savoirs. La formation des enseignants du secondaire en France: entre universitarisation et professionnalisation, quelle mobilisation des savoirs en fonction des contextes ? [Teacher training and knowledge mobilization. The training of secondary school teachers in France: between academicization and professionalization, what mobilization of knowledge according to the contexts?] *Education & Formation* [online], *e-305*, 11–22. https://hal.archives-ouvertes.fr/hal-01710897

Portelance, L., Mukamurera, J., Martineau, S., & Gervais, C. (2008). *L'insertion dans le milieu scolaire: Une phase cruciale du développement professionnel de l'enseignant* [Induction into the school environment: A crucial phase in a teacher's professional development]. PUL.

Rix, G., & Lièvre, P. (2005). Une mise en perspective de modes d'investigation de l'activité humaine [A perspective on modes of investigation of human activity]. In *Actes du 6e congrès européen de Sciences des Systèmes*. ENSAM.

Schön, D. (1993). *Le praticien réflexif. A la recherche du savoir caché dans l'agir professionnel* [The reflective practitioner. In search of knowledge hidden in the professional act]. Editions Logiques.

Shulman, L. S., & Shulman, J. H. (2004). How and what teachers learn: Shifting perspective. *Journal of Curriculum Studies, 36*(2), 256–271.

Snoek, M., Bekebrede, J., Hanna, F., Creton, T., & Edzes, H. (2017). The contribution of graduation research to school development: Graduation research as a boundary practice. *European Journal of Teacher Education, 40,* 361–378.

Strauss, A., & Corbin, J. (1990). *Basics of qualitative research: Grounded theory procedures and techniques.* Sage.

Van der Linden, W., Bakx, A., Ros, A., Beijaard, D., & Vermeulen, M. (2012). Student teachers' development of a positive attitude towards research and research knowledge and skills. *European Journal of Teacher Education, 35,* 401–419.

Van Katwijk, L., Jansen, E., & Van Veen, K. (2021) Pre-service teacher research: A way to future-proof teachers? *European Journal of Teacher Education.* doi:10.1080/02619768.2021.1928070

Van Nieuwenhoven, C., Leroux, L., & Colognesi, S. (2021). Synergies between educational science research and teacher training: An illustration of research as supporting training of future primary school teachers. *Academia, 22,* 147–170.

Vivegnis, I. (2019). Postures d'accompagnement et conceptions : une évidente interrelation ? Quatre cas sous la loupe en contexte d'insertion professionnelle [Coaching postures and conceptions: an obvious interrelation? Four cases under the microscope in a context of professional insertion]. *Phronesis, 1*(1–2), 48–63.

Willegems, V., Consuegra, E., Struyven, K., & Engels, N. (2018). Pre-service teachers as members of a collaborative teacher research team: A steady track to extended professionalism? *Teaching and Teacher Education, 76,* 126–139.

Zeichner, K. (2003). The adequacies and inadequacies of three current strategies to recruit, prepare, and retain the best teachers for all students. *Teachers College Record, 105,* 490–519.

CHAPTER 16

Quality in Teaching and Teacher Education

Key Dilemmas and Implications for Research, Policy and Practice

Joanna Madalinska-Michalak, Björn Åstrand and Marco Snoek

Abstract

The purpose of this final chapter is twofold: (1) to provide a synthesis of learning on quality in teaching and teacher education based on the analyses and discussions of the fifteen chapters collected in this book, and (2) to discuss implications that have emerged for future research on quality in teaching and teacher education, policy and practice. In so doing, we ask: What do we know about quality in teaching and teacher education from the collected chapters, and how can these findings inform future research, policy and practice in these areas? In order to answer these questions, this closing chapter is divided into five main parts. In the first part, we identify and endorse a call that is present in all chapters to move beyond a reductionist notion of education. In the second part, we recognise the growing attention to teaching quality both as a blessing and a burden. In the third part, we identify seven key dilemmas that arise from the different chapters. Next we use these dilemmas to identify implications for teacher education practice, policy and research. We then conclude this chapter with some final reflections on what we have learnt in the collected chapters about reimagining and rethinking teacher education quality and the challenges ahead.

Keywords

quality – quality in teaching and teacher education – teacher – teacher education – key dilemmas – move beyond a reductionist notion of education – resonance

1   Introduction

The preceding chapters in this book reflect the many scholarly perspectives on understanding the complex concept of quality in teaching and teacher education in relation to the current and future conditions of teaching, learning, and learning to teach. The richness of the work of colleagues from a range of geographic, political, economic, cultural, educational, and research contexts has a significant role to play in inspiring researchers, policy-makers and practitioners by identifying some directions, questions, and methods through which we may deepen our exploration and understandings of the issue of quality in teaching and teacher education.

A synthesis of the fifteen chapters organised into the three parts of this volume would allow us to explore the concept of quality in teaching and teacher education through the following seven key dilemmas that emerged from the discussions in these chapters:

– Teacher quality or teaching quality
– A static or dynamic concept
– An isolated or embedded concept
– An individual or collaborative concept
– A narrow or broad concept
– A standardised or contextual concept
– A fixed and defined concept or a dynamic and dialogical concept

Our discussion of these dilemmas is preceded by an indication of our position on how to move beyond the reductionist notion of education and by a short but important discussion on the key role of teachers in societies. We argue that in considerations of the quality in teaching and teacher education, it is essential that we acknowledge the interconnected complexities of teaching and of learning to teach. At the same time, the issue of quality and its meanings in teaching and teacher education needs to be problematised in terms of the context of teacher education reforms, specific features of practice at national, regional and local levels, and serious challenges to the teaching profession in these turbulent times. Establishing essential relationships with a changing world – relations that enable us to live in harmony, meaningfully, and in resonance with others, with the world and with ourselves – has become a priority task for education and teacher education both today and in the future.

2   Beyond a Reductionist Notion of Education

The different contributions to this book show that we cannot look at education in isolation, but must also consider the wider societal context. Education and teacher education have always been influenced by societal challenges and the changing priorities of the times. In this anthology, we have chapters on this with regard to the impacts of the pandemic situation (Hordatt Gentles et al.; Tur Porres & Ires Carrera; Eloff & du Plessis) as well as war (Symenonidis et al.).

The very origin of education as a deliberate activity can be understood to be about responding to certain needs of people and to certain times. Exercises in power and control, as well as more enlightened agendas concerning enablement, have driven education down the years and continue to do so. Compulsory schooling in modern society grew from societal needs for the labour force, competence, etc., but we have to distinguish between articulated purposes, *de facto* functions and how societal challenges permeate into educational discourses, practices and policies. Apparently, substantial frictions are always part of these processes: sometimes these are visible in open clashes, and sometimes more subtle. There will always be tensions around how we perceive the purpose of education as questions 'about the nature and purposes of education are ultimately questions about what it is to be, and about how we understand what it is to be, human' (Standish, 2003, p. 231). Hence, it is important for us to use these occasions as opportunities to build insights into what it is that is most important in our time and in our context. As professionals, we have to approach this not as a battle but as an option for progress by argument. Along that line of thinking, in this volume, Goodwin outlines five domains of knowledge of particular importance for thinking anew – particularly about quality teacher educator preparation.

While endorsing such an approach, we would also point toward a disturbing problem: education increasingly appears to lack the capacity to address the most poignant and agonising peculiarities of our time. Humanity has produced astonishing inventions relating to the quality of life. We now have tools that can make in a blink of an eye what previously took years to accomplish, we have inventions that can effortlessly process in minutes what earlier took not only a huge amount of time but also great labour, we can produce more food than ever, we can cure most diseases, we can communicate over vast distances, and we are experiencing what are probably among the lowest levels of violence since the introduction of agriculture thousands of years ago and the social orders that consequently emerged. And yet, in modern societies, we are experiencing a number of devastating shortcomings like alienation and deep discontent centred on well-being, freedom, and rights. In education, we are in search of ways to address challenges articulated in the UN's sustainable development goals (SDG s), but we appear to be neglecting and failing the wider challenge of human well-being and discontent with it. Irma Eloff and Anna-Barbara du Plessis (Chapter 8) point towards the need for teacher education programmes to address this and how policy could endorse several support factors that hold the promise of at least some mitigation in all of this.

The German sociologist Hartmut Rosa has described in detail the paradoxical contemporary situation in which societal acceleration is frequently the cause of such alienation in our modern world. We are not any happier or more content, and we fail to establish essential relationships with the world – relationships that would allow us to live meaningfully and in resonance with the world and with ourselves (Rosa, 2019). According to Aristotle, happiness or 'living well' should be the informing ethical purpose for humans, and it is hard to understand why such ambitions for human well-being are not employed to direct contemporary education to a greater degree. That said, a central task for teacher education seems to be to reinvent education to properly respond to such fundamentally central but also demanding challenges. Fifty years ago, such approaches were arguably seen as central and implicit within the international policy agenda for education. For instance, the seminal UNESCO report of 1972 on *The world of education today and tomorrow* bore the main title *Learning to be* (UNESCO, 1972). The notion of education in that report was broad, and it offered a profoundly holistic analysis of how education could contribute to individual advancement and societal improvement through science, solidarity and democracy. Along similar lines, the equally seminal 1996 UNESCO report focusing on establishing a learning society outlined many of what still remain challenges for education in the twenty-first century. This was published under the title *Learning: The treasure within* (UNESCO, 1996). These reports echo in their perspectives and concepts an understanding of education and its potential role, a more sincere and more hopeful understanding as they address how societal challenges are also challenges for education, and discuss education from a comparatively more holistic perspective than those that have become the norm of our time.

If education is about 'learning to be in the world' and if learning is 'a treasure within', and if we agree with Aristotle that living well is the purpose and meaning of life, we cannot address issues of teacher quality and quality in teaching and teacher education without paying attention to these perspectives.

As long as education is narrowed into what is easily measurable, and as long as it is reduced to 'only' issues of qualification and employability, it will fail coming generations. The reduction of what education is about can have different features. Kay Livingston points towards standards-based understandings of teacher competence (Chapter 1), Helle Plauborg (Chapter 5) points towards how overly managerial notions about teaching and simplified descriptions based upon certain dichotomies shadow important aspects of teaching that the didactic tradition entails, and Noel Purdy, Kathy Hall, Daria Khanolainen and Conor Galvin (Chapter 3) voice concerns over the growth and impact of a delimiting, economically oriented notion of education.

According to long-standing, more humanistic educational traditions, education is about the whole person and in support of every individual in their search for their singular possibilities, their wider sense of belonging, and in warrants offering at least some agency over their life (Biesta, 2010, pp. 22-25; Biesta & Stengel, 2016, pp. 31-37). Rosa also voices this tradition when he asserts that 'the educational process consists in learning how we relate to or (have to) position ourselves towards [...] various spheres of action and life, these potential axes of resonance' (Rosa, 2019, p. 239). In essence, Rosa argues that during modernity – with all its incredible progress in many societal areas – there have emerged tangible shortcomings, primarily in how humans relate to the world. Within Rosa's terminology, we are failing to develop capacities to live in resonance with the world.

Of course, while education and teacher education need to be mobilised to counter this troublesome development, not every aspect of societal challenges can or should be devolved to education (Tröhler, 2017). That said, education is central to how we perceive the world, and education shapes prospects for individuals as well as society to a high degree. The argument here, therefore, is that education must be sensitive to the world in which we live and responsive to its changing nature and that our response must be values-guided so that we respond *educationally* and *adequately* to changes in human conditions.

Teacher and teaching qualities must be understood within a conjunction of purposes, ambitions and challenges, both technical and ideational. Contemporary education is often considered slightly negatively as 'mass education'. But the fact is that access to education has been transformed – opening it out from the preserve of a tiny elite into being accessible to the many. Along with this, there have been remarkable efforts to move well beyond low-quality offerings and to develop educational opportunities for all that adequately reflect perspectives of changing societal values.

In Europe, much of this has its origins within the *Bildung* tradition of Humbolt and Herder, in which education is about cultivating 'the most harmonious possible development of the whole person' and understanding education as 'a complex process of adaptive transformation of the world' (Rosa, 2019, p. 241, original emphasis). In this perspective, teaching is about 'making the world resound' for students (ibid, p. 243). However, such approaches to education are proving increasingly incompatible with today's reductionist notions of education.

How we understand the emerging purposes and intentions of education and how these catalyse practices in our schools and systems that increasingly fold into narrow economic rationales is definitely a problem. At the core of this shift is a series of values and practices that can detach teachers and students from the most valuable aspects of education: its aim to support children and youngsters to find themselves and their meaning in life or, as Rosa would put it, to be in resonance with the world.

3   Recognising the Key Role of Teachers: A Blessing and a Burden

The authors of the different chapters of this book provide varied perspectives on the concepts of teaching quality and teacher education quality. Regardless of these variations, they all share the same starting point: teachers are crucial actors in the development of children and young people and in providing them opportunities to engage and participate in society and to shape their own future. This starting point can be recognised not only in the different chapters of this book but also more widely in national and European debates and policies on education.

This wide recognition of the key role of teachers can be seen as a blessing, as it confirms the importance and life-changing role of each and every teacher and – connected to that – the importance of teacher education to prepare them for this key role. At the same time, this recognition can also be understood as a burden, as it can easily lead to a strong pre-occupation, sometimes bordering on fixation, among politicians, policy-makers and society with the quality of teachers and teacher education. As education impacts each and every one of us and as national governments have a heavy responsibility to provide quality education for everyone, the quality of teachers and of teacher education can readily become a matter of national and European concern.

This concern helps explain the multitudes of policy initiatives, policy papers, projects, measures and actors that aim to strengthen the quality of teaching and teacher education. However, a key question for all these initiatives and actors is how teaching quality needs to be understood. This is not often adequately addressed. In fact, one could say that teaching quality is a contested concept, with multiple actors bringing oftentimes conflicting perspectives and concerns to the activities. These different perspectives can easily create confusion and misunderstandings and might also lead to a battleground of deeply contested positions regarding what needs to be understood as key elements of quality and which stakeholder group(s) should have a say in this. This, unfortunately, can involve issues of power and interdiction where the preoccupation of policymakers with safe-guarding the quality of education through quality in teaching can threaten to reduce the collective and individual professional autonomy of teachers. This, in turn, can affect teachers' ability to make the pedagogical decisions they need to make for the sake of their students. The ultimate and ironic impact of this can be that the focus on safe-guarding the quality of teaching may reduce the attractiveness of the profession and paradoxically lead to excellent teachers leaving, therby ultimately reducing teaching quality.

This suggests that the debate on teaching quality is of crucial importance and that the key question needs to be the following: How can we support teachers to maintain and develop their quality in such a way that it supports their passion and dedication towards pupils without reducing their professionalism and the attractiveness of the profession?

By creating different and wider perspectives on teaching quality, the authors in this book contribute to finding answers to this question. By foregrounding different viewpoints, they help to make implicit views and intrinsic models of what it is to teach and to be a teacher more explicit and so create the opportunity for an open dialogue on teaching quality and teacher education quality.

4 Key Dilemmas

In this section, we synthesise learnings from the fifteen chapters of this volume. Drawing on the research findings and discussions presented in these chapters, we have identified seven key dilemmas concerning teacher and teacher education quality:
– Teacher quality or teaching quality
– A static or dynamic concept
– An isolated or embedded concept
– An individual or collaborative concept
– A narrow or broad concept
– A standardised or contextual concept
– A fixed and defined concept or a dynamic and dialogical concept

We suggest that these dilemmas provide a useful perspective on the complexity of the concept of quality in the areas of research and policy for/in education and teacher education. These dilemmas acknowledge the dynamic orchestration that teaching involves and the choices that teachers must make in their everyday practice. They also direct our attention to important tensions in national and European debates. To resolve these tensions, these dilemmas need to be discussed in a spirit of engagement, without precondition or vested interest, and in the interest of consensus or at least building a shared understanding of what is essential for quality in teaching and teacher education.

4.1 *Teaching Quality or Teacher Quality*

While addressing quality in education, the preferred terminology of the various participants in the conversation can be confusing as the words used can cover a variety of meanings and interpretations, depending on the implicit or explicit perspective of the speaker/author. One important example in the context of this book is the use of *teacher quality* versus *teaching quality*. Throughout its different chapters and in wider debates on quality in education, both are used frequently and interchangeably – as noted by Livingston in Chapter 1 with reference to Darling-Hammond et al. (2017) and Mockler (2013). This can lead both to fractious debates and misunderstandings on essential perspectives on improving education. However, such debates often ignore that each term – teacher quality and teaching quality – emphasises a specific aspect of a complex profession.

When the focus is on the key purposes of education, it seems fitting to emphasise 'teaching quality', as that will impact learners and learning outcomes. Teaching is the core of professional action: learning takes place in the complex interplay between teachers and learners, mediated by the activities, techniques, tools, genuine interest, and spoken and non-spoken communication that the teacher uses to stimulate, support, invite and entice the learner. Teaching is not a matter of qualifications, diplomas, or certificates, but must be lived in the embodied interaction and engagement between the teacher and the learner. By using the verb 'teaching' in the concept of teaching quality we emphasise that the key to the quality of education is the work of teachers and their active engagement with learners. However, emphasising this concept also runs the risk of reducing the complexity of teaching to an instrumental task that can be controlled and standardised. In this reading – which is more frequent among policy-makers – teaching is understood in a diminished and narrow way and reduced in the understanding of the observer to technical skills that are employed in the classroom and that are open to observation through simplistic checklists.

Emphasising 'teacher quality', on the other hand, stresses that the key asset that teachers use to engage and support learners is themselves and their embodied values and capabilities: 'Consciously, we teach what we know; unconsciously, we teach who we are' (Hamachek, 1999, p. 209). Focusing on teacher quality stresses that the person and their actions cannot be separated when it comes to teaching and so affirms that teaching and learning is a fundamental encounter between human beings, each with their own qualities, values, personalities and characteristics. Teacher quality as terminology can also recognise that the teaching profession is more than simply a classroom instruction-based profession, as the work of teachers is undertaken in a wider sphere than merely classrooms. It recognises the role (and voice!) of teachers in development and innovation, inquiry, networking, policy and management. Teacher quality includes in addition to teaching qualities the qualities that teachers need for these other roles and responsibilities (Snoek, Dengerink & de Wit, 2019).

In summary, what we have seen from the chapters collected in this book implies that both concepts use different perspectives and, as such, emphasise different elements of the complexity of the profession. And, importantly, each has its strengths and place in the wider discourse around teaching and teacher education. We believe the debate on education and teachers is enriched by using both concepts instead of dwelling pointlessly on which of the two should be the more important. The quality of education is defined by the quality of those who develop and discuss education, study its principles and values, engage honestly with learners, and ultimately put teaching into practice through that engagement along the way.

4.2   *A Static or Dynamic Concept*

Studies of teacher qualifications, salaries, recruitment and retention, and professional development almost inevitably connect to some consideration of the quality of teachers as 'an input' to the education system and direct our attention to the concept of quality as a static or fixed concept. The most common manifestation of this relates to competence frameworks and practice standards. Many national policies aim at formulating quality criteria that define the conditions for entrance to the profession and the affirmation of progression once qualified. Such quality criteria serve as guidelines for initial teacher education and are based on what we expect novices to be able to do once they enter the profession. They also connect to perceptions of status – and not always in a positive way. Countries such as Singapore, Finland and South Korea position teaching as a high-status career for cultural reasons and, interestingly, also score well in international tests of students. In these nations, teacher education recruits student teachers with high academic qualifications, which has prompted attempts to research the possible connection between teacher qualifications and student attainment (Darling-Hammond, 2017). It has also spurred considerable policy interest in Europe and, indeed, globally.

One troubling outcome is that policy-makers have too often set out to emulate this perceived link and to improve both student attainment and teacher education by recruiting students of a higher 'standard'. It seems to us, however, that by doing so they are in fact applying a counter-educational presumption – namely that competence/capacity is something you have or do not have – while the more authentically educational approach would be that those qualities are consequences of learning and open to mastery. Exchanging one type of teacher students for another, a type that already is on a 'higher' level, might appear as a radical and positive approach to educational improvement. However, this rests on a conceptually weak and static notion of quality. Rather, we believe the main challenge for teacher education institutions is to embrace more dynamic understandings of professional formation and development and so work to initiate and accelerate learning among the (student) teachers we have, both in initial and post-initial programmes.

Mónica Lourenço and Ana Isabel Andrade, in their chapter on teachers' continuing professional development (CPD) regarding sustainability and citizenship education (Chapter 9), directed our attention to the issue of professional teaching development, which can be understood as professional learning anchored in building the educationally rich everyday practices of teachers as they engage IN problems of teaching and learning. Accordingly to Lourenço and Andrade, meaningful teacher CPD cannot be detached from identifying the knowledge teachers need or from identifying the factors that help teachers deploy this knowledge in practice. In this respect, the role of reflection as a process of teachers' professional learning, as well as the role of motivation to learn, should be highlighted in any consideration of the issue of quality in teaching and teacher education. This leads us to the concept of teacher knowledge and its practices as a dynamic phenomenon. A. Lin Goodwin's considerations on current reform efforts and teacher education for the 31st century (Chapter 11) focused on the value of the concept of quality as a dynamic and positive determinant of better professional practice and how teacher preparation and development must change to meet the needs of an unknown and constantly evolving future. Goodwin proposes that there are knowledges or competencies that are fundamental and enduring enough to serve society long beyond the 21st century. The proposed five domains of knowledge for teaching are helpful for us to think anew about teacher competencies and understandings, with a focus on a teacher preparation curriculum, as well as offering insights for CPD and for teacher educator learning. We agree with Goodwin that these five knowledge domains 'can enable us to reimagine teaching and learning, and reform the teaching profession in ways that can support, nurture and sustain the creative, thinking, agentic professionals we need, not just for the 21st century but for the 31st'.

This tension between static and dynamic visions of teacher action and teacher education is also explored by Marco Snoek when he considers: 'how teacher careers can be understood, and what the implications for such a more dynamic understanding are for education systems, school heads, teachers and for teacher education' (Chapter 13). Snoek's discussion clearly shows the importance of the career-long development of competencies for teachers and the need for initial teacher education institutes to actively support teachers not only during their initial development but throughout the different stages of their careers. At the heart of this argument is a solid logic for focusing on the notion of quality in teaching and teacher education as a dynamic rather than static concept.

4.3 *An Isolated or Embedded Concept*

We know how the learning environment impacts the opportunities for pupils to learn in schools: pupil well-being is very much a condition for learning. The same could be applied to teachers: teacher well-being can be a major determinant of quality teaching. This suggests that we cannot just look at teacher quality in isolation and expect it to function as a predictor for good teaching. We clearly need to take the teaching environment into account as it defines the conditions under which teachers can excel. This better recognises the complexity of the task because 'observed schooling situations represent the outcomes of several interrelated choices – those of parents, teachers, administrators and policy-makers. This complexity makes it difficult to separate the various influences reliably' (Hanushek & Rivkin, 2006, p. 23). As a result, classroom quality is not only dependent on teacher quality but also on other factors (Chapter 2 by Maria Flores). Eloff and du Plessis illustrate this interconnectedness in their chapter on the situational support available to pre-service teachers within their immediate learning environments (Chapter 8), as they evidently show that the situational support for teachers is critical to the teachers' subjective well-being and hence it requires a deeper understanding. Their study indicated a cluster of situational support factors that support the well-being of pre-service teachers. Among the factors, one can find: (i) the campus environment and facilities, (ii) pragmatic student support structures, (iii) the quality of the academic experience and the vital role of lecturers in the learning experience of students, (iv) feelings of safety, and (v) opportunities for socialisation outside of the formal academic programme.

At the same time, the quality of learning concerns more than 'qualification' (knowledge and skills) and test scores measured in standardised tests, as it also includes key broad purposes of education such as the socialisation (family, citizenship and employability) and subjectification of learners (development as a unique individual) (Biesta, 2010). All of this implies an additional need to recognise the agency, hopes, beliefs and values that are developed by learners throughout their school career. Qing Gu in her deliberations on developing teachers and quality retention of teachers indicated how teacher quality is dependent on the context and support provided by the school and the school structure, culture, conditions and leadership (Chapter 12). Gu's explorations of variations in the needs of teachers' professional learning and development over the course of their professional lives, as well as the ways in which the increasingly complex and diverse landscape of teaching supports or hinders their capacity to teach to their best in different schools and in different phases of their professional lives, clearly indicate the key importance of the conditions for sustaining teacher quality through learning and development over the course of their professional lives. Good examples of this are detailed in Plauborg's case study on quality in classroom management practices (Chapter 5). Drawing on agential realism, a theoretical approach that seeks to understand the world as deeply entangled, Plauborg explores the interplay between instruction and management and between the academic and the social, which allows her to show how the distinction between management and instruction can obstruct new insights into classroom management practices, including how classroom management can unite the academic and the social. Based on the case study presented, the concept of classroom management has been re-thought by integrating concerns for thoughtful instruction, and by indicating the inseparability of classroom management and didactics.

It is worth noting, that the terms 'quality' and 'quality assurance' have their origins in the manufacturing industry and within education and have become associated with managerial approaches to leadership (Allais, 2017). These terms have, we suggest, been tainted by a neoliberal emphasis on accountability and performativity during 'the age of measurement' (Biesta, 2010). The danger, as we see it, is that teachers become compliant with a system of quality assurance based on market demands and this constrains the space for professionality (Biesta, 2017). Embracing the complexity of teaching means looking beyond standardising its constituent actions and being flexible in response to context (Darling-Hammond, 2016). But the pressure from policy-makers to tightly codify and control teacher effectiveness tends to reduce teaching to 'what works' (Skourdoumbis, 2017). The language of effectiveness foregrounds teacher practices that impact student attainment in tests (Singh, 2018), and this tends to constrain important wider purposes of education including citizenship and individual development (Biesta, 2010). The related emphasis on data gives influence to data experts and consultants who collate and impose measures of performance on schools and teachers (Fenwick & Edwards, 2016, p.122). The resulting overwhelming emphasis on data also shapes the identity formation and professional learning of teachers who, unfortunately, often feel obliged to respond to the data-driven market by pursuing improved test results above all else (Keddie, 2016).

4.4 *An Individual or Collaborative Concept*
The typical structures of classroom instruction (with one teacher working with a group of pupils) can create a professional context that is characterised by isolation from colleagues and can easily lead to professional loneliness. As a result, teachers often lack the opportunity for collegial consultation and are confronted with (and at the same time tend to hide) professional vulnerability. The consequent risk is that teachers define their own individual norms

while claiming 'autonomy' in their classroom. However, educating pupils and supporting their development, emancipation and transformative agency can never be an individual task but is in its essence a collaborative effort of several teachers – and indeed the whole school. These understandings also impact educational policy in terms of focusing on/developing either individual teacher heroes or a profession which is constantly in search of higher levels of collaborative performance. And, indeed, sometimes pursuing both simultaneously with all the tensions inherent in this.

In her considerations of the importance of collaborative reflection and self-evaluation in schools and the need for professional ethics (see Chapter 4), Hannele Pitkänen exemplifies an image of a profession that is not based on individual norms and personal interpretations of 'quality', nor disciplined by politics, but challenged by social and professional norms by the members of a profession in an ongoing professional dialogue. Pitkänen argues that along with the quality 'evaluation wave', schools and teachers have not only become objects of evaluation, but have also been subjected to increasing demands to self-evaluate. Her analysis of the emergence and formation of the politics of school and teacher self-evaluation and of the power and subjectivities in the case of Finnish comprehensive education indicate the importance of the ethics of self-evaluation not only in the Finnish context but also in educational contexts elsewhere. The ethics of self-evaluation within school teams is closely entangled with and supports the governing of education through quality evaluation. It is not yet, however, well understood for its possibilities in bridging the tension between individualistic and collaborative forces that are experienced in many systems.

4.5 *A Narrow or a Broad Concept*

The authors of several chapters warn against a narrow understanding of teaching quality. Such a narrow understanding can occur when outcomes of the learning process are defined in terms of limited sets of measurable learning outcomes instead of taking a wider perspective of learning in terms of outcomes relating to voice, agency, transformation and social justice. The danger is that these narrow understandings of learning processes can easily lead policy-makers to assume an instrumental approach towards the work of teachers, expecting them to use 'evidence-informed approaches' to pursue deeply problematic prescriptions of 'better' outcomes. This can deprive both teachers and learners of voice and ownership and reduce them to the status of passive objects in the processes of education instead of seeing them as active participants who shape the process of teaching and learning through meaningful interaction and dialogue.

Purdy, Hall, Khanolainen and Galvin, in their considerations of teacher quality driven by equity and social justice (Chapter 3), draw our attention to the overlapping and *sometimes conflicted purposes of education* (Biesta, 2010), which forces us to engage more closely with professional values and principles. Professional educators and other stakeholders increasingly argue that a significant purpose of education is to work towards social justice. From this value-based perspective, a central purpose of formal education is to tackle the attainment gap and broader inequitable outcomes in health, employment and well-being that exist in relation to social disadvantage and its intersectionality with factors including social class, children in care, race/ethnicity, gender, sexuality, religion, citizenship, and prior attainment (Tefera & Powers, 2018). The pursuit of social justice has considerable implications for school organisation, curriculum and pedagogy and adds a contested element to the professional capacities required by teachers, for example, in combining research literacy and professional judgement in deciding what and how to teach to stimulate the 'socialisation' of their students.

In terms of 'socialisation', a quality school education should prepare students for citizenship rather than merely prepare them for employment. This creates a challenge for the traditional subject discipline-based curriculum adopted in many school systems internationally in which we teach maths, science, languages, history, geography, arts and so on as distinct subjects. Many of the big societal challenges we and our students face in modern life are transdisciplinary, for example, poverty, inequity and climate change – and so quality schools should be open to the challenges of mapping student achievement in understanding these, and similar issues across the curriculum (Boyd, 2019). In the case of teacher education, foundation studies are important to include an understanding of social justice issues in education, including equity and intersectionality, with the development of practical strategies, for example, for proactive anti-racist work in classrooms and schools. Beginning teachers need to develop self-awareness so that they do not fall so readily into the traps of the 'shame game', which stigmatises those living in poverty (O'Hara, 2020), 'colour blindness', which ignores white privilege (Bhopal, 2018), or unconscious bias, which holds back gender equality (Bohnet, 2016). Beginning teachers should arguably have a capacity for reflective learning and the development of research-informed practice through professional inquiry.

A narrow understanding of teacher quality might also come from the way in which the work of teachers is understood. When their work is understood as classroom-centred, delivering (readymade) curricula using evidence-based approaches, the potential role of teachers in developing education and curricula, teacher inquiry, involvement in school policy and supporting colleagues is neglected. Such a narrow understanding of the profession not only reduces the voice of teachers but also creates little room for development and variation in the work of teachers during their careers. This might easily lead to a static understanding of the profession, reducing its attractiveness and causing teachers to leave the profession due to a lack of career prospects (not so much in terms of salary, but rather with regard to variation, challenge, growth and recognition).

In Chapter 12, Gu confronts these types of narrow understanding of teaching quality and focuses on the altruistic values and efficacious beliefs of teachers as key conditions for teachers' retention in the profession, defining their ethical character and professional quality. When no attention is given to such essential inner resources for being a teacher – both during initial teacher education and during the professional lives of teachers – the risk is that teachers will simply choose to escape poor and dysfunctional school cultures by leaving the profession.

This risk is also central in the contribution of Snoek, while Colognesi and März (Chapter 15) illustrate a different perspective on the profession by highlighting one particular career path: the path towards being a teacher-researcher. Again, this is an area that is not yet understood well enough but holds out important possibilities for using a practitioner's voice to bridge the policy-practice gap that so often plagues policy work for teaching and teacher education.

In academic, professional and policy debates on the teaching and on the quality of teaching, it is important to be aware of this dilemma and to understand how the concepts used can support a narrow or a wider understanding of teaching quality, recognise or deny the interactive complexity of the profession and so impact its attractiveness either positively or negatively.

4.6 *A Standardised or Contextual Concept*

Many chapters in the present book address the tensions that occur in the implicit understanding of 'quality'. Often, debates on teaching quality are based on the conviction that it can be defined in such a way that it can be used in policies regarding teacher education curricula and quality assurance in education. Policy-makers frequently argue that being able to develop adequate policies requires that they can define teaching quality in clear, measurable criteria and against defined standards. These general and standardised criteria are expected to apply to all teachers and all contexts. However, this disregards that unique and defining element of the teaching profession that we mentioned earlier: that teachers teach who they are. They themselves are the key 'instruments' in supporting pupils. Therefore, it is impossible to make a distinction between teaching quality and teacher quality as it is impossible to separate the teacher from their teaching, as is argued by Livingston in the first chapter.

This questions the movement emphasising 'what works' (see the contribution of Purdy et al.) as it tries to separate teaching from the teacher and its context. At the same time it emphasises the need for ongoing inquiry by teachers to gain insights into the impact of their teaching on pupils and in the factors that make a difference in the specific context they are in (teacher, pupil, school, local environment). Colognesi and März show in Chapter 15 how the development of such an inquiring mindset by the teacher themselves can be strengthened and how that contributes to teaching quality in terms of reflexivity skills and improved classroom practices. It is promising to see how their approach can help to bridge the gap that teachers have long perceived between practice and research.

As a result, teaching quality cannot be adequately defined by standardised competencies and criteria but is fundamentally associated with the identity, professional and altruistic values, mindsets, personal theories, characteristics and personality of the teacher, resulting in a unique pedagogical style (see, for example, the contribution of Gu in Chapter 12). However, it is also associated with the characteristics and needs of pupils, the context in which they live and the conditions created by schools and society. This is illustrated very clearly by Vasileios Symeonidis, Felix Senger, Heike Wendt, Amal Fatah Zedan, Saraa Salim Dawood and Fawzi Habeeb Jabrail in Chapter 10, where they show how teacher education in conflict-affected societies not only has to deal with poor physical conditions in terms of buildings and resources, but also with traumas and issues of well-being affecting both students and teacher educators. Such contexts call for a process of redefining teacher education that takes into account the acute needs of students and teacher educators while, at the same time, society places a moral appeal on (student) teacher and teacher educators to support rebuilding the society.

Two other chapters illustrate the way in which teaching quality is dependent on context by relating the concept to the COVID-19 pandemic. In Chapter 6, Carol Hordatt Gentles, Sarah Younie, Marilyn Leask and Helen Caldwell show how, in the process of transitioning to online delivery and finding creative, offline ways of reaching students, teachers at all levels demonstrated their capacity to be innovative and to take ownership of accelerating changes in how they think and work. This capacity to adapt and the willingness to practice agency and autonomy in developing pedagogical skills, collaborative practices, knowledge, and competencies proved invaluable during their pandemic response. These authors considered this ability to reinvent practice at a fundamental level appropriate for teaching and learning during the pandemic as one of the most important elements of teaching quality now and in the future.

In Chapter 7 Gisselle Tur Porres and Washington Ires Correa also emphasise this perspective – again in the context of COVID-19, where teachers were forced to use online environments to support and engage with their pupils – by phrasing that there are no 'universal' answers 'for good/quality practices, rather, there are local practices that may teach us what works in local contexts and perhaps can be transferred to other contexts as lessons learned'. Just likee in physical classrooms, teachers need to (re)think their purpose, beliefs and pedagogical aims while designing online learning environments and evaluate how such environments might strengthen (or weaken) the voice, ownership, emancipation and agency of their learners. The chapter makes a strong case for this.

4.7   *A Fixed and Defined Concept or a Dynamic and Dialogical Concept*

This brings us to the final dilemma that can be identified in the different contributions in this book: the fact that teaching quality cannot be defined as a fixed and defined concept. This is, on the one hand, caused by the fact that teaching quality can be seen – as Livingston mentioned in Chapter 1– as an elusive concept (Liston et al., 2008): as there are so many possible perspectives and layers related to teaching quality, every definition will lack essential elements, making it hard to express or define. This becomes even more complicated by the fact that within the debate on teaching quality, several stakeholders, claiming authority on the topic of teaching quality can be discerned. Teachers, school leaders, education employers, education ministries, as well as learners and parents all have their own perspectives and their own concerns. This makes the concept not only elusive but also contested. This is illustrated in the contributions of Livingston, Purdy et al., Hordatt Gentles et al., and Galvin et al., who each emphasise the need for an open dialogue in which not only policy-makers at a national or European level claim authority over defining teaching quality, translating these to formal standards for teachers and teacher education, but in which teachers and teacher educators are also given a voice. The Dialogue Labs that are presented by Livingston in Chapter 1 are excellent examples of how such open dialogues can be organised and can enable the engagement of multiple stakeholders and how these contribute to redefining the understanding of teaching quality and teacher education quality from a more developmental approach rather than a judgemental one.

This requires not only a change in mindset from policy makers, recognising the voice of teachers in debates on teaching quality, but also from teachers who need to recognise that policy-makers have a fair claim to be concerned with regard to the quality of their profession from the perspective of system-level quality assurance. For an open dialogue in which every stakeholder is given a voice, it is necessary to avoid an 'us' versus 'them' dichotomy.

This implies that the discourse on teaching quality should not be considered as a temporary intellectual, professional and policy challenge aimed at finding a definitive answer regarding the quality question, but as an ongoing endeavour that is an essential part of strengthening 'quality', not by the aim to find answers, but by the understanding that each context will require a unique answer to the question of what defines quality in this specific situation and context. That answer requires an ongoing dialogue where different stakeholders critically question each other on a continuous basis, not in order to judge each other but to gain a deeper understanding of the multitude of perspectives on our understanding of quality and how that understanding helps us to improve the way in which we support young people to take responsibility for the further development of themselves and the world.

5 Implications for Teacher Education Practice, Policy and Research

The above key dilemmas focus on teaching quality and teacher quality. This raises the question as to the extent to which these key dilemmas also apply to teacher education and, if so, what the possible consequences are for teacher education practice, policy and research.

To answer this question, it is first important to realise that the performance of teachers in the classroom might be positioned both as a 'process' in relation to teaching quality and as an 'output' in relation to teacher education quality. In that sense, supporting the teaching quality of student and novice teachers is one of the purposes of teacher education. However, teacher education itself is a process where teacher educators teach their student(teacher)s, and as such, teaching quality also applies to teacher education as a process relating to the lecture room performance of teacher educators.

In relation to the output of teacher education, key dilemma 1 implies that teacher education curricula should focus both on supporting student teachers in improving their classroom performance in such a way that they are able to provide optimal conditions for pupils to learn effectively in a safe environment (teaching quality) and on supporting the development of a professional identity based on an understanding of education as a human relation and encounter, taking into account the personal dispositions, qualities, values, personalities and characteristics of both teachers and learners (teacher quality).

At the level of the teacher education process, the same applies to teacher educators, who need to critically evaluate both their performance in the lecture room and how they understand their professional identity and relation to student teachers.

Key dilemma 2, relating to a static or dynamic understanding of teacher quality, implies that teacher educators need to be careful not to step into the pitfall whereby society and teacher educators themselves expect to cover all the necessary competencies and skills within the initial teacher education curriculum. Initial teacher education is just the start of a great career in which teachers can and should develop during their whole professional lifespan and to which initial teacher education just contributes the first foundations. When we understand the teaching profession and teacher education as a continuum, this implies that teacher education institutes should not restrict themselves to the initial education of student teachers but should also find ways to use their expertise to support teachers throughout their professional lives.

Again, this also applies to teacher educators, who can and need to develop their expertise as teacher educators during their careers. Being appointed at a university does not imply that someone has reached the top of their career but indicates that they have embarked on a new journey where new horizons and undiscovered areas can and need to be explored.

The third key dilemma on quality as an embedded concept that is dependent on the local conditions in which it takes shape also has implications for teacher education. The teacher education curriculum needs to make student teachers aware that outcomes of research cannot be considered as tips, tricks and guidelines that can be applied in any situation but always require a careful consideration of the wider learning environment that is provided by the school and the way it supports or hinders certain types of learning outcomes. Teachers need to learn to critically assess the learning environment and the way it supports pupils with different backgrounds. At a similar level, heads of teacher education institutions and teacher educators need to critically assess which aspects of teacher educator quality are supported and stimulated by the context of the teacher education institution in terms of structure, culture, conditions and leadership – and which are not.

Key dilemma 4 implies that the teacher education curriculum can strengthen either an isolated or a collaborative perspective in the way it focuses on collaborative activities and forms of peer feedback and peer assessment. At the level of teacher educators, it raises the question of the extent to which the work of teacher educators is understood as a collaborative activity with forms of peer teaching and peer feedback.

Key dilemma 5, regarding a narrow or broad understanding of quality, relates to the way in which the teacher education curriculum not only values and focuses on the acquisition of the necessary knowledge base and skills of teachers but also aims to support student teachers in the development of their voice, agency and transformation and thus contributes to social justice, while at the same time, they are supported to strengthen the voice, agency and transformation of their pupils.

Key dilemma 6, focusing on quality as a contextual concept, challenges teacher education to strengthen its awareness of contexts, both of pupils and student teachers. This requires context-specific teacher education that takes into account local contexts and cultures (see e.g. Matsko & Hammerness, 2014). For teacher educators, it also implies that they need to be aware of the context in which student teachers live and work and how the curriculum and their teaching relates to those contexts.

Finally, key dilemma 7 promotes a dynamic and dialogical perspective on teaching quality. This implies that the concept of teacher education quality also needs to be seen as dynamic and dialogical. Debates on teacher education quality must not aim to find definite answers but instead aim for an ongoing dialogue where clear and defined solutions are constantly questioned and new perspectives are opened. It requires that teacher educators invite other stakeholders into this ongoing dialogue and that policy-makers invite teacher educators to the table not as opponents but as partners striving for the same goal: supporting teachers to become the best supporters of learners.

We believe that the lessons that can be derived by applying each of the key dilemmas to teacher education will create an important and powerful frame of reference for teacher educators, teacher education researchers and policy-makers concerned with teacher education. It also shows that the global diversity in teacher education – as has been made visible in this book through the different contributions from around the world – creates a powerful kaleidoscopic perspective that can enrich us and help us to question the things we take for granted within our national or local contexts and boundaries. However, it is also important for those of us who work in a European context to note the radical and far-reaching changes characterising the teacher education policy activities of the European Commission in pursuit of its teacher and teaching quality agenda over recent years, as outlined by Conor Galvin, Panagiotis Kampylis, Deirbhile Nic Craith, Joanna Madalinska-Michalak and Noel Purdy (Chapter 14). Opportunities for dialogue between the teacher education community and policy-makers can never be assumed; they must be argued for and engaged with positively and from a principled standpoint when they are presented – otherwise, we risk becoming passive observers rather than active participants in the process of addressing dilemmas such as those discussed above.

6   Final Reflections

The purpose of this chapter was twofold: (1) to provide a synthesis of learning on quality in teaching and teacher education based on the analyses and discussions of the chapters collected in this book, and (2) to discuss implications that have emerged for future research on quality in teaching and teacher education, policy and practice. In so doing, we asked: What do we know about quality in teaching and teacher education from the collected chapters and how can these findings inform future research, policy and practice in these areas?

Drawing on the international collection of studies focusing on the nature of quality in teaching and teacher education, and current and future challenges to and possibilities for teaching and teacher education, we highlighted how quality is variously defined and understood and how this is transformed into various practices. A synthesis of the research presented in the volume's fifteen chapters inspired us to explore the concept of quality in teaching and teacher education through the seven key dilemmas discussed in the section *Implications for teacher education practice, police and research* above.

These dilemmas seem to be highly relevant and profoundly generative and relate to the heart of certain tensions regarding education and its quality. From our point of view, every discussion on quality in education must be anchored in ideas on the purpose of education. Accordingly, how we perceive teacher and teaching quality must relate to how we understand what education is about – and why this is of importance in an ever-changing, increasingly complex world. The dilemmas discussed and the perspectives that are offered by the authors direct our attention to finding at least some common ground, if not the more ideal consensus and shared understanding of what is essential in and for education nowadays and in the future. The dilemmas we have foregrounded raise important questions about dated neo-liberal assumptions around performativity embedded in many national and international policies. Although such a performance orientation might seem helpful for policy-makers in getting a grip on assuring quality in schools and taking seemingly strong policy measures contributing to global competitiveness, in essence, the clear messages emerging from the chapters in this book show that such an approach may at best create an illusion of decisiveness and policy vigour but misses the essence of teacher quality and even risks a seriously counterproductive effect.

In sum, the contemporary policy emphasis on teacher quality descriptors emerges from many of the chapters as a limited and reductionist approach, increasingly inadequate for the task of defining quality in contemporary teaching and teacher education.

Teaching quality policies too often prioritise indicators that are easy to measure – for example, level of education, years of professional experience and participation in formal professional development activities – but descriptions of teaching quality really need to capture the true determinants of quality. These concern teaching acts such as the intentional but fluid pedagogical activities teachers deploy; the epistemologically rich learning experiences they direct towards individuals and collectives of students in ways that advance their perception of the world and readiness to engage with it; the insights and competencies teachers impart; and the artfulness with which they pursue Rosa's *resonance* and Aristotle's *living well* – all aligned to the fundamental purpose of education for life in the contemporary world. Accordingly, descriptions of high-quality teaching must entail a holistic range of observations, departing from the purpose of the activity but also recognising the enactment, the interaction, how diverse epistemological dimensions become present in the complex act of teaching, and how they become related to socialisation, subjectification and qualification, not of one student but many.

Some contributions in this anthology have dealt with this complexity, and some also voiced issues regarding the purpose of education, and its implications for teacher education. For example, they point to how educational agendas tend to become influenced, if not dominated, by economic rationales that operate in divergence with the foundational priorities of education.

Anchoring discussions about quality in contemporary teacher education in ideas about the purpose of education is essential for enhanced depth and progress. Unfortunately, our tradition is partly inward-looking, using concepts that come with somewhat taken-for-granted content that, over time, have become placeholders for too many comfortable and uncritical ideas and arguments. As a consequence, the message becomes less relevant, less sharp and less enlightening when it comes to our most central challenges. In addition, we have a tendency to foreground internal policy issues in either teacher education programmes or schooling, while our most problematic current challenges appear to be both more encompassing and more demanding.

Education based on narrow notions and functionalist or neo-liberal concerns does not support resonance but rather the opposite: it generates alienation and the occurrence of muted classrooms. In addition, reductionist notions of education (and hence teacher and teaching qualities) do not draw upon or make use of insights and knowledge from within the teaching profession. Conversely, high-quality teaching creates learning experiences in which resonance can grow and life-related learning can and will occur. This is the well-sustained picture that surfaces in the observations and insights of this anthology. It draws our attention to values and emancipation, and warns against the growth of narrow notions of education, notions that come with perceptions of teachers and teaching as the instrumental delivery of scripted curricula, opening the way for replacing professional teaching with standardised, manual based activities, and so diminishing what it is to be human and the value of human learning.

Our chapters collectively voice strong concerns about the tendency to simplify and narrow teaching, and they present valid arguments for their worries. For us, there remains much in this argumentation that deserves further analysis: the tension between, on the one hand a natural, legitimate and valuable effort towards both clarity and quality (to be able to describe and identify levels of advancement in learning, professional practice, etc.), and on the other, the risk that profound qualities are being reduced through such acts by the processes that these measures intended to improve. This is an area that needs further work in order to be understood and to lessen its potential negative impact. This is an area with which teacher educators have to engage to defend fundamental aspects of the teaching profession as well as to ensure that we build knowledge and insights on how teaching contributes to individuals and to society and how high-quality teaching contributes to happiness, human well-being, the growth of human capabilities and the diversity of understandings of what it is to be human and what a desirable society looks like. As Dewey once wrote, 'democracy is more than a form of government; it is primarily a mode of associated living, of conjoint communicated experience' (Dewey, 1916/2011, ch. 7, 2§; Nussbaum, 2011).

References

Allais, S. M. (2017). *Quality assurance in education.* Centre for Education Policy Development.

Bhopal, K. (2018). *White privilege: The myth of a post-racial society.* Policy Press.

Biesta, G. J. J. (2010). *Good education in an age of measurement. Ethics, politics, democracy.* Routledge.

Biesta, G. J. J. (2017). Education, measurement and the professions: Reclaiming a space for democratic professionality in education, *Educational Philosophy and Theory*, 49(4), 315–330.

Biesta, G. J. J., & Stengel, B. S. (2016). Thinking philosophically about teaching. In D. H. Gitomer & C. A. Bell (Eds.), *Handbook of research on teaching* (pp. 7–68). American Educational Research Association.

Bohnet, I. (2016). *What works: Gender equality by design.* Harvard University Press.

Boyd, P. (2019). Knowledge and ways of knowing. *Journal of the Chartered College of Teaching, 6,* 34–37.

Darling-Hammond, L. (2016). Research on teaching and teacher education and its influences on policy and practice. *Educational Researcher, 45*(2), 83–91.

Darling-Hammond, L. (2017). Teacher education around the world: What can we learn from international practice? *European Journal of Teacher Education, 40*(3), 291–309.

Darling-Hammond, L., Burns, D., Campbell, C., Goodwin, A. L., Hammerness, K., Low, E. L., & Zeichner, K. (2017). *Empowered educators: How high-performing systems shape teaching quality around the world.* Jossey-Bass.

Dewey, J. (2011). *Democracy and education. An introduction to the philosophy of education.* The Free Press. (Original work published 1916)

Fenwick & Edwards. (2016). Exploring the impact of digital technologies on professional responsibilities and education. *European Educational Research Journal, 15*(1), 117–131.

Goodwin, A. L., & Low, E. L. (2021). Rethinking conceptualisations of teacher quality in Singapore and Hong Kong: A comparative analysis. *European Journal of Teacher Education, 44*(3), 365–382.

Hamachek, D. (1999). Effective teachers: What they do, how they do it, and the importance of self-knowledge. In R. L. Lipka, & T. M. Brinthaupt (Eds.), *The role of self in teacher development* (pp. 189–224). State University of New York Press.

Hanushek, E. A., & Rivkin, S. G. (2006). Teacher quality. In E. A. Hanushek & F. Welch (Eds.), *Handbook of the economics of education* (Vol. 2, pp. 1052–1078). North Holland.

Keddie, A. (2016). Conceptions of responsibility within and beyond neoliberal frames: A story of leadership in an English primary school. *Educational Management Administration & Leadership, 46*(1), 124–139.

Liston, D., Borko, H., & Whitcomb, J. (2008). The teacher educator's role in enhancing teacher quality. *Journal of Teacher Education, 59*(2), 111–116.

Matsko, K. K., & Hammerness, K. (2014). Unpacking the 'urban' in urban teacher preparation: Making a case for context-specific teacher preparation. *Journal of Teacher Education, 65,* 128–144.

Mockler, N. (2013). Teacher professional learning in a neoliberal age: Audit, professionalism and identity. *Australian Journal of Teacher Education, 38*(10), 35–47.

Nussbaum, M. C. (2011). *Creating capabilities. The human development approach.* Harvard University Press.

O'Hara, M. (2020). *The shame game: Overturning the toxic poverty narrative.* Policy Press.

Rosa, H. (2019). *Resonance. A Sociology of our relationship to the world.* Polity Press.

Singh, (2018). Performativity, affectivity and pedagogic identities *European Educational Research Journal*, 17(4), 489–506.

Skourdoumbis, A. (2017). Teacher quality, teacher effectiveness and the diminishing returns of current education policy expressions. *Journal for Critical Education Studies*, 15(1), 42–59.

Snoek, M., Dengerink, J., & de Wit, B. (2019). Reframing the teacher profession as a dynamic multifaceted profession: A wider perspective on teacher quality and teacher competence frameworks. *European Journal of Education*, 54(3), 413–425.

Standish, P. (2003). The nature and purposes of education. In R. Curren (Ed.), *A companion to the philosophy of education* (pp. 221–231). Blackwell.

Tefera, A. A., & Powers, J. M. (2018). Introduction: Intersectionality in education: A conceptual aspiration and research imperative. *Review of Research in Education*, 42, vii–xvii.

Tröhler, D. (2017). Educationalization of social problems and educationalization of the modern world. In M. A. Peters (Ed.), *Encyclopedia of educational philosophy and theory.* Springer. https://doi.org/10.1007/978-981-287-588-4_8

UNESCO. (1972). *Learning to be: The world of education today and tomorrow.* International Commission on the Development of Education. UNESCO.

UNESCO. (1996). *Learning: The treasure within.* Report to UNESCO of the International Commission on Education for the Twenty-first Century. UNESCO.

Zimmerman, B. J. (2002). Becoming a self-regulated learner: An overview. *Theory into Practice*, 41(2), 64–70.

Index

academic and social 98–103, 105, 106, 108, 109, 111–114, 363
academic attainment 36, 99, 360, 363
academic learning 99
access to education 55, 142, 204, 205, 356
accountability mechanisms 38, 205
active distance learning 125, 127, 129–131, 137, 139
adaptability 16, 100, 122, 148, 161, 210, 245, 282, 367
agency 24, 54, 55, 57, 58, 60, 80, 102, 123, 126–128, 132, 137, 140, 141, 167, 168, 174, 177, 208, 260, 264–266, 278–280, 288, 289, 292, 293, 295, 299, 314, 356, 362, 364, 367, 368, 371
agency for well-being 167, 168, 177
agent of change 13, 28, 63, 198, 204, 207, 208
agential realism 3, 100–102, 112, 363
agentic teachers 26, 232, 361
ambiguity 1, 12, 20
apprenticeship model 52
archaeology 79
autonomy 22, 28, 54, 55, 76, 82, 123, 128, 132, 137, 141, 151, 191, 205, 223, 279, 282, 292, 295, 357, 364, 367

Bologna Declaration 308
broad concept 353, 358, 364

care 26, 27, 89, 132, 141, 171, 172, 175, 177, 215, 238, 242, 246, 247, 261, 263, 365
career goals 173
career ladders 288, 294, 296, 297
career opportunities 5, 278, 280, 283–287, 289–291, 295–300
career trajectories 167, 244
case study 3, 38, 99–101, 103, 126, 180, 181, 186, 188, 197, 204, 211, 218, 363
child 21, 22, 35, 38, 107, 133, 138, 207, 237, 246, 247
classroom 3, 6, 16, 21, 33, 40, 41, 43, 53, 55, 57–59, 62, 63, 83, 98–102, 104–107, 110–115, 123, 124, 129, 131, 134, 135, 137, 140, 141, 150, 152, 160, 161, 167, 189, 196, 197, 207, 222, 236–239, 243, 245–247, 253, 255–258, 265–268, 281–284, 287, 291–298, 300, 305, 330, 331, 339, 345, 359, 362–367, 369, 370
classroom cultures 33, 99, 207, 255, 256, 265–268, 281, 282, 295, 331, 362, 366, 370
classroom management 3, 98–102, 105, 111–115, 337, 339, 363
classroom teachers 131, 297
collaborative concept 353, 358, 363
collaborative practice 337, 367
collaborative research 6, 331–333, 337, 344–346
community solidarity 54
competence 16, 17, 52–58, 60, 62, 128, 134, 189, 281, 284, 289, 300, 307, 308, 310, 314, 315, 318, 319, 322, 343, 354, 355, 360
conceptual ambiguity 20
conceptualising teacher quality 35, 128
conditions of teachers' work and lives 206, 256, 264, 266, 293, 345
conflict affected societies 3, 4, 203, 223, 367
conflicting values 209
connectivism 125, 126, 137, 141
constructivism 123, 125, 130, 137, 141
context 1–4, 6, 7, 12–18, 20, 21, 28, 29, 34–45, 51–62, 64, 76, 82, 84, 90–92, 101, 110, 122–124, 127, 131, 140, 141, 149–153, 155–159, 162, 167, 168, 174–177, 181, 182, 185–187, 189, 197, 204–212, 222, 223, 235, 237–239, 244, 245, 257, 262–267, 279, 287, 290, 291, 297, 298, 306, 307, 310–312, 320, 322, 323, 330, 331, 336, 339, 343, 345, 353, 354, 358, 362–364, 366–371
contextual concept 353, 358, 366, 371
cooperation 8, 13, 52, 233, 243, 254, 289, 305, 310–312, 316, 320, 324
COVID-19 121, 122, 125, 130, 131, 135, 137, 138, 141, 142, 151, 153, 162, 232, 233, 235, 245, 368
COVID-19 pandemic 18, 26, 56, 124, 127, 129–132, 140, 141, 148, 150, 153, 155, 158, 160–162, 212, 253, 267
craft models of teaching 2, 52

creativity   22, 43, 122, 136, 234, 235, 237, 245
crisis   3, 4, 45, 122, 124, 129, 131, 148, 205, 209, 211, 221
crisis situations   3, 4, 204, 206, 208, 213
crisisification   315
critical awareness   61, 158
critical dialogue   151, 152, 154–158, 161
critical perspective   148, 149
critical thinking   61, 62, 111, 152, 157, 160, 184, 208, 210, 234, 245
cultural diversity   33, 150, 153, 182, 191, 246
curriculum   5, 16, 22, 23, 35, 36, 38–43, 81–84, 86–88, 111, 125, 137, 142, 149, 185, 187, 190–192, 195–197, 204, 208, 211, 212, 214, 218, 219, 222, 232, 234–241, 244, 245, 247, 285, 295, 297, 299, 300, 332, 337, 361, 365, 370, 371

deliberative intellectuals   27
deliberative supranationalism   321
deontology and ethics   337
development   IX, X, 1, 3–8, 13, 16, 21, 22, 24–26, 33, 35, 37, 38, 41–43, 51–55, 63, 74, 76, 81, 84–88, 99, 101, 124, 125, 128, 130, 131, 136, 142, 147, 153, 154, 181, 184, 185, 196, 197, 206–210, 232, 235, 244–247, 264, 267, 281–283, 285, 289, 292, 299, 300, 312, 313, 318, 330, 332, 335, 336, 360, 361, 373
dialogue   IX, 13, 20, 21, 24–28, 128, 131, 137, 151, 152, 154, 155, 157, 158, 161, 181, 186–188, 195, 208, 221, 235, 290, 299, 300, 258, 264, 364, 368, 369, 371
dialogue labs   24, 25, 27–29, 368
Digital Education Action Plan   305, 321
dilemma   1, 281, 352, 353, 358, 366, 368–372
discourse   12, 14, 18, 19, 22, 34, 36, 52, 53, 74, 75, 79, 80, 84–86, 88–91, 99, 128, 149, 188, 211, 234, 241, 262, 265, 309, 321, 323, 354, 360, 369,
discourses of quality   17–20, 26, 33, 39, 89, 150
discursive practices   79–81, 87, 90, 91
discursive spaces   20, 25, 28
discussion circle   156–158
distance learning   125, 127, 129–131, 137, 139
domains of knowledge   2, 220, 232, 354, 361
dynamic and dialogical concept   353, 358, 368

dynamic concept   22, 353, 358, 360
dynamic nature of teaching   17, 38

EC policy   307–309, 312, 315, 316, 321, 323
EC policy work   313, 322, 323
economic policy   18
education   IX, X, 1–8, 11–20, 24–29, 32–45, 50–56, 59–64, 73, 74, 81, 83, 128, 147–151, 153–156, 159, 160, 162, 167, 169, 176, 178, 181, 183, 185–188, 195, 198, 199, 203–213, 217–223, 231, 235–237, 239, 241, 244, 277, 280–282, 289, 299, 300, 304–317, 319–324, 329–337, 343–346, 352–361, 365–373
education as a European Policy Space   311
education for sustainability   4, 181, 182, 186–188, 190, 191, 193, 195
education policy   IX, X, 1, 3, 6, 7, 12, 14, 18, 34, 52, 53, 56, 64, 79, 86, 265, 281, 306, 307, 309, 311–313, 316, 317, 319–323, 371, 372
education reforms   2, 75, 353
educational principles   124, 137, 189, 260, 365
effective teaching   60, 123, 137, 189
emancipation   151, 152, 154, 158, 364, 374
emancipatory pedagogical approaches   4, 148, 149, 151–156, 158–162
emancipatory practices   156
embedded concept   353, 358, 362, 370
empathy   233
employment   177, 205, 206, 238, 318, 365
entanglement   101, 112, 115
equitable quality education   X, 55, 176, 305
equity   2, 12, 50, 51, 54–56, 60, 61, 64, 65, 133, 176, 186, 198, 211, 241, 243, 247, 305, 365
ERASMUS+ Teacher Academies   51, 314, 320–322
ethical purpose for humans   355
ethics of care   3, 72, 76, 78, 89, 91, 364
ethnicity   61, 62, 365
EU TUNING project   52, 307
European Commission   2, 6, 13, 51, 52, 60, 63, 64, 280, 281, 284, 290, 304–306, 310, 311, 313–316, 319, 323, 371
European Education Area   2, 51, 53, 64, 290, 305, 306, 310, 320, 321, 323
European teacher   305, 307, 323
European teacher education   63, 307
Europeification process   52, 64, 311, 316

evaluation of teaching 100, 115
explanatory elements 309

fixed and defined concept 353, 358, 368
flipped classroom teaching 134
fundamental competencies 5, 232, 361, 367, 368
future 1, 3–8, 11, 12, 14, 15, 18, 23–28, 44, 51, 53, 63, 98, 111, 112, 114, 122, 131, 132, 134, 135, 141, 142, 166–168, 176, 177, 182, 183, 189, 190, 192, 194, 211, 231–234, 236, 237, 241, 243, 245, 246, 252, 255, 262, 299, 300, 305, 306, 314, 320, 323, 324, 330, 331, 333, 334, 338, 343–345, 352, 353, 357, 361, 368, 372
future teacher 5, 11, 15, 18, 27, 166, 168, 176, 177, 236, 314, 330, 331, 333, 334, 338, 343–345

genealogical methodology 3, 78
genealogy 72, 78, 91
global citizens 180, 198
global citizenship education 182
global community 232, 243
global education 75, 183
global sustainable development 167
globalisation 18, 33, 184, 208, 232, 242, 311
globalised world 2, 193
good practices 52, 153
good teaching 17, 38, 110, 123, 161, 185, 235, 261, 362
governing 3, 75–78, 80, 90, 91, 311, 315, 364
governmental intervention 33

happiness 355, 374
heterogeneity 60

identity 19, 22, 33, 57, 58, 168, 175, 197, 204, 206, 210, 246, 256, 260, 261, 264–266, 289, 299, 321, 363, 367, 369, 370
improving quality 3, 32, 89
in-career development 51
inclusion 63, 138, 159, 162, 181, 183, 186–188, 195, 208, 209, 243, 309, 317, 318
individual concept 353, 358, 363
initial teacher education IX, 4, 5, 13, 14, 18, 19, 32, 34, 36, 37, 39–42, 44, 45, 51–53, 64, 204, 209, 210, 211, 213, 217, 219, 221, 222, 280–282, 299, 300, 309, 330, 331, 333, 360, 361, 366, 370
injustice 61
inquiry-based working 332, 345
in-service teacher education 186, 305
instruction 3, 16, 35, 36, 39, 98–103, 108–115, 137, 215, 234, 237, 245, 305, 330, 335, 359, 363
integrating instruction 3, 101, 113
international research 1, 3, 14, 61
international studies 39, 52
internationalisation 308
intra-action 101, 102, 113
isolated concept 353, 358, 362

Jean Monnet teacher action 51, 314
joint research centre 312, 314, 317–319, 322
joy of teaching 2, 26
just-in-time learning 130, 141

knowledge domains 5, 212, 220, 232, 235, 236, 241, 244–246, 361

leadership 37, 122, 129, 140, 175, 197, 198, 242, 254, 256–258, 264, 266, 267, 278, 288, 290–292, 294, 298, 362, 363, 370
learning X, 1, 2, 4–6, 8, 12–24, 26–28, 36, 39, 44, 52, 54–61, 63, 64, 74, 85, 87, 99, 100, 102, 112, 114, 122–162, 167, 169, 171, 173, 176–178, 181, 183–185, 187–189, 192, 193, 195, 256, 259–262, 266, 267, 281, 291, 305, 316, 320, 332, 333, 335, 344, 346, 361–363
learning environments 4, 12, 18, 21, 99, 100, 114, 124, 126, 127, 135, 137, 138, 140, 147–156, 158–162, 167, 178, 189, 362, 368, 370
learning materials 124, 134
lesson 63, 84, 99, 100, 103–105, 107–111, 113, 124, 130, 132, 133, 134, 136, 141, 142, 150, 194, 196, 239, 240, 283, 309, 368, 371
lifelong learning opportunities 176
Lisbon Strategy 52, 308, 311, 316
living well 355, 373
looking to the future 4, 26, 27

measurement priorities 23
mentor teacher 21, 22
mobilising policy 130, 304, 306

model for teacher professional development   130
move beyond a reductionist notion of education   353
multicultural competence   60, 62
multicultural teacher education   60
multiple stakeholder collaboration   24, 28, 368

narratives   13, 20, 22, 23, 26–28, 102, 103, 122, 142, 160, 161, 187, 204, 208, 241, 298, 309, 319, 321, 323
narrow concept   293
nature of teacher quality   1, 2, 6, 12, 16, 17, 35, 43, 51
normative discourse   34
normative view of teachers   205

OECD   33, 34, 39, 74, 233, 254, 280, 290, 291, 293, 296, 298, 299, 305, 306, 320
online environments   123, 125, 127, 131, 137, 139, 141, 151, 155, 161, 368
online learning environment   4, 147, 148, 150–156, 158–162, 368
online pedagogies   125, 127, 130, 137, 140, 142, 159, 162
online teacher education courses   24, 195
open method of coordination   281, 315

parent   16, 21, 22, 24, 26, 102, 111, 115, 122, 133, 134, 136, 137, 140, 192, 193, 206, 362, 368
parent's expectations   22
participation   6, 28, 57–60, 111, 126, 133, 151, 154, 155, 157, 169, 184, 209, 215, 243, 293, 296, 331, 344, 373
participatory democracy   54
passion   8, 259, 260, 264, 277, 296–298, 258
pedagogic content knowledge   16, 212
pedagogy   36, 38, 41–43, 56–60, 62, 88, 123–128, 132, 137, 140, 141, 151, 207, 239, 241, 245, 230, 234, 365
pedagogy of discomfort   62
Pedagogy of the oppressed   151
performance   14, 16, 17, 19, 26, 33, 38, 42, 73, 74, 76, 81, 85, 91, 99, 112, 115, 124, 128, 129, 221, 245, 255, 262, 263, 268, 284, 285, 291, 292, 294–296, 363, 364, 369, 370, 372
performative times   20, 22, 23

performativity   19, 20, 22, 26, 141, 255, 256, 363, 372
PISA   14, 33, 52, 75, 236
pluralism   6, 61, 306, 323
policy   2, 3, 6, 7, 13, 14, 20, 24–29, 63, 75, 129, 140, 176, 183, 198, 207, 223, 234, 258, 282, 288, 289, 298, 305, 307, 308, 309, 312, 314, 315, 317, 319, 320, 353, 357, 359, 360, 362, 363, 364, 366, 368, 369, 371, 372
policy development   24, 25, 33, 281, 308
policy experimentations   13, 20, 24, 25, 28, 305, 307, 314, 317, 319–322
policy science   310
policy-maker   IX, 2, 3, 6, 7, 13, 14, 20, 24–29, 63, 75, 129, 140, 176, 183, 198, 207, 223, 234, 258, 282, 288, 289, 298, 308, 309, 312, 314, 315, 317, 319, 320, 353, 357, 359, 360, 362, 363, 364, 366, 368, 369, 371, 372
political aspects of policy work   309
politics of EU policy work   306, 307, 309, 310, 314, 322
post-conflict societies   204, 205, 210, 223
post-COVID-19   150
power relations   91, 133, 152, 157, 158, 210
practice turn   2, 52
practitioner   IX, 6, 13, 18, 20, 25, 27, 29, 73, 74, 210, 244, 247, 330, 332, 344, 353, 366
pragmatic student support   4, 171, 172, 174, 362
praxis   235
preparation of future teacher   11, 12, 15, 27
primary education   212
principles of subsidiarity   315
professional development   IX, 5, 6, 24, 25, 37, 41, 43, 51, 63, 81, 88, 128, 130, 131, 136, 142, 181, 184, 185, 196, 197, 206–210, 232, 235, 244–247, 264, 267, 281–283, 285, 289, 292, 299, 300, 312, 313, 318, 330, 332, 335, 336, 360, 361, 373
professional identity   19, 22, 206, 289, 367, 369, 370
professional knowledge   43, 128, 129, 142, 181, 184–186, 188, 189, 197, 198, 211, 236
professional learning   X, 4, 5, 20, 28, 44, 52, 128, 130, 135, 136, 181, 183–185, 187–190, 192, 193, 195, 256, 266, 267, 291, 305, 332, 333, 335, 344, 346, 361–363
professional learning activities   332, 333, 344, 346

INDEX 381

professional learning and development 5, 188, 256, 266, 333, 362
professional status 206
project IX, 3, 6, 13, 20, 22–28, 42, 43, 52, 103, 130–132, 139, 149, 156, 169, 181, 182, 186–188, 190–192, 194–196, 198, 233, 293, 295, 307–311, 313–315, 320, 322, 323, 332, 333, 339–342, 344, 357
prosocial behaviour 99
pupils' academic performance 99

qualitative research 28, 155, 335
quality IX, X, 1, 2, 4–7, 12–20, 22, 25–27, 33–36, 40, 45, 51, 53–55, 64, 74, 76, 114, 146, 168, 176, 177, 180, 181, 183, 184, 197, 198, 204, 209, 217, 232, 235, 237, 239, 246, 253, 254, 258, 259, 263, 264, 266, 267, 279, 304–307, 309, 311, 323, 324, 353–355, 357–359, 362, 365, 367–373
quality assurance 2, 12–14, 17–20, 26–28, 53, 54, 75, 149, 290, 308, 363, 366, 369
quality assurance in teacher education 11, 12–14, 17–20, 26, 28, 53
quality discourses 19, 22, 150
quality education X, 12–15, 34–36, 40, 55, 74, 76, 148, 168, 176, 177, 180, 183, 184, 204, 235, 253, 254, 305, 311, 324, 357, 358, 368, 369, 371
quality evaluation 3, 73–80, 86, 87, 89, 90, 364
quality evaluation policy 75, 76
quality in classroom management practices 3, 98, 101, 102, 114, 115, 363
quality in teacher education 14, 35, 36, 148, 324, 357, 358, 368, 369, 371
quality in teaching 1, 2, 6, 35, 40, 140, 150, 259, 305, 353, 356–359, 364, 366–369, 371–373
quality indicator 19, 36, 114, 115
quality management 18
quality of pedagogical practices 73
quality of teaching 1, 2, 16, 35, 40, 140, 150, 159, 305, 353, 356–359, 364, 366–369, 371–373
quality of the academic experience 4, 171, 173, 174, 362
quality retention 5, 252, 253, 257, 362
quality teacher education IX, 2, 4, 11–15, 26, 27, 32, 34–36, 38, 40, 64, 147, 148, 155, 176, 181, 198, 217, 218, 222, 306, 323, 324, 357, 358, 368, 369, 371
quality teachers IX, X, 1, 2, 4–7, 12–20, 22, 25–27, 33–36, 40, 45, 51, 53, 54, 64, 114, 181, 183, 197, 198, 209, 217, 232, 237, 239, 246, 253, 254, 258, 259, 263, 264, 266, 267, 279, 304–307, 309, 323, 353–355, 358, 359, 362, 365, 367, 369, 370, 372, 373
quality teaching X, 1–4, 6, 7, 12, 13, 15–17, 19, 20, 34–36, 40, 123, 140, 148–150, 197, 198, 204, 223, 244, 253, 259, 305, 353, 357–359, 362, 364, 366–369, 371–374

reflective practice 151, 160, 333
reflective practitioner 73, 74
reform X, 2, 5, 18, 25, 26, 32, 35, 38, 53, 75, 80, 85, 86, 88, 196, 209, 222, 232, 236, 237, 247, 259, 266, 288, 293–296, 305, 308, 311, 320, 344, 353, 361
reformist teacher 87
reimagine teaching and learning 5, 232, 361
relationships 15, 17, 18, 28, 33, 37, 38, 106–109, 113, 115, 136, 152, 161, 175, 182, 210, 239, 260, 264, 266, 295, 314, 316, 333, 337, 353, 355
research participation 6, 331, 344
researcher IX, 1, 2, 6, 7, 13, 18, 20, 24–27, 29, 91, 105, 115, 131, 170, 186, 189, 197, 198, 258, 283, 300, 317, 322, 330–339, 341–345, 353, 366, 371
research-to-practice gap 330
resilience 122, 140, 257, 259, 264
resonance 353, 355, 356, 373, 374
role diversity 332
role of teacher 4, 17, 54, 126, 204, 205, 207–209, 353, 357, 365

safety 4, 139, 171, 173, 174, 205, 253, 362
school leader 2, 13, 21–27, 198, 256–258, 264, 266, 267, 279, 281, 283, 287–289, 291, 293, 368
school-based teacher education 2, 38, 52
SDG 3 168, 177
SDG 4 168, 176, 177
selection 21, 24, 141, 158, 167, 205, 206, 307, 337
self-discipline 72, 90
self-evaluation 3, 72, 73–82, 84, 86–92, 187, 364

self-evaluative teacher   84, 88, 91
self-inquiry   62
self-reflection   62, 74, 80, 318
situation support   167
situational support   4, 166, 168–174, 176–178, 362
social awareness   233
social constructivism   125, 130
social justice   2, 50, 51, 54–56, 60, 61, 63, 64, 128, 182, 191, 193, 196, 198, 211, 235, 364, 365, 371
social online communities   125
social-emotional learning   99
socialisation   171, 174, 204, 207, 262, 362, 365, 373
sociality   99, 115, 116
socio-cultural theory   56, 60
stakeholders   2, 3, 20, 21, 24–29, 33, 35, 44, 45, 54, 64, 122, 151, 204, 233, 264, 281, 282, 298, 313, 315, 357, 365, 368, 369, 371
standardised concept   129, 353, 358, 366
standards   14, 16–19, 22, 26, 33, 34, 36, 38, 43, 52–55, 62, 76, 128, 222, 233, 236, 240, 253, 255, 265, 267, 278, 292, 293, 355, 360, 366, 368
static concept   361
stress   2, 5, 34, 40, 43, 195, 205, 206, 214, 256, 296, 359
student   x, 1, 3, 4, 6, 8, 13–19, 22–27, 34–36, 38–44, 52, 55–57, 60–64, 74, 76, 86, 99, 100, 106, 107 111, 122, 123, 125–128, 131–140, 148–162, 168–176, 182–187, 189, 190, 192–196, 205–208, 210–212, 214, 215, 217–219, 221, 222, 232, 234–237, 245–247, 253–260, 263, 265, 267, 278, 286, 296, 300, 306, 330–345, 356, 357, 360–363, 365, 367, 369–371, 373
student attainment   23, 52, 360, 363
success   2, 19, 36, 59, 60, 75, 132, 206, 237, 247, 255, 256, 321, 340, 341
successful teaching   17
Summit of European Leaders   323
sustainable development goals   55, 166–168, 176, 177, 181, 182, 354
sustainable peace   205, 207, 209

TALIS   33, 52, 235, 254
teacher   ix, x, 1–8, 11–29, 32–45, 50–57, 59–64, 72–92, 89–100, 102, 106–108, 110, 111, 113–115, 121–137, 140–142, 147–162, 166–169, 171, 173–178, 180–199, 203–223, 231, 232, 234–247, 252–267, 277–300, 307–324, 329–338, 340, 341, 343–346, 352–374
teacher attrition rates   167, 255
teacher career   ix, 244, 278, 280–282, 284–286, 288, 290, 293–296, 298–300, 361
teacher competencies   5, 52, 54, 232, 355, 361
teacher continuum   300
teacher education   ix, x, 1–8, 11–20, 24–29, 32–45, 50–56, 59–64, 73, 74, 81, 83,128, 147–151, 153–156, 159, 160, 162, 167, 169, 176, 178, 181, 183, 185–188, 195, 198, 199, 203–213, 217–223, 231, 235–237, 239, 241, 244, 277, 280–282, 289, 299, 300, 304–317, 319–324, 329–337, 343–346, 352–361, 365–373
teacher education programmes   18, 19, 32, 34–36, 38, 39, 41, 45, 55, 61, 62, 169, 178, 183, 185, 187, 188, 195, 198, 210, 223, 239, 300, 307, 310, 330, 332, 343, 344, 354, 373
teacher educator   ix, 2, 5–7, 12, 13, 15, 18, 19, 20, 24–27, 37, 44, 45, 51, 61–63, 131, 148, 149, 153, 186–188, 197, 204, 208, 211, 222, 223, 232, 237, 240, 244, 283, 331, 334, 335, 337, 345, 346, 354, 361, 367–371, 374
teacher experience   34, 121
teacher policy   52, 307
teacher professionalism   33, 34, 37, 39, 45, 122, 123, 127, 128, 141, 142, 255
teacher qualification   205, 236, 360
teacher quality   ix, x, 1, 2, 4–7, 12–20, 22, 25–27, 33–36, 40, 45, 51, 53, 54, 64, 114, 181, 183, 197, 198, 209, 217, 232, 237, 239, 246, 253, 254, 258, 259, 263, 264, 266, 267, 279, 304–307, 309, 323, 353–355, 358, 359, 362, 365, 367, 369, 370, 372, 373
teacher quality agenda   6, 36, 304, 306
teacher recruitment   44, 205
teacher retention   167, 168, 205, 255–257, 266, 288, 295
teacher satisfaction   256, 262, 263
teacher self-evaluation   3, 72, 74, 76–78, 80–82, 84, 87–89, 91, 364
teacher voice   127, 128

teacher well-being   167, 177, 178, 362
teacher workforce   206, 208, 323
teaching as an occupation   44, 51
teaching for now   135, 234
teaching for the future   142, 234
teaching force   51
teaching portfolio   335, 340
teaching profession   IX, X, 5–8, 41, 44, 45, 52, 64, 122, 128, 185, 198, 204–206, 215, 232, 236, 247, 253, 258, 260, 282, 283, 285, 291, 313, 330, 332, 346, 353, 359, 361, 366, 370, 374
teaching quality   X, 1–4, 6, 7, 12, 13, 15–17, 19, 20, 34–36, 40, 123, 140, 148–150, 197, 198, 204, 223, 244, 253, 259, 305, 353, 357–359, 362, 364, 366–369, 371–374
teaching strategies   4, 148, 153, 155, 160–162, 192, 239, 345
teamwork   234, 337
theoretical knowledge   61, 331
theory-practice gap   330
trainees   52, 187, 192, 193, 196, 338
training   4, 6, 14, 41, 44, 45, 51–53, 62, 129–131, 135, 170, 177, 183, 186, 192, 194, 206, 207, 209, 214, 217, 218, 235, 254, 295, 305, 309–314, 317–320, 324, 330–340, 343–345
transformative power   63

university-based teacher education   2, 52
unknown future   231

values   IX, 2, 6, 7, 12, 15, 16, 18, 20–23, 25, 26, 28, 41–43, 45, 50–57, 62–64, 115, 123, 127–129, 135, 137, 172, 173, 175, 182, 187, 189, 190, 193, 195, 196, 198, 207–211, 214, 238, 241, 255, 258–263, 265–267, 278, 279, 283, 284, 296, 305, 306, 323, 330, 331, 339, 343, 356, 359–362, 365–367, 369, 371, 374
values-centred teacher education   2, 6, 50, 51, 54, 64
war   204, 205, 213, 217, 222, 353
well-being   1, 4, 74, 99, 140, 160, 166–169, 171–178, 205, 221, 252, 256, 261–263, 286, 354, 355, 362, 365, 367, 374
World Bank   13, 233, 320